Dialogues with Dostoevsky
The Overwhelming Questions

Dialogues with Dostoevsky
The Overwhelming Questions

ROBERT LOUIS JACKSON

STANFORD UNIVERSITY PRESS
Stanford, California

Stanford University Press
Stanford, California

© 1993 by the Board of Trustees
of the Leland Stanford Junior University

Printed in the United States of America

CIP data appear at the end of the book

Stanford University Press publications are distributed
exclusively by Stanford University Press within the
United States, Canada, Mexico, and Central America;
they are distributed exclusively by Cambridge University
Press throughout the rest of the world.

Original printing 1993
Last figure below indicates year of this printing:
05   04   03   02   01   00   99   98   97   96

To Leslie

Contents

In every serious philosophical question uncertainty extends to the very roots of the problem. We must always be prepared to learn something *totally* new.

—Ludwig Wittgenstein

Introduction

Dostoevsky in Movement

It is a game of chess; neither side can move without consulting the other.
Allen Tate

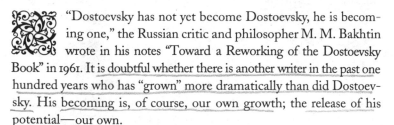 "Dostoevsky has not yet become Dostoevsky, he is becoming one," the Russian critic and philosopher M. M. Bakhtin wrote in his notes "Toward a Reworking of the Dostoevsky Book" in 1961. It is doubtful whether there is another writer in the past one hundred years who has "grown" more dramatically than did Dostoevsky. His becoming is, of course, our own growth; the release of his potential—our own.

Dostoevsky has become an icon—in some respects a cliché—for twentieth-century self-consciousness: to know him has been to know ourselves and our century. Indeed, the nineteenth century ended with an awareness of a special relationship with Dostoevsky. "The anxiety and doubts that flood his works are our anxieties and doubts, and they will remain such for all times," the Russian critic and thinker V. V. Rozanov wrote in his classic study of Dostoevsky's "Legend of the Grand Inquisitor" in 1894. "In those epochs when life flows along particularly smoothly or when people are not conscious of its difficulties, this writer may even be quite forgotten and not read. But whenever anything on the path of human history arouses a sense of confoundment, when the peoples moving along these paths shall be shaken or thrown into confusion—then the name and image of the writer who thought so much about these paths of life will awaken with full undiminished force."[1] The twentieth century was such a time; increasingly it acknowledged in Dostoevsky a contemporary. "He is the great founder and definer of our cultural complexity," wrote Vyacheslav I. Ivanov in 1916.[2]

In the middle of the twentieth century, another Russian, the émigré poet and critic Georgy V. Adamovich, taking stock of Dostoevsky's impact on Western literature and culture, found in him not merely a definer of complexity, but an agent of confoundment. Adamovich held Dostoevsky "responsible for a great deal in contemporary literary and artistic moods—not guilty, but precisely responsible. . . . He is responsible for the ostentatious, uncontrolled anxiety which gushed through the fissure he had broken open—for the imprudence in basic point of view . . . for the certitude that one can imagine and depict whatever one pleases, as the world anyhow every year becomes more and more like a madhouse. In short, he is responsible for the fundamental lawlessness in themes and situation, for the mad metaphysic 'all is permissible' which, once having broken loose, will not easily and quickly be brought under control."[3]

One may take issue with Rozanov and Adamovich: Dostoevsky addresses more than our anxieties; as for his "responsibility" for the "mad metaphysic 'all is permissible,'" one may argue cogently that Dostoevsky's works suggest—in the manner in which they cope with chaos—the possibility of some control over disorder. The comments of Rozanov and Adamovich, though they pass over many aspects of Dostoevsky's art, nonetheless speak eloquently of Dostoevsky's relevance to our century. Indeed, it is possible to say of Dostoevsky what he, summing up Schiller's place in Russian culture, wrote in 1876: He has marked an epoch in the history of our development.[4] It is probably correct to say that the *age of Dostoevsky*—in the sense that Rozanov and Adamovich have defined it—has come to an end, but not his colossal art, his deep understanding of man and history, his artistic vision. Dostoevsky is still "becoming," and we keep discovering, or rediscovering, in him dimensions that both embrace and go beyond his relevance to the nearly apocalyptic events of the twentieth century.

The great Russian satirist M. E. Saltykov-Shchedrin, writing in 1871, a decade before the death of Dostoevsky, observed presciently:

In depth of thought and in the breadth of tasks of the moral world which he has unfolded, this writer stands absolutely unique among us. He not only acknowledges the legitimacy of those interests which stir contemporary society, but goes even further, entering into the realm of previsions and premonitions such as constitute the goal not only of the immediate but of the most distant strivings of mankind.[5]

It is noteworthy that these words were written by one of Dostoevsky's most ardent ideological opponents in the 1860's; indeed, Saltykov-Shchedrin's deep appreciation of Dostoevsky as a writer appears in an article in which the author criticizes the Russian novelist for what he regarded as an unfair representation of radicals in Dostoevsky's work.

Dialogue with Dostoevsky is at the center of the most important encounters with him; it is a mark not merely of the timelessly topical nature of Dostoevsky's work, but of the singularly provocative character of his vision of man and the world. Bakhtin insisted that the "idea" as "seen" by Dostoevsky is a *"live event."* "Like the word, it wants to be heard, understood, and 'answered' by other voices from other positions."[6] This is true not only in the world of Dostoevsky's novels, but in the universe of commentary and criticism. Only through interchange with Dostoevsky does the essential Dostoevsky emerge: not the answer to this or that question, but a sense of Dostoevskian reality, at the center of which lies movement.

Certainly the most direct approach to Dostoevsky's world is through a personal reading of his writings: here we discover where Dostoevsky is and where we are, or think we are. Dostoevsky's work is most protean and most itself at this frontier where the "work" is going on, where we meet it, where writer and reader are obliged to define themselves, each according to their outlook, according to the laws of their own deepest impulses—aesthetic, moral, and philosophical. Yet Dostoevsky exists in a vast and ever-expanding historical context of readings and relationships involving other writers, critics, and thinkers, past and present, in Russian and European literature and thought. Some of the most revealing sides of his artistic thought and personality emerge in this context. *Dialogues with Dostoevsky* seeks to throw light on the Russian novelist by examining moments of contact between him and other writers and thinkers.

Dostoevsky is at the center of the book: his name, his works, his ideas are present in every essay, and it is his manifold art and image, his thought, that gains from the steady focus upon him. At the same time, the point of departure in each essay, and often the lion's share of attention, is upon other critics and writers (Gogol, Turgenev, Tolstoy, Nietzsche, Gorky, etc.) and their contrasting or concurring points of view, literary, critical, or philosophical; the dynamic of each essay is formed through the interaction of the concerns of one or more writers with those of Dostoevsky. Though questions of influence or impact of one writer upon another sometimes constitute the given of the discussion, the main focus is upon the issues—moral-psychological, aesthetic, and historicophilosophical—that engage these writers in their contact with each other's work or emerge from a juxtaposition of their works or ideas. It is these issues that form the fabric of the book and provide a sense not of an a priori, unified field of problems, but a set of recognizable, recurring problems and concerns. Dostoevsky is not the source of these concerns and problems, but he certainly gave vivid expression to many of them.

Simply put, the question underlying the first three essays is How does one look at violence? The notion of the "ethics of vision" raises the question of the accountability of sight. Tolstoy, Dostoevsky, Turgenev, and Chekhov—the writers under discussion—looked at executions with varying degrees of inner necessity and involvement, but they *looked*; and they wrote not only about what they saw, but about how they saw—about the moral-psychological experience of looking at violence. They were not interested in merely depicting horrible things.

The problem of executions and man's disturbed and disturbing response to them is at the center of Turgenev's sketch "The Execution of Tropmann." In Paris in 1870, Turgenev casually accepted the invitation of an acquaintance to attend the beheading of a convicted murderer. The experience as a whole turned out to be traumatic for him. Turgenev was revolted by the spectacle and literally turned his eyes away from the guillotine at the moment of Tropmann's beheading. He came away shocked at the whole affair and at the eagerness with which 25,000 Parisians watched the execution; his sketch "The Execution of Tropmann," an attack on public executions, followed shortly after the occasion. Turgenev's gesture of turning his eyes from the guillotine and his constant questioning in his sketch of his "right" to be present at an execution invited Dostoevsky's scorn: "Man on the surface of the earth does not have the right to turn away and ignore what is taking place on earth, and there are lofty moral reasons for this: *homo sum et nihil humanum*, etc."[7] The very writing of "The Execution of Tropmann" was a demonstration, of course, that Turgenev was facing the issue of violence: for him, the dehumanizing character of such a spectacle. Dostoevsky, relentless in his criticism of Turgenev, will allude in *The Devils* to what he regarded as the self-centered nature of Turgenev's response to the execution of Tropmann.

A close examination of Turgenev's sketch and Dostoevsky's response to executions and violence in his work (Chapter 1, "The Ethics of Vision I: Turgenev's 'Execution of Tropmann' and Dostoevsky's View of the Matter") suggests that the two great writers divided not in their social viewpoint on executions, but in the radically different ways they reacted to violence as human beings: Turgenev literally experiencing revulsion; Dostoevsky in some deep sense being drawn to the experience. "I'm making you suffer," Ivan Karamazov says to Alyosha in the midst of providing vivid accounts of dreadful abuses of children. "I'll leave off, if you like." "Never mind, I want to suffer, too," mutters Alyosha. These lines most exactly define the moral-psychological content of Dostoevsky's insistence that man face every aspect of human reality—here, the reality of violence. This deep emotional involvement in violence was disturbing to Turgenev. He was particularly disturbed by the potential for moral-psychological corruption that seemed to him to accompany the experience of looking at violence. "It is awful to think what is hidden there," he remarks after speculating on the crowd's interest in the execution.

What is "hidden there" is also what is hidden in Turgenev and Dostoevsky as well. Dostoevsky, too, recoils from violence in man. The power of his exploration of violence in his work, however, comes not from a deeply felt dissociation with the act of violence and rejection of complicity, as it does with Turgenev, but from a psychological and, ultimately, metaphysical recognition and acceptance of complicity and guilt. We are all guilty because in one way or another we are making other people suffer and enjoying that suffering; we are guilty because in each of us lies the propensity for violence and evil.

Tolstoy (Chapter 2, "The Ethics of Vision II: The Tolstoyan Synthesis"), together with Sophocles and Shakespeare, is unsurpassed in his artistic and psychological grasp of *looking, sight, vision* as an organic expression of human character and experience. That is certainly true of the way he deals with eyes, looking, and vision throughout *War and Peace*; it is strikingly true of his artistic structuring of the scene in *War and Peace* in which Pierre Bezukhov, a prisoner of the French, is led to a field of execution and obliged to confront the executions of several alleged Russian incendiaries. (Pierre is unaware that he himself has been reprieved.) He twice avoids looking at the execution of his compatriots. Yet, overcome with agitation and curiosity, Pierre turns his eyes on the execution of the fifth and last prisoner. Here there is a visceral desire to look, but here, too, looking takes the form of involuntarily *bearing witness*—an act of moral identification with one's suffering fellow man. Not surprisingly, this solidarity with suffering takes the form of an interaction of glances, a silent communication between Pierre and the prisoners. Like Dostoevsky, Tolstoy is unable to ignore what is taking place on earth; precisely the moral aspects of violence are uppermost in his mind.

Tolstoy's interest in the executions both embraces and goes beyond Turgenev's and Dostoevsky's. On a deeper level of his text, he focuses upon man's instinctive unwillingness to recognize or face the reality of his death—the motif of the blindfold is central to the scene. One prisoner scratches himself a few moments before his execution. The instinct for life to which Tolstoy calls attention is more basic than even the knowledge of death; it may even overcome one's moral feelings, as Tolstoy demonstrates in a later scene in which Pierre, on the forced march from Moscow, turns away from the execution of his friend and spiritual mentor, Platon Karataev. The moment is an extremely painful one for Pierre and, one senses, for Tolstoy as well, for at this moment he introduces into the entire question of the ethics of vision a new and disturbing element: the fact that the organic will to live may in certain circumstances supplant or suppress the moral impulse.

In the January 1876 issue of *Diary of a Writer*, Dostoevsky recalls a scene from his youth—one, he says, that was impressed forever upon his memory: an official smashing his fist upon the neck of his coachman, the coachman in turn lashing his horse with all his might; probably that same day, Dostoevsky adds, the coachman will beat his wife. "This repulsive little scene has remained in my memory all my life," Dostoevsky notes.[8] Dostoevsky had more than enough time in his life to experience and speculate upon violence in Russian life and history. He spent the first forty years of his life in a serf society; his father was murdered by peasants; and he was forced to witness the preparations for his own execution—a piece of theater arranged by Tsar Nicholas I. During his four years in prison, Dostoevsky witnessed violence in a multitude of forms.[9] Cruelty as a way of life, as a by-product of despotism and the universal corruption of social relations, was one of the messages of *Notes from the House of the Dead.*

Chekhov as man and writer certainly felt a greater kinship to Tolstoy than to Dostoevsky; of the two writers, Tolstoy had the profounder impact on him. Nonetheless, Chekhov read Dostoevsky attentively and, above all, shared many of his concerns. We can find echoes of Dostoevsky's works and ideas throughout Chekhov's works; for example, in his philosophically important stories "Ward No. 6" and "In Exile," both of which are linked with Chekhov's visit to the penal colonies on the island of Sakhalin in 1890. Dostoevsky's *Notes from the House of the Dead* was one of the works in the background of Chekhov's mind when he wrote his remarkable account of his visit to the penal colony on the island of Sakhalin (*Island of Sakhalin. Notes from a Journey*, 1893–1894). The two works are radically different in design, style, and focus; Dostoevsky uses a fictitious narrator, a convict, to describe his prison world; Chekhov, a visitor to Sakhalin, writes under his own name. Both writers, however, are concerned with violence as a corrupting feature of Russian life. Chekhov devotes one particularly vivid episode to the flogging of a convict. His approach to this revolting scene is particularly "Chekhovian." As in Turgenev's "The Execution of Tropmann," one senses a narrator-observer for whom violence is objectively and subjectively repugnant. Yet Chekhov's focus in this scene is entirely upon the action; he does not question his "right" to be present like Turgenev; nor does he, like Dostoevsky's narrator in *Notes from the House of the Dead*, call attention to his emotions or his interest in details of punishment. Chekhov depicts the scene with the calmness of a physician and the precision of a chronicler. Yet his attitude is clearly felt. The power of the scene lies not only in its shocking detail, but in the coarse and indifferent attitude of other witnesses to the beating. *This is the way it is*, Chekhov's account seems to say; this is the normal everyday life to which we have long become inured.

"Sakhalin is a place of unbearable suffering, the kind that only man, free or subjugated, is capable of," Chekhov wrote before his journey to Sakhalin to Alexey Suvorin on March 9, 1890. "We have let *millions* of people rot in jails, rot to no purpose, mindlessly, barbarously; we have driven people in the cold in chains, across tens of thousands of versts, we have infected them with syphilis, debauched them, bred criminals, and for all this have heaped blame on red-nosed prison wardens. Now all educated Europe knows that it is not the wardens who are guilty, but all of us, but it's none of our business, it's uninteresting."[10] The island of Sakhalin is a penal colony. Yet the scene is all Russia and all of Russian history. "The landowners flogged our grandfather, and every measly official whacked him on the snout," a character in one of Chekhov's stories remarks. "Grandfather flogged our father, and father flogged you and me. . . . What sort of nerves and what sort of blood have we inherited?"[11]

Chekhov did not have to visit Sakhalin to discover the virus of brutality and sadomasochism in Russian life. That is clear alone from one of the very first of Chekhov's published stories, "Because of Little Apples." The setting of the tale, the narrator remarks, is "somewhere" between the Black Sea and the White Sea. The story, starkly realistic, draws at the same time on Christian mythology (the "Fall" of Adam and Eve) and folklore to make its larger social and historical statement. Chekhov explores the tragedy of violence, cruelty, and sadism in Russian life—one into which everybody has been drawn. In "A Doctor's Visit" (1898), Chekhov touches on this kind of tragedy. The narrator of the story, Korolyov, reflecting on the oppressive and threatening character of life in a factory town, ruminates: "The chief person, for whom everything is being done, is the devil. . . . The strong have to hinder the weak from living—such was the law of nature, but this is comprehensible and acceptable as an idea only in a newspaper article or a textbook; in the muddle which is everyday life, in the tangle of trivialities out of which human relations are woven it was no longer a law but a logical absurdity, when the strong and the weak alike fall victim to their mutual relations, involuntarily submitting to some directing force, unknown, standing outside of life, and apart from man." Korolyov's meditations serve in their own way to rationalize his curious indifference, but they nonetheless call attention to an important thought of Chekhov—that social relations in Russia, indeed human relations in general, cannot be reduced to easy formulas (and to the rectilinear solutions to which such formulas usually lead); that men are victimized in their mutual relations; that man is also his own environment and in the final analysis must undergo a basic change in all aspects of his life.

Chekhov's "Because of Little Apples"—a story saturated with motifs from Dostoevsky's work (in particular, *Notes from the House of the Dead* and *The Brothers Karamazov*, but also Dostoevsky's early story "A Christmas Party and a Wedding")—appeared at the end of 1880. Little more than a year later, N. K. Mikhailovsky published a slight book entitled *A Cruel Talent* in which he attacked the just-deceased Dostoevsky for his alleged predilection for cruel and sadistic scenes. Chekhov's "Because of Little Apples," with its direct allusions to Dostoevsky, is especially valuable to us because it discloses that the young Chekhov had an entirely different understanding than Mikhailovsky and others of the significance of the themes of cruelty and sadism in Dostoevsky's work. These themes were close to Russia's heart.

The general question of Dostoevsky and the abnormal, Dostoevsky and cruelty, Dostoevsky and sadism, preoccupied some writers and critics in the several decades following his death. Some of Dostoevsky's early critics disparaged his work as preoccupied with the "abnormal" or "underground" side of human character; his characters were perceived as "exceptional" if not purely pathological types. Dostoevsky himself was the object of scandalous rumors alleging immoral behavior on his part—raping a child.

Nikolai N. Strakhov, a well-known conservative Russian critic and philosopher, and for many years a friend and journalistic collaborator of Dostoevsky's, certainly was a conduit for rumors about Dostoevsky's alleged immorality. In a letter to Leo Tolstoy little more than a year after Dostoevsky's death in 1881, Strakhov insisted that Dostoevsky was an "evil, envious, debauched" man who created in his own image such characters as the Underground Man, Svidrigailov, and Stavrogin (the letter is cited in full in Chapter 5).

Strakhov's letter, whatever its nonliterary motivations, is certainly a prime illustration of the pitfalls of biographical criticism. Yet a comparison of Strakhov's public commentary on Dostoevsky (he was the author of the first critical biography on the Russian novelist) with his private letter to Tolstoy suggests that the line between creative and destructive biographical criticism is a thin one. In his published biography, Strakhov wrote that the novelist "so easily took his own subjectivity [i.e., his "muse," his "tender and lofty humanity"] for complete realism": "the muse and man came together in an unusually close union." In his letter to Tolstoy, Strakhov does not radically alter this formula; he simply declares the *man* Dostoevsky to have been *immoral* and his humanism *literary*—that is, hypocritical. In the first case, Strakhov wishes to remain with the writer; in the second, with the man Dostoevsky, or what he took to be the man.

Tolstoy wisely and politely refused to be drawn into discussions of Dostoevsky's alleged immorality; he shifted the discussion to Dostoevsky's struggle as an artist between good and evil. Strakhov, however, was unrelenting in his efforts to belittle Dostoevsky's art. In a later letter to Tolstoy on August 21, 1892, Strakhov again sought to put down the Russian novelist's achievement: "Dostoevsky, creating his characters in his image and likeness, wrote about a multitude of half mad and sick people, and was firmly convinced that he was describing them from reality and that the human soul was like that."[12] Tolstoy replied forcefully in a letter of September 3: "You say that Dostoevsky described himself in his heroes, imagining that all people were like him. And so! The result is that even in such exceptional people not only we, his countrymen, but foreigners recognize themselves, their soul. The deeper [the depths from which] you draw, the more general, familiar and close [one is] to everybody."[13] Tolstoy's remark is of special interest because he had just created the highly idiosyncratic character of Pozdnyshev in *The Kreutzer Sonata*—an unusually "Dostoevskian" work in certain respects.

The critique of Dostoevsky as a "sadist," as one who delighted in cruelty, took on broader and more complex dimensions in the mind and work of Maxim Gorky than in Turgenev. Gorky, like Turgenev and Mikhailovsky, finds in Dostoevsky a "great torturer," but he is not primarily concerned with judging Dostoevsky's tastes; nor is he, like Mikhailovsky, concerned with the taxonomic task of cataloging sadistic scenes and characters in Dostoevsky's novels. Gorky is too close to Dostoevsky and his world to take his work lightly. Very much like Chekhov in "Because of Little Apples," Gorky is impressed by the relevance of Dostoevsky's novelistic reality to Russian man and history. In the suffering and disfigured world of Dostoevsky's novels, his tormented heroes and heroines, their sadistic and masochistic roles, Gorky found an epic and terrifying "memory" of "the spiritual illness injected in us by the Mongol, by the mutilation inflicted on our soul by tormenting Moscow history."[14] Gorky believed that Dostoevsky had idealized quite banal social types along with their petty but virulently hostile psychologies—the ideology of the "master" and the ideology of the "slave." Gorky rejected both ideologies, identifying them with the philosophies of Dostoevsky and Tolstoy. These writers, he maintained, call upon man to "humble himself." Gorky, rejecting the "rhetoric" of the "so-called 'higher demands of the spirit,'" called upon the Russian proudly to straighten his back. The work of Dostoevsky, in short, is for Gorky a kind of psychohistory of Russia.

The irony of Gorky's life and work is that it reveals a person who for all his heroic preachment about "proud" man, deeply mistrusted Russian man (both peasant and intellectual) and doubted his capacity to emerge unscathed from his dark past. Gorky himself, in the final analysis, was an immensely complex "Dostoevskian" personage in his constant spiritual torment and searching, his psychological and ideological oscillations, and finally, the tragic way he embodied the role of Dostoevsky's Grand Inquisitor at the end of his life: the role of a man preaching a lie in the name of the truth.

The work and thought of François-René de Chateaubriand and the marquis de Sade—men totally antithetical to each another in their outlook—finds a distinct resonance in Dostoevsky's work and spiritual drama. It is not difficult to see in them an embodiment of the radical tension one finds in Dostoevsky's novelistic universe between an ecstatic spiritual religious ethos—one deeply moral and aesthetic in content and finding embodiment in the image of Christ—and an all-consuming skepticism and rationalism, one finding ultimate expression in the notion that "all is permissible."

The explicit references to Chateaubriand in Dostoevsky's writings are few. The young Dostoevsky, however, appears to have been moved early in his life by Chateaubriand's passionate synthesis of the religious and aesthetic elements in *Le Génie du Christianisme*. Dostoevsky's unfulfilled project to write an article, "Letters About Art," on the "significance of Christianity in art," a work he conceived in prison and called "the fruit of a decade of thought," may indeed have had affinities with Chateaubriand's work.[15] What is striking is the way both men approached the question of the unity of religion and morality. Both are firm in their conviction, as Chateaubriand put it, "qu'il n'y a point de morale, s'il n'y a point d'autre vie" (that there is no virtue if there is no immortality).[16] It is this thought and concise formula, along with Chateaubriand's "proofs" of Christianity, that echo in the ideological drama of Ivan Karamazov. Leonid Grossman has argued that the "fundamental proofs of the atheistic argumentation of Ivan" are to be found in Voltaire's *Candide*. In turn, one may say that Chateaubriand's various "proofs" of Christianity enter into Dostoevsky's refutation of Ivan's atheistic proofs.

Chateaubriand and Sade, each in his own way, recoil from the age of the philosophes: Chateaubriand, believing that "religion is necessary or society will perish," seeks to rescue religion and morality from the Encyclopedists. Sade, with perverse delight and a gift for philosophical parody, arrives at a negation of morality and religion by pushing the conclusions of the philosophes to an extreme. Sade as an erotic fantasist and Sade as a philosopher was ultimately of importance to Dostoevsky as a symptom of the total moral breakdown of individual, the loss of spiritual equilibrium in society, and its consequent plunge into an "underground" of destruction and self-destruction. Sade's cardinal notion that nature provided a justification and model for any and all extreme behavior—his theory, in essence, that "all was permissible"—was for Dostoevsky only the last expression of a society whose moral and religious foundations had been shattered. In Sade Dostoevsky clearly found the bellwether of the philosophes, a creature of the Enlightenment who carried the thought of the philosophes to its logical consequences. "As for me, I have really merely carried to an extreme in my life what you did not dare to carry through halfway," Dostoevsky's Underground Man remarks to his unseen interlocutors, the rationalists and materialists of the "Russian Enlightenment"of the 1860's. Dostoevsky could have put these words into the mouth of any of his "Sadean" characters—for example, Prince Valkovsky in *The Insulted and Injured*, Svidrigailov in *Crime and Punishment*, or Klinevich in "Bobok."

It is the principle of *moderation*—a sense of measure, the striving for equilibrium and compromise, the ideal of what Nicholas Berdyaev called "middle" culture—that informs the art and artistic outlook of Turgenev. In his study on the "Legend of the Grand Inquisitor," Rozanov dismissed Turgenev as old-fashioned and irrelevant to contemporary life. With greater insight, Dmitry Merezhkovsky early recognized that the problem of the reception of Turgenev in fin de siècle Russia was linked with the problem of culture in Russian life and history. In Russia, a "land of all kinds of revolutionary and religious maximalism, a country of self-immolation, of the wildest excesses," Merezhkovsky wrote in 1908, Turgenev, after Pushkin, is "almost the sole genius of measure and, therefore, a genius of culture."[17] The problem of Turgenev and culture is the point of departure and return of the essay "The Root and the Flower: Dostoevsky and Turgenev, a Comparative Aesthetic." The full dimensions of Turgenev as artist-thinker are only now being explored.

The legendary antagonism between Turgenev and Dostoevsky is manifested in their radically different ways of looking at reality. Both Dostoevsky and Turgenev find their roots in German romanticism and culture philosophy, yet they move in different directions. "Nature," with its sense of measure and harmony, its obedience to internal law, is Turgenev's artistic model. Again and again, Turgenev invokes "nature" to define his artistic method. The artist, he insists, must "feel the roots of phenomena, but represent only the phenomena themselves in their flowering and fading." Rich and complex, reality is nonetheless simple and homogeneous to the observing eye. The writer's art, in Turgenev's view, must reflect this paradox. It is for the writer, and ultimately the reader, to interpret and decipher the outwardly casual signs and signals that make up the landscape of reality.

Henry James called Turgenev a "novelist's novelist": this was really only an elitist way of saying that Turgenev is the *reader's writer.*

Turgenev's art of indirection and restraint, his acceptance of the equilibrium of nature as the artist's guiding principle, his insistence that an artist be a psychologist without psychologizing, contrasts radically with the art of Dostoevsky. "I am only a realist in the higher sense, that is, I depict all the depths of the human soul," Dostoevsky wrote in the last year of his life.[18] Dostoevsky's art begins its explorations at the moment of crisis and fragmentation. It depicts a world in a state of tension and hyperbole. Turgenev found Tolstoy's direct psychologizing and philosophizing objectionable; he found Dostoevsky's artistic and spiritual maximalism even more intolerable. Yet, for all their differences in artistic method and ideology, Turgenev and Dostoevsky were drawn to similar problems. In many respects both writers constitute a strange unity of opposites. Dostoevsky craved the spiritual harmony and beauty that Turgenev expressed in his art, while we find in Turgenev psychological and philosophical interests and emphases that are very close to Dostoevsky's.[19] One is tempted to see in the ambience of their artistic sensibility and expression, and in their opposing "Western" and "Slavophile" ideological orientations, the extraordinary spread of nineteenth-century Russian culture. In any case, the longer one reads these two writers, the more one is inclined to see in them mutually supporting complementarities in the life and culture of society.

Gogol's artistic types, Dostoevsky wrote in his *Diary of a Writer*, "oppress the mind with the most profound and unbearable questions, evoke in the Russian mind the most disturbing thoughts—with which, one feels this, it may be possible to cope only in some far-off distant time; indeed, will we ever cope with them?"[20] Dostoevsky had in mind a complex of literary, moral, and social-historical issues that critics found embedded in Gogol's art. Central was the question of the identity, destiny, and historical maturity of the Russian people. The question had been posed not so much by Gogol as by the Gogolian world the reader encountered in his works. What relation to the Russian people and to Russia had Gogol's subculture of grotesque characters, his Breughel-like vision of man and life in general? Was there any connection?

The radical Russian critic Vissarion Belinsky hailed Gogol in the 1840's for his truth and realism. He insisted that Gogol reflected Russian life and reality and that his grotesque literary types were "for the time being the most authentic Russian types."[21] At the end of the century, the conservative critic and philosopher V. V. Rozanov, echoing many earlier critics of Gogol, argued that Gogol's characters in fact were unreal waxen figures lacking any verisimilitude. Dostoevsky's point of view on this question, I argue in Chapter 10, "Two Views of Gogol and the Critical Synthesis," constitutes a synthesis of the two opposing points of view so well articulated by Belinsky and Rozanov. In his first novel, *Poor Folk* (1846), Dostoevsky gave expression to this question through his characterization of the still-forming consciousness of the clerk Makar Devushkin. In Devushkin, Dostoevsky acknowledges both the relevance to Russian reality of Gogol's artistic vision of man and its nearsightedness. Dostoevsky endows his Gogolian hero with a life and soul, and in this way contributes to the reshaping of the Gogol tradition in Russian literature.

Dostoevsky had his differences with Tolstoy, but he profoundly respected him. "In all history, in all of world literature, there never was a greater artistic talent than that of Tolstoy," he is reported to have said.[22] According to Strakhov, Dostoevsky, on reading the final parts of *Anna Karenina*, spoke of Tolstoy as a "god of art."[23] Tolstoy's responses to Dostoevsky were of a reverse order. He had great respect for Dostoevsky as a thinker, but for the most part thought poorly of him as an artist. Berdyaev seems to have taken the judgments of Dostoevsky and Tolstoy on each other and synthesized them: Tolstoy was probably the greater artist, he suggests, but Dostoevsky was a greater thinker.[24] Where one is concerned with such colossal artist-thinkers as Tolstoy and Dostoevsky, however, judgments about the superior merit of one over the other seem unproductive.

Tolstoy's objections to Dostoevsky's artistry, usually expressed in casual comments, reflect the vast differences separating his artistic method from Dostoevsky's. In these objections, however, occasional emphases may contribute to a fuller understanding if not of Dostoevsky's art then of the difficulties Tolstoy had with it. In his response to Strakhov's broadside attack on Dostoevsky, Tolstoy sidesteps the question of Dostoevsky's personal behavior and morality and at once lifts the discussion to a higher plane, one involving Dostoevsky's work at large. What seems to disturb Tolstoy is that Dostoevsky was a man who was "in his entirety struggle."[25] Tolstoy's comments suggest to us that he was disturbed by what he considered a kind of *perpetuum mobile* in Dostoevsky: he does not get you to a destination. In this connection, Tolstoy arrives at the conclusion that "Turgenev will outlive Dostoevsky" not because he is a greater artist, but because he doesn't stumble—that is, he gets you to a destination. Tolstoy's notion that Turgenev would outlive Dostoevsky is idiosyncratic: it seems doubtful that he was seriously concerned with this question. Yet his remarks in his letter seem to touch on something deeper: the question of unresolved, open-ended conflict and movement in Dostoevsky's artistic universe and Dostoevsky's efforts (in Tolstoy's view, unsuccessful) to come to terms with unresolved conflict in his works.

If my analysis of Tolstoy's comments in his letter is correct (Chapter 5, "A View from the Underground"), Tolstoy would seem to be noting critically what Mikhail Bakhtin later was to refer to, approvingly, as the "unfinalized" character of Dostoevsky's artistic worldview. Whether or not Tolstoy fully understood the nature of Dostoevsky's way out of what Bakhtin (with respect to the Underground Man) called "the vicious circle of dialogue which can neither be finished nor finalized," he had touched upon the critical center of Dostoevsky's conception of the universe and found it disturbing. Movement, as I suggest in my discussion of Dostoevsky's and Turgenev's aesthetics, is both the illness and cure in Dostoevsky's universe. The problem of movement, uncontrolled and without direction, is posed by Dostoevsky in his seminal philosophical work, *Notes from the Underground.* Dostoevsky's entire oeuvre is an attempt to come to terms artistically, spiritually, and philosophically with a reality "striving toward fragmentation"—that is, it is an attempt to give creative meaning to open-ended conflict.

Whatever Tolstoy and Dostoevsky thought about each other's art, both were careful and respectful readers of each other's works. The moral-philosophical and topical concerns of Dostoevsky and Tolstoy often run parallel with each other: Raskolnikov, in *Crime and Punishment,* wonders about his "right" to transgress; Pierre, in *War and Peace,* is carried away by the moral utilitarianism of Napoleon, and Prince Andrey is dreaming of emulating Napoleon and rising above everybody. At the moment Aleksey Ivanovich, in Dostoevsky's *The Gambler* (1866), is seeking to dominate lady luck in Roulettenburg, Dolokhov, in *War and Peace*, is seeking through play with chance to impose his will on people or events. In other cases, we find direct or indirect evidence in the fiction of Tolstoy and Dostoevsky of their reading each other's work. Tolstoy may or may not have had *Notes from the Underground* in mind when he worked on *The Kreutzer Sonata*, but the latter is certainly one of his most Dostoevskian works. A juxtaposition of the two works (Chapter 11, "In the Darkness of the Night: Tolstoy's *The Kreutzer Sonata* and Dostoevsky's *Notes from the Underground*) is useful in that it helps clarify a work, *The Kreutzer Sonata*, that has had a troubled critical history in general.

The Kreutzer Sonata (1887–1889; 1890) is one of Tolstoy's most polemical works; it is also one of his most controversial. Criticism for the most part has identified Tolstoy with the hysterical hero, or antihero, of the work and with his extreme ideas on woman, marriage, sex, and the family. Indeed, shortly after the appearance of the work, Tolstoy wrote an "Afterword" in which he unambiguously embraces the ideas of Pozdnyshev, the protagonist of *The Kreutzer Sonata*.

The work has been viewed as a pamphlet masking as a story (an examination of the history of the writing of *The Kreutzer Sonata* clearly discloses Tolstoy's efforts to fuse fiction and polemics) and therefore only partially successful as a work of art. *The Kreutzer Sonata* has evoked contrary attitudes in the same critic. On its appearance, Nikolai N. Strakhov congratulated Tolstoy on a powerful though somber work, but went on to complain about distracting "discussions on general questions" and what he regarded as Tolstoy's unclear characterization of his protagonist.[26] More recently, George Steiner has characterized *The Death of Ivan Ilych* and *The Kreutzer Sonata* as "masterpieces, but masterpieces of a singular order. Their terrible intensity arises not out of a prevalence of imaginative vision, but out of its narrowing." *The Kreutzer Sonata*, he argues, is "technically less perfect [than *The Death of Ivan Ilych*] because the elements of articulate morality have become too massive to be entirely absorbed into the narrative structure. The meaning is enforced upon us, with extraordinary eloquence; but it has not been given complete imaginative form."[27]

Donald Davie carries George Steiner's mildly critical view of *The Kreutzer Sonata* to an uncompromising conclusion. He regards it as "a badly flawed work, one that cannot be categorized as 'novel of ideas' . . . a thoroughly respectable literary kind, having methods and conventions proper to it." *The Kreutzer Sonata*, he argues, is "a novel and a tract at once, or it essays to be both at once. It is both and neither. And the conventions which govern it are confused, so that the reader does not know 'which way to take it.' Nor, so far as we can see, was this ambiguity intended by the author. It is therefore a grossly imperfect work." Davie argues that whereas in the "great works" (*War and Peace*, etc.) "we are concerned with the artist Tolstoy," "with Tolstoy's vision," in *The Kreutzer Sonata* we are concerned with "the conflict inside Tolstoy," with "Tolstoy the agonized titan," with "Tolstoy's life." "The vision is not independent in *The Kreutzer Sonata*, and the novel suffers accordingly."[28]

Yet is the matter one of confused conventions in *The Kreutzer Sonata*, or is it a case of a work of unique artistic integrity not adapting to arbitrary conventions? *The Kreutzer Sonata* is as much an imaginative work as Dostoevsky's *Notes from the Underground*, a work which also combines elements of authorial polemic and fiction, and in addition involved Dostoevsky on a deeply subjective plane. In *The Kreutzer Sonata*, as in *Notes from the Underground*, there is an organic unity between the psychology and ideology of its primary narrator (Pozdnyshev). The "conflict" may be inside the man Tolstoy; indeed, it took on many forms in him at different times in his life. What is important, however, is that the conflict develops independently in the artistic framework of *The Kreutzer Sonata*. The drama of Pozdnyshev's character and ideas acquires a momentum of its own, and as in *Notes from the Underground*, the ideas and character of the anti-hero (whether through authorial design or not) are called into question. *The Kreutzer Sonata* poses a great many questions, but it does so not only or even principally through the direct polemic of the hero, but through his character and fate. These questions—or the artist's view of them—can be evaluated only in the context of a discussion of *The Kreutzer Sonata* as a *work of art*.

In general, the radical distinction between the "conflict inside men" and the "conflict inside Tolstoy,"[29] between "imaginative" art and art with "moralistic and pedagogic strains,"[30] is schematic and arbitrary; it derives, in part at least, from a rude distinction between Tolstoy's earlier "artistic" works and his later "moralistic" writings. Tolstoy's post-"crisis" works do have specific characteristics. Yet works such as *The Death of Ivan Ilych*, "Master and Man," "Father Sergius," and *The Kreutzer Sonata*, for all their "moralistic and pedagogic strains," are colossal works of art. They are remarkable precisely for their perfect mastery of the moral-didactic genre, that is, for their subordination of the genre to both the complexity of life and the requirements of art. The conventions that govern *The Kreutzer Sonata*—that is, the conventions that *it* governs—may be syncretic, as are those which *War and Peace* created for itself, but they are not confused.[31]

Jacques Madaule has noted that some Dostoevskian types inhabit "that uncertain region between good and evil in which one can never be sure how far apparent good overlaps hidden evil, and vice versa. What is certain is that ambiguity in Dostoevsky's universe is a breeding ground for evil." That is certainly true of Ivan Karamazov. From the very beginning of the novel, we learn that he has been living amicably with his father, though (as we learn) he is bursting with anger and resentment. These feelings accumulate as the novel progresses, yet Ivan maintains his surface amiability, concealing his true feelings. Hamlet puts it well:

> O villain, villain, smiling, damned villain!
> My tables—meet it is I set it down,
> That one may smile, and smile, and be a villain;
> At least I'm sure it may be so in Denmark.

It is so in Russia too. Ivan's ability to mask his feelings toward his father is the counterpart of his fatal ability to conceal his true intentions from himself. "Be sure I shall always defend him [Fyodor]," Ivan says to Alyosha. "But in my wishes I reserve full latitude for myself in this case. Don't condemn me, and don't look upon me as a villain."

Dostoevsky puts here the words "he added with a smile." A post-Freudian Ivan, perhaps, would not have so blithely assumed that wishes could so easily be walled off from unconscious readiness to realize them. The greater the self-awareness, however, the more subtle the techniques of self-deception. And that is certainly true of Ivan's conversations with Smerdyakov before leaving his father's house, conversations in which he signals in convoluted ways his assent to actions that may, and indeed do, contribute to the murder of his father.

Shakespeare rivals Dostoevsky in depicting the game of verbal signs and signals, that is, in depicting states of moral ambiguity (Chapter 12, "States of Ambiguity"). The theme of complicity and moral duplicity engages Shakespeare in several scenes involving King John and his chamberlain Hubert in *King John*. John signals to Hubert (the "winking of authority") his desire to do away with Prince Arthur, rightful heir to King Richard I's throne. But when he receives news of Arthur's death, he adopts a line of defense that recalls Smerdyakov in his last meetings with Ivan: "But thou didst understand me by my signs / And didst in signs again parley with sin; / Yes, without stop, didst let thy heart consent." John's words also could have been spoken by a more honest Ivan.[32]

The names of Nietzsche and Dostoevsky have consistently been linked in modern European literature and thought. Dostoevsky knew nothing about Nietzsche or his work. On the other hand, Nietzsche read Dostoevsky and was enamored of his writings. He read *Notes from the House of the Dead*, a garbled version of *Notes from the Underground*, *The Devils*, and probably *The Idiot*. It appears that he did not read *Crime and Punishment* or *The Brothers Karamazov*. The discoveries of Schopenhauer, Stendahl, and Dostoevsky, Nietzsche maintained, were signal events in his life. He prized Dostoevsky's work as the "most valuable psychological material known to me—I am grateful to him in a remarkable way, however much he goes against my deepest instincts."[33] Nietzsche certainly found in Dostoevsky rich material confirming his notion of the crisis of nihilism. Both Dostoevsky and Nietzsche posit, each in his own way, a moral and spiritual crisis in European civilization: the *devaluation of the highest values*. Nietzsche sought a "countermovement" in the creation of new values, in a philosophical outlook that would accept the world as it is—that is, as indifferent to values. Dostoevsky, on the other hand, turned to traditional Christian values for a solution to the problem of nihilism. Dostoevsky's Christian values, however, did not prevent Nietzsche from fully appreciating his work. He placed Dostoevsky's work in the category of affirmative art, the category of tragedians who have the courage "to represent terrible and questionable things," who do not fear them. Defending his view that "there is no such thing as pessimistic art," Nietzsche adds: "Art affirms. Job affirms. . . . How liberating is Dostoevsky!"[34]

The understanding of the complex community of interests between Dostoevsky and Nietzsche has certainly been hampered by a tradition of Nietzsche interpretation that sought directly to translate his *philosophical* insights, concerns, and imagery into concrete social-historical and even political terms. In this perspective, Nietzsche's "Übermensch" has been transformed into the rapacious "immoralist" and "superman" of early-twentieth-century literary and political thought. Along these lines, Dostoevsky's Raskolnikov has been perceived as a prefiguration of Nietzsche's so-called immoralist-superman. The independent life of Nietzsche's thought in twentieth-century culture—what the Russians call Nietzsche-ism (*Nitsshean-stvo*)—cannot be ignored, of course. It, too, is part of the crisis of nihilism the philosopher anticipated, and Nietzsche himself is to blame for neglecting the social and political implications of his thought; but the history of Nietzsche's ideas should not be used to cloud his fundamental philosophical concerns or to obscure the very real kinship that exists between Nietzsche and Dostoevsky as artist-philosophers and philosopher-artists. Not without reason did Nietzsche write apropos his first reading of Dostoevsky: "The instinct of affinity . . . spoke to me instantaneously."[35]

One may, of course, "takes sides" in the Nietzsche-Dostoevsky discussion, as did the Russian philosopher Nicholas Berdyaev when he wrote: "Dostoevsky knew everything that Nietzsche knew, but he also knew something that Nietzsche did not know."[36] Yet what makes a juxtaposition of Dostoevsky and Nietzsche interesting is that they seem to "know" what the other knows; both are continually taking sides against themselves in their explorations of the human condition; both deeply know more than they want to know. They are artist-thinkers who, each in his own way, are unable to reconcile themselves to the world as they see it.

"The investigation of Dostoevsky's religious philosophy remains as a serious task for the future," Vyacheslav I. Ivanov wrote in the chapter "Theological Aspect" toward the end of his study *Dostoevsky* (1932), a work which incorporated and developed parts of earlier studies he had written on Dostoevsky. "In our modern and more sober times," Ivanov complains, "investigation is directed almost exclusively towards matter of fact problems of form."[37] In "Theological Aspect," Ivanov strongly affirmed the Christian character and design of Dostoevsky's art, rooting it deeply in the personal spiritual life and vision of Dostoevsky. Ivanov wrote of the "unshakable rock of scholastic theology, whose name, in the language of St. Thomas Aquinas is 'Sacra Doctrina.'" Ivanov goes on to observe: "We are equally entitled to speak—mutatis mutandis—of a 'doctrine' propounded by Dostoevsky. Both writers make it 'the end of the whole and of each part'—we quote Dante's words concerning his own work . . . to lead [the living] to a state of bliss."[38] Yet Ivanov emphasizes the "dynamic and tragic" character of "Dostoevsky's apologetics."[39] The affirmation of Dostoevsky's art is achieved at continual cost. "The Hell that he vanquishes is a dispersed part of his own self, and the flame of Purgatory sears him with unending torments. His cry to God is ever 'out of the depths I cry to thee' (de profundis clamavi). No signs reach him from a Beatrice awaiting him in Heaven. Only the 'holy sickness' at moments lifts before him the curtain over the entrance to Paradise."[40] Dostoevsky's struggles in his art, or the struggles of his heroes and heroines, are without resolution, but these struggles, Ivanov suggests, are overwhelmingly *indicative* of a way out.

Ivanov's magisterial eloquence or rhetoric in his book can be offputting. The word "doctrine"—Ivanov is provoking his reader—is an unfortunate choice to define what Ivanov plainly recognizes is Dostoevsky's complex artistic vision of the universe. Ivanov believes in the "great organic unity of Dostoevsky's works as a whole." Yet nowhere in his writings, except in "Theological Aspect," does he explore extensively Dostoevsky's religious philosophy and the way in which it finds expression in his poetics. In his several studies on Dostoevsky, however, Ivanov has made extremely valuable contributions to an under-

standing of Dostoevsky's art. Particularly valuable were his early discussions of the form and dynamics of Dostoevsky's "novel-tragedy";
his exploration of strata of myth in Dostoevsky's novels; his perception
of the polyphonic character of Dostoevsky's universe, and, linked with
this notion, his ethical-religious conception of Dostoevsky's realism as
based fundamentally on the notion of "thou art."

The critic and philosopher Mikhail Bakhtin was heir to Ivanov's
deepest religious concerns; he certainly developed Ivanov's thought
most fully in the realm of poetics. In his review of scholarly literature
on Dostoevsky in chapter 1 of *Problems of Dostoevsky's Poetics* (2d ed.
1963), Bakhtin acknowledges in Ivanov the writer who posited the
"fundamental [religioethical] principle" in Dostoevsky's art. However,
Bakhtin observes, while Ivanov "incorporated it into a monologically
formulated authorial worldview . . . he did not show how this principle
of Dostoevsky's worldview becomes the principle behind Dostoevsky's
artistic visualization of the world." Ivanov's "fundamental principle" is
of interest to Bakhtin in his book not as "the ethicoreligious principle
behind an abstract worldview," but only insofar as it governs "concrete
literary construction."

Only this side of the question is "essential for the literary scholar."
Bakhtin speaks of "the fundamental innovation that [Dostoevsky's]
poetics represents; its organic unity within the whole of Dostoevsky's
work" yet disavows any intention in his book to examine that whole.
Indeed, Bakhtin establishes in his "specialized study" a very strict
focus upon Dostoevsky's poetics. Yet Bakhtin's point of departure,
paradoxically, is to "show how this principle [the "ethicoreligious
principle"] becomes the principle behind [Dostoevsky's] *artistic* visualization of the world."[41] It is fair to say that the examination of Dostoevsky's religious philosophy, or what Ivanov calls more generally
Dostoevsky's "philosophy of life," though in fact at the periphery of
Bakhtin's concerns, in essence constitutes its invisible center.

In *Dostoevsky's Quest for Form: A Study of His Philosophy of Art*
(1966) and later in several parts of my study *The Art of Dostoevsky*
(1980), I have set forth my view of the novelist's philosophy of art.
There I focused on Dostoevsky's concept of man's spiritual-religious
quest for the ideal, for beauty, for truth—ultimately, for Christ; I
defined it broadly as a "quest for form." Central to Dostoevsky's

religious-philosophical point of view is the idea of a permanent tension toward the ideal, a permanent process of overcoming and self-overcoming in the face of what Dostoevsky called "opposite proofs." My discussion of Bakhtin (Chapter 15, "Bakhtin's Poetics of Dostoevsky and Dostoevsky's 'Declaration of Religious Faith'") is largely an attempt to correlate my views with Bakhtin's view of Dostoevsky's poetics. In other words, the essay is an effort to elucidate on a connection that the Russian critic in passing establishes between Dostoevsky's poetics and his religious philosophy.

Dostoevsky quite lucidly gives expression to his central religious-philosophical idea in his important letter to N. D. Fonvizina in February 1854, in his notebook (April 16) in 1864, and in several other places in his writings. In his letter to Fonvizina, he characterizes his faith in paradoxical terms: his "thirst to believe" is "all the stronger" in him because of "opposite proofs." Dostoevsky provides a view of himself, "a child of lack of faith and doubt," as a person who is in continual struggle, who has only "moments" of faith and tranquility. Here Dostoevsky returns again to paradox in his definition of his faith: His luminous, spiritually complete, and aesthetically perfect image of Christ is so compelling that even if somebody "proved" to him that "Christ was outside the truth, and it *really* were so that the truth was outside of Christ," then he "would rather remain with Christ than with the truth."[42]

Dostoevsky's personal credo becomes the foundation of his religious philosophy of history and life. The history of humanity and of the individual is "only the development, struggle, striving and achievement" of the goal of "Christ's heaven." Man's existence on earth is necessarily flawed because he "strives on earth for an ideal that is *contrary* to his nature." ("The nature of God is directly contrary to the nature of man.") This existence, however, is rendered viable—by striving or struggle. Man on earth—and here we are touching on Dostoevsky's core belief—is forever "achieving, struggling and, through all defeats, refocusing on the ideal." Spiritual health for Dostoevsky is characterized by movement—not aimless movement, not movement crowned by the achievement of a goal, but movement reflected in a *tension toward an ideal.* (Christ is the "*ideal of man in flesh.*") Dostoevsky posits this "law of striving for the ideal" as a "law of nature."[43]

Bakhtin's view of the unfinalized dialogical character of all aspects of Dostoevsky's novelistic world—or as he puts it, "the dialogicality of the ultimate whole"[44]—is in part a development of Dostoevsky's concept of movement and striving, his concept of man's condition as one marked by permanent spiritual crisis. Some of the key ideas of Bakhtin's conception of Dostoevsky's poetics—the Russian novelist's "new artistic position," one that "affirms the independence, internal unfinalizability, and indeterminacy of the hero"—are fully in accord with Dostoevsky's expressed ideas on the "law of striving." "It is given to all Dostoevsky characters to 'think and seek higher things,'"[45] Bakhtin writes. Dostoevsky, the author, is conceived as a seeker in his own works. Among the "voices," or "world of consciousnesses," Dostoevsky "seeks the highest and most authoritative orientation"; "the image of the ideal human being or the image of Christ represents for him the resolution of ideological questions."

Yet there is no resolution for Dostoevsky or for any of his characters in their striving, Bakhtin stresses. Man is continually seeking the truth in a world of conflicting "truths," other "voices"; his achievement, the achievement of "man" as we find him collectively in Dostoevsky's novels, is *the process of continually striving to surmount other "truths," other "voices," "opposite proofs" inside and outside of himself.* In this struggle, man stands *in relation to* truth—in tension toward it. The "ideal orientation (the true word) and its potential," as Bakhtin puts it, are "never lost sight of," is literally forever "before the eyes."[46] "Not faith (in the sense of a specific faith in orthodoxy)," Bakhtin writes, "but a sense of faith, that is, an integral attitude . . . toward a higher and ultimate value."[47] To the extent that Dostoevsky's novels— that is, man as he is presented in them—give evidence of this continual striving, this conscious or unconscious tension toward the ideal in the face of "opposite proofs," to that extent we may say that Dostoevsky's "declaration of religious faith," as Bakhtin puts it, or his religious "doctrine," as Ivanov put it, plays an organic role in the *artistic* structuring of Dostoevsky's novels.

The final essay, Chapter 16, "Last Stop: Virtue and Immortality in

The Brothers Karamazov," was written some time before the essay on Bakhtin, and it is essentially without an a priori theoretical framework. Nonetheless, it "takes place" in a context explored by Bakhtin, namely, the question of the authorial position in Dostoevsky's works. Bakhtin rigorously affirmed in his foreword to the 1963 edition of his Dostoevsky book: "Critics are apt to forget that Dostoevsky is first and foremost an artist (of a special type, to be sure) and not a philosopher or publicist."[48] Later on, apropos Dostoevsky's journalistic writings in various periodicals and his *Diary of a Writer*, Bakhtin further accents the distinction he finds between Dostoevsky the artist and Dostoevsky the journalist or philosopher.

> In these articles he expressed definite philosophical, religious-philosophical, and sociopolitical *ideas*; he expressed them there (that is, in the articles) as *his own confirmed* ideas in a *systemically monologic* or rhetorically monologic (*in fact, journalistic*) form. These ideas were sometimes expressed by him in letters to various correspondents. What we have in the articles and letters are not, of course, images of ideas, but straightforward monologically confirmed ideas. But we also meet these "Dostoevsky ideas" in his novels. How should we regard them there, that is, in the artistic context of his creative work?[49] [Bakhtin's italics]

Bakhtin bluntly answers his own question: "In exactly the same way we regard the ideas of Napoleon III in *Crime and Punishment* (ideas with which Dostoevsky the thinker was in total disagreement), or the ideas of Chaadaev and Herzen in *The Adolescent* (ideas with which Dostoevsky the thinker was in partial agreement)."[50] Bakhtin's answer is not entirely helpful. If Dostoevsky the thinker is "in partial agreement with [Chaadaev's and Herzen's] ideas" in a novel that is in charge of Dostoevsky the "artist," then the radical distinction between the artist and thinker breaks down. Yet Bakhtin is certainly correct in affirming that "the ideas of Dostoevsky the thinker, upon entering his polyphonic novel, change the very form of their existence, they are translated into artistic images of ideas. . . . They become thoroughly dialogized and enter the great dialogue of the novel on *completely equal terms* with other idea-images."[51]

This process of transformation into dialogue is certainly the fate of an idea that Dostoevsky thundered out in his December 1876 *Diary of a Writer* in an item entitled "Arbitrary Assertions": "I declare (once again *for the time being* without proof) love for humanity is even quite unthinkable, incomprehensible and *quite impossible without concurrent faith in the immortality of the human soul*" (Dostoevsky's italics).[52] On entering *The Brothers Karamazov*, however, this idea does become "thoroughly dialogized." Ivan Karamazov gives expression to essentially the same idea that Dostoevsky does in his *Diary of a Writer*: "There is no virtue if there is no immortality," Ivan declares. This idea, however, comes under sharp scrutiny in *The Brothers Karamazov*, and not surprisingly, it is found wanting precisely because of its arbitrary and dogmatic formulation. One may make "arbitrary assertions," but in life (here, in literature) these assertions may have unexpected consequences quite as arbitrary as the assertions that gave rise to them. It is precisely Ivan's dogmatic insistence on the connection between virtue and immortality (he finds little virtue on earth) that leads him to breakdown. In the final analysis, Dostoevsky dispenses with all formulaic equations and rectilinear attempts to resolve the problem of the interrelations of virtue and immortality. The problem cannot be resolved rationally: it can only be endlessly dissolved in the free effort of love. Love for Dostoevsky is the straightest path to faith.

The essays gathered in this book were written over the past twenty years. Most of them have been published separately in earlier versions. Almost all of these studies have undergone some revision or extension. A few are published here for the first time (Chapters 2, 3, 5, 15). In the end, the connective links between the studies are the crisscrossing paths of my own explorations. I have not been guided, at least consciously, by any particular critical approach or theory, though I should have been glad to subtitle my book "Essays in the Old Criticism" if George Steiner had not preempted that subtitle in his *Dostoevsky or Tolstoy: An Essay in the Old Criticism*. Older than even old criticism, however, are the intractable problems that preoccupy both literature and criticism. Essentially, I have sought no more than to bring into focus and distinguish the shape and movement of some of these problems.

The Ethics of Vision I

Turgenev's "Execution of Tropmann"
and Dostoevsky's View of the Matter

Often and often I blame myself for not having given more attention to
accounts of public executions. One should always take an interest in such
matters. There's never any knowing what one may come to. Like everyone
else I'd read descriptions of executions in the papers.

Albert Camus, *The Stranger*

The full horror of what happened you cannot know for you did not see it.

Sophocles, *Oedipus Rex*

 At the end of Book 4 of Plato's *Republic*, Socrates, pur-
suing his argument that the soul is a unity in diversity, provides an example in which "spiritedness" or "noble wrath"
(*thumos*), appears to be the natural ally of reason:

I once heard something that I trust. Leontius, the son of Aglaion, was
going up from the Piraeus under the outside of the North Wall when he
noticed corpses lying by the public executioner. He desired to look, but at
the same time he was disgusted and made himself turn away; and for a
while he struggled and covered his face. But finally, overpowered by the
desire, he opened his eyes wide, ran towards the corpses and said; "Look,
you damned wretches, take your fill of the fair sight!" [1]

Socrates' interpretation of the story aside, the incident suggests a
basic conflict between man's curiosity or lower instincts and appetites
and his moral nature or instinct to protect himself from realities that
threaten to destabilize the soul or the psyche. Leontius's powerful desire to look comes up against deep resistance in him; he struggles for
a while and makes himself turn away, but in the end, overcome by a
desire that expresses itself almost physiologically in his wide-open
eyes, he *looks*. His angry statement "Look, you damned wretches, take
your fill of the fair sight!" suggests the power of *thumos*, but also the
overwhelming force of the desire to see and know the forbidden.

Socrates' story highlights a phenomenon that is a matter of common experience: the confusion of impulses or instincts that almost invariably accompanies looking at scenes of violence, ugliness, and death. For Turgenev and Dostoevsky (and as we shall see, Tolstoy), looking at such scenes—specifically, looking at public executions—raised serious social, ethical, and psychological questions.[2] Each of these writers is troubled when looking at executions. Each "looks" in his own way, and each provides variants, as it were, of the Platonic model.

Turgenev's and Dostoevsky's discussions of executions certainly bear a direct relation to each other; indeed, they stand in polemical relation to each other. Prince Myshkin's discussion of executions in *The Idiot* turns up in part 1 of the novel, published in January 1868. Turgenev's "Execution of Tropmann" ("Kazn' Tropmana," 1870), though inspired by a real execution he attended in January 1870, certainly was written with an eye to Dostoevsky's approach to this theme in *The Idiot*.[3] Dostoevsky, in turn, responded to Turgenev's article negatively in a letter to N. N. Strakhov on June 11, 1870, and—in a parodic and masked allusion to the sketch—in his novel *The Devils* the following year. Dostoevsky based his parody in part on stories circulating about Turgenev's allegedly self-centered and cowardly behavior as a young man in 1838 on the sinking steamer *Nicholas I*. Turgenev's *Un incendie en mer*, an account of this incident dictated in French to Polina Viardot a few months before his death in 1883, may in some respects be considered his response, unfanciful and unbarbed, to the different accounts (including Dostoevsky's in *The Devils*) of this incident.[4]

In January 1870, Jean Baptiste Tropmann, a young Frenchman under twenty, was publicly beheaded before an eager crowd of 25,000 Parisians, his crime cold-bloodedly killing a family of six—father, pregnant mother, and four children. He insisted to the end that he had had accomplices but adduced no evidence to support that contention.

Turgenev was living in Paris at the time and was invited by officials to attend the execution. He gave an account of the event in "The Execution of Tropmann," a sketch consisting of twelve sections. In his account he describes the time he spent between 12:00 midnight and the execution at 7:00 A.M.: his arrival at the prison; conversations with notables attending the affair; setting up the guillotine and the rehearsal of the event on the square; the final interrogation and preparation of Tropmann for the execution; the walk to the guillotine; and the execution itself.

Waiting through the long hours of the night in the prison governor's apartment for the execution ("We wandered about like condemned souls, 'comme des âmes en peine,' as the French say"), the narrator is unable to sleep. The atmosphere is eerie, frightening, demonic. The horror of the scene is repeatedly conveyed to the narrator in sounds even more threatening and inescapable than sights:

> The distant hollow noise of the crowd was getting louder, deeper and more and more unbroken. At three o'clock [A.M.] . . . there were already more than twenty five thousand people gathered there. The noise struck me by its resemblance to the distant roar of the sea: the same sort of unending Wagnerian crescendo, not rising continuously, but with huge intervals between the ebb and flow; the shrill notes of women's and children's voices rose in the air like thin spray over this enormous rumbling noise; there was the brutal power of some elemental force discernible in it. It would grow quiet and die down for a moment, then the hubbub would start again, grow and swell, and in another moment it seemed about to strike, as though wishing to tear everything down, and then it would again retreat, grow quiet, and again swell—and there seemed to be no end to it... And what, I could not help asking myself, did this noise signify? Impatience, joy, malice?... No! It did not serve as an echo of any separate, any human feeling... It was simply the rumble and the roar of some elemental force. . . .
>
> I still remember the face of a workman, a young fellow of about twenty: he just stood there grinning, with his eyes fixed on the ground, just as though he were thinking of something amusing, then he would suddenly throw back his head, open his mouth wide and begin to shout in a drawn-out voice, without words, and then his head would again drop and he would start grinning again. What was going on inside that man? Why did he consign himself to such a painfully sleepless night, to an almost eight-hour immobility?[5]

Like "phantoms," street urchins inhabit the branches of trees, "whistling and screeching like birds." The guillotine had some "sort of sinister shapeliness, the shapeliness of a long, carefully stretched out swan's neck." Amidst all the shouts, abusive arguments, shrill whistles, hideous bursts of laughter, coarse singing, rank breath of alcoholic fumes, all the ominous preparations for the execution, "the only innocent creatures among us all seemed to be the horses harnessed to the vans and calmly chewing the oats in their nose-bags." "'A bas Pierre Bonaparte!' someone shouted at the top of his voice... Oo-oo-ah-ah! the crowd responded in an incoherent roar." Not surprisingly does one of the gentlemen observers imagine that it was not 1870 but 1794, that the observers were not ordinary citizens but Jacobins, that Tropmann was not a common murderer but a marquis-legitimist. Indeed, the "hoarse roar," the "menacing chorus," the "elemental, that is, senseless" shouting, seems to rise out of depths that threaten all civilization.

Yet integral with the narrator's revulsion for the masses is his growing disgust with his role as gentleman observer of the execution. He is increasingly uncomfortable with his role as witness. "False shame," he tells us at the outset of the sketch, prevented him from going back on his decision to accept the invitation to attend the execution. "As for me," he writes a little later, "I felt one thing: namely that I had no right to be where I was, that no psychological or philosophical considerations excused me." Observing the preparations for the execution, he remarks: "I did not stop to look at this rehearsal, that is, I did not climb onto the platform: the feeling of some unknown transgression committed by myself, of some secret shame, was constantly intensifying in me..." He refuses to partake in the preexecution "collation" for the notables. "'I have no right,' I kept saying to myself for the hundredth time since the beginning of that night." And in the walk to Tropmann's cell before the execution, the thought again flashes through the narrator's mind that "we had no right to do what we were doing, that by being present with an air of hypocritical solemnity at the killing of a being like us, we were participating in some kind of lawless, detestable farce."

The narrator's sense of being in the wrong place intensifies until in the eleventh chapter, the penultimate one that gives an account of the execution, this revulsion expresses itself in a dramatic gesture. At the high point of his description of the last moments preceding the beheading, we learn: "But here I turned away—and began to wait— the ground slowly rising and falling beneath my feet..." The narrator, in short, averts his eyes from the sight of the actual decapitation of

Tropmann.[6] There is a lapse of twenty seconds before he "glances at a companion who had grasped his arm to support him."

The gesture of averting his eyes from the actual beheading is of signal importance in the sketch; it not only gives final embodiment to the narrator's persistent thought that he had no right to be where he was, but points toward one of the principal thoughts of Turgenev's sketch: that the witnessing of violence, crime, the physical or moral degradation of another human being, implicates the observer in the act of violence. The narrator's gesture, then, raises the issue of the ethics of observation, one involving various psychological questions relating to the peculiar interest aroused by scenes of death and violence.

Whatever the man Turgenev missed when he turned away from the actual decapitation of Tropmann on January 7, 1870, it cannot be said that the artist Turgenev either ignored the details of Tropmann's execution or the moral-psychological issues surrounding it. The twenty seconds or less during which the narrator averts his eyes from the guillotine are by no means idle ones. The narrator first listens to the guillotine much as the victim listens.[7] In lines of extraordinary onomatopoetic power, he describes the sound of the descending knife of the guillotine: "*Potom chto-to vdrug glukho zarychalo i pokatilos'—i ukhnulo... tochno ogromnoe zhivotnoe otkharknulos...*" (Then something suddenly began to growl indistinctly and set into motion—and grunted... just as though a huge animal had retched...). The animal sounds of the "monster guillotine" form a counterpart to the animal response of the crowd to the spectacle—"the thunderous squeal of the overjoyed and expectant crowd."

After these twenty seconds—from an artistic point of view that interval serves as a device of dramatic retardation—the narrator picks up his visual account of the beheading. At the beginning of chapter 12, he writes:

> Our group gathered in the guard-house . . . I, too, went in there and learned that, while lying on the plank, Tropmann suddenly and convulsively threw his head sideways, so that it did not fit into the semi-circular hole, and the executioners were forced to drag it there by the hair, and while they were doing it, he bit one of them, the main one, by the finger.

Tropmann's head ("it" is almost a detached object in this description), his bite, are an intimation of the cruel if unequal struggle waged here.

It is almost impossible to describe a beheading as it occurs. The narrator approaches the matter both at his leisure and with the aid of his imagination. In the haircutting ceremony preceding Tropmann's execution, he declares: "*I could not turn my eyes away* . . . particularly from that slender youthful neck... In my imagination I could not help seeing a line cut straight across it... Precisely there, I thought, a five-hundred pound axe would in a few moments pass, smashing the vertebrae and cutting through the veins and muscles... and yet the body did not seem to expect anything of the kind: it was so smooth, so white, so healthy..." (my italics). And in one of several dramatic descriptions of the guillotine, this one during the guillotine "rehearsal," the narrator points out the "large wicker basket, looking like a suitcase" into which "the executioners would throw the warm and still quivering body and the cut-off head..." The *artist* Turgenev, then, does not and cannot turn away from the beheading. He loses nothing in averting the eyes of his narrator from an essentially indescribable moment; rather, he provides the reader in advance with ample material to exercise *his* imagination when the narrator momentarily turns away from the actual decapitation. After the beheading, moreover, the narrator adds a detail that would satisfy even the most eager seeker of sensation:

> [I learned that] immediately after the execution, at the time when the body, thrown into the van, was being driven away at a fast clip, two men taking advantage of the first moments of inevitable confusion, penetrated the lines of the soldiers and, crawling under the guillotine, began soaking their handkerchiefs in the blood that had dripped through the chinks of the planks...

The narrator adds that he listened to all this talk "as though in a dream." But the artist Turgenev was not dreaming; nor was he slow in exercising the artist's "right" to participate in, and reflect upon, a scene from which the narrator—earlier in the sketch—had excluded both psychologist and philosopher. In his sketch, Turgenev does not turn away from the gory visual details of execution. But precisely the problem of *looking*, of sight, of vision in the deepest ethical and psychological sense, preoccupies him. His concern with sight is signaled first by a series of pronounced references to looking in the chapter given over to the execution of Tropmann—chapter ii.

The verb "see" (*videt'*), or "look at" or "glance at" (*vzgljanut'*), appears a number of times. The central passage leading up to the moment the narrator averts his eyes from the scene:

> I suddenly felt cold, cold to the point of nausea... . . . my legs gave way under me. However, I *looked again* at Tropmann. . . . Those who rushed past him in the street wanted to *see* how his head would roll off... I had not enough spirit for that; with a sinking heart I stopped at the gates... I *saw* the executioner rise suddenly like a black tower on the left side of the guillotine platform; I *saw* Tropmann separate from the huddle of the people below, scrambling up the steps (there were ten of them—as many as ten!); I *saw* how he stopped and turned around; I heard him say: "Dites à Monsieur Claude..." I *saw* him appearing above and two men pouncing on him from the right and the left, like spiders on a fly; I *saw* him falling forward suddenly and his heels kicking... But here I turned away—and began to wait—the ground slowly rising and falling beneath my feet. [My italics]

"I saw," "I saw," "I saw," "I saw." Sight here is not that vision that freely orders and reveals the inner significance of things. This is sight assaulted, captive vision, the eye transfixed. At the moment he turns away, the narrator observes the face of a young sentry: "He looked intently at me with a kind of vacant bewilderment and horror." He had probably come from some "humble and kindly family in a distant village,—and now—what did he not have to see!" In such moments of violence and unfreedom and hypnotic spell, to turn away, to avert one's eyes, is to rescue vision from a condition of "eyes without feeling,"[8] to restore to it its ethical function of insight and judgment.

The account in chapter II of Tropmann's last moments is artfully framed by passages at the end of chapter 10 and the beginning of chapter 12—two passages marked by references to sight that raise the moral issue and direction of Turgenev's "Execution of Tropmann." The theme of sight is introduced in a characteristically understated manner at the very end of chapter 10. "'Listen, Tropmann (*Voyons*, Tropmann!),' M. Claude's [the police commissioner's] voice resounded in the death-like stillness, 'soon, in another minute, everything will be at an end. Do you still persist (*vous persistez*) in claiming that you had accomplices?' 'Yes, sir, I do persist (*Oui, monsieur, je persiste*).'" In the subtext of this bit of dialogue, the idiomatic or figurative *voyons* (listen, come now) yields to its literal and core meaning "we look." "We look," "let us look," signals the conscious or unconscious urge and preoccupation of all the observers of the execution of Tropmann, both gentlemen and mob.

But can one look at, visually participate in, violence without becoming an accomplice in the act of violence and without incurring the guilt? Tropmann insists that he was "not guilty" of the terrible crime for which he had been condemned. He maintains that he had had "accomplices." "I did not strike a blow" (*Je n'ai pas frappé*), he repeats, as though the fact that he did not strike a blow (if indeed true) absolves him of guilt. Turgenev brilliantly integrates this bit of dialogue between Tropmann and M. Claude into his artistic text and subtext. Tropmann's argument that he did not strike the blow and is therefore innocent rests on the common notion that guilt or innocence is only a technical or legal issue. Neither Turgenev nor Dostoevsky accepted this way of thinking. Ivan Karamazov never actually struck a blow at his father; he had an accomplice. Ivan's guilt is nonetheless profound. Turgenev's point is clear: Those who come to witness the execution of Tropmann were accomplices in the violence. As Victor Hugo put it, "Qui assiste au crime, assiste le crime."[9] But the narrator finds accomplices not only in the masses of people who came to witness the execution, but in the gentlemen observers and in himself.

The essence of Turgenev's thought is contained in some lines at the beginning of chapter 12, lines that complete the "framing" of chapter 11. Here the notables gather to convey their impressions of the execution:

> But I listened to all that talk as though in a dream. I felt very tired, and indeed, I was not alone to feel that way. Everybody seemed tired, although everybody obviously felt relieved, just as though a burden had fallen from their shoulders. But not one of us, *absolutely no one looked like a person who recognized that he had presided at the performance of an act of social justice*: Everyone tried mentally to turn away and, as it were, to shake off the responsibility for this murder... [Turgenev's italics]

In these lines Turgenev subtly conveys a number of thoughts central to his sketch. The response of those who came to participate visually in the execution is now "mentally to turn away," as it were, to shake off their responsibility for this act of violence; that is, their mental gesture corresponds to the narrator's real gesture of turning away from the sight of the beheading. Their gesture marks a sense of guilt. Their feeling, nonetheless, is one of relief, as though "a burden had fallen from their shoulders." The phrase is noteworthy. After participating vicariously in the murder of Tropmann, the gentlemen spectators experience a sense of relief; they, like Tropmann, Turgenev hints, have *lost their heads*, that is, paid for their crime.

An examination of the passage cited above yields one further subtle suggestion by Turgenev. The central feeling of the gentlemen observers is one of shame, a sense of complicity. "Not one of them looked like a man who recognized that he had presided at the performance of an act of social justice." Buried in this line is a variant thought: Not one of them "looked like a man" (*smotrel chelovekom*); that is, the act of witnessing crime is a symbolic act of self-disfiguration, a kind of moral decapitation.

A difficult paradox arises from Turgenev's "The Execution of Tropmann": Deliberately looking at an execution, vicariously participating in it, is morally speaking a turning away from humaneness; on the other hand, averting one's eyes from such a scene constitutes an equally immoral act, an attempt to shake off responsibility. In both cases, figuratively speaking, *one loses one's head*; that is, one suffers a kind of self-disfiguration.

Yet Turgenev seems to be saying something else as well: It is impossible literally to look at a scene of violence and degradation, to be absorbed by it, and at the same time look into it, that is, cope with it in moral and spiritual terms. But what is impossible for the individual when confronting violence is possible for the artist in the work of art. Turgenev simultaneously *looks at*—that is, depicts the execution of Tropmann in all its absorbing naturalistic detail and horror and *looks into* the ugliness that unites executioner and observers, looks into it and reveals its meaning in the larger frame of moral truth or image (*obraz*)—that is, the truth of man created in the image and likeness of God. "Can one conceive in an image that which has no image?" asks Ippolit Terentiev in *The Idiot*.[10] The answer to this apparently insoluble question is yes—if, that is, one is a supreme artist like Turgenev, Dostoevsky, or Tolstoy.

In the opening chapter of "The Execution of Tropmann," the narrator, recalling the invitation he received from the writer Maxime Du Camp to attend the execution of Tropmann, observes:

> Taken by surprise by M. Du Camp's proposal, I accepted it without giving it much thought. And having promised to arrive at the place fixed for our meeting—at the statue of Prince Eugene, on the boulevard of the same name, at 11 o'clock in the evening—I did not want to go back on my word. A false sense of shame prevented me from doing so... And what if they should think I was a coward? As a punishment of myself—and as a lesson to others—I intend now to tell everything that I saw. I intend to revive in my memory all the painful impressions of that night. Perhaps more than the reader's curiosity will be satisfied; perhaps he may find my story of some use.

What follows these remarks is the account of the narrator's experience, one that is both documentary and confessional in character.

I speak of a "narrator." The narrator, of course, is Turgenev. Yet the recognition of some distinction between Turgenev as artist and Turgenev as character is essential to an understanding of the text as it is to an understanding of Turgenev's early work *Notes of a Hunter* (*Zapiski okhotnika*), 1847–50). The generally autobiographical character of "The Execution of Tropmann" should not blind us to the fact that the artist Turgenev has deliberately turned his experience into a self-reflecting literary artifact and himself into a character open to criticism; that is, he has subordinated all the elements of his experience to an artistic-ideological design.

The narrator critically observes the eager crowds attending the execution, the notables participating in the procedures and ceremonies surrounding that event, and, though more with admiration or awe, the murderer Tropmann. But he also observes himself and the manner in which he is observed by others. "'There he is, there he is—it's him!' a few voices shouted around us. 'Why,' Du Camp said to me suddenly, 'you have been mistaken for the executioner!' . . . The Paris executioner, Monsieur de Paris, whose acquaintance I made during that same night, is as tall and as grey as I."

The motif of self-criticism is consistent throughout the sketch, as, for example, when the narrator comments on the walk through the prison to Tropmann's "collation": "We all felt a little awkward—or did it only seem to me to be so?—a little ashamed, too, though we walked along jauntily, as though on a hunting expedition." Indicting society, the mob, and the cortege of gentlemen for their participation in the execution, the artist Turgenev in his *Bildungsgeschichte* indicts himself in his role as gentleman narrator; that is, he singles out the conventional man of sensibility who has moral scruples about attending executions, is unable to endure the spectacle, and comes away with a sense of guilt. The narrator is the prism through which the artist observes the execution. He candidly records his painful responses to the entire experience, his feeling that he has no "right" to be present. At the core of Turgenev's design, then, is a sacrifice: making himself as narrator, as a social cultural type, vulnerable to the charges he makes as an artist. The artist, then, stands above his narrator. Hence the irony: in this preeminently philosophical and psychological sketch, the narrator is constantly insisting that he has no "right," philosophical or psychological, to attend executions; in this sketch where the narrator speaks of his "inappropriate curiosity," the artist Turgenev has turned that curiosity into an instrument of self-criticism and analysis.

After reading Turgenev's "Execution of Tropmann," Dostoevsky wrote the following to the critic Nikolai Strakhov in a letter dated June 11, 1870:

> You may have a different view, Nikolai Nikolaevich, but this pompous and finicky article exasperated me. Why does he get all flustered and maintain that he had no right to be there [at the execution]? Yes, of course, if he only came for the spectacle; but man on the surface of the earth does not have the right to turn away and ignore what is taking place on earth, and there are lofty *moral* reasons for this: *homo sum et nihil humanum*, etc.[11] The most comic thing of all is that in the end he turns away and doesn't see how [Tropmann] is finally executed. "Just look, gentlemen, how delicately I have been nurtured! I couldn't bear it." Moreover he gives himself away: the chief impression one gets from the article is a frightful concern—fussy to the nth degree—about himself, his integrity, his composure—and all this over a decapitated head![12]

Dostoevsky's final observation recalls Thomas Macaulay's comment that the proponents of the abolition of capital punishment were victims of "effeminate feelings." Dostoevsky's main criticism, however, centers on Turgenev's insistence that he had no *right* to attend executions.

The moral core of Dostoevsky's critique of Turgenev's cowardly

and squeamish approach toward the execution of Tropmann is echoed
in his well-known parody of Turgenev at the beginning of *The Devils*.
Here the chronicler remarks apropos of Karmazinov, the writer:

> About a year ago I read an article of his in a journal written with a fright-
> ful affectation of the most naive poetry and also psychology. He was de-
> scribing the wreck of a steamer somewhere off the English coast, one
> which he himself had witnessed, and how he had watched the drowning
> people being saved and the drowned people being dragged ashore. The
> whole article was long and verbose, written with the sole purpose of put-
> ting himself in the foreground. So that one could read between the lines:
> "Interest yourself in me, how I behaved in those moments. Why be con-
> cerned with the sea, the storm, the cliffs, the smashed fragments of the
> ship? Why are you looking at that drowned woman with the dead child
> in her dead hands? Rather, look at me, how I was unable to endure this
> spectacle and turned away from it. Here was I with my back to it; here
> was I full of horror and incapable of looking back; I closed my eyes—isn't
> that really interesting."

Dostoevsky's thought is clear: the writer, Karmazinov-Turgenev,
in describing the shipwreck (read also the execution of Tropmann),
should have kept his eyes on the disaster itself and, above all, on the
human tragedy—the dead woman and child (and in Paris he should
have kept his eyes on Tropmann's head). In short, no one has a right
to ignore what is taking place on earth.

How justified is Dostoevsky's criticism? And what underlies his
nervous irritability and sarcasm? Turgenev can in no way be accused
either of sidestepping the brutal and gruesome details of the execution, be they physical or psychological, or "ignoring" in the broad social and moral-philosophical sense what is taking place on the face of
the earth. Indeed, what Dostoevsky accuses him of ignoring is the
precise center of Turgenev's attention. How could Dostoevsky ignore
this fact? What offense or challenge did he find in "The Execution of
Tropmann"?

Dostoevsky's exasperation was understandable. He had been condemned to death in 1849 for subversive activities. The sentence was
commuted to prison and exile only seconds before he was to be executed. "What do you suppose is going on in such a man's soul at this
moment, what agonies must it be experiencing?" Prince Myshkin asks
in *The Idiot*. "It's an outrage on the soul, that's what it is!" Dostoevsky
clearly resented in "The Execution of Tropmann" the narrator's "con-

cern . . . about himself." Reading Turgenev's text, he surely recalled Victor Hugo's *Le Dernier Jour d'un Condamné* (1829)—a work he had remembered at the time he had awaited execution and one that he was later to call Hugo's "masterpiece"—a story told by a man about to be guillotined. Hugo's objective was to compel the viewer to see the spectacle, and himself, through the eyes of the condemned man— a human being like himself.

Turgenev recognizes in Tropmann "a being like us"; his angle of vision, however, is not that of the condemned man. In the humiliating *toilette du condamné*, the narrator takes note of Tropmann's apparent composure, even cheerfulness. He views him almost as a scientific curiosity, an aberration, that is, precisely as a being *not* like us. "If Tropmann had begun to howl and weep, my nerves would certainly not have stood it and I should have run away." But at the sight of "*such* composure," simplicity, even modesty, his feelings of "disgust" over a pitiless murderer and "compassion" for a man about to be executed disappeared in a "feeling of astonishment."

Increasing anguish and alienation mark Hugo's condemned man. Toward the end of his ordeal he bitterly complains of the priest's routine spiritual consolations: "Nothing felt, nothing pitying, nothing born of tears, nothing torn from the soul, nothing that came from his heart to go to mine, nothing that was from him to me." Were these also Dostoevsky's feelings as he read Turgenev's sketch, a work in which the narrator speaks about his own sensibilities, anguish, and nausea, but nothing about the condemned man's? Turgenev morally recoils from the role of spectator, yet he remains the quintessential observer, faithful to things seen, heard, and felt.

"Why does he get all flustered and maintain that he had no right to be there [at the execution]? Yes, of course, if he only came for the spectacle." In his letter to Strakhov, Dostoevsky accidentally touched on an important aspect of the narrator's self-concern in "Execution of Tropmann," one that helps explain his irritation with Turgenev. To judge by Turgenev's curious letter of January 19, 1870, to the seventeen-year-old Claudie Viardot, daughter of the opera singer Pauline Viardot-Garcia, written in the Roquette prison six or seven hours before Tropmann's execution, Turgenev came unprepared for how he would face the full impact of that whole experience.

Dear Didie, my little idol

I have just returned from the theater where I took [the parents of Pau-linette's husband]; it was not "The Princess of Trébizonde" (there was a misunderstanding with the tickets), but a theatrical extravaganza—"Paris Revue"—rather amusing; many magnificent costumes, beautiful scenery, etc. I laughed but I wasn't carried away. . . . I've had enough of Paris. . . . Thursday at 10 I'll see you all at the station, and at 9, Tulipatan, Tulipatan! I am bringing some contredanses [musical scores], etc. etc.

It will soon be one in the morning and they will cut off Tropmann's head at 7 a.m. He is now sleeping a nasty sleep troubled and timor-ous—and he will abruptly raise his head when he hears the door of his cell open at 5 a.m. What a terror will clutch at his throat and stomach—he will want to speak and his lips will stick together. If I were younger or if I were not afraid of catching a cold—which would perhaps prevent me from returning (to Baden-Baden) good God! I believe I would have gone down there to see this crowd. But why have I spoken to you of all these horrors—to you, my dear angel all white as a little lamb! (I speak in the moral sense.) I don't really know; perhaps because I tell you everything that goes through my head, everything I'm taken up with.[13]

Turgenev's letter is valuable to us precisely because he is telling Clau-die all that goes through his head and occupies him.[14]

One senses, perhaps, a certain nervous levity in Turgenev's letter. On the surface he seems to place no distance between the theater he had just watched and the open-air performance he had been invited to attend at La Place de la Roquette, one in which Tropmann would play the leading role and all of Paris was audience. Yet the uncomfort-able irony of his situation could not have been lost on him, though he was perhaps not directly conscious of it at the moment. Here in La Place de la Roquette was indeed a "contredanse" in the baldly literal sense of the two French words joined into one. The execution of Tropmann was certainly no laughing matter. One did not have to be advanced in years and to fear catching a cold to be reluctant to go "down there" to see the crowd and to witness the execution. Behind the suspicious lightness of his efforts to visualize Tropmann's awak-ening at dawn, one senses an incipient terror clutching at Turgenev's throat and stomach.

Was Turgenev's letter to Claudie a last effort to gain some self-control, to establish some aesthetic distance from the ominous event crowding in upon him? Did not he too, like Tropmann in Turgenev's letter, "want to speak"? However we are to understand the motivations and motifs of Turgenev's letter, he clearly took a very different view of Tropmann and Tropmann's execution after a night spent in the Roquette prison and on La Place de la Roquette. Risking catching cold—more accurately, risking trauma of a psychic kind—Turgenev nonetheless went "down there to see this crowd," a step that turned out to be a descent into hell, as his own language and imagery in "The Execution of Tropmann" suggest. "I will not forget this terrible night in the course of which 'I have supp'd full of horrors,'[15] and acquired a definite aversion for capital punishment in general and for how it is carried out in France in particular," Turgenev wrote to his friend Pavel Annenkov on January 22, 1870, apropos of what he termed his "unexpected" experience. "I can only say one thing now: such courage, such scorn for death as Tropmann had I simply could not have imagined. But the whole business is horrible... horrible."[16]

The execution of Tropmann, the epic theater that Turgenev witnessed on a Paris square, turned out to be an entirely different *revue féerie*, or theatrical extravaganza, than the "Paris Revue" he had attended a few hours earlier. Indeed, the whole scene that Turgenev presents in "Execution of Tropmann" comes across to the reader as eerie, nightmarish, unforgettable theater of life. What Turgenev had feared consciously or unconsciously, what during and after the event had placed such a burden on his sight and conscience, he dramatized in his truly extraordinary sketch "The Execution of Tropmann."

Dostoevsky without question sensed intuitively, if not the confessional aspect of Turgenev's sketch, at least something special in Turgenev's sense of guilt and distress in being present at Tropmann's execution, a guilt that surely extended back to his letter to Claudie. Turgenev certainly had not come to the Roquette prison, like the Parisian masses, for the "spectacle"; yet he quickly found himself cast in precisely the role of a spectator, somebody who had left one theater and had dropped in at another for a late-night performance. He was indeed "flustered." Dostoevsky, then, had noted an odd personal side to Turgenev's narrator and in the process disclosed something intimate of Dostoevsky's nature. In focusing on the strictly personal side of Turgenev's narrative, however, Dostoevsky ignored the multidimensional social-psychological and moral-philosophical aspects of "The Execution of Tropmann."

Dostoevsky's reference in his letter to Turgenev's "composure" (Turgenev was hardly composed in the Roquette prison) illuminated another important element in his irritation with the writer of "The Execution of Tropmann": It not only signals the vast stretch between Dostoevsky's turbulent personality and poetics and those of Turgenev, but also points to his early envy and admiration of the youthful aristocrat Turgenev in the 1840's[17]—that same Turgenev who had addressed some barbed epigrams at the then youthful and morbidly self-conscious Dostoevsky.

Finally, one cannot exclude an element of pure jealousy on Dostoevsky's part. Turgenev's "Execution of Tropmann" not only takes up issues that are the heart of some of Dostoevsky's concerns in *Notes from the House of the Dead* and *The Idiot*, but contains pages that rival Dostoevsky's in their artistic brilliance.

Yet we must turn to other areas of genuine distress, conflict, and creative inspiration for Dostoevsky if we are to get to the bottom of his highly charged response to Turgenev's sketch. I have in mind the question that is at the heart of Turgenev's sketch, as it is of Dostoevsky's works: the problem of man's attraction to violence, crime, ugliness, evil. Like Turgenev, and indeed more intensively than he, Dostoevsky was deeply and painfully concerned with the relation of the observer to crime and violence. Precisely in this realm, and finally in his religious-philosophical approach to evil in man, we shall find the deepest source for Dostoevsky's malevolent discontent with Turgenev.

In *Notes from the House of the Dead* (1861–1862) the narrator not only raises the question of the sadomasochistic involvement of the guards and convicts in executions, but directs attention to his own obsessive interest in beatings and executions. "The attributes of the executioner are to be found in almost every contemporary man," he remarks, striking a note that will be central in Turgenev's "Execution of Tropmann." "In that first period in the hospital," the narrator recalls, "I would listen spellbound to all these stories [about beatings] of the convicts." "I was agitated, disturbed and frightened," he observes again. The stories told by the convicts made his heart "rise in his throat and thump heavily and violently." Yet he eagerly probed into all the gruesome details of punishments, the nature of the pain of beatings, beatings that sometimes excited the nerves beyond endurance. "I really don't know why I was after all this," the narrator writes almost evasively. "I only remember one thing, that it was not from idle curiosity. I repeat that I was agitated and shaken." Why *was* the narrator of *Notes from the House of the Dead*, "after all this," as he puts it? We can with assurance say only that it was obviously not out of moral indignation that the narrator's heart thumped heavily and violently, that his eyes were riveted to the suffering backs of his fellow convicts, and that he devotes so much time to the sadistic and masochistic dimension of punishment. What is involved is what Charles Dickens called man's "horrible fascination" with executions.

"The example of violence is a temptation," the narrator writes in a justly famous passage of *Notes from the House of the Dead*, one that opens significantly with a reference to the names of the notorious marquis de Sade (1740–1814) and marquise de Brinvilliers (1651–1675): "Blood and power intoxicate, coarseness and debauchery follow, the most abnormal phenomena begin to appeal to the mind and feelings, become sweet to them." Not only torturer and victim succumb to the disease of violence, Dostoevsky makes clear in *House of the Dead*, but the observer as well; even the most educated, artistic, and scientific observer is not immune to the spectacle of violence, may find something to identify with, or enjoy, in torturer or victim. How shall we put it? *Homo sum et nihil humanum?* We are not trying to subvert Latindom's noble formula. Dostoevsky himself recognizes that Terence's line could be used ironically (as indeed it is used in Terence's work) in a purely psychological and negative sense. Thus Svidrigailov in *Crime and Punishment* employs the expression in defense of his special carnal appetite:

> Now let's just assume, now, that I, too am a man, *et nihil humanum*... in a word, that I am capable of being attracted and falling in love (which, of course, doesn't happen according to our will), that everything can be explained in a most natural way. The whole question is: am I a monster or am I myself a victim? Well, and what if I am a victim?

What we are saying, then, is what Dostoevsky suggests: the narrator's special interest in violence, though permeated by an ethos of moral and social concern, may also be explained, in Svidrigailov's words, "in a most natural way." Here, of course, our distinction between Dostoevsky and his narrator in *Notes from the House of the Dead* is as vital as the distinction between Turgenev and his narrator in "The Execution of Tropmann."

The reader of the first dream of Raskolnikov—the episode in which an old horse is methodically beaten to death in front of an enthusiastic crowd of peasants—is treated to an orgy of violence. The episode is traumatic for the boy in the dream. "Let's go, let's go!" says the boy's father, "they're drunk, they're fooling around, the idiots: let's go, don't look! . . . It's not our business, let's go!" Dostoevsky is saying, of course, that it *is* the business of man to look. Violence, from the moral and social point of view, is our business. We cannot and must not "ignore what is taking place on earth, and there are lofty *moral* reasons for this."

Dostoevsky's point, however, is not that we—above all, children—should passively watch old horses being beaten to death by drunken peasants with crowbars, that we should literally keep our eyes on such scenes of human degradation. That kind of looking points again to other, more "natural" interests and pleasures. Indeed, one of the main points Dostoevsky makes in his account of Raskolnikov's dream is that looking at violence is a form of vicarious and corrupt participation in it. The adult observers, peasant men and women alike, fully enjoy the spectacle of the beating of the horse. Like the crowd of Parisians watching Tropmann's execution, they have not the slightest inclination to turn away, not until the performance is over. As Svidrigailov would cynically say: *homo sum et nihil humanum*; we are involved with a case of the common "brotherhood" of all men.

The complex questions involved in witnessing violence—the ethics and psychology of observation—are taken up again by Dostoevsky in part 1, chapter 5 of *The Idiot*. It is in this chapter that Prince Myshkin meets Mrs. Epanchin and her daughters, and expatiates at length on executions. The chapter opens with a general focus on the aesthetics of sight. The theme of looking which does not *see into* reality—that is, looking that is morally and spiritually blind—is raised here obliquely in the second paragraph of the chapter. In moments of crisis, we are told, Mrs. Epanchin would open her eyes wide and look vacantly before her. "Her rather large grey eyes sometimes had a most unexpected expression. A long time ago she had the weakness to imagine that her gaze was extraordinarily striking." Mrs. Epanchin, however, lacks the capacity to see, a fact that is indirectly indicated by her remark to Myshkin: "Sit down here, Prince, in this armchair, opposite me—no, here—move nearer to the light—in the sun, so that I may see you."

The problem of seeing is raised a moment later in connection with Adelaida's painting. Characteristically, she is "copying a landscape she had already begun from an engraving." She complains that for two years she hasn't been able to find a subject for a picture. "Do find me a subject for a picture, Prince," she asks. But Myshkin, who has his own problems of seeing, especially in Russia[18] (he is even uncertain whether when abroad he actually "learned to look"), does not have much advice to give. "I know nothing about it. It seems to me you just look and paint." "I don't know how to look," Adelaida rejoins quite candidly. Mrs. Epanchin's response is what we would expect from her: "Why are you talking in riddles? Can't understand a word! . . . What do you mean, you don't know how to look? You have eyes and you look." But whether you are involved in painting or simply observing reality, looking involves more than the mechanical act of seeing. Mrs. Epanchin's advice is as useless as Myshkin's: "It seems to me you just look and paint." Myshkin's limitations as an observer, at least at this point in the narrative, are signaled by Aglaya: "Besides, he is a complete child, one could still play blind man's bluff with him." Myshkin, childlike, is groping about in the darkness. For his own sake, too, it is important that he "move nearer to the light."

These discussions form an important background to Myshkin's descriptions of executions. The theme of executions seems to obsess Myshkin. The following conversation between Aglaya and Myshkin poses some of the questions raised by Turgenev in "The Execution of Tropmann":

> "It's a pity, Prince, that you didn't see an execution. I'd have liked to ask you something." "I have seen an execution," replied the prince. "You've seen one?" exclaimed Aglaya. "I might have guessed it! . . ." "I saw one at Lyons, I went there with Schneider, he took me there. No sooner did I get there than the execution took place." "Well, did you like it very much? Was there much that was edifying? Useful?" asked Aglaya. "I didn't like

it at all, and afterwards I was a little sick, but I confess that I looked as though rooted to the spot. I couldn't tear my eyes from it." "I too would have been unable to tear my eyes from it," replied Aglaya.

What keeps Myshkin from tearing his eyes from the guillotine has nothing to do with lofty moral principles, although he is deeply opposed to capital punishment. He is transfixed by the scene. What is more, the execution disturbs him as it disturbs Turgenev's narrator. "Tell us about the execution," Adelaida asks him. "I would really rather not..." Myshkin replies, confused and almost frowning. Like the gentlemen observers after Tropmann's execution, one might say, Myshkin at this moment tries to turn away in spirit from his feeling of guilt and confusion.

Myshkin, however, does go on to describe the execution scene. Not surprisingly, he proposes that the amateur painter Adelaida— precisely Adelaida the copyist ("You most of all," he emphasizes)— paint the face of a man at the moment he is about to be executed. "Just a moment ago . . . when you asked me for a subject for a painting the idea really occurred to me to give you a theme: to depict the face of a condemned man a minute before the blow of the guillotine blade." "I thought at the time that such a picture would be a useful one," Myshkin remarks.

> Paint the scaffold so that only the last step is clearly visible and in the foreground; the criminal stepping on it: his head, his face as white as paper, the priest extending the cross, the man greedily extending his blue lips; he looks, and— *knows everything.* The cross and the head—that's the picture, the priest's face, the faces of the executioner and his two assistants, and several heads and eyes below—all this can be painted as background, in half light, as setting... That's the picture.

But what exactly does Myshkin want to teach by such a picture—beyond instilling in the spectator a horror of capital punishment? Is it the moment of harmony and eternity, the moment of the highest "perception of life" he experiences in the first stage of his epileptic fit? Such a vision might be termed "useful." Yet Myshkin's vision of light and eternity is followed quickly by darkness. Darkness is the obverse side of his vision. Indeed, we must ask what *does* the condemned man see and know? Is his a vision of light or darkness? Or both—and in that order. Perhaps he has seen the light? Is this Myshkin's idea of the painting? The "cross and the head," after all—"that's the picture." The condemned man is "greedily extending his lips" to the cross. Yet here there seems more a terrible desire to believe than belief. More important, we have here only an idea of a painting. Will the talented Adelaida overcome the darkness, that darkness which Myshkin himself cannot overcome and imbues his painting with its grim and morbid theme? "Such a painting," Myshkin later remarks in connection with Hans Holbein's *Christ in the Tomb*, "could make one lose one's faith." Holbein's representation of Christ, presumably, strikes Myshkin as a naturalistic one that carries no intimation of resurrection.

In this connection it is noteworthy that in an essay attributed to Dostoevsky, "An Exhibition in the Academy of Sciences for 1860–1861," the writer sharply criticizes the Russian painter Mikhail P. Klodt's *The Last Spring* for representing in his painting the "agony" of a dying girl in a spiritually crushing way. This "beautifully executed, but unfortunate picture," the critic insists, will "eternally perpetuate this agony" and will drive the spectator away. "No, artistic truth is not at all this, it is something quite different from naturalistic truth." Myshkin may indeed wish his painting to embody the useful idea of pointing to "the highest perception of life," but the image that strikes the reader's eye does not overcome the stark and naturalistic material of the subject. There is no transfiguration, only a passionate wish for it. Will Adelaida transfigure Myshkin's subject by simply *looking* and painting?[19] Or will people run away from her painting? However we interpret Myshkin's idea for a painting, he remains a prisoner of his subject. Quite rightly he recommends that the picture be painted in "half light."

Myshkin's remarks, his references to the details of the painting, come only as an afterword to the main description of the execution, one interestingly enough that does *not* provide the reader with a visual description of the actual decapitation. Like Turgenev in "The Execution of Tropmann," but from the vantage point of the victim, Dostoevsky focuses on the sound of the falling blade. But whereas Turgenev graphically anthropomorphizes the sound of the falling blade, Dostoevsky concentrates on the way the victim hears the blade descending upon him.

Suddenly he *hears* [*uslyshit*] the iron come slithering down over his head! He must certainly *hear* that! If I were lying there, I'd listen for it on purpose and I would *hear* it. There is only perhaps one tenth of second left, but one would certainly *hear* it. And imagine, there are still some people who maintain that when the head is cut off, it knows for a second perhaps that it has been cut off—what a thought! And what if it knows for five seconds! [My italics]

Instead of Turgenev's horrifying "*ja videl*," "*ja videl*," "*ja videl*" "*ja videl*" ("I saw"), we have Dostoevsky's "*uslyshit*," "*uslyshit*," "*uslyshish*," "*uslyshal*," "*uslyshish*"—sounds capturing the slithering and swishing sound of the blade. "As soon as you finished your story," Aglaya remarks to Myshkin, "you suddenly became ashamed of what you've said. Why is that?" Myshkin remains silent. Silence here is eloquent. Myshkin's sense of shame is linked with a deeper sense of complicity and guilt, the same kind of feelings experienced by the narrator and notables at Tropmann's execution.

Dostoevsky's whole approach to the question—to look or not to look?—is marked by ambiguity. On the one hand, he indicts Turgenev directly in his letter to Strakhov and indirectly in the figure of Karmazinov in *The Devils* for turning away from the scene of horror and, as it were, directing attention to his own delicate feelings. Yet in the same novel the narrator with obvious disapproval calls attention to the "greedy curiosity," the "pleasure" with which a group of people look at a corpse, a recent suicide. "In general," the narrator notes, "there is always something that gives pleasure to an outsider's eye in misfortunes that afflict one's fellow man—and *that* applies to everybody." It is noteworthy, however, that in the scene involving the suicide, a few people remain behind, resist yielding to the general curiosity and pleasure. Dostoevsky, then, insists that it is man's moral duty not to ignore what is taking place on earth. At the same time, he is deeply conscious of the more unattractive and dangerous aspects of the instinct to look upon execution and death.

What, then, may we conclude from our discussion of Turgenev's "Execution of Tropmann" and Dostoevsky's approach to executions? The authors appear to have similar concerns and attitudes. Both are troubled by man's attraction to violence and death, and both examine that problem in a broad social and moral-psychological framework.

What is more, Turgenev and Dostoevsky implicitly distinguish between obsessive *looking*, one captivated and fascinated by horror, and artistic or spiritual vision that looks *into* a phenomenon, contextualizes it in a moral sense, and thereby brings it under control. Turgenev's repeated expression "I saw," "I saw," "I saw" and Myshkin's transfixed gaze are psychologically of the same order.

Why, then, was Dostoevsky so upset by Turgenev's sketch? The answer, I believe, is twofold. First, and in the most immediate sense, Dostoevsky was, like Myshkin and Aglaya, himself literally "unable to tear his eyes" from scenes of violence and execution. The reasons have nothing to do with high-mindedness. Turgenev's gesture of turning away, whether one of will or weakness, must have reminded Dostoevsky of his own fascination with violence. What troubled Dostoevsky in the first instance, I suggest, is what troubled Hamlet's mother when, under the force of Hamlet's reproach that she had "eyes without feeling," she exclaimed:

> O Hamlet, speak no more!
> Thou turn'st mine eyes into my very soul,
> And there I see such black and grained spots
> As will not leave their tinct.

Yet there is another aspect of the matter that deserves equal attention. Dostoevsky seized upon a literal gesture of recoil on Turgenev's part—one not at all characteristic of his own nature—and interpreted it figuratively, proclaiming that Turgenev was ignoring what was taking place on earth. Nothing was further from the truth. Yet Turgenev's narrator—though he expresses a sense of "shame" at having allowed himself to play the spectator; though in general he places the spectator on no higher moral plane than Tropmann (who in fact emerges in this sketch as a more integral and admirable figure than the spectators); though he suggests finally that the executioner exists in all of us— does not identify himself with the crowd and their lower instincts. "Why, for the sake of what sensations, had *they* left the rut of everyday life for a few hours?" the narrator asks at the end of the sketch (my italics). "It is awful to think what is hidden there."

The signal characteristic of Dostoevsky is that he asks this question of himself and compels the reader to examine his own deepest instincts. Dostoevsky, who felt the force of evil perhaps more closely than any other Russian writer, clearly understood that the fact that we note in ourselves the same brutal and degrading impulses and responses that we find in others is not in itself a cause for self-congratulation. Yet the cornerstone of his religious-philosophical outlook is his insistence that human solidarity begins at the point we recognize our solidarity in evil with others. All efforts at redemption, he believes, must begin with this recognition. Dostoevsky clearly identified himself with the crowd in its corrupt tastes and its craving for sensation, but he also identified himself with it in its countercraving for redemption from sin. And this craving for sensation, suffering, and redemption was very different in character from Turgenev's deepseated disgust with the crowd and his instinctive need to separate himself from the violence, corruption, and evil that threaten to engulf, and do indeed engulf in one degree or another, the witness of violence.

Here it is worth noting that Turgenev has his narrator turn away from the beheading in chapter II of his sketch of twelve chapters; that is, he turns away in the symbolic eleventh hour, the hour of salvation. For Dostoevsky, however, the drama of salvation lay in the Crucifixion (an event that dominates Dostoevsky's whole preoccupation with executions in *The Idiot*). One cannot turn away from the crucifixion, from the supreme drama of suffering, even at the risk of losing one's faith. "I like to look at this picture," Rogozhin remarks in *The Idiot* apropos of a copy of Hans Holbein's *Christ in the Tomb* on the wall. To which Myshkin replies, as I have noted earlier: "Really, looking at this picture a person might lose his faith." Later, Ippolit Terentiev again links the problem of looking with the problem of faith when he notes that "Christ suffered not figuratively [*ne obrazno*] but in a real way. . . . His body on the cross, therefore, was subjected absolutely to the law of nature." "How could one believe, looking at such a corpse, that this sufferer would be resurrected?" Literally—with what image (*kakim obrazom*) could one believe, that is, have faith, looking at such a corpse? As Ippolit puts it a moment later, "Can one conceive in an image (*obraz*) that which has no image?"

With what *image*—with what sense of form or perfection, inner and outer—can one look at death and disfiguration and still retain one's faith, or, more generally, maintain one's moral-psychological and spiritual integrity? Dostoevsky fully recognizes the problems raised by the sight of death and disfiguration. Such a sight—here, the sight of the disfigured Christ—arouses "anguish and confusion," and despair. Yet Dostoevsky's point is that one cannot, one must not, turn away, however painful the sight, or one separates oneself from humanity and the drama of suffering and salvation.

At the moment Tropmann loses his head, Turgenev's narrator averts his face from the sight. The symbolism of both occurrences is identical: a separation from the human condition. Turgenev and Dostoevsky, each in his own way, recognizes this fact. Yet both also recognize the obverse side of this truth, that looking at disfiguration is a dangerous act arousing moral and psychological confusion and despair.

In Socrates' discussion of the unity-in-diversity of the three constituent components of the soul—reason, desire, and "spiritedness" or "noble wrath" (*thumos*)—the example of Leontius first covering and then cursing his eyes is intended to illustrate the power of spiritedness as an ally of reason in coping with desire. One might take the story, however, as an example of the triumph of irrational desire over reason. In any case, Turgenev and Dostoevsky would seem to illustrate both halves of this paradoxical example. Turgenev's gesture of averting his eyes might be viewed as a triumphant exemplification of reason supported by "spiritedness" in the name of the harmony of the whole, and Dostoevsky's fixed gaze might be said to betoken the triumph of desire and the lower instincts at the expense of harmony.

It is clear, however, that virtue and vice do not neatly take their places on one side or the other of the Platonic paradox. There is an indication in *The Republic* that Plato himself did not approach his example in a one-sided manner. Socrates hints that the punishment of offending desire may also be harmful and stand in the way of the soul's development, indeed may constitute a threat to philosophy, for "spiritedness," or *thumos*, in the example given, is fighting curiosity, the kin of the desire to *know*. As Allan Bloom notes in his discussion of the Leontius story: "The soul in which reason is most developed will—like Leontius' eyes—desire to see all kinds of things which the citizen is forbidden to see; it will abound with thoughts usually connected with selfishness, lust and vice. Such a soul will be like that banished poetry which contains images of vice as well as virtue."[20] Such a soul, of course, was Dostoevsky's, one that went very far in an effort to see all kinds of things the citizen is forbidden to see. "Everywhere and in everything I go to the uttermost limits, all my life I have crossed the last line."[21]

As even the most cursory reading of "The Execution of Tropmann" will demonstrate, the artist Turgenev, in spite of his narrator's persistent doubts about his "right" to witness the execution, presents the totality of the execution in all its brutal detail and significance. Yet the narrator's honest gesture of turning away, acknowledged by Turgenev as providing no solution to the moral issues of complicity in crime, was nonetheless characteristic of Turgenev the man and his poetics. For nothing was more alien to him than crossing the "last line." His art is a poetry and philosophy of equilibrium. The narrator's turning away from the beheading of Tropmann was emblematic in the deepest sense of a moral and artistic nature that viewed measure, temperance, and self-limitation as the attribute of all nature and as the safeguard of civilization.

2　　*The Ethics of Vision II*

The Tolstoyan Synthesis

> The memory of Tolstoy contains *everything*. This man had done
> everything, passed through all experiences.
>
> Romain Rolland

 Leo Tolstoy, unlike Dostoevsky, but like Turgenev, actually attended a guillotining—in Paris in 1857. Like Prince Myshkin in *The Idiot*, however, but unlike Turgenev, Tolstoy did not turn his head away at the last moment. He watched the decapitation of the victim. He left us a brief description of that moment in the opening words of his recollection of the Paris execution in his *Confession* (1884):

> When I saw the head part from the body and how they thumped separately into the box, I understood, not with my mind but with my whole being, that no theories of the rationality of the existing order and of progress could justify this act, and that if all the people in the world, by whatever theories, from the beginning of the world, found that it was necessary—I knew that it was not necessary, that it was bad, and that therefore the judge of what is good and necessary is not what people say and do, and not progress, but I with my own heart.[1]

Tolstoy's response to the execution deserves close attention. He arrived in Paris in the middle of March 1857. Although he enjoyed the cultural life of Paris for a while, he experienced increasing inner dissatisfactions and turmoil. "Last night," he jotted down in his diary March 19, "I was tormented by a sudden doubt *in everything*. And now, although it does not torment me, it is sitting in me. Why? And why am I like that?"[2] On April 5 he wrote again of his spiritual condition: "Anguish, which I cannot get rid of."[3] On the same day, he learned that an execution was to take place the following morning in front of one of the Parisian prisons. A certain Francis Richeux, a man who had killed and robbed two people, was to be guillotined. In order to "test himself," Tolstoy decided to attend the execution.[4] Early in the morning April 6 he joined a crowd of 12,000 to 15,000 spectators, one that included women and children. Later that day he wrote in his diary:

> Sick, I got up at seven 'clock and went to see an execution. A stout, robust white neck and breast. He kissed the Gospels and then—death, how senseless! A strong impression and one that will not be wasted. I am not a man of politics. Morals and art. [These,] I know, I can also love. I am not well, melancholy. . . . The guillotine long prevented my sleeping and obliged me to reflect.[5]

Tolstoy was shaken by his experience. Out of sorts, unable to eat for a long time, he reportedly had nightmares in which he "dreamed of the guillotine" and imagined that he was being executed.[6] Yet it was not only personal shock that preoccupied Tolstoy. The execution also aroused thoughts of a broad ethical, social, and political nature, reflections which quite plainly fitted in with his mood of doubting everything. These reflections found immediate expression in a letter to V. P. Botkin March 24–25, 1857, one that he had begun the day before the execution but had left unfinished. At the beginning of his letter, Tolstoy had spoken of his "enjoyment of the arts" in Paris and "all the social freedom of which I had not the slightest conception in Russia; all this means that I will not leave Paris, or the village near Paris where I want to settle shortly for another two months at the earliest." After witnessing the execution, however, Tolstoy thought differently of the matter. Resuming his letter to Botkin on April 6, he noted that his mood had radically changed: he had had the "stupidity and cruelty" to attend an execution.

> The spectacle made such an impression on me that it will be long before I get over it. I have seen many horrors in war and in the Caucasus, but if a man were torn to pieces in my presence, it would not have been so repulsive as this ingenious and elegant machine by means of which they killed a strong, hale, healthy man in an·instant. There [in war] it is not a question of the rational [will], but the human feeling of passion, while

here it is a question of calm and convenient murder finely worked out, and there's nothing grand about it. The insolent, arrogant desire to carry out justice, the law of God. Justice, which is determined by lawyers every one of whom, basing himself on honor, religion, and truth, contradicts each other. . . . Then the repulsive crowd, the father explaining to his daughter what a convenient and ingenious mechanism it is, and so forth. The law of man—rubbish! The truth is that the state is a conspiracy not only for exploitation, but chiefly to corrupt its citizens. But all the same states exist, and moreover in this imperfect form. And they cannot pass from this system into socialism. . . . For my part, I can only see in all this repulsive lie what is loathsome, evil, and I do not want to, and cannot, sort out where there is more and where there is less. I understand moral laws, the laws of morality and religion, binding on no one, that lead people forward and promise a harmonious future; I feel the laws of art which always bring happiness; but the laws of politics constitute for me such an awful lie that I cannot see in them a better or worse. All this is what I felt, understood, and recognized today. And this recognition at least to some extent relieves the burden of the impression for me. . . . From this day forward I will not only never go to see such a thing again, but I will never serve *any* government anywhere.[7]

The following day Tolstoy wrote in his diary: "Got up late, unwell, read, and suddenly a simple and sensible idea occurred to me—to leave Paris."[8]

Tolstoy had gone to the execution with the idea of testing himself. The experience shattered whatever detachment he had brought to the scene. His response to the execution was direct and self-condemnatory: it was stupid and cruel. Like Turgenev's narrator in "The Execution of Tropmann," he appears to have come away from the execution with the recognition that in this realm there is no such thing as a neutral witness. Complicity accompanies observation.

Turgenev was horribly impressed by the idea of the guillotine's knife cutting through a strong, healthy neck. Especially "revolting" to Tolstoy is the "ingenious and elegant machine" that so efficiently kills "a strong, hale, healthy man." Tolstoy, however, does not dwell on the guillotine as a machine or upon the details of the execution. Unlike Turgenev, he directs little attention in his letter to his own sensations as he watched the execution or those of the crowd. Nor does he give any attention, as does Dostoevsky, to what the victim must have been experiencing. His main focus is upon the broad moral, social, and political implications of the execution. And in this realm he arrives at some definite and devastating conclusions about the "laws of politics" and the nature of government. "And this recognition at least to some extent relieves the burden of the impression for me." Mentally, it would seem, one wants to turn away from contemplating such a horrible sight.

On the face of it, Tolstoy does not seem to have been preoccupied with the question *to look or not to look?* Yet an analysis of the execution scene that Pierre Bezukhov witnesses in *War and Peace* (vol. 4, part 1, chap. 12) suggests that the Paris execution had indeed raised for Tolstoy many of the issues of looking that concerned Turgenev and Dostoevsky and had found a classical point of departure in Plato. The problem of looking—and its moral implications—is an important component in Tolstoy's whole approach to the execution scene on Maiden Field in *War and Peace*.

Before taking up Tolstoy's structural and thematic use of sight in the execution scene in *War and Peace*, it is worth attending to a curious linguistic detail in Tolstoy's diary account of the 1857 execution, a detail that constitutes a special link between Tolstoy's actual experience and his fictional account of an execution in *War and Peace*. "The guillotine long prevented my sleeping and obliged me to reflect [*ogljady-vat'sja*]," Tolstoy had written in his notebook after witnessing the execution in Paris. The English verb *reflect* (for which there are a number of closely corresponding Russian verbs) inadequately conveys the meaning of *ogljadyvat'sja*, the Russian verb Tolstoy employs. This verb means "to look around or about"; it sometimes conveys the sense of "looking about fearfully or apprehensively." Tolstoy's choice of this verb to convey the abstract notion of reflecting suggests the poetic concreteness of his use of language. Also, his choice of *ogljadyvat'sja* surely relates back to the actual moment of looking at the execution and glancing about, even fearfully or apprehensively, not only at the victim, but at the priest, the guillotine, the repulsive crowd, and the father instructing his daughter. The literal act of looking, of registering the action around him, however, cannot be separated from the mental process of reacting and reflecting on the meaning of what he saw—that is, from the act of reviewing, indeed *re-viewing*—the execution in its wider context: "lawyers," "formalities," "political laws," the "law of man," people who believe in lies and laws, government, the state itself. The execution, in short, compels Tolstoy to look around apprehensively at the execution scene and society in the light of higher "laws of morality and religion" and the "laws of art." "All this is what I felt, understood, and recognized today," Tolstoy had written in his letter to Botkin.

One discovers in Tolstoy's use of language evidence of a direct and organic connection, deeply felt, between the aesthetic act of looking at an execution and the moral act of re-viewing or reflecting on the society and institutions that sanction such horrible deeds. To summarize Tolstoy's remarks in his *Confession* on the execution he witnessed: "I saw [the execution] . . . I understood . . . I knew . . . that it was bad . . . with my own heart." Of this kind of direct apprehension of good and evil Dostoevsky wrote in 1864 in his notebook: "In what does the law of this ideal [of humanity, of Christ] consist? A return to a sense of immediacy, to the mass of the people, but—a free one, and not even one that is willed, not through reason, not through consciousness, but through a direct, terribly strong, unconquerable feeling that *this* is terribly *good*."[9] In Tolstoy's case, the unconquerable feeling that emerged from witnessing an execution was that *this* was terribly *bad*.

The events leading up to the execution scene introduce the problem under discussion—the problem of looking in its ethical context. Pierre, alone in Moscow after the battle of Borodino, is arrested by the French as an incendiary. Fearing for his life, he conceals his background and thus precipitates his crisis of identity. Put in with people of the lowest class, he is interrogated as defendants are questioned in legal procedures: "Who are you? Where were you? With what intentions?" All of Pierre's answers relating to his effort to save a child are greeted by one question, "Who are you?" and each time he repeats "that he could not say." From Pierre Bezukhov, wealthy and well-known count in Moscow and Petersburg social circles, Pierre now becomes simply "No. 17." Faced with the possibility of execution, Pierre, who is identified only as "*celui qui n'avoue pas son nom*," is brought before General Davoust. "Pierre felt like an insignificant chip that had fallen into the wheel of some strange but perfectly functioning machine." Again the question is put: "Qui êtes vous?" Again Pierre is silent because "he wasn't capable of uttering any words." "I know that man," General Davoust says in a cold and measured voice. "Mon général, vous ne pouvez pas me connaître, je ne vous ai jamais vu," Pierre responds. Pierre finally gives his name, "Bezukhov." He pleads again with Davoust, maintaining that he is a militia officer and not a spy. "Davoust raised his eyes and attentively looked at Pierre. For several seconds they looked at one another, and this glance saved Pierre." In this glance both Pierre and Davoust "established human relations. At that moment both of them vaguely experienced a countless multitude of things and understood that they were children of humanity, that they were brothers. . . . Davoust . . . saw in him a man."

Tolstoy suggests here an ideal truth: To *see* a person is to *know* him. The act of seeing in this sense is active, cognitive, and ethical. But this act of seeing-in-depth, Tolstoy suggests again, is not single-directional; it is not the action of subject upon an object but a mutual interaction of persons or personalities in which their reality as "subjects" is confirmed and their common identity as human beings is affirmed. General Davoust thinks that he knows Pierre ("I know that man"). Pierre's response is that General Davoust could not "know" him because Pierre has never seen him (*je ne vous ai jamais vu*). They have never seen each other. Immediately after Pierre's remark, Davoust "raised his eyes" and looks attentively at Pierre.

What is important here is that Pierre and General Davoust "look at each other" and "establish human relations." Out of this exchange comes the fleeting recognition, conscious or unconscious, that "they were brothers." The act of two people genuinely looking at each other, Tolstoy suggests, is at root an ethical act.[10] Tolstoy's thought is even signaled by the Russian phrase used here: "*oni smotreli drug na druga*" (they looked at one another; literally, looked friend upon friend). To see truly, in Tolstoy's conception, is to *know*; and to know deeply is to *love and unite*. Man is his integral self only when he is completed by another. Such is the ethic of vision that will triumph in Pierre in the course of the execution scene he witnesses on Maiden Field.

Pierre's brief encounter with Davoust is interrupted. He emerges from his interview uncertain whether he had been condemned to death or reprieved (only later does Pierre learn that he had been reprieved). "One thought all this time was in Pierre's head: this was the thought about who, yes who, in the last analysis, condemned him to be executed?" He concludes that it was not the people who questioned him, not Davoust who looked at him in such a human way, nor the adjutant. "Then who, in the final analysis, was executing, killing, depriving him of life—him, Pierre with all his memories, strivings, hopes, thoughts. Who was doing this? And Pierre felt that it was nobody. It was the system, the concatenation of circumstances. A system of some sort was killing him, Pierre, depriving him of life, of everything, annihilating him."

The question of personal identity for Pierre in captivity (here he is the nameless "No. 17," that is, nobody) is augmented by the question of the identity of the forces condemning him to death. And the answer to this new question is, again, "nobody." The dominion of Nobody—where "nobody" executes "nobody"—signals the disintegration of all bonds, personal or social. The moment of execution in which neither executioner (traditionally masked) nor victim (traditionally blindfolded) sees or knows the other prefigures, literally and figuratively, the triumph of darkness and death.

To Look or Not to Look?

Pierre, walking mechanically and in a state of "absolute stupor and numbness," arrives at the execution grounds with its execution post, freshly dug pit, and the crowd of people around it awaiting the executions. The condemned men were placed in a "certain order" determined by a list (Pierre was sixth in position) and led up to the post. Pierre had "lost all capacity to think or take things in. He could only see and hear." The sentence is read, and the first two prisoners are taken to the execution post. The entire scene that follows is dominated by the motifs of looking, seeing, and knowing:

> On nearing the post, the convicts stopped and while the sacks were being brought, silently looked about them, as an injured animal looks at the approaching huntsman. One of them kept crossing himself, another scratched his back and made a movement with his lips resembling a smile. With hasty fingers the soldiers began to bind his eyes, drawing sacks over their heads, and tying them to the post.
>
> A dozen sharpshooters with muskets stepped out of the ranks with a firm, regular tread, and halted eight paces from the post. Pierre turned away in order not to see what would happen. Suddenly there was heard a

crash and roar that seemed to Pierre louder than the most terrific thunderclaps, and he glanced about him. There was smoke, and the French soldiers, with pale faces and trembling hands, were doing something near the pit. Two more prisoners were led up. In the very same way, with the very same eyes, they looked at everybody, vainly, with their eyes alone, silently asking protection, and, visibly, not understanding, not believing what was about to happen. They could not believe because they alone knew what their life meant to them and because they did not understand and did not believe that it could be possible to take it away.

Pierre wanted not to look and again turned away; but again some kind of terrible explosion crashed against his ears, and along with these sounds he saw smoke, some blood, and the pale frightened faces of the Frenchmen, who again were doing something at the post, their trembling hands knocking against each other. Pierre, breathing heavily, glanced about, as though asking: what is this all about? The very same question was in all the glances that met Pierre's glance.

On all the faces of the Russians, on the faces of the French soldiers, officers, all without exception, he read the same fright, horror, and struggle that were in his heart. "But just who, then, is doing all this? They are all suffering the way I am. Yes, who, who?"—there flashed for a second in Pierre's soul.

"Tirailleurs du 86-me, en avant!" cried someone. The fifth one standing alongside Pierre was led up to the post—alone. Pierre did not understand that he had been saved: that he and all the others had been led here only to be present at the execution. With ever mounting horror, experiencing neither joy nor relief, he looked at what was being done. The fifth one was a workman in a loose coat. No sooner did they touch him than he sprang away in horror and seized Pierre (Pierre shuddered and tore himself away). The workman was unable to walk. They dragged him, holding him under the arms, and he cried out something. When they led him up to the post, he suddenly fell silent. It was as though he suddenly understood something. Whether he understood that it was useless to scream or that it was impossible that people could kill him, he all the same stood by the post, awaiting the blindfold as the others had and, like a wounded animal, looked about him with glittering eyes.

Pierre could no longer take it upon himself to turn away and close his eyes. With this fifth murder his curiosity and agitation and that of the whole crowd had reached the highest pitch. Just like the others, this fifth prisoner seemed composed: he drew his coat around and rubbed one bare foot against the other.

When they began to bind his eyes, he himself adjusted at the back the knot which cut into him; then when they placed him against the bloody post, he leaned back, and since it was awkward for him in this position, he made an adjustment and, getting an even stance with his feet, leaned back. Pierre did not take his eyes off him, did not miss the slightest movement.

The word of command must have sounded out, the volleys of eight muskets must have echoed after the command. But Pierre, much as he tried later to remember, heard not the slightest sound of the shots. He saw only how for some reason the workman suddenly slumped in the ropes, how blood appeared in two places and how the ropes themselves, from the weight of the body hanging on it, came loose, and the workman, his head unnaturally drooping and one leg bent under him, came down into a sitting position. Pierre rushed up to the post. Nobody restrained him. Frightened pale people were doing something around the workman. The lower jaw of one old mustached Frenchman shook as he untied the ropes. The body collapsed. The soldiers awkwardly and hastily dragged it from the post and began shoving it into the pit. Everybody, obviously, knew without a doubt that they were criminals who had to hide the traces of their crime as quickly as possible.

Pierre looked into the pit and saw that the workman was lying there with his knees pointing up to his head, one shoulder higher than the other. And this shoulder convulsively, evenly sank and rose up. But the shovels of earth were already covering the whole body. One of the soldiers shouted in an angry, ill-tempered, and tormented voice for Pierre to get back. But Pierre did not understand him and stood at the post, and nobody drove him away.

At the center of this episode is a dialogue of glances that affirms the fellowship of all men and declares that to see and to know in the deepest sense is to bear witness to the bond that ties all men together—that is, to our ineluctable humanity.

As he faces the executions, Pierre experiences all the conflicts and impulses of Plato's Leontius: the desire to turn away and the desire to look. The terror of the moment is underscored by the first pair of prisoners, who before they are blindfolded, "looked silently about them as an injured animal watches the approaching huntsman." Pierre seems unable to face either the prisoners' looks or the event about to take place. "Pierre turned away so as not to see what was about to happen." Only after the first executions does he look about, but then merely to register the actions of the French soldiers. Pierre's inability to look at the executions is countered, as it were, by the second pair of victims, who "looked at everybody" and silently asked protection "with the very same eyes" of the first victims, "with their eyes alone." The prisoners look about "vainly," visibly "not understanding, not believing what was about to happen." The prisoners' failure to get any sympathetic response or help seems reflected in Pierre's refusal, for a second time, to look at the executions. "Pierre wanted not to look and again turned away." Tolstoy's use here of the words "wanted not to look," as opposed to "did not want to look," even more strongly accents Pierre's will to turn away from the scene.

Yet at this point Pierre again "glanced about him." Now, however, his looking about is not merely confined, as before, to registering passively the "pale, frightened faces" of the French and Russians. Like Tolstoy, who felt compelled in Paris to reflect on the meaning of the execution he witnessed, Pierre's glancing about involves the beginning of a review of the meaning of the events that are transpiring. He "glanced about, as though asking: what is this all about?" Looking about, Pierre significantly finds this same question "in all the glances" of the other French and Russian observers.

Pierre's transition from refusal and inability to look to willingness to look is directly linked with his looking about, literally and figuratively; it arises out of his recognition of the suffering of others ("they are all suffering the way I am") and the appearance in him of vital questions. It is at this point, Tolstoy writes, that Pierre "with ever mounting horror, experiencing neither joy nor relief . . . looked at what was being done."

Pierre, who twice has been unable or unwilling to look at the execution of other prisoners, first goes through a terrifying experience, one that finds embodiment in the medieval representations of the danse macabre and other medieval paintings: death seizing his victim (death here is the equalizer among men). The prisoner about to be executed seizes Pierre, who in turn tears himself from the doomed man's grasp. Yet Pierre has been compelled, if only vicariously, to experience man's brotherhood in death.

Pierre's decision to look at the execution of the fifth prisoner significantly follows that moment when the man who is about to die, like a wounded animal, looks about "with glittering eyes." It is at this significant moment that "Pierre could no longer take it upon himself to turn away and close his eyes." There are, to be sure, some familiar motivations for looking. "With this fifth murder his curiosity and agitation and that of the whole crowd had reached the highest pitch." Yet Pierre's looking goes beyond curiosity and agitation. It is noteworthy that Pierre "could no longer take it upon himself to turn away and close his eyes." The Russian phrase *vzjat' na sebja* (take it upon oneself), like the parallel structure in French, *prendre sur soi*, carries the connotation of a moral act. Pierre cannot take on himself the responsibility of *not* looking. Not looking, now, is no longer merely physically closing one's eyes to a set of visual images but ignoring the meaning of the scene, a meaning that has now been established by the dialogue of glances. These glances between victims and observers make it impossible to turn away.

Pierre at the field of execution is, in a manner of speaking, both subject and object, observer and observed, a witness of the executions and a person about to be executed. His vision, his knowing, therefore, is a double one. This ambiguity of position, however, does not prevent the reader from identifying with Pierre as observer and from experiencing as his own Pierre's conflict of feelings on the issue of looking at the execution. Through Pierre, Tolstoy establishes a dialogue of glances not only between the observer and the observed, but between the observers themselves. The effect of the reader's bond as observer with Pierre is to compel the reader not only to look at the execution through Pierre's eyes and to make contact with the "glittering eyes" of the suffering prisoners, but to look at himself and to become aware of his own ambivalent impulses: his desire not to look, yet his enjoyment of the role of voyeur—that callousness or cruelty that Tolstoy discovered in his own attitude as he watched the guillotining of Francis Richeux in Paris.

Yet while Tolstoy gives a certain emphasis to this aspect of looking (the intensifying "curiosity and agitation" of Pierre and the crowd), it is clear that looking has become a moral imperative for Pierre; it is impossible to turn away from the glittering eyes of suffering man. Thus the whole configuration of human actions and responses in the execution scene compels the reader-spectator, along with Pierre, to look about himself, to look not only *at* the executions but like Pierre, to reflect with fear and pity on their meaning, to identify himself with his fellow man.

In this connection, the image of the blindfold (*povjazka*) is of central importance in the execution scene. Man does not want to look truth—here, death—in the face. The murderer does not wish to look into the eyes of the man he is murdering; he does not want to face himself, his guilt and responsibility. Neither does the victim wish to face his death. The prisoner adjusts his blindfold or scratches his feet, seeks out a more comfortable position only several seconds before death; he looks around, unable to believe in the possibility of his death. Even in the face of death, the body, the organic self, instinctually rejects death as abnormal and continues to respond to normal needs. Whether with respect to the victim or victimizer, Tolstoy ruthlessly removes all blindfolds, dispels all illusions, insists finally on man's moral responsibility before his fellow man.

Pierre's decision to look—figuratively speaking, his decision not to blindfold himself—comes but a moment before the glittering eyes of the prisoner are about to be blindfolded. Pierre had been physically "saved" when he made contact with the eyes of his judge, General Davoust, when both men recognized in each other a human being and not merely judge and defendant. So now, on the symbolic plane of the narrative, the possibility of spiritual salvation is signaled to Pierre by the glittering eyes of the workman, a man who also was apprehensively "looking about him" vainly trying to understand the meaning of the events at whose center he stands.

Pierre watches every detail of the execution of the workman. Immediately after the execution, in a gesture of profound significance, he rushes up to the execution post and looks down into the pit at the still-living victim.[11] Pierre's world is shattered. "Such a painting," Prince Myshkin in *The Idiot* remarks about Hans Holbein's *Christ in the Tomb*, "could make one lose one's faith." So too, Pierre, who finally has looked into the face of death, who has come to *see* and know all, looks about with "senseless eyes." Here the paradox of looking at violence and death comes dramatically to the fore: The very same looking—the tearing away of all blindfolds—that establishes a human bond between the observer and victim may also lead the observer to psychological and spiritual breakdown:

> From the moment Pierre had witnessed that hideous murder committed by people who had no desire to do it, it was as if the spring in his soul, by which everything was held together and acquired life, had been suddenly

pulled out and all had collapsed into a heap of senseless refuse. Though he did not realize it, his faith in the right ordering of the universe, in humanity, in his own soul, and in God had been destroyed. He had experienced this state of mind before, but never with such force as now. Formerly, when similar doubts had come upon Pierre, these doubts had had their origin in his own guilt. And in the depths of his soul Pierre had felt that salvation from this despair and those doubts was to be found within himself. But this time he felt that it was not his guilt that caused the world to crumble before his eyes, leaving only meaningless ruins. He felt that it was not in his power to get back to faith in life.

When Pierre looks into the pit, he sees the dying workman in the fetal position. Pierre's spiritual rebirth, as Tolstoy represents it in the chapter following the execution scene, Pierre's first meeting with Platon Karataev, is represented as that of a child who through organic attractions and responses, is drawn back again into the orbit of personal and social relations.[12]

Pierre's response to the executions in the episode on Maiden Field embraces all aspects of the Platonic model. At first, he turns away from the scene of violence and death. Here, Pierre's resistance to looking is of the same order as the resistance of Turgenev's narrator in "The Execution of Tropmann." The third time, however, Pierre looks avidly and fixedly at the execution. "Man on the surface of the earth," Dostoevsky had written, "does not have the right to turn away and ignore what is taking place on earth, and there are lofty *moral* reasons for this: *homo sum et nihil humanum*, etc." Undeniably, Tolstoy is closer to Dostoevsky than Turgenev in his resolution of the problem of the ethics of vision in the execution scene in *War and Peace*. In the final analysis, Pierre *looks*, and like Myshkin, discovers both his humanity and despair. Tolstoy came away from the execution in Paris with the decision that he would never look again—a decision that perhaps may have been reflected in Pierre's initial resistance to watching the executions. Nonetheless, Tolstoy seems to have concluded that man must face the terrible reality of execution and violence, must face *what is taking place on earth*. The price of seeing and knowing all may be, for the witness, darkness and despair. Yet the act of witnessing, the act of suffering, may be the only way the darkness can be redeemed.

It was, of course, the darkness in the human soul that preoccupied

Turgenev on the field of execution. Regardless of their differences in their personal responses to the spectacle of execution, Turgenev and Dostoevsky are deeply concerned with the problem of man's attraction to the spectacle of violence and suffering; they are troubled by the problem of evil in man. Tolstoy does not deny evil in *War and Peace.* Yet radical skepticism such as we find in Prince Andrey toward the end of his life is not in the ascendant in Tolstoy's epic work. For all their potential for evil and corruption, people are disclosed in *War and Peace* as basically good. It was not corrupt or ill-intentioned men who condemned him to death, Pierre reasons. "Not one of the men on the commission who had first examined him wanted and, indeed, was able to do this. . . . It was not Davoust, who had looked at him in such a human fashion . . . and that adjutant, clearly, wished no harm. . . . Then who was it who was executing, killing, depriving him of life?"

Pierre's optimism with respect to Davoust and others, of course, bears the mark of *his* peculiarly generous and indeed curiously naive nature. Yet with the exception of the French officer who "in a voice of cold indifference" gives the command to shoot the prisoners, there is not a single suggestion that the French soldiers, or for that matter anybody on the field of execution, experiences either malice, enjoyment, or indifference in carrying out their activities. When the French officer gives his command, "there was a stir in the ranks of the soldiers and it was observable that they were all in a hurry—not as men hurry to execute an order they understand but as people hurry to have done with a necessary but unpleasant and incomprehensible task." The Russians and the French soldiers are as upset as Pierre by the executions. When the crowd of Russian and Frenchmen began to disperse, "they all walked off in silence, with lowered heads."

The Frenchmen may feel guilt, may even feel that they are criminals, but in Tolstoy's representation they are as much victims as perpetrators of evil. On Tolstoy's grand canvas, the executioners, like the executed, are victims of a "system." "Nobody" has executed "nobody." Here is the root of the terror, the meaninglessness and alienation, that Pierre experiences.

Tolstoy may be singularly modern in his perception of the individual's true isolation and alienation in the face of his fate. However, the sense of depersonalization, aloneness, or ontological isolation that an individual may experience is not the same as the dehumanization that accompanies the corruption of the human spirit. In this respect, Tolstoy's representation of the execution scene in *War and Peace*—that is, his representation of the psychology of the soldiers and the people witnessing the executions—in no way prepares the reader for the twentieth-century drama of mass executions and exterminations carried out by men who unlike the French soldiers on Maiden's Field in *War and Peace*, at best fulfilled their tasks with indifference and at worst with zest. In this particular respect, the approach of Turgenev and Dostoevsky to executions seems more germane to the twentieth century than Tolstoy's. Twentieth-century experience, not to speak of the long history of mankind, seems to have validated Turgenev's exclamation about the Frenchmen who witnessed the execution of Tropmann: "It is awful to think what is hidden there." It seems to have validated Dostoevsky's remark in *Notes from the House of the Dead*: "The attributes of the executioner are found in embryo in almost every person today." Tolstoy, of course, was fully aware of the "repulsive crowd"; in the execution scene in *War and Peace*, however, this repulsive side of the crowd, this dark side of human nature, did not come to the fore.

In his essay "Creative Suffering," the philosopher-theologian E. F. F. Hill observes:

> Historical knowledge is the intuitive grasp of the lived experience of others. The creative possibility of suffering is precisely the possibility of entering into, and of drawing into oneself, the entire composition of an act which involves another, whether it be evil or good, whether it inflict suffering beyond measure or bring the perfection of peace, both from the side of him who performs it and of him who suffers it.
>
> This is not to be confused with a sensitiveness to suffering and to the evils from which it springs. It is not this attribute raised to a higher power but one which, while it includes this, is of an entirely different order. In sensitiveness, life is not lived through; in it a man does not touch and move with the deeper course of reality and gather it into himself. With it, the danger of perversion is never far away.
>
> Sensitiveness is a state—of the soul or the mind or the nervous system: whichever you will—but the creative possibility of suffering is an orientation of the will towards (and here a metaphor must serve) the light.[13]

It is Pierre in the execution scene, not Turgenev's narrator and perhaps not even Dostoevsky's Myshkin, who seems to exemplify most "the creative possibility of suffering." Pierre's rush to the pit where the fifth prisoner has been dumped, still alive, is not merely a supreme moment of bearing witness, but a taking responsibility, an acceptance of suffering. Here there are no *words*, as there are in Dostoevsky's "The Dream of a Ridiculous Man" when, "accusing, cursing, and despising himself," the ridiculous man calls upon the inhabitants of the paradise he has corrupted to crucify him. Here there is no moving and melodramatic declamation about divine injustice, as in Ivan Karamazov's great peroration over the suffering of children. Here there is no "sensitiveness" leading to the "perversion" of either turning away from suffering or enjoying it too much. Here there is only an instinctive gathering into self of reality, an organic gesture, a direct response to what has been seen, heard, and felt. Here the question *to look or not to look?* dissolves in the ethics of action.

Pierre's Limp

"Everything changes and moves," the voice of Pierre's Swiss teacher of geography tells him in a dream after the death of his beloved Platon Karataev. This is true of Tolstoy's position on the ethics of vision. In the execution scene, Pierre moves in the direction of finally confronting the horror of the execution, taking off the blindfold, facing death, looking at it. Yet the high point of Pierre's witnessing the executions, a lofty moment when he bears witness to what is taking place on earth, is also a moment of despair. Pierre is overcome by a sense of the meaninglessness of human existence. It is in part through contact with the earthly and motherly Platon Karataev and his philosophy of acceptance of all life processes, a philosophy that Karataev embodies in his existence, that Pierre recovers his faith in life. It is one of the paradoxes of his recovery, a necessary albeit painful paradox in the view of Tolstoy, that Pierre now looks upon death—specifically, the execution and death of Platon—differently than he looked upon the executions on Maiden Field. This extraordinary, deeply ambiguous moment in Pierre's destiny, one that will test of the very foundations of Pierre's will to life, is one of the most philosophically important and in certain respects troubling scenes in

War and Peace. We are in the presence of a point of view, pervasive throughout *War and Peace*, that places the organic *life striving* in conflict with ethical behavior.

In the march from Moscow, Pierre and Platon Karataev are together in the party of Russian prisoners under French guard. Karataev is ailing, and as he loses strength, Pierre distances himself from him. During this period of retreat, the French soldiers, to free themselves of the burden of guarding Russian prisoners, shoot those who lag behind. The same fate befalls Karataev. Prior to the moment when two French soldiers shoot Platon, Pierre notices him leaning against a tree:

> Karataev *looked at* Pierre with his kindly round eyes which were now filled with tears, and, obviously, was beckoning to him, wanted to say something. But Pierre was too afraid for himself. He acted *as though he had not seen his glance* and hastily moved away. When the prisoners again set off, Pierre *looked back*. Karataev was sitting at the edge of the road, near a birch tree, and two Frenchmen were saying something over him. Pierre *looked no longer*. He went on, limping [Pierre's feet were lacerated from the march], up the hill. From behind, from the place where Karataev was sitting, came the sound of a shot. Pierre heard the shot distinctly, but at the same moment that he heard it, Pierre remembered that he had not finished reckoning up how many stages were left to Smolensk—a calculation he had begun before the marshal rode by. And he began to count. Two French soldiers, one holding a still smoking gun in his hand, ran by Pierre. They were both pale, and in the expression of their faces—one of them timidly *looked at* Pierre—there was something similar to what *he had seen* on the face of the young soldier at the execution. Pierre *looked at* the soldier and remembered how the other day this soldier had scorched his shirt while drying it by the fire, and how they had all laughed at him. A dog was howling behind, at the spot where Karataev had been sitting. "Silly creature, why is she howling?" thought Pierre. Pierre's fellow prisoners, marching at his side, like him *did not look back* at the spot from which a shot had been heard and a dog howling; but there was a grim expression on their faces. [My italics]

How is one to understand Pierre's apparent recreancy—his avoidance of Karataev's glance, his unwillingness to look back at him, his unwillingness to face the awful truth of Karataev's execution? Pierre's behavior is motivated in part by fear: "Pierre was too afraid for himself." There is something else, however, which is deeper than fear. Pierre's behavior is linked with his will to live, with an organic life force called forth by the terrible suffering, the terrible circumstances of the forced march. Pierre thought it would be impossible to walk on his lacerated feet, Tolstoy observes in one of the chapters preceding the death of Karataev, but when everybody got up to move on, Pierre managed to limp along: he even "walked without pain, although by evening it was more fearful than ever. Only now Pierre understood the full strength of the vitality of man and the saving power innate in him—something similar to the safety valve in a boiler that lets off the surplus steam as soon as the pressure exceeds a certain point."

The issue confronting Pierre in the march, literally a march of life, is nothing more or less than *going on*. Pierre is not a spectator at an execution faced with the question to look or not to look? His own survival is at stake; he does not even risk looking at his fearfully lacerated feet but thinks of something else. He has shut out of his mind what lies beyond his capacities. "He did not see and did not hear how the lagging prisoners were shot, although more than a hundred of them had perished this way," Tolstoy notes immediately after conveying Pierre's thoughts on the vitality of man. "He did not think of Karataev, who weakened with each day and obviously would soon be subject himself to the same fate. Even less did Pierre think about himself. The more difficult his situation became, the more terrible the future, the more independent from the present situation in which he found himself were the joyous and consoling thoughts, recollections, and imaginings that came to him."

Pierre did not think of Platon Karataev. In fact, however, at this critical juncture in his life, Pierre is under the mystical influence and power of Karataev's life and thoughts on the organic processes of life. He is under the influence of Karataev's story, listened to the night before, of a merchant who had suffered innocently. "Not the story itself, but its mysterious meaning, that ecstatic joy which shone in the face of Karataev when he told this story, the mysterious significance of this joy; precisely all this vaguely and joyously filled the soul of Pierre now." It is under the influence of Karataev that Pierre turns away from the beckoning Karataev and *goes on*, almost involuntarily chooses life. Pierre's response to Karataev's death is an imitation of Karataev's response to the terrible questions that tormented Pierre after the executions on Maiden Field. Pierre is reborn under the mystical influence of Platon Karataev in the shed after the executions. The death of Platon Karataev, a kind of mother surrogate for Pierre, completes his rebirth.

Pierre's dream of Karataev immediately after the latter's death is, significantly, not a dream of guilt but one involving the joyous discovery of life and God, one celebrating the endless flow of existence. "Life is everything. Life is God. Everything changes and moves, and this movement is God. And while there is life, there is delight in the consciousness of divinity. More difficult and more blessed than everything is to love this life in one's sufferings, in undeserved sufferings. 'Karataev!' Pierre remembered."

Everything moves and changes. Things grow, merge, press together, and are destroyed on the surface, pass into depths, and again reemerge. These thoughts press upon Pierre in his dream, and he attributes them to his old teacher in Switzerland, who shows Pierre a globe, "a quivering ball with no fixed dimensions" whose surface consisted of drops pressed closely together, moving about, changing places, expanding, coalescing, splitting. "That's life," said the teacher. "That was the case with Karataev: he overflowed and vanished," the voice concludes. "'Vous avez compris, mon enfant,' said the teacher. 'Vous avez compris, sacré nom,' cried a voice, and Pierre awoke."

Death is absorbed into the ocean of life; guilt and conscience, the memory of all that happened to his beloved Platon Karataev, are washed away finally by the recollection of a "beautiful Polish lady on the veranda of his house in Kiev." Finally "a picture of the country in summer time mingled with a memory of bathing and of that liquid, quivering globe, and he sank deeply into water, so that the waters closed over his head." Pierre's awakening, accompanied by real liberation from the French, resembles that of Goethe's Faust at the beginning of part 2 of *Faust* when Goethe's hero awakens cleansed of guilt: "Life's pulses beat again, with living freshness / mildly greeting the ethereal dawn; / earth, you have lasted out this night as well, / and new-revived lie breathing at my feet." In Pierre as in Goethe's Faust, it is precisely the earthly life forces that outlasts the night.

The moral problem of not looking is dissolved (though never resolved) in the necessary plunge into the ocean of life, the continuum of existence, one that is beyond good and evil. Life must go on. Yet as Pierre's relation to Karataev during the march discloses, it is indeed "more difficult" than anything else to love life in the midst of "undeserved suffering," to turn one's glance away from suffering, violence, and death. Pierre's imitation of Platon Karataev—really a very poor and transparent one—is an excruciating experience. His every gesture, as Tolstoy demonstrates with unparalleled artistic mastery, betrays his pain and shame before his self-concern and self-deception. Here, Tolstoy's remark about Pierre—"He went on, limping, up the hill"—is of great symbolic significance; it subtly defines Pierre's dilemma: Even in the necessary process of going on and not looking back, even in the necessary acceptance of evil, even in the necessary plunge into life, man cannot get away from the ethical demands of conscience. Love of life, the need for life, the inborn impulse to survive, carries with it forgetfulness, the blurring of ethical memory, the tragic potential for moral compromise and even betrayal. Thus man can only limp toward the light.

A long tradition has applied the metaphor of feet to the faculties of the soul.[14] "He did not look at [his feet] and thought of something else." Tolstoy lays the groundwork here for the central metaphor of the scene: "He went on, limping, up the hill." There is a clear allusion here to Golgotha—place of the crucifixion, place of the skulls, place of executions. Even in his necessary escape to life, one approved by his teachers, Pierre labors laboriously in the shadow of love, sacrifice, and death.

Tolstoy's final statement on the ethics of vision is unfinal: he has explored the gamut of the question to look or not to look? and has validated each option, all the while insisting that the options are not mutually exclusive, that whatever choice man thinks he makes, he lives with both as he limps along.

3 The Ethics of Vision III

The Punishment of the Tramp Prokhorov in Chekhov's *The Island of Sakhalin*

"Do you live well here?" I asked the lady.
"We live well, except for the mosquitoes."

The Island of Sakhalin

 Toward the beginning of his *The Island of Sakhalin. Notes from a Journey* (1893–1894), in chapter 2, Chekhov writes of his domestic quarters in Alexandrovsk on the island:

Up to the time of the arrival of the governor-general, I lived in Alexandrovsk, in the doctor's apartment. Life was not quite normal. When I awoke in the morning, the most diverse sounds reminded me where I was. Past the windows that opened on the street convicts were moving, slowly, to the measured clanging of their irons. In the military barracks opposite our apartment musicians from the army band were practicing the marches with which they would greet the governor-general; the flute played passages from one song, the trombone from another, and the bassoon from still another, and the result was unimaginable chaos. In our rooms the canaries whistled incessantly, and my doctor host paced from one corner to another, leafing through a law book as he moved, and thinking out loud: "If on the basis of such and such a section I submit a request to this particular department," and so on. Or he would be sitting down with his son to write up some kind of litigious statement.

The passage is almost wholly descriptive. There is hardly any direct commentary in it, but the elements in the scene add up to a somber commentary. There is a cacophony of "voices" not only in the band, but in the scene as a whole. The canaries are singing as convicts march along outside. The doctor and his son are mired down in petty legal technicalities. None of this is "quite normal" for an outsider, and yet this situation in which everyday life goes chirping along within the ordered disorder of a penal society is really quite normal. Chekhov never gets used to it.

Toward the end of his book (chap. 20), and directly following an observation by Chekhov that Sakhalin's "new history" was still noticeably influenced by a "mixture of Derzhimordas and Iagos—gentlemen who in relating to their inferiors recognize nothing but fists, lashes, and abusive language"[1]—Chekhov remarks casually: "Be that as it may, the 'House of the Dead' no longer exists." This remark is an obvious allusion to the prison world depicted in *Notes from the House of the Dead*. It is typical of Chekhov's restrained, laconic, often ironic style of commentary in *The Island of Sakhalin*. The remark is noteworthy in that it comes but a few pages before Chekhov's discussion of punishments (chap. 21) in the island penal colony. Central in this discussion is Chekhov's eye-witness account of a horrendous, yet typical flogging, the kind about which Dostoevsky has much to say in *Notes from the House of the Dead*. Chekhov introduces this flogging scene—it includes a medical examination of Prokhorov, a detailed description of the flogging (ninety strokes), and the removal of the now shattered convict—with "How they punish with the lash I saw in Dué." Indeed, the scene that unfolds before the reader's eyes has a stark documentary character. Except for a commentary at the end of the scene, the narrator Chekhov maintains the stance of an observer. The "picture" carries the message.

Chekhov records the terrible physical and physiological details of the beating with the clinical precision of a physician. As in *Notes from the House of the Dead*, however, Chekhov's focus is not alone upon the brutal laceration of the convict's body, but also upon the cruel mentality of those attending the punishment. The young German doctor "listened to the convict's heart to determine how many blows this convict can endure." "'Oh, poor fellow!' he says dolefully with a thick German accent, dipping the pen in an inkwell. 'I dare say the chains must weigh on you! Now why don't you plead with the honorable warden over there, he will order them removed.' Prokhorov is silent; his lips are pale and trembling. 'Your hope is in vain,' the doctor persists. 'You all have vain hopes. So many suspicious people in Russia!

Oh, poor fellow, poor fellow!'" The warden asks Prokhorov, who still doesn't know what this inquiry is all about, "What did you dream last night?" "I forgot, your honor." "Well, listen"—and the warden reads out to him the crime for which he will be given ninety strokes. "And, clapping the convict on the forehead with the flat of his hand, the warden says didactically: 'And why all this? Because, head, you want to be smarter than you are.'"

The executioner, Tolstykh ("the Fat One"), tall and "built solidly like an acrobat," ties up Prokhorov for the punishment, "slowly" prepares the lash with three leather thongs, "softly" calls upon the convict to "brace" himself, and, "without overdoing it, as though only taking measurement, delivers the first blow. 'One,' says the warden, with the voice of a deacon." Consecutive blows mangle the body of Prokhorov. He goes into convulsions, shrieks, vomits. "I am an unfortunate man, I am a miserable man... Why am I being punished like this?" Prokhorov cries out in the middle of his punishment. Prokhorov's cry—every Russian reader would recognize it—is that of the "little man" in Russian literature, beginning with Gogol's Akaky Akakievich, who responds to his fellow clerks' ragging and ridicule with "Why do you insult me?"

Midway in his account Chekhov remarks: "A whole eternity seems to have passed since the beginning of the punishment, but the warden just keeps on shouting out: 'Forty two! Forty three!' It is a long way to 90. I go outside." Chekhov does not *say* why he steps outside (he twice leaves the scene and twice returns), but the degrading spectacle provides the answer. Chekhov's reaction—horror? disgust? nausea?—is not shared by the four other men attending the flogging. The military medical assistant looks upon the flogging quite differently. His comments on the floggings frame the entire scene. He is at the entrance to the building when the flogging is about to take place, and at that moment he "pleads in a wheedling voice as though asking alms: 'Your honor, please let me see how they punish a man!'" And at the end of the flogging, when the half-dead Prokhorov is led away, we hear his words again: "'I love to see how people are punished!' the medical assistant says joyfully, very pleased because he has satiated himself with the abominable spectacle. 'I love it! They are such scoundrels, villains... They should be hanged!'" The word *abominable*, one should note, is the only epithet Chekhov uses to describe his attitude toward the flogging.

The motif of delight in punishing dominates Chekhov's Garden of Eden scene in his early story "Because of Little Apples" (1880): the sadistic play of the landowner and his overseer with the girl and boy who have been caught stealing apples in the estate apple orchard; the delight of the landowners' daughter, who witnesses the scene; and the delight in cruelty of the victims toward each other (they are forced to beat each other). "Because of Little Apples" is saturated with reminiscences from *Notes from the House of the Dead* and other works. The Chekhov who visited Sakhalin in 1890, however, did not have to read Dostoevsky's to find his material. The "dead house" was Russia: Dostoevsky had made this amply clear in *Notes from the House of the Dead*.[2] Dostoevsky explored the disfigured and disfiguring lives of Russians both inside and outside the prison walls. The demonic guard Zherebyatnikov, who howled with laughter when his victims were flogged, or the guard Smekalov, whose wrath was preceded by mock sympathy and sadistic play, were exceptional types, though how exceptional they were is a real question. What is certain is that they were carriers of a disease that had infected all of Russian society. The vicious and depraved guards in *Notes from the House of the Dead* were no less depraved than some of the characters in the Russian village Dostoevsky writes about in "Akulka's Husband," a chapter in *Notes from the House of the Dead*. The cruel scenes and characters Dostoevsky wrote about were certainly not mere projections of a writer who "enjoyed cruelty."

In Chekhov's flogging scene, the behavior of the medical assistant is repulsive and shocking. The German medical doctor, the warden, and the executioner, however, are no less repellent. Yet in contrast to some of Dostoevsky's torturers, the participants in Chekhov's flogging scene do not strike us as melodramatically "wicked," "Sadean," or "evil" (as the main characters do in "Because of Little Apples" or some of Dostoevsky's works). We perceive the men in Chekhov's flogging scene (as we perceive for the most part Chekhov's ordinary human beings in his works) not as villains but as people who have grown coarse, insensitive, indifferent in an indifferent and coarse society. The world of Sakhalin, like the everyday world of Russia, is not a law-abiding society run amok; it is a world of disordered social relations, a world that has never known rule by law—a world in which arbitrary rule and violence from time immemorial have constituted normal, everyday life and behavior. For inhabitants of this world, nothing is exceptional or fantastic, and this is perhaps the best definition of the centuries-old life of Russia (as Gogol, Dostoevsky, and Saltykov-Shchedrin understood better than anyone else). Only to the outside eye are things "not quite normal." Chekhov's recognition of this paradox determines much of his artistic method in *The Island of Sakhalin.*

In presenting the flogging scene, Chekhov the narrator "speaks" through the artful ordering, juxtaposition, and presentation of action, dialogue, and detail. Somewhat like Turgenev's hunter-observer in *The Sportsman's Notebook* or Turgenev's narrator in "The Execution of Tropmann," Chekhov comes across to the reader as an outside observer. Unlike Turgenev's narrator in the Tropmann sketch, however, Chekhov does not question his "right" to be present. He is not a gentleman writer who has casually accepted an invitation to an execution only to find himself alone with his conscience. Chekhov on Sakhalin is a professional writer who in advance of his trip had explored thoroughly the history and life of Sakhalin; he has come to the island to see and describe it. The roles of historian, chronicler, and scientist only lightly mask Chekhov the artist and moralist.

"Man on the surface of the earth does not have the right to turn away and ignore what is taking place on earth, and there are lofty *moral* reasons for this: *homo sum et nihil humanum,*" Dostoevsky wrote. In a sense, one might say that Chekhov accepted Dostoevsky's injunction both literally and figuratively. Chekhov does not turn away from what is taking place on earth. And yet, as I have noted, Chekhov twice walks away from the spectacle of the flogging. This gesture, more than the single word *abominable* he uses overtly to signal his sense of revulsion at the flogging, speaks also of Chekhov's connection with Turgenev and his difficult struggle to maintain his integrity as artist-observer—that is, not to be seduced by the abominable spectacle.

Dostoevsky's narrator in *Notes from the House of the Dead,* as I have noted in the opening chapter, gives evidence of his deep subjective interest or involvement in the drama of punishments. He recalls his "agitated, confused, and frightened" state of mind. "I remember that at that time I quite suddenly and impatiently began to look into all the details of these new phenomena, to listen to the conversations and stories on this theme of other convicts." The narrator sought to find out "all the degrees of sentences and punishments, all the subtleties of these punishments. . . . I tried to imagine the psychological state of those going to an execution." In the midst of his somewhat agitated discussion of the details of corporal punishment in *Notes from the House of the Dead*, the narrator suddenly launches into a lengthy discourse on the degrading effects of punishment on both individual and society. Strong in idea, the passage is marked by a lofty eloquence.[3] The narrator speaks of "gentlemen" in the recent past who obtained a satisfaction from flogging a victim, a satisfaction "resembling that of the marquis de Sade." "Blood and power intoxicate . . . ," the narrator declares, "man and citizen perish in the tyrant forever, and a return to human dignity, regeneration, repentance, now becomes for him almost impossible. . . . A society that regards indifferently such a phenomenon is already corrupt at its foundations."

Dostoevsky's narrator writes not only movingly and powerfully about the corrupting character of punishment and violence, but also with the knowledge of a man who has experienced with strange excitement the convicts' stories of punishments, all that he can see on the backs of convicts who have been flogged.[4] Dostoevsky's narrator, then, not only writes about executioners and their victims, about artist-executioners who enjoy flogging other people, but affirms that the "attributes of the executioner are found in embryo in almost every contemporary man."

At the end of the flogging scene and immediately after the medical assistant expresses his delight in witnessing a flogging ("I love it!"), Chekhov remarks blandly, matter-of-factly:

> Not only do the convicts become coarsened and brutalized by the corporal punishments, but also those who inflict the punishment and attend the punishment. Educated people are no exception either. At least I did not observe that officials with a university education related to the scene of corporal punishment differently than military medical assistants or those who have finished courses in a military school or an ecclesiastical semi-

nary. Others become so accustomed to birch rods and lashes and so brutalized that in the end even they begin to find pleasure in the floggings.

Chekhov's commentary, in contrast to Dostoevsky's, seems devoid
of all emotion or indignation. His "rhetoric" (if that word is appropriate when speaking of Chekhov) might be said to have been exhausted
in the stark and terrifying scene he has just depicted (he will conclude
the chapter with factual accounts of even more fearful brutality he had
heard of from others). What can one "say" after such a scene? What
room is there for a moving disquisition on the evils of violence? One
may argue that the example of Dostoevsky's lofty discourse on the
corrupting influence of violence made it impossible for Chekhov to
wax eloquent over the evils of corporal punishment. That is only the
outer side of the matter, however. Chekhov is not Dostoevsky. Any
flight of rhetoric at this point would have violated the poetics of Chekhov and of the *The Island of Sakhalin*. More specifically, Chekhov
had no need, either personal or artistic, to launch into an eloquent
moral discourse or to express heated indignation. Prokhorov, a character out of Russian life, said it all: "I am an unfortunate man, I am a
miserable man... Why am I being punished like this?"

The art of Chekhov in the flogging scene lies in its avoidance of
sentiment and rhetoric. The flat calm of Chekhov's commentary at
the end of the flogging scene is a case of dramatic anticlimax. Chekhov's matter-of-fact comments, following on the words "I love it!"
not only jolts the consciousness of the reader, but reminds him of a
central point that Chekhov is making: violence is so much a part of
everyday Russian life that it no longer moves a person to indignation
or rhetoric. Chekhov's deliberately unnatural calm, following on the
devastating action of the flogging scene, parodies the indifference that
is so much a part of the participants' response to the flogging scene in
particular and the condition of Russian life in general.

Turgenev, Dostoevsky, Tolstoy, and Chekhov "look at" executions
and violence in distinctive ways. Yet whatever their personal reactions
to violence—indignation, horror, disgust, squeamishness, scientific
interest, obsessive preoccupation, pleasure, or any combination of
these responses—as artists, their art of seeing is flawless. Inseparable
from this artistry is the absolute honesty with which they look not

only upon the world, but upon themselves. Beyond this, and permeating everything, is their depth of moral vision, what might otherwise be described simply as an extraordinary vulnerability to human experience and suffering. They do not separate themselves from what they see. They see with the eyes of the soul. In the end, their vision is ethical not because it is moral but because it is vision in the highest sense, because in them, as in Dante, mind is "smitten by a flash."[5]

4   *Dostoevsky in Chekhov's Garden of Eden*

"Because of Little Apples"

> In the large fruit orchard, a black thick acrid smoke spread out across the earth.
>
> Chekhov, "The Black Monk"

I

 One of the saddest, indeed most tragic tales of Chekhov is one of the first: "Because of Little Apples" (1880). The story was first published in the Russian humor magazine *Dragon Fly*. It was reprinted in a collection entitled *In the World of Laughter and Jokes* in 1900. There is laughter and jest in "Because of Little Apples," but it is of a very grim order. Like so many of Chekhov's early so-called humorous stories, "Because of Little Apples" opens up a world of cruelty and tears.

The story's realism is sharp and unsentimental. The narratorial voice is full of irony. "Because of Little Apples" is particularly responsive to some of the central concerns of Dostoevsky; indeed, the impact of Dostoevsky may be clearly felt in this work. The story has a certain heaviness, yet it gives full evidence of Chekhov's artistic powers as well as of deep social-historical consciousness.

The plot of the story is simple. A landowner, Trifon Semyonovich, and his bailiff, Karp, are walking through the estate orchards. They encounter a peasant boy and girl stealing apples. By way of punishment, the girl is induced to beat the boy; in turn, the boy is commanded to beat the girl. Both then leave the garden—in opposite directions.

The power of the story lies in part in the skill with which Chekhov interweaves everyday life and myth and arrives at a broad statement of the Russian "condition." Trifon Semyonovich is the autocratic lord of his estate "garden" in tsarist Russia; but we recognize in him also the "Lord" walking in the Garden of Eden in Genesis (3:8). "And they heard the voice of the Lord God walking in the garden in the cool of the day: and Adam and his wife hid themselves from the presence of the Lord God amongst the trees of the garden." His bailiff, Karpushka, is nicknamed "*oprichnik*"—the name of the hated guards of Ivan the Terrible. Karpushka, with his "smirking little mug," is not cherubic but demonic. Trifon Semyonovich likes to walk with him because "he feels more secure and finds it more cheerful." The peasant boy and girl are both representatives of an oppressed peasant class, but they are also "Adam and Eve." Their unique punishment—which forever divides them—reenacts the drama of the "Fall" with its foreshadowing of catastrophe in the family of man. But what specifically characterizes Chekhov's use of the biblical story is his "reduction" of the biblical statement on the human condition to a concrete social statement on the Russian condition. Throughout his story Chekhov parodies Genesis and its traditional religious interpretation. Yet the mood of tragedy that dominates the biblical story of Adam and Eve permeates the conclusion of Chekhov's anecdote.

The opening lines of "Because of Little Apples" underscore the national context of the story.

> Somewhere between the Euxine Pontus [The Black Sea] and the Solovetsky Islands [The White Sea], at certain degrees of latitude and longitude, on his own black earth, a landowner by the name of Trifon Semyonovich has been living for a long time. Trifon Semyonovich's name is long, like the word "natural scientist" [*estestvoispytatel*], and derives from a very sonorous Latin word signifying one of the numerous human virtues. [Possibly *benevolensky*; in Russian, *dobrozhelatel*]

Chekhov goes on to characterize this typical Russian landowner in precise social and economic terms. He is the owner of a mortgaged estate which has been on sale for ages. But because of his financial "wiliness" and the gullibility of the bank, Trifon Semyonovich, "like so many others of his kind," has been living on loans and evading interest payments. "His name is legion." He has been around, moreover, for "three-quarters of a century."

Trifon Semyonovich, then, is not merely a landowner in the post-emancipation world of the 1870's and 1880's, that is, a neighbor of Fyodor Pavlovich Karamazov or Saltykov-Shchedrin's Yudushka Golovlyov, but a contemporary of the strange landowners that also inhabit the world of Gogol's *Dead Souls*. He is a social and national type whose career spans all the nineteenth century. His "estate," or "garden," is the traditional Russia of autocracy and serfdom. The moral and social thrust of "Because of Little Apples" is directed against this social and historical edifice.

The narrator of the story, though he adopts a somewhat facetious manner in discussing Trifon Semyonovich's character, makes no effort to conceal his real views. He not only castigates him as a member of a moribund landowning class and a thief, but he bluntly "names" him:

> If this world was not this world, and things were named by their real names, then Trifon Semyonovich would not be called Trifon Semyonovich, but something else: they would call him by the name given to horses and cows. Frankly speaking Trifon Semyonovich was an out-and-out beast [*skotina*].

But at this point the narrator, still maintaining a thin facade of humor, suggests that he has refrained from "letting his long name loose in the world" because he hopes that Trifon Semyonovich will send him some of his Antonov apples in the fall. Therefore, the narrator limits himself to the name and patronymic—Trifon Semyonovich. "I am not going to describe all the virtues of Trifon Semyonovich: the topic is a big one." A complete description of Trifon Semyonovich would take as long as Eugène Sue took over his "Eternal Jew."

The first paragraph concludes with some brief references of the narrator to the kind of thing he will *not* have the time to speak about: Trifon's cheating at cards; his habit of not paying his debts or interest; tricks played on priest and deacon; or finally his horseback ride "through the village in the attire of Cain and Abel." The reference to Cain and Abel not only anticipates the broad mythopoetic context of "About Little Apples," but it signals one of its underlying themes: fratricide.

The narrator limits himself to only "one little scene" that characterizes Trifon Semyonovich's "relation to people." "On one thoroughly splendid morning . . . Trifon Semyonovich was walking up and down the paths of his luxuriant garden." Poetry and myth are on the narrator's mind as he introduces the reader to Trifon Semyonovich's garden. This luxuriant garden, he observes, "inspires gentlemen poets"; everything in it seems to say, "go ahead, take it, man! Enjoy yourself before autumn is upon us!" The taste for poetry and myth, however, is not the exclusive property of the poets. Both the lord of this garden and his hired man have a penchant for the literary. Karpushka is "an inexhaustible source of various tales, anecdotes and fables . . . he is always telling stories." Indeed, at the very moment he is walking in the garden with his master he is telling him a "long story" of how two high school boys in white caps had tried to bribe him to "let them into the garden to hunt," but he had refused and had sicced his dogs on them. Neither the lord of this garden nor Karpushka is noted for his generosity. And just as Karpushka is about to depict in vivid colors the "revolting way of life of the village feldscher," suspicious sounds are heard in one corner of the garden.

Both Trifon Semyonovich and Karpushka rush off to seek out the intruders. They come upon a "peasant girl standing under an old spreading apple tree, munching"; and, at her feet, a young broad-shouldered fellow (her betrothed) crawling about picking up windfalls and offering the ripe ones to his "Dulcinea." As in the biblical story, she eggs him on to take an apple directly from the tree. Though reluctant, the boy jumps high, picks an apple, and hands it to her. "But the lad and his lass," remarks the narrator, "like the ancient Adam and Eve, had no luck with their apple." No sooner did they taste the apples than their faces blanched: "not because the apple was tart but because they saw before them the strict face of Trifon Semyonovich and the maliciously smirking little mug of Karpushka."

The action in Chekhov's Russian garden sharply parodies the biblical scene in the Garden of Eden even as it remains faithful to it in detail. The mock politeness and solicitude with which Trifon Semyonovich and his smirking hired hand greet the Russian "Adam and Eve" veil a sadistic delight in cruelty and humiliation. Here the distinction between God and Satan is erased. "Well, how is your health, Grigory . . . And how is your health, my sweet? . . . You haven't celebrated your wedding yet, have you?" Grigory, well aware of the menace hidden in the words of Trifon Semyonovich, protests that he took only one apple, and that one from the ground. But the all-knowing lord of the garden is not taken in. He maliciously pokes fun at the ignorance of the Russian Adam. "You don't know how to read, but you can steal . . . You're certainly not weighed down with knowledge." Trifon Semyonovich sets about instilling "knowledge" of good and evil in Grigory and his girl. "Come, now, Grigory," he remarks, "tell us a tale." Grigory protests that he "knows no fairy tales" and doesn't need his master's apples. But Trifon Semyonovich insists. "Tell us some tale. I will listen. Karp will listen, even your beautiful betrothed will listen. Don't be embarrassed, be bold! A thieving soul must be bold," he remarks bluntly. "Is it possible you don't know? But you know how to steal? How does the 8th commandment go?" As Karpushka pointedly sets about picking nettles with which to thrash him, Grigory hastily begins "spinning a tale about how in olden times the Russian *bogatyr'* [folk hero] would thrash the *koshchey* [the evil one] and marry the beautiful maiden." Grigory's tale, of course, tells a story that in its outcome is the reverse of what happens in "Because of Little Apples." In his fairy tale, the Russian *bogatyr'* defeats the *koshchey* and marries his Dulcinea; in Chekhov's story, it is Trifon Semyonovich who thrashes Grigory. Chekhov's use of the term *koshchey* is not accidental. For the mythic *koshchey* in Russian folklore is a thin, bony old man possessing the secret of longevity, a man who is rich and evil, and, of course, a miser. Trifon Semyonovich, lord of the Russian garden, is, of course, the *koshchey* of Russia. He lives "between the Euxine Pontus and the Solovetsky Island"; he is of extraordinary longevity—the heir of a thousand years of autocracy and serfdom; he is a man whose "name is legion."

The demonic Trifon Semyonovich, then, is a parody of the benevolent but stern Old Testament God. But, in turn, one of his victims, Grigory, is a parody of the Russian folk hero, the Russian *bogatyr'*. He is not even a Don Quixote. (It is interesting that at no point in the story does Chekhov use the name Don Quixote to refer to Grigory, whereas he has Trifon Semyonovich twice use the name Dulcinea in reference to the peasant girl.) Here in the Russian garden there can be no question even of a token conflict between Trifon Semyonovich and Grigory. The utopian Russian tale in which the *bogatyr'* defeats the *koshchey* is only a dream in the Russian tsarist dystopia. It is noteworthy that Grigory does not end his tale. As the narrator observes, Grigory finally lost the thread of the tale: it ended by his "talking rubbish." Similarly, the story of the Russian Adam and Eve in their confrontation with the *koshchey* of Russia, Trifon Semyonovich, ends, like Grigory's tale, "in rubbish," that is, not in the triumph of the moral-aesthetic ideal embodied in idea of the handsome man [*krasavets*] and beautiful woman [*krasavitsa*], or in the untarnished image of the Russian "Dulcinea" before her "fall," but in desecration. The unfinished tale, then, plays a symbolic role in Chekhov's modern allegory; it prefigures the defeat and "fall" of Grigory and his betrothed, of the Russian Adam and Eve.[1]

After Grigory's catastrophic recitation, Trifon Semyonovich compels the Russian Dulcinea to recite the prayer "Our Father who art in heaven" with its motifs of veneration for the heavenly father and his "will," its anticipation of his "kingdom"; with its "give us this day our daily bread" and its pleas for "forgiveness" of sins; its entreaty, finally, that man not be "led into temptation" and that he be saved from the "evil one." The actual words of the prayer are not present in "Because of Little Apples" ("The beautiful lass blushed and barely audibly, scarcely breathing, recited "Our Father who art in Heaven"), just as Grigory's fairy tale is not spelled out in detail. But the irony of the episode is plain to view: the lord of the garden, the tsarist Russian landowner Trifon Semyonovich, though masking himself in the cloak of religion and morality, is himself the "evil one" who not only withholds "bread" and "forgiveness" but leads his Adam and Eve into "temptation." The parodic motif of antitheodicy here serves Chekhov's sharp indictment of a corrupt social order. The myth of the benevolent, stern but just "Father" explodes in the Russian landscape along with the image of the just "tsar father." Here in Chekhov's modern social allegory, it is not "God" who is good and Adam and Eve guilty, but God who is guilty and Adam and Eve who are innocent.

The "fall" of the Russian Adam and Eve is presented by Chekhov with grim realism. Trifon Semyonovich complains that neither Grigory nor his betrothed have learned the Eighth Commandment. His punishment for "stealing" is to have each one, in turn, beat the other. "It's a bad thing, my dear children, that you don't know the commandments," Trifon Semyonovich observes. "You must be taught. My beautiful one [*krasavitsa*], did he teach you to steal? Why don't you answer, my little cherub? You must answer. Speak! You are silent? Silence means assent. Well, my beauty [*krasavitsa*], then beat your handsome one [*krasavets*] for teaching you how to steal!" The girl balks at beating Grigory, but Trifon Semyonovich is implacable. "Beat him a little . . . give him a beating, my darling!" When Trifon Semyonovich threatens to call his hired man, Matvey, to give her a beating, the girl rushes up to Grigory and slaps him. Grigory "smiled foolishly and burst into tears," while Trifon Semyonovich, wild with excitement, eggs on the girl: "'Well done, my beauty! And now go after his hair! Go at him!' The girl started to drag him about. Karpushka went mad with ecstasy, howling and squealing." Finally, Trifon Semyonovich calls a halt to the beating ("Thank you, darling, for punishing evil") and invites Grigory to beat his betrothed:

> "After all, she beat you, and now you beat her! It will do her good. You don't want to? You'll avoid nothing that way. Karp, call Matvey!" The lad spat, wheezed, grasped his betrothed's braid and began to punish evil. But in punishing evil he, without realizing it, became inflamed with ecstasy, was carried away, and forgot that he was beating not Trifon but his bride. The girl started screaming. He kept on beating her for a long time.

It is only the sudden appearance of Trifon's "pretty daughter" and her announcement of the hour for "tea" that puts an end to the beating of the girl. On seeing her "papa's little escapade she burst out into peals of laughter." "Enough," said Trifon Semyonovich. "You can go now, my little darlings." "And Trifon Semyonovich bowed deeply to the punished ones. The boy and girl set themselves straight and went off. The boy went to the right and the girl to the left, and... to this day have not met again."

Chekhov's Russian garden, of course, is not a garden of paradise but a garden of hell. Its lord is Satan. The peasant boy Grigory and his betrothed are his victims. Their "fall" is their participation in the process of their alienation from one another—participation in a process of sadistic cruelty and humiliation. The final episode gives expression to the theme of fratricide—of Cain and Abel—a theme obliquely introduced at the beginning of the story. The tragedy of fratricide in the Russian village is concretely conveyed by Chekhov in his story "The Lady" (1883). Here the tragedy of fratricide—the theme of Cain and Abel—is in the foreground. The role of the *koshchey-landowner* Trifon Semyonovich is replaced here by the landowner Elena Egorovna Strelkova, who wishes to have sexual relations with a married man in a peasant family. The young man at first resists living with the landowner and betraying his wife. Finally, under the pressure of his brother and father, he yields. The ultimate result is the total disintegration of the family in a drama of fratricide and crime.

2

"Our age-old, direct and intimate pleasure is obtained through the torture of beating," remarks Ivan in *The Brothers Karamazov*. Chekhov's garden scene—with its motifs of physical cruelty and spiritual disfiguration, the absolute humiliation of the individual and sadistic delight in cruelty—is closely connected with Dostoevsky's works in its moral and psychological problem content. In *Notes from the House of the Dead* Dostoevsky explores the consequences of brutality in Russian life. In the central section of the book—the hospital scenes ending with the Russian village tale "Akulka's Husband"—Dostoevsky descends step by step into the deepest regions of his hell. Here the central social and moral motif of beatings and brutality ("all is permissible") merges with the psychological-aesthetic motif of uncontrolled "delight" in cruelty. This is a realm of total corruption of the human spirit, a realm bordering on demonism and madness. The guard Zherebyatnikov "was something of a refined connoisseur of executions. He loved, passionately loved the art of executions, and loved it purely as an art." Dostoevsky recalls the deceptively "tender" yet diabolical manner in which Zherebyatnikov would address a prisoner who was about to be beaten mercilessly, how he would offer to lighten his punishment, but how he would suddenly yell: "Let him have it! . . . Scorch him! Lay on, lay on! Flay him! Again, again! Give it to him hot, the orphan, the sneakthief! Cut him down, beat him down!" And Zherebyatnikov would run after the prisoner along the column of soldiers who were doing the beating, "laughing, laughing, helpless with laughter, holding both his sides, so doubled up with laughter that in the end one must be sorry for the kind-hearted creature."

Or Dostoevsky would recall the "fatherly" Lieutenant Smekalov, who would come to the execution scene "with a smile and a joke." While the rods were being brought, Smekalov would sit down and light his pipe.

> The prisoner would begin to beg for mercy.... "Oh, no, brother, lie down; what is the use?" Smekalov would say. The prisoner would sigh and lie down. "Now, my dear fellow, do you know such-and-such verses by heart?" "Of course I do, your honor; we are Christians and we learnt them as children." "Say them, then."

The prisoner would then begin to recite "Our Father who art in heaven." But when he reached the well-known words "in heaven," Lieutenant Smekalov, "blazing with excitement," would shout "Enough!" and order the terrible beatings to begin. "And he would roar with laughter." Smekalov would repeat his joke as though it were a ritual. This ritual, of course, is repeated by Trifon Semyonovich and his hired hand Karp in Chekhov's story. The pathos, and indictment, of the scene depicted by Chekhov and Dostoevsky is deepened, of course, by the fact that cruelty emerges not only as a hypocritical instrument of social oppression, but almost as part of the ritual of religion itself.

In the well-known chapter "Rebellion," Ivan Karamazov remarks that "a beast could never be so cruel as a man, so artistically, so aesthetically cruel." In "Because of Little Apples" Chekhov strongly accents the aesthetic motif of delight in cruelty. One recognizes in Trifon Semyonovich and Karp the successors of Zherebyatnikov and Smekalov. The boy Grigory is frighteningly caught up in the mad "ecstasy" of physical brutality. The "peals of laughter," finally, of the "pretty daughter" of Trifon Semyonovich complete this terrible scene of the degradation of man. Dostoevsky calls such examples of individual and social degradation a "disease." Recalling in this connection the names of the marquis de Sade and marquise de Brinvilliers, Dostoevsky writes in *Notes from the House of the Dead* that

> whoever has once experienced this power and boundless opportunity to humiliate with the deepest degradation another being carrying in himself the image of god—such a person whether he wills it or not has somehow lost control over his sensations. Tyranny is a habit; it has the capacity to develop and does develop, finally, into a disease. I maintain that the finest person through habit can be reduced to the crude and coarse state of a

beast. Blood and power intoxicate: coarseness and debauchery follow. . . . A society that regards indifferently such a phenomenon is already corrupt at its foundations.

Trifon Semyonovich and Karp, clearly, are social embodiments of this "disease" in which, according to Dostoevsky, the "most abnormal phenomena" "become sweet." Trifon Semyonovich is one of the morally and psychologically corrupt jailers of tsarist society: "Trifon Semyonovich, like many of his kind, quite beautifully took the law into his hands. He either locked the thief up in a cellar for twenty-four hours, or flogged him with nettles, or set him free—preliminarily stripping him bare... Is this news to you?"

The theme of beating, of flogging, of course, is central to the social and aesthetic-philosophical problem content of *The Brothers Karamazov*. In one episode of this novel ("Over the Brandy"), Fyodor Pavlovich drunkenly expatiates upon the theme of beating in Russian life:

> "And as for what he's concocting, the Russian peasant, generally speaking, ought to be whipped. . . . Our peasants are swindlers, and aren't worth pitying, and it's good that even today they're being flogged now and then. The Russian land is rich in its birches. . . . We've stopped thrashing the peasants, we're so high-minded, but they go on whipping themselves. And a good thing, too. . . . Russia's all swinishness. My friend, if you only knew how I hate Russia... that is, not Russia, but all these vices... but maybe I mean Russia. . . . On my way through Mokroe I asked an old man, and he told me: 'More than anything,' he said, 'we're very fond of sentencing the girls to be thrashed, and we let the young fellows do the thrashing. And the girl he has thrashed today, he takes as his bride tomorrow. So it seems,' he says, 'that the girls themselves like it.' There's a set of marquis de Sades, eh?"

We find summed up here a number of motifs that are to be found in "Because of Little Apples": the social contempt of the gentry for the peasants and for Russia; the notion that the peasants themselves have taken on the task of "thrashing each other"; and the Sadean motif of delight in flogging (here associated with the fellows who thrash their betrothed).

The theme of the drunken Fyodor Pavlovich is profanation, the disfiguring of all that is beautiful in form and spirit.[2] The underlying tragedy of "Adam and Eve" in "Because of Little Apples" is the disfiguration of goodness and beauty. Not without reason does Trifon

Semyonovich use such terms as "beautiful one" (*krasavitsa*) and "handsome one" (*krasavets*), "cherubim," Dulcinea, to refer to Grigory and his girl. But the tragedy of goodness and beauty, as I have already noted, is a tragedy of self-spoliation. "Adam and Eve" are drawn into the dialectics of evil, made to participate in it, and—spiritually—to fall. In Chekhov's parody of the biblical fall, of course, the sexual motif lies hidden in the Sadean response of Trifon Semyonovich, Karp, and Grigory to the beatings. The "awakening" of Grigory and his girl from innocence is an awakening of shame before their inner disfiguration. "The boy went to the right, and the girl to the left, and... to this day have not met again."

Yet in Chekhov's garden scene, "original sin" lies not with the Russian Adam and Eve, not with the peasants, but with Trifon Semyonovich. Clearly, the source of evil—its genesis—is the *koshchey* Trifon Semyonovich, the demonic embodiment of centuries of autocracy and serfdom. Man and woman are originally good and beautiful (as in Rousseau's conception) but have been subverted and corrupted by the social order.

Who, then, is Trifon Semyonovich? Chekhov, I think, "names" him on three separate but interacting planes: mythopoetic, social-historical, and social-literary. He is, first of all, the *devil*—precisely the "natural scientist" (*estestvoispytatel'*) or one who "tests" nature (*ispytatel' prirody*) that Chekhov mentions in his first paragraph: that is, one who not only "tests" (*ispytyvajushchij*), but also "torments" (*pytajushchij*) and "tempts" nature, leads Russian Rousseauesque man "into temptation"; he is, secondly, on the social-historical plane that equally evil "tsar father" who rules over Russia; finally, on the literary-social plane Trifon Semyonovich is certainly a blood-relative of Fyodor Pavlovich Karamazov, a Sadean character who in his own words is inhabited by the "unclean spirit": "Verily I am the lie and the father of the lie!"

3

Chekhov could hardly have missed reading *The Brothers Karamazov*. "Because of Little Apples" was first published August 17, 1880, in *Strekoza* (no. 33). *The Brothers Karamazov* was printed serially in 1879 and 1880 in the *Russkij vestnik*. The chapter "Over the Brandy," cited above, appeared in the very early part of 1879. Chekhov himself seems to have wished to emphasize the link connecting Trifon Semyonovich with Fyodor Pavlovich. He writes in the final paragraph of his story:

> That's how Trifon Semyonovich amuses himself in his old age. And his little family is not far behind him. . . . His little son Mitya, a retired second lieutenant, one winter surpassed even his papa: together with Karpushka he tarred the gates of a former private because this private did not want to make a gift of a wolf cub to him, and because this private allegedly put his daughters on guard against the candy and gingerbread of the gentleman lieutenant...

There is every reason to regard this detail about "retired second lieutenant Mitya" as evidence of the literary ancestry of Trifon Semyonovich. Chekhov concludes the above-cited passage, and the story itself, with the line "Now after this call Trifon Semyonovich—Trifon Semyonovich!"

4

The narrator of Dostoevsky's "A Christmas Party and a Wedding" opens the story with this remark: "The other day I saw a wedding... but no! I had better tell you about the Christmas party." He recalls a Christmas party and children's ball he had attended as an "outsider" five years earlier at the house of a wealthy man with influence and connections. "It might be supposed that the children's ball was a pretext for getting the parents together and discussing various interesting matters in an innocent, accidental, and casual way." The scene of innocent play of children, in fact, provides a setting for adult concerns of a very uninnocent character. One of these concerns turns out to be the mortgaging of the future of the eleven-year-old daughter of a wealthy contractor. We learn that she will inherit 300,000 rubles when she comes of age in five years. It turns out that one of the guests, the pompous and influential Julian Mastakovich, on hearing of the dowry, immediately calculates the interest on this money in five year's time and makes up his mind to marry the future sixteen-year-old. As the narrator remarks: "Either his calculations had had an effect upon him, or something else, but he rubbed his hands and could not stay still."

Julian Mastakovich, it should be noted, also appears in Dostoevsky's early story "A Weak Heart" (1848) as patron of the unfortunate clerk Vasya Shumkov. He also appears in Dostoevsky's "Petersburg Chronicle" (April 27, 1847), where he is presented as a rapacious voluptuary who pretends to be a decent and respectable man about town. The narrator in "Petersburg Chronicle" speaks with scathing irony of this "very good soul." "You know this gentleman very well, gentlemen. His name is legion."

> My good friend, former well-wisher [*dobrozhelatel'*] and even to a certain extent patron, Julian Mastakovich, intends to get married. . . . He still hasn't gotten married, there is still three weeks before the wedding. But every evening he puts on his white waistcoat, wig, and all his finery, buys a bouquet of flowers and some sweets, and goes off to enjoy Glafira Petrovna, his fiancée, a seventeen-year-old girl who is full of innocence and completely ignorant of evil. The very thought of this latter fact evokes the most cloying smile on the sugary lips of Julian Mastakovich. Yes, indeed, it is truly very nice to marry at such an [advanced] age in life! . . . "In the flower of his advanced years," I thought to myself, "a man finds a friend who understands him completely, a seventeen-year-old girl, innocent, educated, and just one month out of boarding school. And this man will live, and he will live out his life in pleasure and happiness!" I was overcome with envy.

It is the narrator of "Christmas Party and a Wedding" who provides us with a full view of the *dobrozhelatel'* Julian Mastakovich in action.

The core of Dostoevsky's story is a seduction scene involving three people: Julian Mastakovich, the wealthy eleven-year-old future heiress, and a poor abased boy, the son of the governess of the household where the Christmas party is taking place.

The boy and girl in Dostoevsky's story are seen playing alone with a doll in a room apart from the rest of the children. Clearly excited by the monetary and sexual prospects of his future marriage, Julian Mastakovich tiptoes into the room. He approaches the beautiful little girl (*krasavitsa*) with a smile, bends down, and kisses her on the head. The girl, not expecting this "attack," utters a cry of alarm. "And what are you doing here, sweet child?" he asks in a whisper, patting the girl on the cheek and glancing around. "We are playing..." "Ah, with him?" Julian Mastakovich looks askance at the little boy. "You had better go into the drawing room, my dear," he says to the boy. "But the boy and girl," the narrator notes, "frowned and clutched at each other. They did not want to be separated." More excited than ever, Julian Mastakovich again glances around and lowering his voice, asks in an almost inaudible voice broken with emotion and impatience: "And will you love me, my darling, when I visit your parents?" He attempts to kiss the girl, but the little boy, his apparent rival, begins to cry and whimper, and sympathetically clutches the hand of the girl. But Julian Mastakovich, overcome by his rapacious and voluptuous feelings and increasingly upset at the boy's stubbornness, orders him to leave the room. "No, he needn't, he needn't," the girl insists, "it is you who should go away. . . . Leave him alone, leave him alone," she says, almost crying. Suddenly sounds are heard in the doorway. The frightened boy stealthily makes his way out of the room into the dining room. His persecutor, afraid of being seen, also leaves the room, disconcerted and embarrassed by his own "excitement and impatience."

I have omitted for the moment some important details from my description of this scene. Nonetheless, we can discern the mythopoetic setting. The little boy and girl, alone with their innocent play-acting, are like Adam and Eve in the Garden of Eden. Julian Mastakovich, full of voluptuous thoughts and feelings, emerges as the archetypal tempter or devil. He wishes to separate the boy and girl. He persecutes his rival, the boy, and at the same time relates to the little girl like a seducer.

Dostoevsky underscores the motif of Eden in the denouement of this scene. Frustrated and angry, Julian Mastakovich pursues the boy into the dining room. "Be off, what are you doing here? Be off, you good-for-nothing, be off," he exclaims. "Are you trying to steal fruit, is that it? So you're trying to steal fruit? Be off, you good-for-nothing, be off!" The frightened boy crawls under the table, but his persecutor, flushed with excitement, takes out his large handkerchief and tries to drive the boy out from under the table.

The boy, of course, is not trying to steal fruit. His relationship to the girl is one of total innocence. It is rather Julian Mastakovich who has eaten from the tree of good and evil and who now, again in the room with the girl, is attempting to eat forbidden fruits. He is clearly projecting his own guilt upon the boy (though the boy's innocence, as I shall note later, is reviewed by Dostoevsky in another light). Not without reason does Julian Mastakovich enter the room "on tiptoe as though feeling himself guilty." It is he who seeks to destroy the childrens' illusions (linked significantly with the idea of the family); it is he who separates them from each other in anticipation of some kind of erotic encounter with his future bride; it is he who seeks to expel both boy and girl from their garden of innocence.

Julian Mastakovich's attempt to flush the boy out from under the table is interrupted by the laughter of the narrator, who has observed this whole episode in silence from his hiding place. A few moments later, the host of the party, unaware of all that has taken place, asks Julian Mastakovich to become the patron of the little boy. But the boy's persecutor haughtily refuses. In the context of the preceding episode, his unwillingness to be the boy's patron is of special significance: he not only expels the boy from the playroom, the garden of innocence, but by refusing to become his patron, he literally drives the poor boy out into the Petersburg wilderness.

The final attack on the girl takes place when she has reached the age of sixteen and is married off to Julian Mastakovich. The innocence of the girl—"charming, like a cupid, quiet, contemplative, pale, with wide-open thoughtful eyes"—had been violated on the symbolic plane in her first encounter with Julian Mastakovich. "And what is that you've got, a dolly, my child?" he asks her. "A dolly," she answers timidly. "A dolly... And do you know what your dolly is made of, my child?" "I don't know," she answers in a whisper, head bowed. "It's made of rags, darling." Julian Mastakovich, anticipating his marriage, seeks to destroy not only the vital creative illusions of the boy and girl as they pertain to the family, but to debase and destroy the sacred notion of the child itself. The doll has living reality to the children; it is, moreover, a symbol of pure beauty and innocence. Through his remark, Julian Mastakovich seeks to "reduce," as it were, the image of the child to a mere object or rag.

The scene in which Julian Mastakovich questions the girl about the doll is one of barely restrained sexual aggression. The narrator himself notes in this connection: "Possibly he was at first so much impressed by his calculations, so seduced and inspired by them, that in spite of all his dignity and importance he decided to act like a bad boy and directly assault the object of his intentions, in spite of the fact that this object could become a real object only after some five more years at least." The concept of the girl—whether at the age of eleven or sixteen—as an "object" leaves little doubt as to the kind of marriage Julian Mastakovich anticipates.

The final fall of the girl, her expulsion from her Eden, takes place five years later. The narrator witnesses the wedding of Julian Mastakovich and his now nearly matured bride. The girl who at eleven was described by the narrator as "a beauty" is now described as "a miraculous beauty whose first spring had barely arrived." But there is nothing springlike or joyous about this bride. Pale and sad, she has the face of a Madonna. "The classical severity of every line on her face endowed her beauty with dignity and solemnity," the narrator observes. "But through this dignity and solemnity, through this sadness there peered the original child-like, innocent face; something was expressed there that was intensely naive, uncertain, youthful, something, it seemed, that implored mercy without asking anything for itself."

No sooner does the narrator recognize the bride and bridegroom than he rushes out of the church as fast as he can. And with good reason: the church has become a symbolic scene for a new sacrifice of innocence to evil. In a subtle way, Dostoevsky hints at the desecration involved in this marriage. "In the crowd," the narrator remarks, "people said that the bride was wealthy, that she had a dowry of five-hundred thousand and rags galore." The reappearance of the word *triapki* (here, clothes, or colloquially, rags) is not accidental. In the seduction scene, Julian Mastakovich had sought to reduce the child's doll to "rags," to the status of an "object." Now, at his wedding, Dostoevsky indirectly makes plain, Julian Mastakovich's dream of reducing the girl to an object or rag is finally within reach.

5

In the stories of both Chekhov and Dostoevsky, the biblical Garden of Eden constitutes the subtext of the core scenes. Adam and Eve find reincarnation in Dostoevsky's innocent preadolescents and in Chekhov's innocent and handsome adolescents. In both stories evil comes masked in a person who poses as a well-meaning respectable citizen. In both Julian Mastakovich and Trifon Semyonovich, the dulcet tones of the seducer mask the sinister intention of a person who takes pleasure in the destruction of beauty and innocence.

Both stories are narrated by anonymous observers. The narrative tone is ironical, at times sarcastic. The narrators focus on a central figure who affects an attitude of outward morality and respectability but who is inwardly corrupt and rapacious. Chekhov's narrator plays no role in the story. Dostoevsky's narrator, the "unknown person" of the story's title, describes himself as an "outsider" at the party. He witnesses the action of the story and at the same time plays a marginal but significant role in it.

In the core scene of the story, the boy and girl are playing alone with the doll in a room apart from the rest of the Christmas festivities. Dostoevsky's description of the narrator's situation at this point is not without symbolic significance in the mythopoetic context of the story. "I had been sitting for more than half an hour, almost slumbering, in an ivy-covered arbor," says the narrator, "listening to the chatter of the red-haired boy and the beautiful girl with the dowry of three hundred thousand, both so busy with their doll, when Julian Mastakovich suddenly entered the room." Like Satan, Julian Mastakovich tiptoes into the children's garden of innocence. Yet the narrator, too, acquires a certain sinister presence as he remains concealed, like the slumbering serpent, nearby in his ivy-covered arbor.[4] He too is an alien presence, and the scene he witnesses (it might almost be a fantasy of semi-slumber) is charged with erotic tension. Here the narrator is not only a detached observer with a moral point of view, but a voyeur. The drama that he witnesses and vicariously participates in is a complex one. Here plot—the account of Julian Mastakovich's "attack" on the girl—is conjoined with subplot—Julian Mastakovich's relationship to the "terribly cowed and frightened boy."

Dostoevsky's interest in the socially abased and psychologically disturbed child was not confined to "A Christmas Party and a Wedding." In the original edition of *Netochka Nezvanova* (1849), a work which began to appear in print only a few months after the publication of "A Christmas Party and a Wedding," Dostoevsky explored the psychology of this type of child in the figure of the orphan boy Larenka. This boy of eleven, "pale, thin and red-haired" (like the boy in "A Christmas Party and a Wedding"), is a "wounded heart," an orphan who comes into contact with Netochka Nezvanova, a girl roughly of his own age. Netochka speaks of him as my "little criminal" in her recollections. At one point she dwells on the psychological character of humiliated children like Larenka:

> First, they are all sensitive by nature, tender, but egotists and sensual. They are, for example, miserly and greedy, sensualists in the highest degree. . . . Now the child is a despot by nature. And who knows, perhaps

Larya had already begun to take a pusillanimous pleasure in taking out on another person his innocent sense of humiliation, quite in the same manner of those adult egotists whom I encountered in the world so often later on, people who carried their egotism to the point of a refined sensualism and would take out on others all the insults they had suffered in life. . . . I have observed many such children who, for the sake of gratifying a depraved sensualism, the outgrowth of a falsely developed sensitivity, have emerged as utter tyrants at home, and have brought their refinement of pleasure to such a point as, for example, intentionally to torture domestic animals in order that they might, at the moment of the very process of torment, experience a certain inexplicable pleasure comprised of the sensation of feeling remorse, pity and the awareness of their own inhumanity.

The little boy in "A Christmas Party and a Wedding" would appear to be, in embryo, a variant of the type of child described by Netochka. The narrator observes the children in their play at the Christmas party. His attention is drawn in particular to the behavior of a cowed and frightened boy, the son of the governess, among his more fortunate companions. Poor and socially inferior, the boy was the last to receive a present, nothing but a book of stories with descriptions on the grandeurs of nature, and without even pictures. The narrator observes the boy wandering around among the other toys.

He wanted terribly to play with the other children, but he did not dare: it was obvious that he felt and understood his position. I very much like to observe children. Their first manifestation of independence in life is extraordinarily interesting. I noticed that the red-haired boy was so tempted by the expensive toys of the other children, especially by the theater in which he wanted very badly to take some part, that he decided to do a little bootlicking. He smiled and ingratiated himself with the other children, gave away his apple to a puffy-faced boy whose handkerchief was already tied up full with presents, and he even decided to give a piggyback ride to another boy so as not to be driven away from the theater. But a minute later some rascal of a boy gave him a first-rate thrashing.

This episode appears at first sight to serve merely as background or introduction to the subsequent temptation scene involving the girl and boy and Julian Mastakovich. Yet when we juxtapose the behavior of the boy in this scene with the behavior with Julian Mastakovich in the temptation scene, we become aware of a carefully concealed subplot.

The narrator, it will be recalled, describes Julian Mastakovich as so "tempted" and "inspired" by his calculations that he resolved to behave like "a bad boy" and "assault the object of his intentions" even though it was a good five years before his "object" would be ready for him. He ingratiates himself with the girl (as he does later before her mother and father) with the object of taking advantage of her. He is motivated by both greed and sensuality. His accusation that the boy is stealing fruit only masks his own desire to taste forbidden fruits. Clearly, he projects his own guilt upon the boy (later he calls him "a naughty child") when he persecutes him and tries to thrash him. Nobody punishes Julian Mastakovich for his vile behavior, but the narrator's laughter may be said objectively to constitute a form of retribution.

The boy also is seen as behaving like a bad boy in his "first manifestation of independence," that is, his first step out of the nursery into the real world. Of what is he guilty? He is "tempted" by other children's toys, in particular the theater, but also the girl's doll. He behaves in a servile way, ingratiates himself with other children, gives away his apple, and lets others take advantage of him. Finally he is thrashed.

The parallel situations of Julian Mastakovich and the boy are so striking as to compel the reader to wonder whether Dostoevsky is not alluding here to vileness of another kind on the boy's part. In the context of the temptation scene involving Julian Mastakovich and the girl, the boy's giving away his apple would appear to have a certain symbolic significance. Here it would seem to suggest a giving away of innocence, some kind of sexual misbehavior. The reference to letting others take advantage of him, ride piggyback on him, certainly is suggestive of sexual relations with another boy or man. In this light the thorough thrashing that the boy receives at the hands of another boy would appear to constitute a kind of symbolic retribution for vile behavior.

The surface plot of "A Christmas Party and Wedding" in no way supports the notion that the boy *actually* engages in any kind of sexual misbehavior. Yet an examination of the text suggests an underlying subplot involving the type of child-sensualist that is discussed in the discarded variant of *Netochka Nezvanova*. This subplot is inactive. Yet whatever light this subplot throws upon Dostoevsky and the theme of child violation from the psychoanalytical point of view, it serves to suggest that such children as the little boy may easily develop, in the words of Netochka Nezvanova, into adult egotists who "carry their egotism to the point of a refined sensualism"; that is, they may develop into types like Julian Mastakovich.

Julian Mastakovich and the boy, then, stand in apposite relation to one another as preadolescent and adult "sensualist" types. But at this point one may ask one further question: Do the boy and Julian Mastakovich stand in any other relationship to each other on the level of the story's subplot? Does Dostoevsky's plot in which a man is tempted to abuse a little girl mask a subplot in which a boy is abused by a man? The direct development of such a theme in fiction would have been unthinkable for Dostoevsky at the time. Did he cannily put it into the subplot of "A Christmas Party and a Wedding"? The subtext of Dostoevsky's story, in any case, certainly lends itself to analysis. In this connection, what is the significance of the narrator's comment earlier in the party? "One little blackeyed, curly haired boy, who kept trying to shoot me with his little gun, was particularly lovely to look at. But my attention was drawn most of all to his sister, a girl of eleven, charming, like a cupid, quiet, contemplative, pale, with wide-open thoughtful eyes." This girl, of course, is the object of Julian Mastakovich's attentions.

The narrator surely deserves close scrutiny. It is noteworthy that he maintains complete silence throughout the temptation scene. He then follows Julian Mastakovich and the boy into the dining room. At the point when Julian Mastakovich attempts to drive the boy out from under the table, the narrator recalls, "I burst out into loud laughter." Julian Mastakovich is taken aback and in a gesture of guilt and embarrassment, puts his handkerchief to his nose. A short while later, the narrator again laughs in the face of the abashed Julian Mastakovich. At this juncture the latter turns to his host with a question that the reader, too, has begun to ask: "Who is this strange young man?" Indeed, who is this supposedly neutral observer and outsider?

In "Because of Little Apples," the boy and girl are forced to beat each other. This moment, so delightful to Trifon Semyonovich, is interrupted when his daughter comes running "from behind the bushes." "Papa, come and have tea!" she cries, "and seeing her papa's escapade she burst out laughing." Her laughter points to her full acceptance and enjoyment of the scene in which the boy and girl have been humiliating each other. Her point of view does not differ morally or psychologically from that of her father. The narrator of "A Christmas Party and a Wedding," of course, morally condemns the action he witnesses. Yet from a psychological point of view, his laughter may also signal a de facto complicity with Julian Mastakovich. Both observer and observed, each one an alien presence in the garden of innocence, share a secret.

Dostoevsky, of course, was also observing his observer. Did he also have a secret? Was he involved in his story in some kind of elusive and allusive literary-psychological play with plot and subplot? In concealing his narrator in an ivy-covered arbor, was he not also implicating him in the entire drama of temptation involving the boy and girl and Julian Mastakovich? Whether the plot and subplot have roots in Dostoevsky's autobiography is a matter for speculation. What is certain for the literary analyst is that the interwoven plot and subplot of his story had roots in his creative imagination and that it found a certain ingenious expression in his story.

Is the laughter of Trifon Semyonovich's daughter as she emerges from behind the bushes a literary reminiscence of the laughter of Dostoevsky's narrator-voyeur? Did Chekhov view the laughter of Dostoevsky's narrator as the laughter of complicity with, as well as indictment of, the temptation scene? Whatever the answer, a comparison of "A Christmas Party and a Wedding" and "Because of Little Apples" provides further evidence that the nineteen-year-old Chekhov had already read Dostoevsky thoroughly, that he was deeply responsive to the social and psychological problem content of Dostoevsky's work. "Because of Little Apples" is an early acknowledgment on Chekhov's part of the deep relevance of Dostoevsky's work for Russian literature, life, and history.

5   A View from the Underground

On Nikolai Nikolaevich Strakhov's Letter
About His Good Friend Fyodor Mikhailovich
Dostoevsky and on Leo Nikolaevich Tolstoy's
Cautious Response to It

 On November 28, 1883, the prominent Russian critic, essay-
ist, and philosopher N. N. Strakhov, Dostoevsky's friend
and journalistic collaborator in the 1860's,[1] dispatched a letter to Leo Tolstoy in which he savagely attacked Dostoevsky as grossly
immoral and ridiculed what he called his "cerebral and literary humanism."[2] Shortly before writing his letter, Strakhov had sent Tolstoy
the first posthumous miscellany of biographic materials on Dostoevsky (1883), which included Strakhov's memoir.[3] Summing up at one
point in his memoir, Strakhov wrote of Dostoevsky's "muse" as the
distinctive element in the Russian novelist's work. Dostoevsky, he
observed, had discovered flashes of beauty under the disfigured
and repulsive exterior of man, and for this he forgave people and
loved them.

> This tender and lofty humanism can be called his muse, and it gave him
> the measure of good and evil with which he descended into the most
> terrible spiritual abysses. He firmly believed in himself and in man, and
> that is why he was so sincere, so easily took his own subjectivity for com-
> plete realism. . . . By muse I understand that idealized character, that
> formation of mind and heart which a man takes when he begins to write
> and create. The muse and the man himself are two different creatures,
> although they have grown out of one and the same root. . . . From what I

have said, it is evident that in Dostoevsky the muse and man came together in an unusually close union.[4]

In an introduction to Dostoevsky's works in 1883, Strakhov wrote
again: "It was terrible to see how Dostoevsky would go down deeper
and deeper into the spiritual abysses, into the frightful abysses of
moral and physical corruption (this is his own word). But he comes
out of them unharmed, that is, without losing the measure of good
and evil, of the beautiful and the monstrous."[5] Strakhov's eloquent
observations are wholly in the spirit of his memoir as a whole. Yet as
his letter to Tolstoy amply attests, he had not expressed in his published recollections his private feelings about Dostoevsky. Strakhov's
letter is certainly one of the most arresting commentaries ever written
on Dostoevsky by a person who knew him well.

Strakhov opens with the observation that he considers the theme
of Dostoevsky "a most rich" one, one that he had wanted for a long
time to "develop fully." He takes this occasion to "make a confession"
to Tolstoy. "All during the writing [of the memoir] I was conflicted, I
struggled with rising revulsion, I tried to repress in myself this bad
feeling." With an anguished, if not quite sincere, appeal for Tolstoy's
aid—"Help me find a way out of it"—Strakhov launches into a violent attack on the man Dostoevsky and his muse.

> I cannot consider Dostoevsky either a good or a happy man (two things
> that in essence coincide). He was evil, envious, debauched, and he con-
> ducted his whole life in the kind of turmoil that made him pitiful and
> would have made him ridiculous if at the same time he had not been so
> evil and so clever. But he considered himself, as did Rousseau, the very
> best of people and the happiest. I vividly recalled all these features on the
> occasion of the biography. In Switzerland, in my presence, he so bossed
> about a servant that the latter took offense and rebuked him: "After all I
> too am a human being!" I remember how at that time I was struck that
> this was directed at a preacher of *humanism* and that there was an echo
> here of notions of free Switzerland *on the rights of man.*
>
> Such scenes were constant, because he could not restrain his malice.
> Many times I remained silent in the presence of these outbursts which
> came about with him in quite a womanish way, unexpectedly and devi-
> ously; but on two occasions I said some very insulting things to him.
> But of course where insults were concerned, he in general was superior
> to ordinary people, and what is worse, he took pleasure in [insulting],
> to the end never repented of all his vilenesses. He was drawn to vilenesses

and boasted of them. Viskovatov once started to tell me how Dostoevsky boasted that . . . [in a bathhouse he had screwed a little girl who had been brought to him by her governess.][6] Note in this connection that with all his animal sensuality, he had no taste, no feeling for feminine beauty and charm. This may be seen in his novels. The characters whom he most resembles are the hero of *Notes from the Underground*, Svidrigailov in *Crime and Punishment*, and Stavrogin in *The Devils*; Katkov did not want to print one scene from Stavrogin's [life] (debauchery and other things), but Dostoevsky read it to many people at the time.

With such a nature he was particularly disposed to sweet sentimentality, to lofty and humane reveries, and these reveries constitute his tendency, his literary muse and path. In essence, however, all his novels represent *self-justification*, demonstrate that all kinds of vileness can coexist in a man alongside nobility.

How difficult it is for me that I cannot get rid of these thoughts, that I am unable to find some point of reconciliation! Am I full of spite? Do I envy him? Do I wish him evil? In no way; I am only ready to weep that this recollection, which *might have been* a bright one, only oppresses me!

I recall your words that people who know us too well naturally do not like us. But sometimes it happens differently. It is possible in [a long] close acquaintance to find in a person a feature for which you would afterwards forgive him everything. *The movement of true goodness, the spark of real heartfelt warmth*, even one moment of real repentance, would wipe out everything; and if I recalled something similar in Dostoevsky, I would have forgiven him and rejoiced for him. Yet [I saw] nothing but the elevation of himself into a splendid man, nothing but cerebral and literary humanism—God, how disgusting this is!

Here truly was an unhappy and bad man who imagined himself happy, a hero, and tenderly loved himself alone.

As I have known about myself that I myself am capable of arousing revulsion, and as I have learned to understand and forgive in others this feeling, I thought that I would find a way out with respect to Dostoevsky. But I do not find it, I do not find it!

Well, there's my little commentary to my biography; I might have put down and related this side of Dostoevsky; many instances present themselves to me far more vividly than those which I have described, and the story would have come out far more truthfully; but let this truth perish, we will parade about only the facade of life as we do everywhere and in everything![7] [Strakhov's italics]

Dostoevsky's widow, Anna Grigorievna, read Strakhov's letter on its publication in 1913. "My sight darkened from horror and indignation," she told Leonid Grossman shortly before her death in 1918.

"What unheard-of slander! And from whom does it come? From our best friend, from our steady visitor, the witness at our wedding—from Nikolai Nikolaevich Strakhov, who after Fyodor Mikhailovich's death asked me to charge him with writing Dostoevsky's biography in a posthumous edition of his works. If Nikolai Nikolaevich were alive, I would at once in spite of my declining years go to him and strike him in the face for this baseness."[8] Anna Grigorievna was particularly outraged at Strakhov's repetition to Tolstoy of the rumor, widespread in the late 1870's and early 1880's, that Dostoevsky had raped a girl in a bathhouse.[9] In her conversation with Leonid Grossman, she recalls that Tolstoy asked her after Dostoevsky's death, "What kind of a man was Dostoevsky?" She answered, "He was the kindest, most tender, most intelligent and magnanimous man whom I have ever known."[10]

Certainly Strakhov's letter as a whole is marked by deep malice and a desire to strike a wounding blow at Dostoevsky. A personal motive, revenge, cannot be excluded in explaining the particularly vicious character of Strakhov's comments and his peculiarly smug moral posture. Strakhov had access to Dostoevsky's archives in the period when he was writing his memoir and in all probability read in one of Dostoevsky's notebooks for the *Diary of a Writer* (1977) the novelist's devastating portrait of Strakhov as a man and type.[11] "[His] literary career gave him four readers, I think, and no more, and a thirst for fame," Dostoevsky wrote. "He leads a cushy life, likes to feed on turkeys, and not at his own but at other people's tables." In old age this type of writer becomes "touchy and exacting." Of Strakhov, a priest's son who as a young man attended a seminary before entering St. Petersburg University, Dostoevsky further wrote:

> The purest strain of the seminarian. There is no hiding one's origin. No civic feeling or sense of duty, no indignation in the face of vileness, but, on the contrary, he himself does vile things; in spite of his strict moral air, he is secretly a voluptuary, and ready in the name of some fatty and coarse sensual vileness to sell everybody and everything, both civic duty, for which he has no feeling, and work, about which he is quite indifferent, and the ideal, which he does not have, and not because he doesn't believe in an ideal but because of the coarse layer of fat which prevents him from feeling anything. Later I'll have more to say about these literary types of ours; one must ceaselessly expose and unmask them.[12]

Dostoevsky's evaluation of Strakhov was strangely prescient. Strakhov, a kind of a moral Tartuffe, seems to have projected on Dostoevsky (whatever the novelist's weaknesses) his own shortcomings ("I have known about myself that I myself am capable of arousing revulsion"). Strakhov's notion that goodness and happiness essentially go together suggests a strange parochialism. Yet while remarking both the banal and sensational aspect of Strakhov's letter, it would be a mistake to set aside his "little commentary" as worthless. The allegation that Dostoevsky raped a child aside, there are elements of truth, albeit distorted, in Strakhov's letter. Dostoevsky was unquestionably a difficult, irascible, tortured human being; the individual cases of rudeness of which Strakhov speaks undoubtedly occurred. Dostoevsky well understood, as he once wrote in a letter describing his prison experiences, how under pressure an individual can behave badly toward other people. "The most intolerable misery is when you yourself become unjust, evil, foul; you recognize all this, you even reproach yourself—but you can't control yourself. I experienced it all." [13]

The problem in general of the disjunction between personal attitudes and behavior on the one hand and abstract humanism and literary attitudes and poses on the other was one of the central problems that Dostoevsky explored in his works. "I love humanity . . . but I really wonder at myself: the more I love humanity in general, the less I love people in particular, that is, as separate individual people," remarks a doctor friend of Zosima in *The Brothers Karamazov*. "I become an enemy of people . . . the very moment they come close to me. On the other hand, it always happens that the more I hate people in particular, the more passionate becomes my love for humanity in general." Could Dostoevsky's description of the doctor's contradictions have been a case of self-parody? Perhaps. But as parody it surely had nothing in common with the "self-justification" of an unhappy "evil, envious and debauched man," as Strakhov puts it. In general, Strakhov's effort to identify Dostoevsky with some of his heroes—with their immorality and failure to live up to their lofty humanism—suggests not only malice, but a simplistic view of the creative process, of the relation of an author to his creation.

In his memoir Strakhov affirms that Dostoevsky the man and his muse constituted a moral and aesthetic unity ("the muse and the man came together in an unusually close union"). In his letter to Tolstoy, however, Strakhov suggests that that unity was only psychological—"self-justification." Surely what Dostoevsky called the "purest strain of the seminarian" is revealed here: to the strict moralist, any disjunction between man and his muse is intolerable and above all reprehensible and unforgivable. For Strakhov, *the good man is a happy man*; this notion he appears to have carried over into the realm of aesthetics.

"From your book," Tolstoy wrote in response to Strakhov's letter about Dostoevsky, "I learned for the first time the full measure of [Dostoevsky's] mind."[14] Tolstoy's reaction to Strakhov's violent personal attack on Dostoevsky was in general cautious and restrained. Tolstoy had never met Dostoevsky. He had never written about him. His responses over the years to Dostoevsky and his works are fragmentary, haphazard: occasional comments in his works on Dostoevsky; remarks in letters; jottings in his notebooks; spoken observations noted or recalled by people who knew Tolstoy. These remarks can only infrequently be judged in context; sometimes they are colored by the point of view of the person making note of the remarks. The observations are sometimes admiring, sometimes slighting, and occasionally capricious; they suggest strongly conflicting attitudes, reservations of Tolstoy that impede a clear point of view or straightforward judgment. Gorky maintained that Tolstoy spoke of Dostoevsky "reluctantly, constrainedly, evading or suppressing something."[15] Nonetheless, a certain pattern of oppositions and emphases may be discerned in Tolstoy's responses to Dostoevsky.

Gorky, who all his life was trying to settle accounts with Dostoevsky, records Tolstoy as saying about Dostoevsky: "There was something Jewish in his blood. He was mistrustful, vain, difficult, and unfortunate. It is strange that he is so much read, I can't understand why! Really it's painful and useless, because all these Idiots, Adolescents, Raskolnikovs, and the rest of them, they weren't like that; it's all much simpler, more understandable."[16] Tolstoy is certainly dismissive in these remarks. Yet on learning of Dostoevsky's death in early February 1881, the same Tolstoy could write to Strakhov:

How I should like to be able to say everything that I feel about Dostoevsky. You, describing your feeling, expressed a part of mine. I never saw this man and never had direct relations with him, and suddenly, when he died, I understood that he was the very, very closest, the dearest and most necessary man to me. I am a writer, and writers are all vain, envious. I at least am such a writer. And it never entered into my head to measure myself with him—never. Everything that he did (the good, the authentic that he did) was of the kind that the more he did it, the better it was for me. Art evokes in me envy, intellect also, but the work of the heart only joy. Thus I considered him my friend and could not think otherwise than that we should meet some time, and that if it hadn't come about, this was something pertaining to me. And suddenly at dinner—I was dining alone, late—I read that he died. Some kind of support gave way under me. I was dismayed, and then it became clear how he had been dear to me, and I wept and weep now.[17]

"I wrote sincerely what I felt," Tolstoy told Dostoevsky's widow in 1885, apropos his letter to Strakhov, which she had seen. "Dostoevsky was for me a precious man and perhaps the only person whom I could ask about much and who might have answered much for me!"[18]

In these comments to Strakhov and Anna Grigorievna, Tolstoy's attitude toward Dostoevsky is decidedly positive. Clearly, he has read Dostoevsky closely, pondered his writings, and admired them. Yet even here there are qualifications. In the letter to Strakhov, Tolstoy's words—"everything that he did . . . was of the kind that the more he did it, the better it was for me"—are interrupted by the qualifying remark "the good, the authentic that he did." Tolstoy, clearly, was not receptive to everything Dostoevsky wrote; even in a moment of grief, he does not fail to define his position precisely. We note, too, that Tolstoy's remarks to Anna Grigorievna about Dostoevsky, significantly, place the emphasis upon *questions and answers*, not Dostoevsky's artistry.

Reviewing the various remarks made by Tolstoy on Dostoevsky, remarks that span half a century, one discerns a deep and abiding interest in and respect for Dostoevsky. "Everything that touches on Dostoevsky, all this is of interest to me," Tolstoy remarked a year before he died.[19] Tolstoy's interest, however, is more in the thinker Dostoevsky than in the artist. Tolstoy is consistent throughout the years in his dissatisfaction with what he regards as Dostoevsky's flawed artistry, what he called in 1910 Dostoevsky's "antiartistry."[20] He appears to have regarded only a few of Dostoevsky's works as fully successful in the artistic sense: *Crime and Punishment* (particularly the first part); the beginning of *The Idiot*; above all, the semiautobiographical *Notes from the House of the Dead*, arguably the least typical of Dostoevsky's works. Shortly before Dostoevsky's death, Tolstoy reread *Notes from the House of the Dead* and wrote Strakhov: "I do not know a better book in all of modern literature, including Pushkin." Tolstoy was impressed by its "sincere, natural, and Christian point of view. . . . If you see Dostoevsky, tell him that I love him."[21] Tolstoy will always be impressed by the ethical emphasis in Dostoevsky's work. In the case of *Notes from the House of the Dead*, however, Tolstoy's judgment was also an aesthetic one. He told his disciple V. G. Chertkov in 1906 that this work was the "best" that Dostoevsky had written "because it is integral in an artistic sense. As for *The Idiot*—the beginning is splendid, but then comes an awful mishmash. And that's the way it is in almost all his works."[22]

Yet Tolstoy's enormous respect for Dostoevsky as psychologist and thinker is unmistakable. Late in life he spoke of Dostoevsky as "an inimitable psychologist-seer and a completely independent writer for whose independent convictions he was not forgiven for a long time in certain literary circles, like that German, in the words of Carlyle, who was unable to forgive the sun because he could not at any moment light up his cigar with it."[23] Tolstoy remarked to A. F. Koni that Dostoevsky was a writer with "tremendous content," adding characteristically, "but no technique."[24] Tolstoy even found a connection between what he considered Dostoevsky's lamentable lack of artistry on the one hand and his valuable content on the other: "Dostoevsky couldn't write well," Tolstoy remarked to A. V. Tsinger, "because he had too many thoughts, he had too much of his own to say."[25] For Tolstoy, however, these thoughts far outweighed Dostoevsky's so-called artistic flaws. "Dostoevsky is the kind of writer in whom it is necessary without fail to steep oneself, forgetting for the moment the imperfection of his form, in order to seek out the real beauty that lies beneath," he remarked to V. F. Lazursky. "Dostoevsky's carelessness in form, however, was striking—monotonous devices, monotony in language."[26]

Yet the same Tolstoy, late in his life, remarked that "sometimes even a careless page of Dostoevsky is worth many volumes of present-day writers."[27]

Not everything in Dostoevsky—especially his views on the church and government—was congenial to Tolstoy. Yet the longer he lived, Tolstoy remarked, the more strongly he felt "how close Dostoevsky is to me in spirit."[28] The "real beauty" Tolstoy found in Dostoevsky certainly was ethical and religious in content. In *What is Art?* Tolstoy placed Dostoevsky, chiefly his *Notes from the House of the Dead*, among the "models" of "religious art" that express the most lofty love for man and God.[29] V. G. Chertkov records the aging Tolstoy as saying, "Dostoevsky, yes—he was a great writer. Or rather it's not so much that he was a great writer as that he had a great *heart*. He was *profound*. I have never ceased to respect him."[30] These remarks came closest to defining Tolstoy's deep interest in, and involvement with, Dostoevsky's work. That interest, finally, is fully disclosed not so much in Tolstoy's casual remarks about Dostoevsky but in his fictional works. Here we find convincing evidence of his creative dialogue with Dostoevsky.[31]

Tolstoy's response to Strakhov's extraordinary letter was brief and like many of his comments on Dostoevsky, does not provide a great deal of material from which to draw hard and fast conclusions on the nature of his reservations about Dostoevsky's works. Tolstoy's remarks, however, are rich in content: they hint at a deeper structure underlying his reservations about Dostoevsky.

"Your letter acted on me in a melancholy way, disillusioned me," Tolstoy wrote in his reply to Strakhov's attack on Dostoevsky. "But I understand you perfectly and, regretfully, almost believe you." Tolstoy understands Strakhov. He "almost" believes him. Almost, but not quite. Strakhov had appealed to Tolstoy to help him "find a way out" of his unflattering views of Dostoevsky and his art. Pressed to the wall by Strakhov's disclosures about Dostoevsky's allegedly "evil" character, Tolstoy seeks to find more general causes for Strakhov's distress.

> It seems to me that you are the victim of a wrong, false relation to Dostoevsky, not yours alone but everybody's—an exaggeration of his significance and a cliché exaggeration and elevation into a prophet and saint of a man who died in the most intense process of an inner struggle between

good and evil. He was touching, interesting, but one cannot place on a
pedestal for the instruction of posterity a man who was in his entirety
struggle [*ves' bor'ba*].[32]

In some notes on Byron in 1825, the poet Alexander S. Pushkin
cites the "crowd" as saying: "He is petty like us, he is vile like us!"
Pushkin rejoins: "You lie, villains: he is petty and vile—but not like
you—differently."[33] Tolstoy does not respond to the rumor, passed on
by Strakhov, that Dostoevsky raped a child. Too, there is no indication
in his letter that he, like Strakhov, regards Dostoevsky as a "bad"
or "evil" man.[34] As always, Tolstoy is concerned with the *writer*
Dostoevsky. Significantly, he shifts the discourse from Strakhov's low
level of attacks on Dostoevsky's character to a higher level of moral-
aesthetic discourse: Dostoevsky was a writer who died "in the process
of a most intense struggle between good and evil." Tolstoy certainly
had in mind here not Dostoevsky's outbursts with servants or his alleged rape of a child but Dostoevsky's intense preoccupation with
good and evil in his novelistic world. Tolstoy is impressed by the pervasiveness of struggle in Dostoevsky. This is not the case merely of a
writer whose subject involves conflict and struggle; this is the case of
a writer who embodied conflict, or the principle of conflict. Here is
a writer who was struggle *in his entirety*, in all aspects of his being.
Tolstoy concludes—and the point is a crucial one—that one cannot
elevate to the rank of a prophet or saint a writer who is all struggle.
The ideal writer, or writer-prophet, Tolstoy would seem to suggest,
cannot himself be trapped in a permanent struggle over fundamental
questions of good and evil.

We might say of a writer who is struggle in his entirety that he is
seeking; but we might also say of such a writer that his seeking appears
to be endless, to have led nowhere, to have had no issue. Tolstoy's
remaining observations on Dostoevsky in his letter to Strakhov move
in this direction.

After his remarks on Dostoevsky and struggle, Tolstoy moves on
to mention another book that Strakhov had sent to him, one by
the French protestant theologian Edmond Déhault Pressensé (1824–
1891).[35] "I also read Pressensé's book, but all its scholarliness comes to
naught because of a snag." To clarify his thought, Tolstoy resorts to a
metaphor:

There are splendid horses: a 1,000-ruble trotter, but suddenly—a stumble [*zaminka*—stumble, hitch, a break in movement], and the splendid horse and powerhouse is not worth a cent. The longer I live, the more I value people who don't stumble. You say that you reconciled yourself with Turgenev.[36] But I was very fond of him. And, interestingly, because he doesn't stumble and gets you where you are going, while a trotter will get you nowhere if he lands you in a ditch. Both Pressensé and Dostoevsky stumble. With one it was all scholarliness, with the other   mind and heart comes to naught. Really, Turgenev will outlive Dostoevsky and not because of his artistry but because he doesn't stumble.[37]

The sequence of Tolstoy's thoughts is interesting: the notion of Pressensé's flawed scholarliness leads him to develop the image of a splendid horse that is suddenly rendered worthless because of a stumble. (The reader recalls the stumble of Vronsky's splendid horse, Frou-Frou, at the race track in *Anna Karenina*.) This thought leads Tolstoy to compare Turgenev to a horse who does not stumble and land you in a ditch but gets you where you are going. Tolstoy, as though tracking Dostoevsky all the time in his unconscious, then returns to him: Dostoevsky, by contrast with Turgenev, lands you in a ditch. Tolstoy seems to have felt that his opening remarks on Dostoevsky were insufficient, that the notion of Dostoevsky's being "in his entirety struggle" needed further development. His reference to Pressensé opened the way to a clarification, one that makes use of the horse as a metaphor for the artist.

The perfect artist is like a horse without a hitch or flaw in his movement, a horse that does not stumble and land you in a ditch, a horse that gets you where you are going. Turgenev's art has this attribute.[38] Dostoevsky does not fit Tolstoy's category of the "splendid horse," or perfect artist. The imperfection he has in mind, it should be noted, does not pertain to Dostoevsky's artistry, the area of Tolstoy's usual complaint about Dostoevsky; nor is it Turgenev's artistry that will enable him to outlive Dostoevsky. It is most certainly not Dostoevsky's alleged immorality or irritability—Strakhov's bête noire—that bothers Tolstoy. The imperfection he has in mind would seem to pertain to Dostoevsky's vision of the universe and to the function of art, as Tolstoy sees it. In Tolstoy's view Dostoevsky does not get himself, his art, or the rider-reader to their destination, figuratively speaking, Dostoevsky's movement does not get us anywhere; we are involved with endless struggle, movement.

Was Tolstoy critically remarking on what Bakhtin later, but approvingly, was to call the "unfinalized" character of Dostoevsky's artistic worldview, the "internal open-endedness of the characters and dialogue"?[39] In the introductory chapter to his revised study of Dostoevsky published in 1963, Bakhtin, summarizing Victor Shklovsky's views on Dostoevsky in Shklovsky's *For and Against* (1957), writes:

> Drawing on large amounts of the most varied historical, historico-literary and biographical material, Shklovsky brings to light, in that lively and witty way characteristic of him, the conflict of historical forces and voices of the epoch—social, political, ideological; it is a conflict, permeating all events of his life and organizing both the form and the content of all his works. This conflict remained open-ended both for Dostoevsky's epoch and for Dostoevsky himself. Thus Dostoevsky died, having resolved nothing, avoiding denouements and not reconciling himself to the wall.[40]

Shklovsky's notion that Dostoevsky died "having resolved nothing" might almost be a reformulation of Tolstoy's remarks (with which Shklovsky was certainly familiar). Bakhtin expresses general agreement with Shklovsky's observations, adding, however, parenthetically: "although it is possible to take issue with some of [his] positions." Bakhtin, in fact, is clearly dissatisfied with Shklovsky's flippant and derogatory "Dostoevsky died . . . having resolved nothing," for he goes on to say: "But we must emphasize here that if Dostoevsky died 'having resolved nothing' of the ideological problems posed by his epoch, then nevertheless he died having created a new form of artistic visualization, the polyphonic novel—and it will retain its artistic significance when the epoch, with all its contradictions, has faded into the past."[41]

The reader familiar with Bakhtin's argument on Dostoevsky recognizes, of course, that from Bakhtin's point of view, Dostoevsky's so-called failure to resolve anything was at the heart of Dostoevsky's poetics; even more, the reader following Bakhtin's book attentively recognizes that in Bakhtin's view, Dostoevsky opened the way to a new concept of "resolution" in which *direction*, or the *potential for resolution* finds expression in and through continuous conflict, struggle, dialogue, movement.[42] Bakhtin, it is true, deals only in the most sketchy way with this aspect of Dostoevsky's artistic outlook in his book. In any case, what I have called potential for resolution in Dostoevsky's novelistic universe was something quite different, in Bakhtin's view,

from the kind of resolution found in what Bakhtin termed "monological" novels (he placed Tolstoy in this category). Bakhtin regarded
as inauthentic—as far as the laws of Dostoevsky's poetics were concerned—the Russian novelist's "conventionally literary, conventionally monologic" endings, or resolutions, to many of his novels; that is,
Dostoevsky's attempts to resolve or "finalize" this dialogue, to add his
own "final word" to it (for example, the epilogue to *Crime and Punishment*).[43] In such epilogues, according to Bakhtin, Dostoevsky was vio-
lating his own poetics.

Shklovsky compares Dostoevsky's life and creative activity to that
of a writer who did not reconcile himself to the "wall"—a familiar
allusion to the Underground Man who finds himself in a *perpetuum
mobile* of actions and reactions that are made in self-defense but turn
out only to deepen his sense of vulnerability and humiliation before
others—abstractly, before the "wall" or "laws of nature."[44] It is no accident that Bakhtin finds the perfect structural model for the dialogical principle, though not in its ultimate *ethical* embodiment, in the
Underground Man's confession. "In the confession of the Underground Man what strikes us first of all is its extreme and acute dia-
logization: there is not a single monologically firm, undissociated
word."[45] Apropos of the Underground Man's constant "anticipation of
another's response," Bakhtin calls attention to the peculiar structural
trait of such anticipation: "It tends toward a *vicious circle*."

> But precisely in this act of anticipating the other's response and in re-
> sponding to it [the Underground Man] again demonstrates to the other
> (and to himself) his own dependence on this other. . . . Hence the *ines-
> capable circle* in which the hero's self-consciousness and discourse are
> trapped. . . . A peculiar perpetuum mobile is achieved, made up of his
> internal polemic with another and with himself, an endless dialogue
> where one reply begets another, which begets a third, and so on to in-
> finity, and *all of this without any forward motion.*[46] [My italics]

Bakhtin, offering a well-known illustration from part 2, chapter 2
of *Notes from the Underground*, refers to it as

> an example of that inescapable perpetuum mobile of the dialogized self-
> consciousness . . . an example of *a vicious circle of dialogue which can neither
> be finished nor finalized.* The formal significance of such inescapable dia-
> logic oppositions in Dostoevsky's work is very great. But nowhere in his

subsequent works does this opposition appear in such naked, abstractly precise, one could even say directly mathematical, form.[47] [My italics]

Making use of the language and imagery of Tolstoy, one could say that the Underground Man is "in his entirety struggle," is continually in movement (this is true of his psychology and his philosophy of will) but "gets you nowhere": laborers take their wages to a tavern, then end up in the clink, declares the Underground Man, "but where can man go?" One could say of the Underground Man, of the tragedy of the "underground" (again borrowing words from Tolstoy), that "mind and heart went to nought." The Underground Man, as he himself puts it, "thirsts" for something quite different from the "underground," but what he thirsts for he has never found. He has never found the "ideal"—for Dostoevsky, a religious one—that gives meaning to his, and man's, endless quest.[48] The tragedy of the underground, as Dostoevsky conceives it, is that the Underground Man *does not believe.*[49] The Underground Man lands himself and the reader in a ditch; that is, figuratively speaking, he keeps beating his head against the wall.

As a work of art, *Notes from the Underground* (as opposed to the Underground Man's vicious circle of dialogue which can neither be finished nor finalized) does not—or at least, if understood in terms of Dostoevsky's intentional design, should not—land the reader in a ditch. It is nonetheless a work in which it is not easy to discern Dostoevsky's idea that perpetual struggle is meaningful only if it is directed toward, or guided by, a higher, luminous, religious ideal. "It is really too somber," Dostoevsky reportedly said about *Notes from the Underground* years later. "Es ist schon ein überwundener Standpunkt. I *can* write now in a brighter, more conciliatory way."[50] All of Dostoevsky's works plunge the reader in a *perpetuum mobile* of movement and struggle. Yet at the same time his great novels, the ones following *Notes from the Underground,* represent an attempt to transform into a creative principle of life, into a positive unending quest for the ideal, what Bakhtin, referring to *Notes from the Underground,* calls the "vicious circle of dialogue."

The dialogic principle that structures Dostoevsky's artistic vision is not static; it does not presuppose either a dead end or endless movement in a dead universe. It was for Dostoevsky an attempt to find a way out of the underground, out of the endless circle of dialogue, out of the dead end of perpetual movement—the movement, in short, of a person who is in his entirety struggle. Tolstoy certainly recognized the profound ethical and religious content of Dostoevsky's art and heart. Yet it seems that Tolstoy, with unease, also took note of the problematic of perpetual movement in Dostoevsky's work, took note of it and felt that it led nowhere except to more struggle—in the "underground" sense. "Dostoevsky died . . . having resolved nothing," Shklovsky wrote. Shklovsky did not have in mind here "the ideological problems of the epoch," as Bakhtin oddly suggests. Shklovsky's words suggest a deeper failure, the kind that Tolstoy hinted at when he wrote that Dostoevsky was "in his entirety struggle."

Tolstoy certainly viewed human nature and human existence as dynamic and full of conflict. In Tolstoy's novels—in particular, his works written before 1880—we find open-ended, inconclusive, non-finalized "dialogue," in spite of the author's own efforts to invade his own works with hard and fast conclusions. Certainly Tolstoy's *War and Peace* is the supreme expression of such a worldview. How, then, could Tolstoy be troubled by Dostoevsky's intense struggles? If Tolstoy, like Dostoevsky, ultimately presents to us a world that defies closure, what could he have meant when he suggested that Dostoevsky, unlike Turgenev, did not "get you where you are going"? It is one thing to view the human experience and the problems of life as without closure; it is another specifically to postulate conflict, fragmentation, explosiveness, as the essence of reality. "There are no *foundations* to our society," Dostoevsky wrote in his notebook in 1875, "no principles of conduct that have been lived through, because there have been none in life even. A colossal eruption and all is crumbling, falling, being negated, as though it had not even existed. And not only externally, as in the West, but *internally, morally.*"[51]

Dostoevsky's remarks are specifically directed to Russian society in its historical roots and development. Yet the impression we have of Russian society and its inhabitants in Dostoevsky's novels is the impression we have of the Dostoevskian universe. What is the *given* in Tolstoy, "foundations," is in dispute in Dostoevsky. "Reality" itself is both without foundations or any assurance. "Reality strives toward fragmentation," observes the narrator of *Notes from the House of the Dead*. Such a notion is profoundly characteristic of Dostoevsky. Man strives, vacillates, doubts, falls, agonizes, rises again, and moves on in the universe of Tolstoy. Yet Tolstoyan "reality," the matrix, is not itself exploding. Discussing the affinities between the Homeric and Tolstoyan points of view, George Steiner speaks of

> the archaic and pastoral setting; the poetry of war and agriculture; the primacy of the senses and of physical gesture; the luminous, all-reconciling background of the cycle of the year; the recognition that energy and aliveness are, of themselves, holy; the acceptance of a chain of being extending from brutal matter to the stars and along which men have their apportioned places; deepest of all, an essential sanity, a determination to follow what Coleridge called "the high road of life," rather than those dark obliquities in which the genius of a Dostoevsky was most thoroughly at home.[52]

There are "dark obliquities" in abundance in Tolstoy's works, but Steiner's listing of some of the epic features of Tolstoy's (and Homer's) art stands. Citing Schiller's view that certain poets "are Nature" while others only "seek her," Steiner writes: "Tolstoy is nature." Language for him is not a mirror or a magnifying glass, "but as a window through which all light passes and yet is gathered and given permanence."[53] Dostoevskian reality is alienated from this nature. Tolstoyan reality encompasses growth as well as decay; the "high road of life" and "dark obliquities"; health as well as illness; peace as well as war. "The memory of Tolstoy contains *everything*. This man had done everything, passed through all experiences," Romain Rolland once observed. One could go further and say that Tolstoy *is* reality—ever disintegrating and ever reshaping itself. Like the millionfold "linkages" that go to create his gigantic tapestry of human motive, action, and event, Tolstoyan reality, in all its diversity, all its complexity and internal turmoil, *strives toward unity*, as opposed to Dostoevskian reality that *strives toward fragmentation*. The unity of Tolstoy's world, as opposed to his art, is of course never achieved, but it is envisaged and even embodied in great moments. Tolstoyan reality, like Pushkinian reality, *holds*. Tolstoy does not stumble. He "gets you where you are going."

"'Turgenev will outlive Dostoevsky.' . . . What does this mean?" asked Georgy Adamovich, citing Tolstoy's words in his letter to Strakhov but not informing the reader about Tolstoy's next phrase: "and not because of his artistry, but because he doesn't stumble." "Really, couldn't [Tolstoy] understand that Dostoevsky still was greater, in all respects, than Turgenev, even as an artist? Obviously," Adamovich wittily continues, "Tolstoy was thinking about something else, and while comparing a comparatively modest and monotonous cuisine with another elegant but excessively spicy one, expressed confidence in the first."[54] Tolstoy, as I have suggested, was pondering in his letter the fundamentals of Dostoevsky's art as he understood them, an art that differed radically from his own. He was surely thinking, too, about the fundamentals of his own art. One feels, then, that behind Tolstoy's suggestion that Turgenev would outlive Dostoevsky was not a preference for a monotonous cuisine as opposed to a spicy one (Adamovich in any case vastly underestimates the significance of Turgenev's "cuisine"), but a preference for a particular artistic vision of man, nature, and the universe, a preference for his own vision. In the last analysis, the words "Turgenev will outlive Dostoevsky" may simply be a way of saying that Tolstoy will outlive Dostoevsky.

6 *In the Interests of Social Pedagogy*

Gorky's Polemic Against the Staging of *The Devils*
in 1913 and the Aftermath in 1917

I remember an expressive gesture of Aleksey Maksimovich during a conversation about Dostoevsky. The talk was about the integral and monumental character of the novelist-tragedian's work, about the verbal magic
of his genius. Gorky sat silently, listening, and suddenly, threatening somebody with his fist, said: "Thus do various gracious sovereigns in Moscow
convince themselves and others that Gorky doesn't give a brass farthing for
Dostoevsky"—and Gorky cast his head upwards, frozen in prayerful ecstasy—"that's how he looks upon Dostoevsky."

    A. A. Zolatarev, *Gorky, Denizen of Capri*

 Three things may be said about Gorky's lifelong polemic
with Dostoevsky: first, that it had deep psychological roots
in a confrontation with aspects of his own nature (overcoming Dostoevsky, for Gorky, was a process of self-overcoming); second,
that this process of self-overcoming became linked with a central effort of Gorky's literary and cultural writings—the task of overcoming
Russian history, the painful legacy of violence and disorder in Russian
man and life, all that he once called "our most implacable enemy—our
past";[1] and third, that these processes of overcoming ultimately took
on the dimensions of a struggle between worldviews, a struggle, as
Gorky conceived it, over whether man is good or evil.

"It is clear and comprehensible to the point of obviousness," Dostoevsky wrote in a review of Tolstoy's *Anna Karenina*, "that evil is
more deeply rooted in mankind than the socialist quacks believe."[2]
Gorky's greatest fear, we suggest, was that Dostoevsky was right; a
good deal of his life was spent trying to prove him wrong.

One of Gorky's lively concerns in the period between the upheav-
als of 1905 and 1917 was that Russian intellectual and cultural consciousness would get bogged down in the moral-psychological turmoil
of Dostoevsky's novels and in particular in the ideology of that
"preacher of passivism and social indifference," Dostoevsky.[3] Gorky,

like many of his contemporaries, did not clearly distinguish between Dostoevsky and his heroes and heroines, between the artist-thinker and his complex statement, and the world he sought to decipher in his art. Thus, in a letter to the editor of *Russkoe slovo* in 1913—one accompanying his first article of protest "About Karamazovism," against the staging of Dostoevsky's *The Devils* (*Besy*)—Gorky wrote: "I am deeply convinced that the preaching of Dostoevskij's sick ideas from the stage can only further unsettle the already unhealthy nerves of society."[4] In his article Gorky speaks out against the Moscow Art Theater's announced plan to stage what he calls the "sadistic and sick" novel *The Devils*.[5] The Moscow Art Theater earlier in 1910 had staged *The Brothers Karamazov*, it was now preparing a new Dostoevsky production under the title *Nikolai Stavrogin*. Gorky's concern is frankly utilitarian and social in character. "Does Russian society," he asks, "think that the depiction on stage of events and people described in the novel *The Devils* is necessary and useful and in the interests of social pedagogy?"[6]

"About Karamazovism" aroused a storm of indignation, including charges of censorship. In a reply, "Once Again About 'Karamazovism,'" Gorky defended his position, arguing vigorously for society's right to protest against the "tendencies of Dostoevsky and in general against any artist whatever his preachment."[7] At the same time he insisted that "Gorky is not against Dostoevsky but against his novels being put on stage."[8] Gorky's effort to join issues of social pedagogy with questions of aesthetics throws light on his own ambivalent attitude toward Dostoevsky.

"As gestures, on the stage of a theater," Gorky argues, "an author's thoughts are not so clear." Impoverished by cuts Dostoevsky's novels will emerge on stage as "nothing but nervous convulsions."[9] Gorky is preoccupied with the *pictorial* representation of Dostoevsky's world. In the opening paragraph of his first article, he questions the significance of showing "pictures" from *The Devils*. The Moscow Art Theater, he writes again, proposes to present Dostoevsky's ideas "in images." "Do we need this mutilating 'performance'?"[10] "This 'performance' is doubtful aesthetically and unconditionally harmful in a social sense."[11] Thus, in staging *The Idiot* (a work produced by another Russian theater at the time), one sees in the foreground the "agony of the tubercular Ippolit, the epilepsy of Prince Myshkin, the cruelty of Rogozhin, the histrionics of Nastasya Filippovna, and other instructive pictures of all kinds of illness of body and spirit." [12]

"Pictures," "images," "performance"—all this visual representation constitutes a disfiguration, "nervous convulsions."

In his second article, Gorky expands on his aesthetic argument. He clearly distinguishes between "reading the books of Dostoevsky" and "seeing images of him on the stage." [13] Reading, for Gorky, is not a passive performance. In reading the books of Dostoevsky, the attentive reader perceives clearly the "reactionary tendency of Dostoevsky and all his contradictions." [14] He can "correct the thoughts of his heroes as a result of which they significantly gain in beauty, depth and humanity. But when a person is shown an image of Dostoevsky on the stage, even in an exceptionally talented performance, the skill of the artist, enhancing the talent of Dostoevsky, imparts to his images a particular significance and a great finality." [15]

Gorky's article has its subtleties. He acknowledges that the Dostoevsky novel as text, even one as tendentious as *The Devils*, essentially does not offer a one-sided view of reality, come up with absolute conclusions. The novel of Dostoevsky read as text, he suggests, is open, or, in the language used later on by Bakhtin, "dialogical." The stage representation of a Dostoevsky novel, on the other hand, "carries the viewer from the sphere of thought, freely admitting argument, to the sphere of suggestions, hypnosis, to the dark region of the peculiar Karamazov-like emotions and feelings, emphasized and concentrated with malicious pleasure." "On the stage the audience sees man created by Dostoevsky in the image of 'a wild and evil animal.'" [16] The Moscow Art Theater, "this gloomy institution," Gorky wrote in the same vein to I. P. Ladyzhnikov August 29, 1913, "exhibits the naked Dostoevsky." [17]

The sense of Gorky's argument is ambiguous: On the one hand, he suggests that a stage performance distorts or narrows Dostoevsky's novelistic universe through naturalistic or visual stage representation; on the other hand, he suggests that a stage representation brings out precisely Dostoevsky's naked truth, that is, the notion that man is "a wild and evil animal." The distinction between the novelist Dostoevsky and his truth and the naked Dostoevsky's truth is one that is central to Gorky's approach to his antagonist. It takes different forms in his writing. Thus Lyutov, in *The Life of Klim Samgin* (1925–1936) at one point outlines the theory that the Russian people only want the kind of freedom that is given by priests: the freedom to commit terrible sins in order to become frightened and then find peace within themselves. "A strange theory..." remarks Turoboev, adding after a moment of apparent inner uncertainty and debate: "All the same, this is Dostoevsky. If not according to his thoughts, then according to his spirit..."[18]

Lyutov's theory, in short, is not in accord with Dostoevsky's thoughts—that is, all that we may ascertain from a reading of his novels. The theory, according to Gorky, does find support in the world of Dostoevsky's characters' experiences and thoughts; a realm in which Dostoevsky, Gorky believed, invested his deepest fears and anguish; a domain, in Gorky's view, where we encounter precisely the "spirit" of Dostoevsky, the "naked Dostoevsky," the "permanent terror" of Dostoevsky, all that that writer sought to come to grips with through religion, but in reality only "justified." "Dostoevsky has been called 'a seeker of truth,'" Gorky observed in a speech before the First All-Union Congress of Soviet Writers August 17, 1934. "If he searched for truth he found it in the bestial, animal element in man, and he found it not in order to refute it, but in order to justify it."[19]

Precisely here we are at the core of Gorky's polemic with Dostoevsky, one linked with despair over Russian history and brutalized Russian man and his desire to redeem Russian man from the chaos of his past. At the center of his solicitude for the moral and spiritual health of Russian man and his polemic with Dostoevsky is a notion of the disorder of the Russian national character. "Bear in mind," Gorky wrote in a letter to I. D. Surguchev in December 1911, "that our evil genius Fyodor Dostoevsky, 'the knight of the woeful countenance,' by no means popped up on the nose of literature like some unexpected odd pimple: his is a face fully justified by Russian life, by our history and, I may say, not a very original face."[20] The very same year Gorky wrote the literary and cultural historian D. Ovsyaniko-Kulikovsky the following apropos of some recent writings of the historian:

> This is the first time, I say, that I have encountered in such sharp and precise form this sad but long-needed and surprisingly contemporary in-

dication of the organic tendency of the Great Russian to eastern passivity which, combined with the famed "breadth of the Russian soul"—or rather with the formless, chaotic nature of this soul—brings forth that quality so typical of us—"swaggering nihilism," always ruinous, especially ruinous, in our austere times. Precisely here, my dear Dmitry Nikolaevich, lies—I am certain—the foundation of such sick and disfigured phenomena as Karamazovism and Karataevism. "My idea is a corner," repeatedly said F. Dostoevsky, the evil genius of cultured Russia, a man who with the greatest power and clarity depicted the spiritual illnesses injected in us by the Mongol, by the mutilation inflicted on our soul by tormenting Moscow history.[21]

In his 1913 article "About Karamazovism," Gorky spells out the spiritual illnesses of Russia as "the sadistic savagery of the completely disillusioned nihilist and, its opposite, the masochism of the beaten, frightened creature who is capable of enjoying his suffering, not without malicious pleasure, however, parading it before himself; he has been beaten mercilessly, and he brags about it."[22] Fyodor Karamazov and the Underground Man emerge in Gorky's writings as typical carriers of these two illnesses.

The word *sadism* appears three times in the opening three sentences of "About Karamazovism." Gorky clearly follows N. Mikhailovsky (*A Cruel Talent*, 1882) in finding in Dostoevsky a cruel or sadistic talent.[23] "Dostoevsky himself was a great torturer and a man of sick conscience," Gorky writes.[24] But it is the social-historical dimension of sadomasochism that interests Gorky. He writes in his article "About Karamazovism":

> The main person, and the one most subtly understood by Dostoevsky, repeated countless times in all the novels of this "cruel talent," sometimes as a whole and sometimes partially, was Fyodor Karamazov. Here is unquestionably the Russian soul, formless and diverse, simultaneously cowardly and insolent, but chiefly morbidly sick: the soul of Ivan the Terrible, Saltychikhi, the landlord who baited dogs with children; the peasant who beats his pregnant wife to death; the soul of the Philistine who raped his bride and there and then handed her over to be raped by a gang of hooligans.[25]

"Here is unquestionably the Russian soul." Gorky insists, however, that Fyodor Karamazov, the Underground Man, Foma Opiskin, Svidrigailov, and Peter Verkhovensky "are still not our sum and substance; after all, it is not just the beastly and crooked that holds sway in us. Yet Dostoevsky saw only those features, and desiring to depict something else showed us the 'Idiot' or Alyosha, transforming sadism into masochism, Karamazovism and Karataevism."[26]

On the stage the audience "sees man created . . . in the image and likeness of 'a wild and evil animal.' But man is not like that," Gorky maintains. "I know. . . . He is far simpler, nicer than he has been conjured up by the Russian wise men."[27] But what does Gorky *know*? Is he so sure about the niceness of Russian man? In the very same article, he warns the reader about the Russian national character. "I know the fragility of Russian national character. I know the pitiful instability of the Russian soul and its inclination—tormented, tired and despairing—toward every kind of plague."[28] Gorky himself exhibits an extreme "instability" in his judgment of the Russian people.

Thus we are confronted by a paradox. On the one hand, Gorky affirms that "all of Dostoevsky's work is a generalization of the negative attributes and qualities of Russian national character."[29] On the other hand, he implies that precisely in Fyodor Karamazov Dostoevsky has most subtly embodied the Russian national character.

In *The Life of Klim Samgin*, Lyutov maintains that Dostoevsky was "seduced by prison. What is his prison? A parade. He was an inspector at a [prison] parade. And for the rest of his life he was unable to write about anybody but convicts, while the righteous man for him was the Idiot. He did not know the people."[30] But in turning to Gorky's own works, one finds a parade of characters and personalities that offers a far from flattering portrait of the Russian people. In his brutally frank essay "On the Russian Peasantry" (1922), Gorky asks:

> Now once and for all—just where is that good-natured, meditative Russian peasant, the inexhaustible seeker of truth and justice, about whom nineteenth century Russian literature so convincingly and eloquently told the world? In my youth I earnestly sought out this person in the villages of Russia and—I didn't find him. I found instead a grim and cunning realist who—when it served his purposes—was marvellously capable of playing the role of a simpleton. By nature he was not stupid, and he himself knew that very well. He created a multitude of sad songs, rude and cruel tales, created thousands of proverbs in which he embodied the experience of his hard life. . . . He says: "Don't fear devils, fear people." "Beat those near you—others will be afraid." He doesn't have a high opinion about truth: "You won't get full on truth." ". . . A truthful person, like a fool, is also harmful."[31]

Gloomy is Gorky's marvellous *Notes from my Diary* (1923), a work with a suspiciously Dostoevskian title, in which he reviews a parade of troubled and troubling Russian types. "They are a gifted people—but only for anecdotes," he observes in one of the sketches. This was a bitter judgment. One wonders if Gorky was not responding with this phrase to Dostoevsky's well-known reference at the end of *Notes from the House of the Dead* to the Russian convict as "really the most highly gifted and strongest of all our people." Gorky's conclusion to *Notes from my Diary* is a startling one: "I have lived among such people for half a century. I hope that this book provides ample evidence that I am not shy about writing the truth when I want to write about it."

Gorky in 1913 was not trying to avoid the truth of Russian man, a truth that he found exemplified in Fyodor Karamazov and in the Underground Man. He saw too much of this truth and did not wish to see it displayed on stage. As he wrote in "Once Again About Karamazovism":

> Things are not well in Rus', gentlemen! Not Stavrogins should be shown to it now, but something different. What is necessary is a preachment of vitality, what is needed is spiritual health, deeds, and not narcissism; what is needed is a return to the source of energy—to democracy, to the people, to a sense of civic duty and science. We've had enough of that self-denigration which among us replaces self-criticism; we've had enough of squabbling among ourselves, senseless anarchism and all kinds of convulsions.[32]

Gorky sees no reason in 1913 to dwell on these "two sick phenomena [sadism and masochism] of our national psyche and its disfigurations."[33] Rather one must struggle to create a healthy atmosphere in which these diseases will not flourish. Russia is in crisis. "Our tormented country is experiencing a deeply tragic time."[34] Prophetically, Gorky writes: "Once again clouds are moving upon Rus', auguring great storms and disasters. . . . Russian society, having experienced too many dramas shattering to the heart, is exhausted, disillusioned, apathetic." He rejects both "social pessimism" and the "rhetoric" of the "so-called 'higher demands of the spirit,' which among us, in Rus', contribute nothing to ethics, do not improve our relations with each other." Will not a production of *The Devils*, he asks, "intensify savage drunkenness, the dark cruelty of our life, the sadism of deeds and words, our feebleness, our sad lack of attention to the life of the world, to the fate of the country and to each other?" In all this Gorky turns to Pushkin, "a man who knew his country but was not poisoned by it." [35] Dostoevsky, clearly, for Gorky, was a man who knew his country but was poisoned by it; Dostoevsky was unable to deliver himself or his art from its subject: *dostoevshchina*.

Did Gorky in 1913 sense the relevance of *The Devils* and its demons to the unfolding revolutionary movement? He appended to his article "Once Again About Karamazovism" an excerpt from an article signed by "Independent," entitled "Contemporary Reality and F. M. Dostoevsky." The author of that article regards *The Devils* as a very contemporary work. One cannot, he writes, make out "where revolutionary party work ends and where the filthy provocation of these filthy operators begins. How contemporary all this is! And how instructive! . . . Here he is, Azef [a notorious police agent working simultaneously for the revolutionaries and the police], a [version of] Peter Verkhovensky. . . . Do we not see all this in our times? . . . What a pity that Dostoevsky's *The Devils* is not a reference book for our sensitive youth?" For Gorky, this article is proof of the "complete satisfaction that the Moscow Art Theater's performance of *The Devils* evoked in the "reactionary press." [36] But Gorky himself could not have failed to recognize the parallel between Azef and other corrupt revolutionaries of the period and Dostoevsky's "devils." Was this one of those cases in which Gorky avoided an unpleasant truth because he wished to avoid it? Or, by publishing "Independent's" observations, was Gorky, obliquely, introducing some counterpoint into his own arguments? Whatever the answer to these questions, Gorky in 1917, barely a few years later, publicly began to criticize the contemporary "devils" of the revolution in the style of "Independent."

Gorky welcomed the February revolution but simultaneously expressed fears that the Russian people were not prepared for freedom and democracy. Russia had been corrupted by its past. "The most terrible enemy of freedom and justice is within us," he wrote in the Petrograd newspaper *Novaya Zhizn* in April 1917. "This is our stupidity, our cruelty and the whole chaos of dark, anarchic feelings nurtured in our soul by the shameless yoke of monarchy." [37] "The conditions of the people's life," he wrote again in May, "have not been able to develop in it either respect for the human being or the consciousness of the right of the citizen or the feeling of justice."[38] The fact remains that "the Russian people is organically inclined to anarchism, that the renowned goodness of its soul is a Karamazov-like sentimentalism, that it is terribly unreceptive to suggestions of humanism and culture."[39]

Gorky does not mention Dostoevsky by name in his articles in *Novaya Zhizn* in 1917–1918. Dostoevsky, however, is clearly on his mind. Gorky's thoughts about the arbitrariness, cruelty, and anarchy in Russian man and life echo the themes of his polemic with Dostoevsky in his articles on "Karamazovism" in 1913 and in his other critical writings and fiction in the prerevolutionary period. In these writings the "underground" type (Karamazov, the Underground Man, etc.) is an individual in whom sadism and masochism form a syndrome of destruction and self-destruction. *Notes from the Underground* for Gorky is always a psychohistorical document that gives expression to the historically shaped tragedy of the individual in Russian history and society, a tragedy of suffering, one in which the tortured becomes the torturer, the slave—a despot. The revolution as Gorky perceives it in 1917–1918 is a reenactment on an epic scale of this tragedy. Defending himself in *Novaya Zhizn* in December 1917 against the charge that he spoke the "language of the enemies of the working class,"[40] Gorky insists on his right to regard the working class critically, no matter who was in power. "And," he went on, "I regard Russian man in power with particular suspicion, with particular distrust; a recent slave himself, he becomes the most unbridled despot as soon as he gets a chance to be his neighbor's master."[41] "The animal, exasperated by its long imprisonment, tormented by centuries-old sufferings, has opened wide its vengeful jaws," Gorky writes again in December. "Yesterday's slave sees its master prostrate in the dust, impotent, frightened—a spectacle of the greatest joy for the slave who has not yet known a joy more worthy of man."[42] The revolution is a period of "monstrous contradictions," Gorky writes despairingly. "At the present-time Russian man is not well—even less well than ever."[43]

As the October revolution unfolds, Gorky becomes increasingly pessimistic and harsh in his comments in *Novaya Zhizn*. Referring to the "poisonous inheritance of the Tartar yoke and of serfdom," Gorky sees Russia as undergoing "a severe revenge for the sins of the past:

for our Asiatic inertia, for the passivity with which we suffered the violence done to us."[44]

In his brilliant story "Karamora," published in 1921—some of his finest prose is written in this period—Gorky continues his polemic with Dostoevsky; but he stands closer to him; he now mercilessly calls attention to the links connecting corrupted revolutionaries with the moral-psychological "underground" of Dostoevsky.[45]

The story sums up a feeling of disillusionment that Gorky had begun to experience in the earliest days of the February revolution. The publication of lists of people who had worked for the tsarist police, people whose hands he had shook, had come as a shock to Gorky. "This is one of the most ignominious mockeries of my faith in man," he wrote in a sketch entitled "Nightmare" in May 1917. There he describes his revulsion at a woman spy who entreated him to protect her from the revolutionary authorities. The experience is a depressing one for Gorky and casts "a dark shadow" over his spirit. "Am I not responsible for all this vileness of life seething about me; is it not I who am responsible for this life that at dawn is so foully smeared with the filth of treachery?" Somber thoughts weigh upon Gorky. Outside in the streets he hears the elemental hum of the "liberated populace." He hears the "sharp smell of new words"; he rejoices. "But I feel myself nailed to some kind of rotten wall, crucified on it by bitter thoughts about disfigured man whom I cannot, I cannot help in any way, ever."[46]

These lines poignantly sum up Gorky's deep affinity with a central feature of Dostoevsky as man and artist: a profound anguish over human nature. Gorky's image of himself as a suffering Christ (nailed not to a cross but to some "rotten wall" of human existence) brings to mind Dostoevsky's ridiculous man ("The Dream of a Ridiculous Man") at the moment he becomes fully aware that he has corrupted the paradise about him. Full of anguish and guilt over the Fall of Man, weeping and accusing himself, he asks to be crucified. On awakening from his nightmare, however, the ridiculous man, transfigured by his dream, sets forth preaching love. He appeals not to the "monstrous earthly truth" of his nightmare, however, but to the "eternal Truth" of his utopian vision of paradise. So, too, Gorky in the late 1920's, returning to Russia, awoke to his old desire to redeem Russian man and history; awoke with a vengeance to "pedagogy," to his fatal urge to romanticize reality; awoke to his recurrent enmity against Dostoevsky.

Noting in his speech at the First All-Union Congress of Soviet Writers August 17, 1934, that Dostoevsky had found truth in the "bestial, animal element in man," Gorky went on to compare Dostoevsky's artistic genius to that of Shakespeare. But "as a personality," Gorky added, "as a 'judge of the world and of people' he is easy to imagine in the role of a medieval inquisitor."[47] Gorky explains why he has given so much space to Dostoevsky in his speech: "Without the influence of his ideas it would be almost impossible to understand the radical turnabout of Russian literature and a large part of the intelligentsia after the years 1905–1906 from radicalism and democracy in favor of the preservation and defense of the bourgeois 'order.'"[48] However crude, wrong, and simplistic this judgment, it attests once again to the central linkage between Dostoevsky and Russian history and culture in Gorky's mind. Not without reason, finally, do these words of Gorky signal the radical turnabout of Maxim Gorky in favor of the preservation and defense of the Soviet "order."

In 1906, after reading Leonid Andreyev's "Lazarus," Gorky wrote the author that he considered the work "the best . . . that has been written about death in all the world's literature." He praised "Lazarus" for its style and insight. "In general, as literature, as a work of art, this work gives me immense enjoyment." However, Gorky adds, "philosophically I cannot accept it. I am infected by life and by its drives for six hundred years, and the longer I live the more optimistically I look on life, although my stomach and teeth hurt unbearably."[49]

The image Gorky projects here of himself is singularly Dostoevskian, even "underground" in its suggestion of pleasure and optimism in the face of severe toothache. Yet a split is always present in Gorky between his "philosophy," that is, what he wanted to believe about "proud" man, and his bitter experience about man and life, all that his stomach and teeth told him. Gorky's affinity here, too, with Dostoevsky's heroes could only have added tension to his strained relations with him. Gorky wrote ironically to Andreyev in 1902 about a certain public figure who "preaches love, the scoundrel, so that his life might not be disturbed by the tragedy of his contradictions."[50] The same might be said of Gorky's dogged faith in reason and in the creation of a new social reality through culture and the arts.

V. Bryusov cites Gorky in his notebook for October 1900:

> Here's what is dear to me in Dostoevsky. You remember in *Notes from the Underground*, in Part I, that man who, in the midst of the reign of universal common sense, will suddenly say: "Well, now oughtn't we to send all this common sense to the devil?" And Gorky with a movement of his leg showed how this man would kick that common sense into the abyss. Indeed, he himself is capable of doing this.[51]

Citing this same passage from *Notes from the Underground* in which common sense is sent to the devil, Gorky wrote in his projected *History of Russian Literature*:

> Here, I say are concentrated all the fundamental motifs of Dostoevsky's creative work—creative work most agonizing and, I would say, fruitless, for it does not clarify anything, it does not enhance the positive in life, rather, by emphasizing merely the negative aspects it strengthens them in man's memory, it always depicts him as helpless in the chaos of dark forces and can lead him to pessimism, mysticism, etc.[52]

Gorky, taking his distance from the "dark forces" within himself, and correctly perceiving the objective historical meaning of the Underground Man as a social type, nonetheless was unable, or more likely unwilling, to discern the inner pro and contra of *Notes from the Underground*, that is, to distinguish Dostoevsky's complex critical stance vis-à-vis the Underground Man from the views of the Underground Man himself. Equally important, in his later polemics with Dostoevsky, he was unwilling publicly to acknowledge his deep affinity with Dostoevsky in many though not all areas. In all of Russian literature, there is perhaps no other writer who more closely approximated Dostoevsky in his deeply ambivalent nature and his torment over human suffering than Gorky. Unlike Dostoevsky, however, Gorky as critic and ideologist increasingly embraced the "elevating deception" of a bankrupt rational humanism. Grasping for utopian solutions to the dilemmas of Russian man, life, and history, turning a blind eye in his last years to tragic Soviet Russian reality, he failed to comprehend the profoundly affirmative and active character of Dostoevsky's religious humanism, one that posited a transcendental moral imperative. In ceaselessly and wrongly pointing to Dostoevsky as a preacher of passivity, Gorky concealed a larger truth about Dostoevsky and that writer's impact on him as a young man, a truth that the Russian writer Leonid Andreyev underscored in a scathing letter to Gorky, March 28, 1912:

> *The West has distorted your view by the instruments of its own struggle, and you have ceased to understand that our instruments for struggle are entirely different,* and that our evil genius Dostoevsky is actually a rebel, a teacher of action, and that he taught you rebellion. The glossy bourgeoisie of the West, like every bourgeoisie, falls to ashes in Dostoevsky's presence, and this is the most genuine and the most permanent revolution.[53]

Andreyev might have added that the final lesson Dostoevsky taught his pupil Gorky was rebellion against his teacher. That act of rebellion obscured on every level the complex, intimate, and dramatic relationship between teacher and pupil. It grievously distorted the image of Dostoevsky as man and writer, but it released Gorky from thralldom to one of the most powerful writers in world history. On the psychological plane, it made possible the independent growth of one of Russia's great modern writers.

7 Chateaubriand and Dostoevsky
Elective Affinities

 In an interesting essay, "The Russian Candide," written some fifty years ago, the Russian scholar Leonid Grossman suggests that some of the elements of Ivan Karamazov's "rebellion" against God, his protest against human suffering, may be found in Voltaire's writings. "The author of *Candide*, deepening in Dostoevsky the protests against world evil and human suffering which he had already conceived independently, communicated to him the fundamental proofs of the atheistic argumentation of Ivan Karamazov."[1] Now it appears possible that at the opposite end of the philosophical spectrum, the writing of another French writer, François-René de Chateaubriand (1768–1848), may have contributed to Dostoevsky's formation of the case against atheism in *The Brothers Karamazov*. The specific work I have in mind is *The Genius of Christianity* (*Le génie du christianisme*, 1802).

In the introduction of this work, Chateaubriand singles out Voltaire as the sophist who had done so much to make atheism fashionable and religion ridiculous. "It is this ridicule that the author of *The Genius of Christianity* has tried to wipe out," Chateaubriand wrote later in his *Defense of the Genius of Christianity*. "That is the goal of all his work."[2] Chateaubriand's *Genius of Christianity* was conceived as an apology for the Christian religion; it was at the same time an attack on the century of the philosophes—in the words of Chateaubriand, "the glorious century of the Diderots and the d'Alemberts . . . when the documents of human wisdom were arranged in alphabetical order in the Encyclopedia, that tower of Babel of science and reason."[3] Chateaubriand rebels against the hegemony of reason. "The heart has its reasons that reason does not know," he observed in his *Defense* (quoting Pascal), apropos of the thought that religious proofs are not always those which one must employ in matters of religion.[4]

Chateaubriand is concerned with proofs of another order in *The Genius of Christianity*: the proofs of divinely inspired beauty. The author described himself as "one who wanted Christianity to be loved for the beauty of its worship."[5] He proposes to reconcile to religion not the sophists, however, but the world they led astray. He wishes to "prove" (Chateaubriand, after all, is a child of the eighteenth century) that the Christian religion is the most poetic, most humane, and most favorable to liberty; that it was the foundation for morality and good taste; that it was, in short, the basis for the elaboration of all culture.[6] It is in its aesthetic and moral dimensions, in the last analysis, that Chateaubriand finds the ultimate proof and justification of Christianity. He writes at the conclusion of *The Genius of Christianity*: "Even if you would deny to Christianity all supernatural proofs, there would still remain—in the sublimity of its moral doctrine, in the vast extent of its benefits, in the beauty of its ritual—quite enough to prove that it is the most divine and the purest religion that men have ever espoused."[7]

2

At first glance, there would seem to be little in common between Chateaubriand and Dostoevsky: the first an aristocrat and royalist by background, bred in the feudal shadows of Combourg; the second a plebeian by nature and son of a doctor, raised in a wing of the Marinsky Hospital in Moscow. The self-limiting pride of Chateaubriand contrasts sharply with the nervous, self-illuminating insecurity of Dostoevsky. Both men were passionate dreamers in their youth; while Chateaubriand bears the marks of the fantast and actor to the end of his days, however, Dostoevsky passes on to a more profound appraisal of self and reality.

The similarities between Chateaubriand and Dostoevsky become apparent when one turns to their spiritual development, their religious-philosophical outlook, and the message each writer conveyed to his age. Both writers were deeply preoccupied with religion and with the eighteenth-century rationalist and materialist negation of religion;[8] both passed through phases of doubt and skepticism in their youth; and both reaffirmed their religious faith through an apprehension of Christianity that in part accented its embodiment of a higher beauty. "You must know that my madness is to see *Jesus Christ* everywhere as Madame de Staël saw perfectibility," Chateaubriand wrote in his *Lettre à M. de Fontanes*. "I have the misfortune to believe, with Pascal, that only the Christian religion has explained the problem of mankind."[9] On his release from prison in 1854, Dostoevsky wrote to Madame N. D. Fonvizina of his "symbol of faith": "to believe that there is nothing more beautiful, profound, sympathetic, intelligent, manly and perfect than Christ, and not only is not but . . . cannot be. Even more, if somebody proved to me that Christ was outside the truth, and it *really* were so that the truth was outside Christ, then I would rather remain with Christ than with the truth."[10] Chateaubriand wrote in *Discourse on Pascal's* Pensées (*Discours sur les* Pensées *de Pascal*) that even if miracle and prophecies were not associated with Jesus Christ, one could not but be captivated by the element of the divine in his doctrine and in his life. He further noted that "as there is neither true goodness nor honesty of inner being without love for Jesus Christ, neither can there be no depth of intelligence nor sensitivity of feeling without admiration for Him."[11]

It would be difficult to find two writers more alike in their paradoxical affirmation of faith than Chateaubriand and Dostoevsky. "As my religious faith grew, it swallowed up my other convictions," Chateaubriand wrote at the end of his life, adding: "There does not exist on this earth a more believing Christian or a more unbelieving man than I."[12] Dostoevsky fervently affirmed his faith in Christ in his letter to Fonvizina in 1854, but in that same letter he prefaces his remarks on his faith with "I am a child of the age, a child of lack of faith and doubt till now, and (this I know) this will be true till the coffin closes over."[13]

3

Against the proofs of the nonexistence of God, Chateaubriand marshals the "proofs" of immortality. A section of *The Genius of Christianity* is entitled "Immortality of the Soul, Proved by Moral Principles and Feeling." Here Chateaubriand advances four proofs of immortality. First, the desire for happiness in man: "Give the poorest man all the wealth in the world, let him stop working, his needs satisfied; before a few months have gone by, he will again be at the mercy of boredom and hope." Man's spirit yearns for the infinite (Chateaubriand alludes to a "melancholy instinct"), for that which is intangible and of God.[14] The second is the presence of conscience in man. Chateaubriand cites Cicero: "Man has within himself a power that leads to good and away from evil."[15] The third is morality. "Morality alone is a proof of immortality," as Chateaubriand puts it at the conclusion of *The Genius of Christianity*.[16] The fourth and final proof advanced in this section is man's veneration for tombs. The third and fourth proofs are considered in a brief chapter entitled "There Is No Morality If There Is No Other Life" and subtitled "Presumption in Favor of the Soul, Derived from Man's Respect for Tombs." Chateaubriand writes:

> Morality is the basis of social life; but if everything is material in us, there really is neither vice nor virtue, and consequently no morality. Our laws, always *relative* and *shifting*, cannot serve as a support for morality, which is always *absolute* and *unalterable*; morality must then have its origin in a world more stable than this one, and more certain safeguards than fragile rewards or fleeting punishments. Some philosophers have maintained that religion was *invented* to uphold it; they were not aware that they were taking the effect for the cause. It is not religion that emerges from morality; it is morality which is born from religion, since it is certain, as we have just said, that morality cannot have its beginning in *physical* man or in *simple matter*; since it is certain that when men lose the idea of God, they plunge into all sorts of crimes in spite of laws and executioners.[17]

The problem of the relation between religious faith and morality—or put another way, the relation between atheism and crime—is posed in *The Brothers Karamazov*. This problem, at the heart of Ivan Karamazov's article on church and state jurisdiction, is the subject of lively discussion in two scenes at the monastery early in the novel. Ivan affirms: "There is no virtue if there is no immortality."[18] It is Miusov, however, who sets forth the main content of Ivan's thought. Ivan is quoted as believing that "there is absolutely nothing on earth that could compel people to love each other, that a law of nature saying that man must love mankind simply does not exist, and that if there is and ever has been love on earth, this is not from any natural law but simply because people believed in immortality." Ivan added parenthetically (Miusov relates) that "precisely in this consists the whole natural law, so that if you destroy humanity's faith in immortality, there will immediately dry up in it not only love, but also every living force necessary to perpetuate life on earth." Then "everything will be permissible, even cannibalism." "For every individual . . . who does not believe in God or in his immortality the moral law of nature immediately must be transformed into the exact contrary of former religious law, and . . . egoism—even to the point of crime—not only must be permitted to man, but even recognized necessary."

Ivan's thought closely parallels the three major points advanced by Chateaubriand: the concept of a moral foundation to society (Ivan's "natural law," "moral law of nature"); the view that morality is based on religious faith; and the view that absence of faith in God inexorably leads to crime. But unlike Chateaubriand in *The Genius of Christianity*, it is not as a believer that Ivan advances these ideas. The formulation that is a source of happiness for Chateaubriand is for Ivan a tormenting paradox. The elder Zosima instantly perceives that Ivan's whole position in his article constitutes a dialectic, that his conviction that "there is not virtue if there is no immortality" is a formulation that cuts both ways: "You are blessed if you so believe, or really very unhappy!" Ivan, as Zosima grasps, does not believe in the immortality of his soul or entirely believe in what he had written of the church and the church question.

Chateaubriand confidently asserts, as I have noted, that morality by itself alone proves immortality. Such an affirmation is part of a chain of circular reasoning, since Chateaubriand believes that morality is born of religion. Ivan, in contrast, takes as his philosophical point of departure the human condition. He is concerned not with the beauties of nature, art, or Christianity, but with the ugliness of human nature as it presents itself to his "Euclidian mind." It is precisely the absence of morality or virtue in man that leads Ivan to doubt the existence of God. His unconscious line of reasoning, at least as it is reflected in his action (or inaction), can be summed up as follows: the absence of morality in man proves the nonexistence of God; therefore, all is permissible; therefore, one is not responsible for his actions.

Chateaubriand was quite conscious of objections raised by Voltaire against the existence of God. In one copy of his *Essay on the Revolutions* (*Essai sur les révolutions*, 1793), for example, next to reflections on God's cruelty in creating beings destined only for misfortune, Chateaubriand noted in his own hand: "This objection is unanswerable and turns the Christian system upside down from top to bottom."[19] Nonetheless, in this skeptical and strangely confused essay, the force of renewal of faith is plainly evident. "What Religion Will Replace Christianity?" one of the last chapters of the book is entitled. Chateaubriand does not answer this question, but he is firm in one conviction: "Without religion, society must perish."[20] This thought is at the basis of *The Genius of Christianity*; it is the theme of the final chapter, entitled "What the State of Society Would Be If Christianity Had Not Appeared on Earth." Chateaubriand expatiates here on the moral degeneration of Rome in its decadent period and posits the Christian religion as the only restraint against crime and the central force in the moral development of modern man. "Destroy the evangelical religion, and in every village you will need a police force, prisons, and executioners."[21] One has a sense in reading this line of how close Chateaubriand stood to the Karamazov abyss of skepticism and despair.

The Christian religion "is an institution which can stand in for every other and become, in the hands of saints and wise men, a universal way to happiness." Chateaubriand suggests that someday the various forms of government "will appear to be immaterial, and people will adhere to simple moral and religious laws which represent the permanent basis for societies and the real government of men."[22] But in the present order of things, it is only the religion of the gospel that acts as a restraint upon the masses and forestalls crime among them. The religion of Christ serves as a second conscience, an evangelical conscience "for the guilty person who has had the misfortune to lose his natural conscience."[23] Chateaubriand's thought recalls the remarks of Zosima apropos Ivan's idea of a church-state. Zosima also anticipates a society in which Christian law will be all-permeating and omnipotent, but he notes that "if anything preserves society even in our times and even corrects the criminal and transforms him into another person, then this again is solely and only the law of Christ speaking in the consciousness of his own conscience."

"Is the tomb an abyss with no outlet or the gateway to another world?" Chateaubriand asks in his *Essay on the Revolutions.*[24] The question is unambiguously answered in *The Genius of Christianity.* Chateaubriand concludes his chapter on morality as a proof of immortality with the observation that in the last analysis there is another proof of the immortality of the soul upon which one must insist: man's veneration for tombs. It is here that human nature shows itself superior to the rest of creation and proclaims its lofty destiny. "We respect the ashes of our ancestors because a voice tells us that all [fire] is not extinguished in them." Everyone one is persuaded "that death is only a glorious transfiguration."[25]

The theme of respect for tombs is a basic one in *The Brothers Karamazov,* and with it is linked, as in *The Genius of Christianity,* the idea of resurrection. Alyosha returns to his home with the specific purpose of seeking out the tomb of his mother. Fyodor, affected by all this, gives a thousand rubles to the monastery so that prayers for his deceased first wife might be read. The novel concludes in an atmosphere of symbolic rebirth and brotherhood with Alyosha's speech at Ilusha's "stone," "under which they wanted to bury him." "Karamazov!" shouts Kolya, "does religion really and truly say that we will all rise from the dead and revivify ourselves and see each other again, all of us, and Ilushechka?" "We will be resurrected of a certainty," replies Alyosha.

The theme of respect for the tomb in all its implications of belief in immortality extends, paradoxically, to Ivan himself. Ivan remarks to Alyosha in the chapter "The Brothers Get Acquainted":

> "I want to travel to Europe . . . and yet I know that I am only going to a graveyard, but to a most, most precious graveyard, that's what! Precious are the dead that lie there, every stone over them speaks of such burning life in the past, of such passionate faith in their exploits, in their truth, in

their struggle, and in their science that I, I know this beforehand, I will fall on the earth and will kiss these stones and weep over them—at the same time convinced with all my heart that all this has long been only a graveyard and nothing more. And I shall weep not from despair, but only because I will be happy to shed my tears."

Ivan's feelings, however, contradict his finite conception of the precious life buried in the tombs of Europe. It is not accidental that Ivan's nostalgic veneration for the tombs is linked expressly with his visceral love of life, his "thirst for life in spite of everything," his love of nature, his notion of the irrational love of a person or honor for a great deed. The first half of Ivan's task, Alyosha significantly remarks, is to love life; this half is already accomplished. "Now it is necessary for you to strive for your second half, and you will be saved . . . it is necessary to resurrect your dead who, perhaps, never even died."

"Religion was born with the tombs," remarks Chateaubriand, "and cannot do without it."[26] It is in this light, perhaps, that a remark of Alyosha's, one that immediately precedes Ivan's comments on the "precious graveyard," must be evaluated. Alyosha recalls Dmitry's statement "Ivan is a tomb." This characterization undoubtedly expresses, in the context of Dostoevsky's tomb symbolism, the peculiar contradiction of Ivan's spiritual and religious nature: this tomb that is Ivan in all its appearances negates the idea of immortality, yet within it may be found the evidences of belief in eternal life. Thus Ivan is himself the supreme refutation of his own religious doubts. Love of life, conscience (manifested most strongly in the final breakdown of Ivan), veneration of tombs, and finally Ivan's recognition (itself a moral awareness) that "there is no virtue if there is no immortality" all point to the presence in Ivan of powerful forces of regeneration. Ivan himself in large measure is evidence of Chateaubriand's "proofs" of immortality.

4

Dostoevsky was certainly directly familiar with Chateaubriand's writings. He had in his library at the time of his death two separate editions of *Mémoires d'outre-tombe*.[27] Dostoevsky mentions Chateaubriand's *Atala* in a letter to his brother Mikhail May 4, 1845.[28] The earliest reference to Chateaubriand is in a single line in a letter to his brother Mikhail October 31, 1838. "Yes! Write me about the chief idea of Chateaubriand's *The Genius of Christianity*."[29] It is a singular fact: the conception of Christianity not only as truth, but as beauty—the chief idea of *The Genius of Christianity*—is at the core of Dostoevsky's religious-aesthetic outlook.

Dostoevsky wrote in a letter in 1856 of his intention to write an essay "essentially on the significance of Christianity in art." He notes that he had conceived his article in prison and that it was "the fruit of a decade of careful thought. I thought through the whole thing down to the last word as far back as Omsk."[30] Judging from Dostoevsky's general views on art in his later writings, he could not have failed in his projected essay to give expression to some of the ideas in *The Genius of Christianity*, certainly one of the most influential works in the nineteenth century on the poetics of Christianity.

There are many points of correspondence in aesthetic thought between Chateaubriand and Dostoevsky:[31] the central place accorded to the aesthetic element in the development of man (an idea which permeates Schiller's writings but which in Chateaubriand is linked directly with Christianity); the synthesis of the antique cult of form with a Christian aesthetic symbolism; the theory of the *beau idéal*, especially as applied to the fine arts; the medieval sentiment for beauty (the nostalgia for the infinite); the conception of close correspondence between morality and religion and between these and taste; the concept of the "perfect hero" (Chateaubriand's Christian *chevalier*) as the embodiment of the "beautiful ideal." However, it is in the general mood, construction, and application of Chateaubriand's ideas, in his passionate synthesis of aesthetics and religion, beauty and faith, and in his mobilization of the full force of Christian aesthetic against eighteenth-century skepticism and rationalism that we find a bridge to Dostoevsky.

"Ivan Karamazov," Leonid Grossman observed, "is unquestionably a convinced Voltairian."[32] Dostoevsky set out to refute the ideas of his Voltairian hero. It is at this point that Chateaubriand's *The Genius of Christianity*, with its rebuttal of Voltairian skepticism and atheism, may have moved again into the foreground of Dostoevsky's consciousness. The evidence of his acquaintance with Chateaubriand's writings—curious similarities in their religious and even moral personalities; parallels in their esthetic thought; finally, what appear to be distinct echoes in *The Brothers Karamazov* of certain formulations that appear in *The Genius of Christianity*—suggests that we may pose the question of Chateaubriand's impact upon Dostoevsky if not provide a conclusive answer to the question.

5

Chateaubriand calls attention in *The Genius of Christianity* to two categories of atheists: To the first belong those who simply declare "that there is no God at all, consequently there is no essential difference at all between good and evil; that the world is in the hands of the strongest and the most clever, etc." The French writer finds these atheists loathsome, but at least candid. (Dostoevsky's Shigalyov in *The Devils* and to some extent Raskolnikov in *Crime and Punishment* fall into this category.) It is the second group of atheists who arouse Chateaubriand's special ire; here are to be found

> the good fellows of atheism, the hypocrites of unbelief. Absurd folk who, with a false sweetness, would go to any lengths to maintain their system; they would call you *my brother* while they would cut your throat; words of morality and humanity are always on their lips; they are wicked three times over; because they bring together with the vices of the atheist the intolerance of the sectarian and the pride of the author.[33]

Chateaubriand mordantly assails a type of Voltairian eighteenth-century atheist; but he anticipates, albeit a little crudely, a late-nineteenth-century disciple of Voltaire, the author and poet-philosopher Ivan Karamazov, and the tragedy of atheistic humanism which is the dynamic core of his characterization.

8 Dostoevsky and the Marquis de Sade

The Final Encounter

Quelle sera la réligion qui remplacera le christianisme?

Chateaubriand, *Essai sur les révolutions* (1793)

You, negators of God and Christ, have not even thought of how filthy
and sinful everything would become in the world without Christ. . . .
People without an image.

Notebooks for *The Devils*

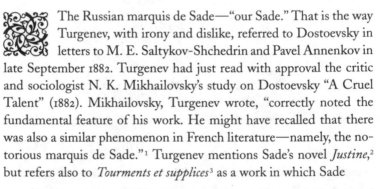 The Russian marquis de Sade—"our Sade." That is the way
Turgenev, with irony and dislike, referred to Dostoevsky in
letters to M. E. Saltykov-Shchedrin and Pavel Annenkov in
late September 1882. Turgenev had just read with approval the critic
and sociologist N. K. Mikhailovsky's study on Dostoevsky "A Cruel
Talent" (1882). Mikhailovsky, Turgenev wrote, "correctly noted the
fundamental feature of his work. He might have recalled that there
was also a similar phenomenon in French literature—namely, the notorious marquis de Sade."[1] Turgenev mentions Sade's novel *Justine*,[2]
but refers also to *Tourments et supplices*[3] as a work in which Sade

> with spasms of sensuality insists on the pleasure obtained through inflict-
> ing wounds, suffering, torture, etc. In one of his works Dostoevsky de-
> scribes in great detail the pleasure of a lover... and just think: all our Rus-
> sian bishops have performed requiems over this de Sade of ours, and even
> sermons have been read about the embracing love of this universal man!
> Truly we live in a strange time![4]

The concept of Dostoevsky as the "Russian Sade," as a "cruel talent" who chooses his subjects for the perverse pleasure he obtains
from them, cannot but strike us as limited. Here there is an expression
of subjective malice in Turgenev, not insight. Even if we were to allow
for a special personal sadistic interest of Dostoevsky in suffering, cru-

elty, and violence, we should in no way be making a statement on the literary and philosophical significance of his use of this material in his work. We should be making a moral judgment, and one which completely muddles the distinction between the man and the artist.

Dostoevsky in general distinguished between the use of erotic material for pornographic purposes and its serious use in literature.[5] Thus in a journalistic piece entitled "Answer to *Russkij vestnik*" in 1861, Dostoevsky rebukes a critic for placing Pushkin's unfinished story "Egyptian Nights," specifically the passages relating to Cleopatra and her lovers, on the same level as the works of the marquis de Sade:

> Are you really equating "Egyptian Nights" with the works of the marquis de Sade? . . . Here there is an impression of fearful horror, and not an impression of the "last expression" [of passion]. We are absolutely certain now that you take this "last expression" as something scabrous and in the manner of the marquis de Sade. But really this is not so, not at all so. This means losing the real, pure view of the matter. This *last expression* that you are talking so much about for you really may be seductive, but for us it is only a representation of a corruption of human nature that has attained frightful proportions and is presented by the poet *from such a point of view* (and just this point of view is the main thing), so that it produces by no means a scabrous impression, but a shocking one.[6]

Dostoevsky's defense of Pushkin's representation of the "last expression" of passion in "Egyptian Nights" is directly relevant to any consideration of his deep interest in Sade. "Sadism" in the work of Dostoevsky—the representation and exploration of cruelty, suffering, and violence—posed for Dostoevsky fundamental social, moral, and philosophical questions, as it did in the works of Sade. But whereas Sade finds in cruelty and violence proof of the irrational and absurd character of all law, morality, and religion, and therefore justification for his view that "everything is permitted," Dostoevsky finds in the human propensity for violence and cruelty only a partial truth—a truth that is counteracted by fundamental moral and spiritual strivings of man.

Dostoevsky found in Sade the archetypal ideologist of destruction and disintegration in society, and it is from this point of view that he approaches Sade and "sadism" in his work.[7] D. S. Savage, discussing Dostoevsky's exploration of the gambler's cruel eroticism in the novel *The Gambler*, excellently defines Dostoevsky's approach to sadism:

Dostoevsky's psychological insight here has nothing to do with the crude notion of "the appetite for cruelty and the appetite for suffering, the sadistic and the masochistic, as alternating manifestations of the sexual impulse." He perceives clearly that the "sexual impulse" cannot be considered as a force in itself, that it is related to the primary spiritual condition of the participants in the sexual relationship, which is thus not physically but metaphysically determined. When a limitless egotism, acknowledging no authority and therefore deprived of meaning and value, is brought into an erotic relationship, there result the convulsive lacerations described by Dostoevsky—the writhings of the disintegrating self in the throes of the knowledge of its own nothingness.[8]

Dostoevsky's references to Sade and his characterization of people like Prince Valkovsky, Svidrigailov, and others suggests that he had either firsthand familiarity with Sade's works or a very close knowledge of their content. Dostoevsky's omnivorous interest in all kinds of literature, high and low, is well known. Of interest in this connection are the recollections of Dostoevsky's wife, Anna Grigorievna:

> Now in general, Fyodor Mikhailovich took pains to shield me from all corrupting impressions. I recall in one instance coming into Fyodor Mikhailovich's study and leafing through some French novel that was on his table. Fyodor Mikhailovich came up to me and quietly took the book from my hands. "But I understand French," I said. "Let me read this novel." "Any one but this one! Why besmirch your imagination!" he replied. Even after our wedding, Fyodor Mikhailovich, wishing to guide my literary development, would himself select books for me and would on no account permit me to read frivolous novels. I was sometimes vexed by this supervision and would protest: "But why do you read these books yourself? Why do you besmirch your imagination?" "I am hardened in these matters," he would answer, "some books are necessary to me as material for my work. A writer must know everything and experience much. But I assure you, I do not relish cynical scenes, and they often arouse in me a sense of revulsion."[9]

Anna Grigorievna concludes with this remark: "I have always been deeply convinced that [Dostoevsky] was one of the most chaste of men, and how bitter it was for me to read that I. S. Turgenev, a writer who was such a favorite of mine, considered Dostoevsky a cynic and went so far as to call him the 'Russian Sade.'"[10]

What Anna Grigorievna has to say of the "chasteness" of her husband is as unconvincing as Turgenev's view of Dostoevsky as "our de Sade" or Nikolai N. Strakhov's view that the Russian novelist resembled his creations Stavrogin and the Underground Man in character.[11] Her testimony is nonetheless valuable. Dostoevsky's attitude toward the world of books was the same as his approach to life. Nothing lay outside his interests. "Some books are necessary to me as material for my work." Sade clearly was one of the authors "necessary" to Dostoevsky.

Sade's name appears in Dostoevsky's writings with significant frequency. Some of Dostoevsky's references to Sade come up in connection with characters in his works (Prince Valkovsky, Stavrogin, Fyodor Karamazov) who behave, philosophize, and even look like some of the denizens of Sade's fictional world.[12] Prince Valkovsky, in *The Insulted and Injured*, mentions the French writer in his confrontation with Ivan Petrovich: "My lady's sensuality was such that even the marquis de Sade might have learned from her." This remark is echoed in *The Devils* where Shatov asks Stavrogin: "Is it true that the marquis de Sade might have learned from you?" In this same conversation Shatov asks Stavrogin whether he had in fact affirmed that he "knew no difference in beauty between some sensual, bestial jest and some act of heroism, such as sacrificing one's life for mankind."

In his discussion of Pushkin's "Egyptian Nights," Dostoevsky observes that the "hyena Cleopatra knew all the mysteries of love and pleasure; compared to her, perhaps, the marquis de Sade might have seemed a child." Pushkin's Cleopatra in Dostoevsky's conception is not merely a corrupt human being, but the representative of a decadent, stagnant society whose foundations had long ago begun to crumble.

> All faith has been already lost; hope seems a useless deceit; thought is paling and disappearing; the divine fire has left it; society has lost its sense of direction and in cold despair senses an abyss ahead of it and is ready to topple into it. Life is suffocating through lack of a goal. The future offers nothing; one must demand everything from the present, one must fill one's life only with the necessities of the moment. Everything passes into the body, everything is used up in physical debauchery, and in order to compensate for the higher spiritual impressions which are lacking, people aggravate their nerves, their whole body with whatever is capable of arousing sensations. The most monstrous perversions, the most abnormal phenomena, gradually are taken for granted. Even the feeling of self-preservation disappears. Cleopatra is the representative of this society.[13]

Debauchery is characteristically understood and depicted by Dostoevsky not merely as erotic excess or perversion, but as a signal and symptom of the breakdown of society. Cleopatra, like the marquis de Sade, is the representative of a decadent, stagnant society without faith or morals. There is no "goal," that is, no social, spiritual, or religious ideal. For want of a spiritual life, all energies are directed to material things, "the necessities of the moment"; "everything passes into the body." Such a state of affairs is suicidal and can only end in destruction and self-destruction. Erotic excess, then, is only the "last expression" of the decline of a materialistic civilization. Thus, the narrator in "The Dream of a Ridiculous Man," speaking of the corruption of man and history after the "fall," notes that "the feeling of self-preservation rapidly began to weaken, proud men and sensualists appeared who bluntly demanded all or nothing."

The motifs of cruelty, sadism, and tyranny pervade *Notes from the House of the Dead*.[14] The problem of violence is always in the foreground. Although *Notes from the House of the Dead* as a social document constitutes a profound critique not only of Russian prisons, but of Russian society, Dostoevsky's most important message is that man is his own environment, that the very real problem of social evil is compounded by the problem of evil in man. "The attributes of the executioner," observes the narrator, "are found in embryo in almost every person today." Those attributes emerge in Dostoevsky's depiction of beatings in prison. He describes the horrible beatings inflicted upon the convicts by such demonic figures as Zherebyatnikov and Smekalov, guards who loved their work "purely as art," men who accompany their beatings with howls of laughter. It is no accident that precisely in his description of the prison punishments Sade is mentioned. Once again, the question of erotic excess is linked with violence and social disintegration:

> I don't know how it is now, but in the not too distant past there were gentlemen to whom the possibility of flogging a victim afforded a satisfaction resembling that of the marquis de Sade and the marquise de Brinvilliers [1630–1676]. I think there is something in this sensation, both sweet and painful, that sends a thrill through the hearts of these gentlemen. There are people who like tigers thirst for the taste of blood. Whoever has once experienced this power, this boundless domination over the body, blood and spirit of a person like himself, created like himself, a

brother in the law of Christ; whoever has once experienced this power and boundless opportunity to humiliate with the deepest degradation another being carrying in himself the image of God—such a person whether he wills it or not has somehow lost control over his sensations. Tyranny is a habit; it has the capacity to develop and does develop, finally, into a disease. I maintain that the finest person through habit can be reduced to the crude and coarse state of a beast. Blood and power intoxicate: coarseness and debauchery follow; the most abnormal phenomena begin to appeal to the mind and feelings, and, finally, become sweet to them. Man and citizen perish in the tyrant forever, and a return to human dignity, regeneration, repentance, now becomes for him almost impossible. What is more, the example, the possibility of such arbitrariness, has a corrupting influence on all society: such power is a temptation. A society that regards indifferently such a phenomenon is already corrupt at its foundations. In a word, the right of corporal punishment given to one man over another is one of the ulcers of society, one of the most powerful means for destroying every germ, every effort in society toward civic feeling, and full cause for its inevitable and irretrievable destruction.

This is the same sick world of Cleopatra, but a more contemporary one—Russia.[15]

In Dostoevsky's notebook in 1864, one finds these interesting jottings:

Catholicism (the power of hell). Celibacy, the attitude to women at confession. Erotic diseases. Here there is a certain subtlety that can best be grasped only in the most inveterate underground debauchery (the marquis de Sade). It is remarkable that all these debauched vile books are attributed to debauched abbots sitting in the bastille, later in the revolution [writing these books] for tobacco or a bottle of wine.[16]

In the notebook to *The Brothers Karamazov*, Dostoevsky invokes the name of Sade as a symbol of the most extreme renunciation of morality and religion. "How do you want to live?" Alyosha asks Ivan. "In a Karamazov way," answers Ivan. "That is, all is permitted?" asks Alyosha. "All is permitted. I would like to totally annihilate the idea of God." Meanwhile, Ivan can conceive of living on for thirty years and then destroying himself. "The idea won't die. It will live like a worm. Only one thing remains: swinish sensuality with all its consequences, sensuality to the point of cruelty, to crime, to the marquis de Sade."[17] Not surprisingly, the name of Sade appears on the profaning lips of Ivan's father. Fyodor Karamazov, compared significantly to a "Roman patrician," speaks of the pleasure of sentencing girls to be thrashed and of the lads who do the thrashing: "A fine set of marquis de Sades, eh?" The reference to Sade, significantly, emerges not only in connection with the theme of beatings, but in the context of Fyodor's most extreme moment of profanation in the novel—when he recalls spitting on an icon.[18]

A final reference to Sade appears in Dostoevsky's notebook in 1881. Here Dostoevsky observes that "conscience without God is a horror, it can go astray and lead to the utmost immorality." A few lines later, Dostoevsky writes: "Conscience, the conscience of a marquis de Sade!—this is an absurdity."[19]

Dostoevsky responded positively, as I have noted earlier, to Chateaubriand's refutation of the Enlightenment; to the French writer's passionate synthesis of esthetics and religion, beauty and faith; to his mobilization in *The Genius of Christianity* of the full force of Christian aesthetic against eighteenth-century materialism, skepticism, and rationalism, in particular, against Voltaire and Diderot. If Chateaubriand may be said to represent the positive complementarity of Dostoevsky's outlook, the marquis de Sade represents the embodiment of a point of view, or philosophical outlook on the world, with which Dostoevsky enters into moral conflict.

Albert Camus, in *The Rebel*, has called Sade the "first theoretician of absolute rebellion," the one who "musters into one vast war machine the argument of the free thinkers up to Father Meslier and Voltaire."[20] In Sade, indeed, the Enlightenment found its most crooked mirror and yet in some respects its most perversely loyal follower. One is reminded of the Underground Man's final remarks directed at the rationalists and utopian socialist thinkers whose theories are so cruelly parodied in both his life and confession. "For my part, I have merely carried to extremes what you have not dared to carry even half-way." Sade, whose motto was "Extreme in Everything," in effect said the same to the *philosophes* of his century:

> *Aimable* La Mettrie, profound Helvétius, wise and learned Montesquieu, why then, so penetrated with this truth [the truth that nature is contented with the "crime of destruction"], have you only hinted at it in your divine books? O century of ignorance and of tyranny, how you have harmed human knowledge and in what slavery you confined the greatest geniuses

of the universe! Let us dare then to speak today, since we can, and since we owe men the truth, let us dare to unveil it completely.[21]

Sade sought to turn the cult of nature into a monster that would devour its creators. He justified every violence and desecration in his criminal utopia with the word *nature* and carried eighteenth-century rationalism and materialism to diabolical conclusions. He put "Nature" into the service of an aggressive imperialism of the ego, the ideology of the debauched libertine, the doctrine that "absolutely everything is permitted."

The extreme conclusions Sade drew in his novels, of course, were not the conclusions of the philosophes, any more than the extreme conclusions of the Underground Man are those of Chernyshevky and the so-called Russian Enlightenment of the 1860's. The philosophes had no intention of abolishing a universal code of morality. Armed with an unshakable faith in reason and a rational ordering of society, they envisaged a new, harmonious society, a triumphant humanistic ethic based on man's moral needs and nature. It was in the name of these philosophes that Sade, exploiting the weaknesses of their outlook and fully grasping the morally explosive character of the "revaluation of values" in eighteenth-century France, with malicious pleasure proclaimed a philosophy of moral nihilism, absolute relativism, and subjectivism. He was, as a thinker, the Underground Man of the eighteenth century, a brilliant dialectician and parodist, but without the sense of bankruptcy, the real ambivalence and despair that characterized the consciousness of Dostoevsky's strange "paradoxicalist."

Sade's philosophy, like a faithful dog, everywhere accompanies the outpourings of his erotic fantasy. The key word in Sade's lexicon, as among the philosophes, is *nature*. In its name Sade struggles against God and every form of personal and social morality. Crime, in his view, only reflects the true state of nature in which destruction holds a necessarily equal place with creation. When nature's "secret inspirations dispose us to evil, it is evil she wishes, it is evil she requires, for the sum of crimes not being complete, not sufficient to the laws of equilibrium, the only laws whereby she is governed, she demands that there be crimes to dress the scales."[22] It follows, for Sade, that "destruction being one of the laws of Nature, nothing that destroys can be criminal."[23] Indeed, crime itself is an impossibility in the order of

Nature; criminals are nothing but the "agents of her caprice." The only crime would be to conflict with Nature's will, and anything that would disturb Nature is beyond man's reach. "Be sure that all the rest is entirely permitted [*tout . . . est absolument permis*]."[24] So-called depravity "is neither more nor less than the natural state of man and its particular details usually the result of the environment into which Nature has cast him."[25]

Sade recognizes no distinction between criminal and virtuous deeds. With the supporting detail of a fanatical ethnographer, Sade insists that "all is relative to our manners and the climate we inhabit; what is a crime here is often a virtue several hundred leagues hence." "There is nothing on earth as indifferent as the committing of good or evil."[26] Sade has a purely historical or cultural understanding of the feelings of revulsion or guilt we may experience over any given act or situation. He finds no *natural* basis for guilt or conscience. The loathing we experience for certain misdeeds "is not dictated by Nature. . . . Its one source is in the total lack of habit; does not the same hold for certain foods?"[27] "Guilt is an illusion . . . naught but the idiotic murmuring of a soul too debilitated to dare to annihilate it."[28] Or again: "Guilt [*le remords*] . . . is merely an unpleasant reminiscence; it crops out of the customs and conventions one happens to have adopted, but it never results from, never has any connection with, the character of the deed one happens to have performed."[29]

What others call crime, Sade insists, is really virtue, energy that civilization has not yet altogether corrupted. He sees an absolute contradiction between the indifference of nature and natural instinct on the one hand and the moral and religious codes of society on the other. In place of Christian ethics he affirms an ethics of sexuality. For Sade, lust is an inspiration of nature, "the secret means whereby [man] exhales the dose of despotism Nature instilled in the depths of his heart." This despotic impulse must be given expression, or man will seek other outlets for it: "It will be vented upon nearby objects; it will trouble the government." To avoid this danger, Sade urges that man be given freedom for his tyrannical desires, which "despite himself" torment him ceaselessly.[30] Sade, it is interesting to note, for all his efforts to declare guilt and conscience obsolete, the function of culturally or socially determined moral and religious codes of society, concedes that man remains inwardly divided.

On the basis of nature, then, Sade establishes a philosophy of self-interest, of absolute egoism, of man in absolute solitude limited only by the law of his own pleasure. "Have we ever felt a single natural impulse advising us to prefer others to ourselves, and is not each of us alone, and for himself in this world?" Nothing is more egoistic than the voice of Nature; her immutable and sacred counsel is to "delight in ourselves, to prefer ourselves, to love ourselves, no matter at whose expense."[31] To be an egoist, then, is to live in harmony with nature.[32] And with this in mind, Sade proposes instead of religious instruction something resembling a doctrine of rational self-interest: Egoism, he believes, is more likely than anything to turn men into "honest people."[33]

Finally, Sade calls upon us to step forward, ax in hand, to "deal the final blow to the tree of superstition."[34] By implication, God does not exist: a just god, Sade believes, would never have put up with the injustices of nature. Religion, finally, is an annoying stumbling block for Sade. "Yes, citizens, religion is incompatible with the libertarian system; you have sensed as much." In general, he wants no more of a God "who is at loggerheads with Nature, who is the father of confusion, who moves man at the moment man abandons himself to horrors."[35] But atheism in Sade, as Pierre Klossowski has noted, is not cold-blooded; it is the atheism of "effervescence and therefore of resentment; his atheism is only a form of sacrilege. Only the profanation of religious symbols is able to convince him of his apparent atheism."[36] The same might be said of Fyodor Karamazov.

However Sade's ideas relate to his disordered personality, these ideas are the partly serious, partly cynical, partly mocking reflections of a philosophic mind on the one hand upon the disorder of a society whose age-old foundations are crumbling and on the other, upon the ideas, or implications of many of the ideas, arising from the debacle of that society. One has no difficulty in singling out in Sade's thought notions and problems that Dostoevsky with so much agony explores in his work: the notion that "everything is permitted," the appeal to science and sociology in dealing with moral questions, the affirmation of the solitude of man, the doctrine of self-interest, the view that all love is self-love, unbridled sensuality—all this turns up in Dostoevsky's work, not as self-evident falsehoods that have only to be counteracted by dramatizations of virtue but as relative truths that must be given broader definition and above all integrated into larger truths about the nature of man. Both Dostoevsky's libertines and intellectuals pose the problems raised by Sade—the problems of a society without moral foundations.

Sade's criminal utopia, in Dostoevsky's view, is the direct outcome of man without God. Sade rejoices in pure nature in man; Dostoevsky recoils from this idea. Yet heroes (or anti-heroes) like Ivan Karamazov can come dangerously close to Sade. For both Sade and Dostoevsky, debauched libertinism raises directly the problem of moral and aesthetic criteria, the question of the distinction between good and evil, beauty and ugliness. Dostoevsky's libertines and sensualists resolve these problems in the manner of Sade. The Russian novelist's divided intellectuals often try to come to grips with these problems in abstract philosophical terms. Ivan, who is obsessed with the "national" habit of beatings, despairingly asserts: "There is absolutely nothing on earth that could compel people to love each other . . . a law of nature saying that man should love mankind simply doesn't exist, and . . . if there is and ever has been any love on earth, then it is not from any natural law but solely because people believed in immortality." Destroy this faith, and "there will no longer be anything immoral, everything will be permissible, even cannibalism." Ivan, of course, suffers over these conclusions, as indeed does Dostoevsky. Sade, on the other hand, arrives at these conclusions cynically, triumphantly. He not only proclaims these conclusions, but like the engineer Klinevich in Dostoevsky's "Bobok," lives them out. Klinevich, in the raw sense, is perhaps the most Sadean of all figures in Dostoevsky's work, a candidate for any role in a Sade novel. He calls upon everybody to "make themselves naked":

> "The devil take it, after all the grave means something! We'll all read our stories aloud and abandon all sense of shame. I'll be the first to tell about myself. I am, you know, one of the carnal types. Everything up on top there was bound with rotten ropes. Away with the ropes, and let us live these final two months in the most shameless truth! Let us bare ourselves and make ourselves naked!"

In the underworld of "Bobok"—a new order based on "rational foundations"—we find ourselves, of course, in Sade's criminal utopia. Dostoevsky parodies a world which has yielded entirely in its life and philosophy to the dictates of Sadean "Nature."[37]

Ippolit Terentiev, in *The Idiot*, expresses the terror before pure nature, nature that is indifferent to good and evil, that destroys and disfigures even that which is most divine in human history: Christ. Versilov, in *The Raw Youth*, insists that love for humanity is a kind of contradiction in terms and must be understood as self-love.

Ivan Karamazov, Ippolit Terentiev, and Versilov, of course, hardly embody full truth in the Dostoevsky novel, but they dramatize important aspects of the author's thought, everything he seeks to overcome. They disclose the deepest level of Dostoevsky's concerns and fears for humanity. In his notebook in 1864, for example, Dostoevsky writes frankly: "To love man, according to Christ's commandment, *as [one loves] oneself* is impossible. The law of individuality on earth is binding." But "man strives on earth for an ideal which is *contrary* to his nature," Dostoevsky states in almost Manichean fashion. "The nature of God is directly contrary to the nature of man." For this reason, Dostoevsky views man's tension toward the ideal—man's life as a permanent process of "achieving, struggling and, through all defeats, refocusing on the ideal [Christ] and struggling for it"—as the only thing that saves life on earth from senselessness.[38]

Man's "nature" here—that is, that which is distinct from the "nature of God"—would seem to be in the same category as the "vile nature" about which Ivan speaks in the notebooks to *The Brothers Karamazov*. But Dostoevsky's view of man's earthly nature is more complex than would appear at first glance. In the notebooks Dostoevsky identifies "vile nature," Ivan's "thirst for life," with Sade; in the novel, however, the reference to Sade disappears, and Dostoevsky (through Ivan) emphasizes the contradictory, dynamic character of earthly nature and the thirst for life with which it is connected. Ivan speaks of his "thirst for life," "frenzied and, perhaps, indecent."

> "Some feeble sniveling moralists, poets, especially, often call this thirst for life vile. It is in part a Karamazov feature, that's true, this thirst for life in spite of everything; you have it in you, too, without a doubt. But why is it vile? There's still a fearful amount of centripetal force on our planet, Alyosha. I want to live, and I go on living, even if its against logic."

At the end of the novel, Dmitry says to Alyosha: "You have no idea how much I want to live now, what a thirst I have to exist and be conscious."

In the final analysis, then, raw Sadean "Nature" is itself antinomian in character, the embodiment (as Sade himself recognized) of a constructive as well as destructive force and principle. Here in man's nature is the terrifying, explosive, centrifugal reality of life which cannot be denied ("Reality strives toward fragmentation," remarks the narrator of *Notes from the House of the Dead*). But there is not only destruction here. "There's still a great deal of the centripetal force on our planet." But nature and the thirst for life, if it is to be formative, if it is to give meaning and center to existence, must be sublimated, must be wedded to striving, must be reborn in moral and spiritual energy. Ivan's thirst for life, his very understanding of that thirst, promises the possibility in him of such sublimation and rebirth.

Sadean nature, with its destructive potential, is not denied in Dostoevsky. At the same time, the Russian novelist accented an aspect of human nature that Sade scoffed at and sought to evade. Sade wanted no more of a "God" (here we may read conscience as well) who is "at loggerheads with Nature, who is father of confusion, who moves man at the moment man abandons himself to horrors." Dostoevsky, though recognizing a point of contact between man's being and Sade's nature, nonetheless posits as central in him precisely that "moment" of conflict that surfaces in man when he "abandons himself to horrors," precisely that all-important moment of transition in him from the elemental to the transcendental, that moment of "confusion" that marks the first step of man in the moral realm toward sublimation of the destructive force of nature.

The libertine in Dostoevsky is the one in whom nature in its destructive aspects has acquired the upper hand, the one in whom sensuality (so often linked with violence and acquisitiveness in Dostoevsky's novelistic universe) has acquired terrifying force. "Sensuality is the root of all evil," the Ridiculous Man asserts. And in his notebook Dostoevsky views marriage and sexuality as a manifestation of egoism and therefore of the "greatest deviation from humanism."[39]

The debauched libertine in Dostoevsky's universe, as in Sade's, is simply the man or woman who has most consistently lived out the logic of an exclusively natural or instinctual existence, one of animal solitude in "harmony" with the jungle of earthly nature in himself or herself. Not without reason does Fyodor Karamazov warn Zosima: "Don't invite me to be my natural self, don't take the risk. . . . As a matter of fact, I won't go so far as to be my natural self."

In some of these "natural" types, celebration of nature and self takes on the character of an often frenzied desecration of moral and spiritual form, of the image of man, of God himself. Fyodor Karamazov and Prince Valkovsky's lover belong to this category of libertine. Valkovsky's lover might have emerged from one of the corrupt convents in Sade's novels. She is extraordinarily beautiful, but in public behavior and reputation, forbidding; she is menacingly virtuous, "like the abbess of a medieval convent," Valkovsky notes. A single hint from her could ruin a reputation. Yet in her secret private life, "you could not have found a debauchee more debauched than she was, and I had the happiness of earning her complete confidence. I was her secret and mysterious lover. My lady's sensuality was such that even the marquis de Sade might have learned from her."

The central trait of character in this woman's sensuality is profanation. In the heat of the most passionate pleasures, she would suddenly laugh like one possessed. But the "strongest, keenest, most devastating element in this pleasure," according to Valkovsky, was the

> "secrecy, the audacity of the deception. This jeering at everything which in public the countess preached as being lofty, transcendent, and inviolable, and finally, this inner diabolical laughter and conscious trampling upon everything that it is forbidden to trample upon, and all this unbridled, carried to extraordinary extremes, such extremes as even the most fevered imagination would not dare to conceive—in that, above all, lay the keenness of the pleasure. Yes, this was the devil incarnate, but she was irresistibly fascinating. That woman understood life and knew how to make the most of it."

"Life," here, it is clear, means nothing more or less than giving free reign to one's "natural" instincts. "But why descend to such beastliness?" asks Valkovsky's interlocutor, Ivan Petrovich. "What beastliness?" responds Valkovsky. "To which that woman descended, and you with her," Ivan Petrovich adds. "Ah, you call that beastliness—a sign that you are still in the apron-string stage," continues Valkovsky. "Of course, I admit that independence might appear as completely the opposite thing."

In Valkovsky's view, Ivan Petrovich's morality is "nonsense." "What isn't nonsense is personality—myself. All is for me, and the whole world is created for me." Valkovsky's philosophy is Sadean to the letter:

I only recognize obligations when I have something to gain by them. . . . At the root of all human virtues lies the completest egoism. And the more virtuous the affair may be, the more egoism is to be found there. Love yourself—that's the one rule I recognize. Life is a commercial transaction: don't uselessly throw your money away, but kindly pay for your entertainment, and you will be doing your whole duty to your neighbor: that's my morality.

These are the cynical "morals" of the marquis de Sade. "I have no ideals and I don't want any."

In Svidrigailov—"a debauched, low, sensual person," in the words of Raskolnikov—the Sadean type and philosophy finds clear embodiment. Although he asserts that he is not a "master at philosophizing," he defends himself with the skill of Sade. When Raskolnikov accuses Svidrigailov of having faith in debauchery alone, Svidrigailov blandly asks what reason there is to restrain oneself, and he adds that "in this debauchery, at least, there is something constant, based even on nature and not subject to fantasy, something that exists in the blood as an eternal flame . . . an occupation." Raskolnikov calls this debauchery "a disease and a dangerous one." Svidrigailov, fending off the moral thrust of Raskolnikov's remark, turns the moral issue into an aesthetic one, arguing that "[debauchery] is a disease like everything else that goes to extremes—and that is an essential part of it," but "to begin with, it is one thing with one person, and something different with another." He argues further that "one must of course observe measure in all things, and make calculations, however mean." Debauchery, in short, is an art.[40]

Svidrigailov, in his own words, "pins his hope on anatomy alone." The words *nature* and *natural* crop up in his conversations with Raskolnikov; they are his answer to the demands of morality. "Now let's just assume, now, that I too am a man, et nihil humanum... in a word, that I am capable of being attracted and falling in love (which, of course, doesn't happen according to our will), that everything can be explained in a most natural way. The whole question is: am I a monster or am I myself a victim? Well, and what if I am a victim?"

The import of this question is clear: are we really responsible for our behavior in such affairs as "love" (and we know what love is to Svidrigailov)? Can we be judged, morally, as monsters? Are we not simply creatures of nature, victims of our "natural" instincts and therefore absolved of any responsibility? Is debauchery really definable in any absolute way? Or is it not something which means one thing to one person and another to someone else? In an untitled page of dialogue that was found in the notebooks of Dostoevsky's *Diary of a Writer*, a character argues that "morality is a relative thing . . . and grounded on nothing. In addition it is everywhere different . . . but it's really not worth while talking about the differences in the centuries and ages. Once again, all this is because we are dealing here with an old habit, a law—and one couldn't say more about it. We have finished with law. . . . We have finished with morality. . . . Really, morality is the same egoism, the same feeling of self-preservation, which means again only my fault. And please let me worry about what is to my own advantage."[41] These remarks are pure Sade and could have been taken directly from any one of his works where these notions are repeated again and again.

If we turn to Sade again, we shall find ourselves in the underground of Prince Valkovsky and Svidrigailov where the "sewers are filthy." Clément's discussion with Thérèse in *Justine* seems to anticipate the conversations of Valkovsky and Svidrigailov with their interlocutors. His cruel tastes, Clément argues in *Justine*, are given to him by nature. "Oh, Thérèse, is there any crime here? Is this the name to designate what serves Nature? Is it in man's power to commit crimes?" Nature's "primary and most imperious inspirations," according to Clément, enjoin man "to pursue his happiness at no matter whose expense. The doctrine of brotherly love is a fiction we owe to Christianity and not to Nature." "But the man you describe is a monster," Thérèse protests. Clément rejoins, "The man I describe is in tune with Nature." "He is a savage beast," insists Thérèse. At this point Clément retorts: "Why, is not the tiger or the leopard, of whom this man is, if you wish, a replica, like man created by Nature and created to prosecute Nature's intentions?"[42]

Brotherly love and virtue are a "fiction" to Sade. Dostoevsky—the words are those of Ivan Karamazov—finds no "law of nature saying that man should love humanity." Dostoevsky is clearly skeptical about the existence of "natural" good in man. Yet it is clear that Sade's "fiction" of brotherly love and good is to Dostoevsky the most important fiction in human existence, a fiction that separates Dostoevskian man from Sadean man. Dostoevsky distinguishes sharply between the "nature of man" and the "nature of God," between man's earthly nature and his existential striving to transcend nature in himself, a striving Dostoevsky ultimately linked with an explicit or implicit belief in immortality.

What conclusions may be drawn from this discussion of Dostoevsky and Sade? Dostoevsky was undoubtedly fully familiar, first- or secondhand, with the general content of Sade's novels and the philosophical argumentation of Sade's debauched libertine.[43] What is certain is that he rejected the Sadean worldview as amoral, disfigured, and destructive of the moral and social fabric of men and society. But what seems equally certain is that he appreciated the gravity of the moral and psychological questions raised by Sade, questions so similar to those he raised in his own novels.

Sade's moral nihilism was a response to the problematic, still immature character of the enormous scientific and philosophic revolution of the eighteenth century. His work, in the most exact sense, constitutes a crisis of rational humanism. Dostoevsky's novels also respond to the weak and contradictory aspects of the eighteenth-century Enlightenment, particularly as it was reflected and continued in the Russian Enlightenment of the 1860's. Yet in his resolution of the questions raised by Sade, Dostoevsky remained, firmly, a religious humanist.

Sade, we may conclude, was the madman who cried out on Nietzsche's marketplace that "God is dead!"—not with Nietzsche's deeply humanistic concern for the consequences of this event but with a frenzied joy. Chateaubriand, viewing with alarm the disintegration in France at the end of the eighteenth century, exclaimed: "Il faut une réligion ou la société périt." Sade was certainly a harbinger of the crisis of nihilism that was to overtake European society. His insights not only disclosed the inherent weaknesses in Enlightenment philosophy, but anticipated in their radical skepticism the critical consciousness of the twentieth century.

Yet as F. Kautman rightly observed in his discussion of Dostoevsky and Sade, "Sade in all his works carries out a far-reaching destruction of the world, of all its phenomena and values, discloses the ab-

surdity of its laws, morals, and practices, stands the world on its head
. . . [but] with this negativity his experiment ends."[44] In the final
analysis, the challenge of Sadean man and philosophy could be met
only by one who recognized man's earthly truth as well as his passion
for transcendence, one who had explored the Sadean abyss and yet,
like Dante, had reached the "other shore." Such a writer was Dostoevsky, who wove the diverse threads of an entire epoch, beginning with
the Enlightenment and ending with the age of nihilism, into an unforgettable epic design. In this design the work of the marquis de
Sade, scion of a decadent nobility, would seem to occupy a significant
though somber place.

9   *The Root and the Flower*

Dostoevsky and Turgenev,
a Comparative Aesthetic

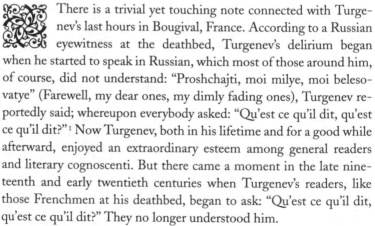 There is a trivial yet touching note connected with Turgenev's last hours in Bougival, France. According to a Russian eyewitness at the deathbed, Turgenev's delirium began when he started to speak in Russian, which most of those around him, of course, did not understand: "Proshchajti, moi milye, moi belesovatye" (Farewell, my dear ones, my dimly fading ones), Turgenev reportedly said; whereupon everybody asked: "Qu'est ce qu'il dit, qu'est ce qu'il dit?"[1] Now Turgenev, both in his lifetime and for a good while afterward, enjoyed an extraordinary esteem among general readers and literary cognoscenti. But there came a moment in the late nineteenth and early twentieth centuries when Turgenev's readers, like those Frenchmen at his deathbed, began to ask: "Qu'est ce qu'il dit, qu'est ce qu'il dit?" They no longer understood him.

The difficulty lay not only in the special character of Turgenev's art, its unique features, but also in the fact that a whole epoch had begun to break, anxiously yet decisively, with a whole vision, or perhaps one should say illusion, of life and art. Not without reason has the novelistic universe of Dostoevsky been linked with this break. "Dostoevsky was the crisis of culture," the Russian philosopher Nicholas Berdyaev maintains at the end of his study of Dostoevsky's metaphysical thought. Though himself "a supreme manifestation of Russian culture, its summit," though leaving us an incomparable spiritual legacy, Dostoevsky's work, or "creative image," gave expression to the "Russian dislike of middle culture." "The crisis of culture," Berdyaev insists, "reveals itself in a longing to escape from the middle course into some sort of all-resolving end. There is an apocalyptic tendency in the crisis of culture. It is present in Nietzsche and it is present in the highest degree in Dostoevsky."[2] This apocalyptic tendency in Dostoevsky—the concomitant, no doubt, of a "maximalism" in all areas of his life and personality—was not only uncharacteristic of Turgenev, but alien to him as a man and artist.

Dmitry N. Merezhkovsky was perhaps the first to suggest that the *question of culture*, of measure and of beauty ("the measure of all measures," as he put it), underlay the "Turgenev question," at least in Russian literature. Merezhkovsky's speech on Turgenev on the twenty-fifth anniversary of the writer's death in 1908 opened with these words:

> Turgenev, people say, is out of date. But forever? Two giant caryatids of Russian literature, Tolstoy and Dostoevsky, really have hidden Turgenev from us. But for how long? Are we not destined to return to him through them? In Russia, in the land of all kinds of revolutionary and religious maximalism, a country of self-immolation, of the wildest excesses, Turgenev, after Pushkin, is almost the sole *genius of measure* and therefore a genius of culture. For what is culture if not the *measuring*, the accumulation and preservation of values?[3]

Merezhkovsky went on to define the opposition between Turgenev and Russia's "two giant caryatids." To Russia's maximalists—Tolstoy with his cultural iconoclasm, his desire to save Russia "peasant style, holy fool style," and Dostoevsky with his contempt for the "godless, rotten West" and his conception of Russia as the "only God-bearing people"—Merezhkovsky opposes the "minimalist" Turgenev, Russia's "true conservator," Pushkin's legatee who first revealed to Europe that "Russia is also Europe." If the Russian revolution of 1905 went awry, Merezhkovsky argues, it was because there was "too much of Tolstoy and Dostoevsky in it, and too little of Turgenev."[4]

It was measure—by which Turgenev understood the temperate, open-end, equitable vision of life and not merely political or social compromise—that fell victim to the twentieth century. "In truth,"

Conrad wrote in his elegaic foreword to Edward Garnett's study of Turgenev in 1917, "it is not the convulsed terror-haunted Dostoevsky but the serene Turgenev who is under a curse."[5] He was right, but he might have added that serenity itself had come under a curse.

The Turgenev-Dostoevsky antinomy resolves itself finally into a cultural metaphor for the twentieth century. The profound differences between the art of the one and the other lie not so much in their conscious ideologies and philosophy as in their underlying vision of "nature," essential reality, being. Here, perhaps, one might posit a primary, deeply organic, and personal response to reality, a kind of *Urphilosophie* which determines the dynamics of a complex body of artistic thought and imagery, but not necessarily the final authorial point of view emerging from that dynamics. With Turgenev, we are certainly in the presence of an archetypal vision of the epic unity, wholeness, and organic character of nature and the vital life processes, one in which "beauty" (in the classical sense of "harmony," "clarity," and "serenity") is in the foreground; with Dostoevsky, a tragic vision of turbulence and fragmentation. One might say that the novel of Dostoevsky, which posits an ideal nonterrestrial unity and beatitude very classical in its formulation, is essentially an effort to contain and structure this turbulence, to find in man, or in man's relation to his universe, a structure of freedom and moral order. Turgenev's art, on the other hand, begins with a vision of a real order and beatitude in nature. The pathos of his art, however, emerges from a permanent contradiction between his aesthetic vision and his tragic sense of life, between the artist who is content to see and enjoy life in its wholeness and the subjective philosopher who is painfully aware of man's unfavored rank-and-file place in the ideal aesthetic order of nature.

The vision of unity and the vision of turbulence—the one centripetal, the other centrifugal—are not only points of departure for each artist: they translate into the very texture and forms of the artists' art, into their manner of representing reality, their style of writing, and finally into the impact of their art on the reader.

Some observations of the narrator of Turgenev's "Journey to the Woodlands" (1857) bring into sharp focus the whole character of Turgenev's vision of nature, essential being. A consideration of nature and life's meaning lies at the center of this brilliantly conceived and executed philosophical tale. The narrator travels through a dense virgin forest for two days. On the philosophical plane, the story moves from lyrical despair to sober optimistic insight; from a subjective, frightening view of nature to an objective understanding and acceptance of the life processes; from the troubled "first day" of a real yet also allegorical journey through the forest of life to the "second day" of liberated vision and form.

Symbolically, the narrator's hands cover his eyes as, sunk in self-contemplation on the first day, he self-pityingly reviews the melancholy fate of man before the implacable dread force of nature and death. But as he prepares for night at the end of the second day, his attention is drawn to an insect on a branch. He peers intently at the insect and offers an explanation of nature and the life processes. Here the narrator's aesthetics of nature—quite literally an "aesthetic of observation," in the phrase of Paul Bourget[6]—constitutes an introduction to Turgenev's poetics:

> I raised my head and saw at the very end of a slender branch one of those large flies with an emerald head, a long body, and four transparent wings which the coquettish French call "virgins" but our ingenuous peasant people call "bucket yokes." For a long time, over an hour, I did not remove my eyes from it. Baked through and through by the sun, it did not move, and only from time to time did it turn its little head from side to side and flutter its upraised wings—that was all. Looking at it, it suddenly seemed to me that I understood the life of nature, understood its clear and manifest, though for many still mysterious, meaning. A quiet and slow animation, a leisureliness and restraint of feelings and forces, an equilibrium of health in every individual creature—that is nature's very foundation, its unalterable law; that is what maintains it and keeps it going. Everything that lies outside this equilibrium—whether from above or from below, it is all the same—is hurled aside by nature as something worthless. Many insects die as soon as they experience those joys of love which violate the equilibrium of life.

Nature, in the narrator's vision, is eminently positive in its preoccupation with, and embodiment of, the life processes. It is fundamentally conservative, centripetal, with a preponderant movement toward the creation of form; it is the "universal mother," as Turgenev calls it in another philosophically important sketch, "Enough: An Excerpt from the Notes of a Deceased Artist" (1862). She is almost pregnant in her "slow and quiet animation," her "restraint of feelings and forces," her embodiment of inner unalterable law, health, and equilibrium. In her state of permanent gestation, she hurls aside all that upsets the "equilibrium of life."

Nature, then, is life; it embraces both growth and decay. It is evenhanded in its distribution of fruits, indifferent in its striving for balance. "Man is the child of Nature," we read in "Enough," but "she is the universal mother who knows no preferences: everything that exists in her realm arises only at the expense of another and must in its time yield place to another; she creates as she destroys, and it is all the same to her whether she creates, whether she destroys, so long as life does not cease, so long as death does not lose its rights." "But what about good, reason, justice?" ("Nature," in *Senilia*, 1879) stammers the dreamer, in a state of shock on learning that man's welfare is not the especial concern of the universal mother. But Nature is amoral. "I know neither good nor evil," the woman in the dream retorts. "Reason is not a law to me, and what is justice? I gave you life, and I will take it away and give it to another, to worms or people, it's all the same to me."

Nature's only criterion, in the deepest sense biological, is equality and "justice" for all. But man, placing himself at the center of the universe, finds injustice here. He anthropomorphizes Nature, valorizes her actions, bewails her indifference to him. It is Nature in the light of human consciousness that nourishes Turgenev's philosophical pessimism. In his remarkable sketch, "Enough" (which he later disparaged for its excess of "subjectivity"), the narrator gloomily speaks of the "deaf dumb blind elemental force of nature which does not even celebrate its victories, but relentlessly moves forward devouring everything." This image of a frightening, threatening, and implacable nature finds expression, though in a controlled and balanced way, in "Journey to the Woodlands" and some other works. Nature in this aspect is implacable fate. But it cannot be overemphasized: it is not Nature that changes her face, the face revealed to the narrator of the "Journey to the Woodlands" as he contemplates the "bucket yoke," but man who restlessly shuttles between a painfully subjective and properly objective perspective of Nature.

Turgenev, then, could respond darkly to Nature and man's fate.

But as artist he accepts Nature as a guide. Nature's evenhanded justice may be bad news for the little Faustian earth god, but this same Nature provides a model for art and the artist precisely in her equilibrium, her restraint, her Olympian tranquility and objectivity.

"Simplicity, tranquility, clarity of lines, conscientious craftsmanship"—these were the aesthetic ideals Turgenev early held out before himself.[7] The artist, he believed, must strive for simplicity and clarity, he must follow Nature in her sense of measure and harmonious simplicity.[8] Indeed, the artist in his innermost being *is* nature. "Fortunate is that person," he wrote, "who, concentrating his focus, finds nature once again in the center—and all nature—because he himself is nature."[9] "Shakespeare," Turgenev insists in a letter to Leo Tolstoy, "is like Nature," even when she has a "vile physiognomy . . . even then she is an embodiment of necessity, truth, and . . . expediency."[10] In a speech honoring Shakespeare in 1864, Turgenev again pursues this comparison between the English dramatist, Nature, and organic form. "Like her, he is simple and multilayered—all, so to speak, on the palm of the hand and endlessly deep, free to the point of annihilating all fetters, and constantly full of internal harmony and that unerring sense of inner law, logical necessity, which lies at the base of everything living."[11] In his eulogy to Pushkin in 1880, finally, Turgenev posits in his beloved model the "classical feeling for measure and harmony."[12] The central attributes of Pushkin's poetic talent are in equilibrium: "the blend of passion and tranquility," that "objectivity of his gift in which the subjectivity of his personality is revealed only through an inner heat and fire."[13]

Turgenev's explanation of the rejection or neglect of Pushkin in the generation that followed the poet's death involves imagery and emphases that are revealing of his own aesthetic preferences and values. The worldview of Pushkin seemed narrow to the new generation, Turgenev remarked in his Pushkin speech, his classical feeling for measure and harmony—"a cold anachronism." "The poet-echo—in the expression of Pushkin, the poet-centered, drawing all to himself, positive, like life in repose, was replaced by the poet-herald, centrifugal, gravitating to others, negative, like life in movement."[14] While attempting to show why this "neglect of Pushkin" had been inevitable," Turgenev at the same time pointed to the renewed interest in

Pushkin, a poet whom people had become accustomed to think of as a kind of "mellifluous singer, a nightingale." Yet those who had forgotten Pushkin could not be blamed entirely. Even such a keen person as the poet Baratynsky, Turgenev notes, called upon to look over the papers of Pushkin after the latter's death, could not help exclaiming in a letter: "Can you imagine what amazes me most of all in these works? The abundance of thought! Pushkin—a thinker! Could one have expected this?"[15] Turgenev was convinced that Pushkin would reemerge from the shadows. "Under the influence of the old, but not yet obsolete master . . . the laws of art . . . will again exert their power."[16]

One could draw upon Turgenev's remarks in speaking of his eclipse by Dostoevsky in the late nineteenth and twentieth centuries. Criticism in the late nineteenth and twentieth centuries increasingly stressed the "exquisite" "artist" and "poet" in Turgenev, the "beauty" of his language. Turgenev came to be admired by many essentially as a "mellifluous singer or nightingale," but with nothing to say. The conception of Turgenev as a thinker would be slow to take root. Turgenev's opposition of the classical "poet-echo" to the centrifugal "poet-herald" would seem to define in part the opposing responses to Turgenev and Dostoevsky. It is noteworthy that in his own Pushkin speech in 1880, Dostoevsky admired in Pushkin precisely the elements of poet-herald and saw in him both prophet and prophecy of Russia's self-consciousness reaching out and incorporating universal archetypes.

The two writers' speeches on Pushkin reflected their distinctive styles and general differences as artists and personalities. Dostoevsky's Pushkin speech was electrifying in the grandeur of its conception of Pushkin; above all, it was charismatic in its eloquence and wholly subordinated to the rhetorical explication of a single idea. Dostoevsky, speaking of Pushkin as a prophet, emerged himself as prophet. Twice he emphasized that he was not approaching Pushkin as a literary critic. Dostoevsky spoke as an artist carried away by his artistic idea. In contrast, Turgenev's speech on the "first Russian artist-poet," Pushkin, was characteristically low key, for the most part devoid of rhetorical device; only once, when speaking of Russia ("and Russia is developing, not declining") did Turgenev rise to heights of pathos, but then only momentarily, quickly tempering his thought with the caution that "growth . . . is inevitably linked with illnesses, painful crises, the most evil and at first glance hopeless contradictions."[17] Overall, Turgenev speaks soberly as a literary and cultural critic with a historical perspective; he speaks as one who conceives of art as ethical in its sources and power yet distinct from prophecy. His remarks have a complexity and a depth that are not present in Dostoevsky's speech.

A. F. Koni, a distinguished Russian jurist, recalls in his memoirs that "the chief living hero of the [Pushkin] celebrations, was, by general acclamation, Turgenev. But on the third day he was replaced in this role by Fyodor Mikhailovich Dostoevsky. Whoever heard his well-known speech on that day, of course, had a very clear idea of the tremendous power and influence human speech possesses when it is spoken with passionate sincerity before an audience that is spiritually prepared." But "Dostoevsky's speech when read," Koni adds, "does not produce a tenth of the impression it evoked when it was delivered."[18] However, Dostoevsky's speech as a work of art, as an artifact entering the stream of Russian culture, is an impressive document.

The artist par excellence for Turgenev, as we have noted, finds nature in himself, and with nature's calm and measure apprehends life in its essential relationships, laws, and continuities. He will see life, as it were, "as God sees it," under the aspect of eternity; his deepest vision, perhaps resembling that of Spinoza, will be marked by objectivity, epic detachment, a predilection for reconciliation and armistice rather than sharp-edged tragic resolution. Certainly the art of Turgenev is strongly shaped by this ideal.

Turgenev's short masterpiece "Live Relics" (1874)[19] is an outstanding realization of this ideal. The withered, hideous body of the servant girl Lukeriya is the very epitome of that dread and indifferent force of nature before which the narrator of "Enough" recoils in horror and despair. Yet though she is withered in body, her last days are a triumph of spirit and simultaneously the aesthetic element in her. She grows inwardly transformed in her contact with the living life of nature around her. "I see beautifully," she remarks at one point. The epiphany of Lukeriya is paradigmatic of the epiphany of Turgenev's art. He "sees beautifully," his vision is active, transitive; and what he sees and gives form to is not merely landscape or flowers, but the inner dynamics of human relations and strivings. The Russian poet Fyodor

Tyutchev, apropos Turgenev's *Sportsman's Notebook* (1852), observed
that one found in Turgenev "in complete equilibrium two elements
difficult to combine: sympathy for man and artistic feeling," as well as
a "no less remarkable union of the most intimate sense of the reality
of human life and a profound understanding of nature in all its poetry." [20] This observation holds for Turgenev's work at large.

What the narrator of "Journey to the Woodlands" sees as he peers
at the bucket yoke can only be described as a vision. His eyes riveted
almost hypnotically on the bucket yoke, he sees into nature's processes
and reveals to the reader his direct "understanding" of them. But in
the art of Turgenev understanding emerges more often through the
objective representation of phenomena and not through the author's
demonstratively burrowing into their significance. One continually
notes in Turgenev's criticism and correspondence an emphasis upon
the artist's interest in the "living person," "the living truth of human physiognomy," the "physiognomy of life," the "physiognomy of
Russians of the cultured class." To Vladimir L. Kign, who asked
Turgenev about the nature of "objective writing," Turgenev replied,
June 16, 1876:

> If the study of human physiognomy, of other people's lives, interests you
> *more* than the exposition of your own feelings and thoughts; if, for ex-
> ample, it is more pleasant for you faithfully and accurately to convey the
> exterior not only of a person but even of a simple thing than it is elo-
> quently and passionately to express what you feel when you see that thing
> or that person, then it means that you are an objective writer and may
> undertake a story or a novel. [21]

Yet it is important to recognize that Turgenev's accent on the "exterior," the surface, always carries with it the assumption that the eye
of the artist will perceive depths through those surfaces. Turgenev's
understanding of the relationship between surfaces and depths in life
is relevant to his aesthetic of observation in art. In a letter to Countess
Lambert, October 14, 1859, Turgenev writes:

> It recently occurred to me that there's something tragic in the fate of al-
> most every person—only often this tragic element is concealed from a
> person himself by the banal surface of life. The person who remains on
> the surface (and there are many such people) often fails even to suspect
> that he is the hero of a tragedy. A certain woman will complain of indi-

gestion and not even know that what she means is that her whole life has been shattered. For example, here [Turgenev's estate]: all around me are peaceful, quiet existences, yet if you take a close look, you see something tragic in each of them—something either their own or imposed on them by history, by the development of the people.[22]

Turgenev, of course, does not remain on the surface; as writer and thinker, he takes a close look at man and reality. Surface life or detail, whether animate or inanimate, always signals for Turgenev the inner world of man, society, or history. What he calls for in art is the revelation of psychology and philosophy in character; in gesture, line, action; in the configuration of human relations; in everything that passes, so to speak, before the eyes. "*The poet thinks in imagery*—this saying is absolutely indisputable and correct," Turgenev writes in his 1880 preface to his novels.[23] In many respects, Turgenev demands from the writer the art of a painter or sculptor for whom visual observation and representation are central; the fine artist must rely on visual imagery alone to explain his subject. Turgenev's early sketch "My Neighbor Radilov," in *A Sportsman's Notebook*, like so many of the sketches in that collection, provides a brilliant example of Turgenev's method, his uncanny sensitivity to surfaces and supposedly "unimportant detail" and their revelations of meanings in life and character. Turgenev's approach is almost cinematographic: what the reader learns about the characters is almost entirely what the narrator sees and hears. Yet what the narrator records is pregnant with meaning and drama. The narrator, significantly, often emerges in his *Sportsman's Notebook* as a voyeur: he secretly observes characters or happenings in the stance of an outsider, but his unexpected angle of vision permits him to grasp the moment of meaning in all its depths.

The writer must explore these depths, the souls and psychology of his characters, fully, but *before* presenting his characters to the reader, Turgenev insists. "'But 'this is psychology,' people will tell us. I daresay," Turgenev answers in his review of the playwright A. N. Ostrovsky's *The Poor Bride* in 1852, "but the psychologist must disappear in the artist, just as the skeleton disappears from the eyes under the living and warm body which it serves with firm but invisible support."[24] The same thoughts, buttressed again by reference to organic imagery, recurs almost ten years later in a letter to Konstantin Leontiev. "A poet must be a psychologist, but a secret one," he stipulates. In words which go to the heart of his artistic method, Turgenev adds: "He must know and feel the roots of phenomena, but represent only the phenomena themselves in their flowering and fading." [25]

Turgenev fully recognized, as did Tolstoy and Dostoevsky, the existence of a determining subsurface reality; he knew that the artist must "strive not only to grasp life in all its manifestations, but also to understand it, understand those laws which guide it, laws which do not always come to the surface." [26] To understand, however, does not mean to focus on the invisible. Thus he warns an amateur writer against trying to "capture all the oscillations of psychic states" [27] and Leontiev against losing himself in a maze of subtle thoughts, in the "unnecessary wealth of the arrière-pensée, secondary feelings and allusions. . . . Remember that however subtle and complex the inner structure of some tissue in the human body, the skin, for example, nonetheless its appearance is comprehensible and homogeneous." Carried away by his organic metaphor, Turgenev adds: "As a doctor, you ought to find this comparison congenial; yet you sometimes get lost, and you get lost in yourself. Look around you and busy yourself less with yourself. 'Greift nur hinaus in's volle Menschenleben. . . . Und wo Ihr's packt, da ist's interessant.'" [28] Noteworthy is the error Turgenev makes in citing lines from Goethe's "Prologue in the Theater" from *Faust*: instead of the word *hinein*, Turgenev uses *hinaus*: "Reach *out* into the fullness of human existence," rather than "*into*" that fullness.

Finally, Turgenev justifies his method by suggesting that the same device that conceals material also serves to maintain the reader's interest. In "psychological work," he writes in a letter, "two or three strokes which strike at the essence of character are all that are necessary, car le secret d'ennuyer est celui de tout dire." [29]

"Art is a plant," Turgenev once wrote. [30] The central images in this romantic organism metaphor are the root and the flower. In Turgenev's art, as in the plant, all energy flows into the visible and evocative form, and it is the flower, its flowering and fading, that is for Turgenev the fullest expression of the mission of art, the artist's preoccupation with beauty in form and form in beauty, and the pathos of human existence.

Turgenev, it is not surprising to learn, had difficulty with Tolstoy's psychological method, his "dialectics of the soul." He finds tedious, he writes in connection with *War and Peace*, "these quasi-subtle reflections and meditations and observations over his own feelings!"[31] Even more alien to him was Dostoevsky's psychological method. Dostoevsky's novel *The Raw Youth* struck Turgenev as "chaos." "My God, what a sour smell, and hospital stench, and perfectly pointless mumbling and psychological nit-picking!!" he exclaims in a letter to the Russian writer M. E. Saltykov-Shchedrin at the publication of Dostoevsky's novel.[32] In spite of the uncongeniality of certain aspects of Tolstoy's artistic method, Turgenev remained a devoted admirer of the man whom, on his deathbed, he called the "great writer of the Russian land."[33] Tolstoy was ultimately great to Turgenev because of his "*truth*."[34] Turgenev's general antipathy to Dostoevsky and his art remained firm.

Many western European critics in the late nineteenth and early twentieth centuries were attracted to the very elements which were alien to Turgenev's artistic method. The art of Turgenev, by comparison with that of Tolstoy or Dostoevsky, seemed limited to many writers and readers. The Irish novelist and critic George Moore, though defending Turgenev's art, gave vivid expression in 1891 to the restive mood of the new generation of readers and critics that was discovering Tolstoy and Dostoevsky: "In reading [Turgenev] we are conscious of a thinness, of an irritating reserve. He has often seemed to us to have left much unsaid, to have, as it were, only drawn the skin from his subject. Magnificently well is the task performed; but we should like to have seen the carcass disembowelled and hung up."[35] In Dostoevsky Europe certainly found an artist who dealt with human psychology and stress in a more radical way than did Turgenev: it found an artist who met head-on the impending tragedy of violence and social disintegration in western civilization, a tragedy of which Moore's naturalistic "carcass disembowelled and hung up" seems in retrospect to give some fearful hint.

Nearly thirty years later, A. Clutton-Brock, ridiculing Edward Garnett's efforts (admittedly not very successful) in a study of Turgenev (1927) to uphold the Russian writer against a tide of adverse criticism, compared Turgenev to "a very big man playing a very small instrument." Turgenev's books, Clutton-Brock smartly declared, are "exquisitely empty, like a Japanese room." He complains of Turgenev's "austere inhibition." "What passion, what knowledge, what obstinate questioning is implied in Bazarov, the hero of *Fathers and Sons*! But it is all implied. Turgenev will not speak out about it."[36]

Turgenev's "austere inhibition," his reluctance to "speak out," lay in an artistic method that preferred to convey thought through the veil of character, gesture, and action, through *artistic* thought; the obverse side of this preference was a skepticism toward *words*, a skepticism that finds its roots in part in Turgenev's rejection of the highflown rhetoric, the "eloquence" and "loud words" of romanticism and German philosophical idealism that found fertile soil in Russia in the 1830's and early 1840's.

In *Rudin*, a work deeply concerned with the inadequacies of language, the eloquent hero is not only involved in a dangerous "game of words" (very much like Dostoevsky's later Underground Man), but is under the illusion that he is the master of words.[37] "This word expresses my thought," Rudin remarks at one point. No, it does not, Turgenev insists on the deepest level of his novel. Rudin's thought is in the control of his language, in the control of words that can "confuse, destroy"; in control of a lofty eloquence that finds no firm support in his behavior or actions. Rudin, Lezhnev remarks, has the "cursed habit of pinning down every movement of life, his own and others', with words, like a butterfly with a pin." But life, like language, escapes him. In his art in general, Turgenev seems to have taken seriously the injunction of Jesus: "But I say unto you, That every idle word that men shall speak, they shall give account thereof in the day of judgment. For by thy words thou shalt be justified, and by thy words thou shalt be condemned" (Matthew 12:36–37).

Dostoevsky also looked upon the uncontrolled rhetoric of romanticism and philosophical idealism with deep skepticism, but he was drawn, often with parodic intent, to explosions of rhetoric and verbosity that drew their strength, paradoxically, from the very romantic sources he sought to negate. The Underground Man's preaching to Liza or Ivan Karamazov's "rebellion" over the suffering of children might serve as two examples. The verbal art of Turgenev moved increasingly in the direction of verbal limitation and understatement, one which accorded with his skeptical attitude over the possibility of possessing full truth and over man's capacity, in any case, to encompass it in words. "Thank God, there's more than one side to Truth," Turgenev writes in a letter to A. V. Druzhinin. The "full truth," he suggests, is inaccessible.[38] "You seek completeness and clarity in everything," Turgenev gently reproves Leo Tolstoy, "and you want all this immediately."[39] Such an optimal state of knowing and seeing, Turgenev believed, was not to be obtained, certainly not through mere words.

Clutton-Brock—a child, perhaps, of Victorian clutter—confused the silence of the Japanese room with emptiness. Yet the comparison of Turgenev's artistic world with that of a Japanese room is an apt one. Turgenev perceived a philosophical fullness and meaning in silence, an intimation of the complexity of "full truth." Turgenev conveyed that sense of complexity at the end of *Rudin* when his hero, chastened by his own unhappy experiences, confesses to Lezhnev: "I have spoiled my life and did not serve thought, as I ought to have done." There is considerable justice to Rudin's view that he had spoiled his life, though his notion that he might have "served thought" is a continuation of an illusion. His old friend Lezhnev cuts him short, however, with a compassionate "Molchi!" (literally, be silent! but here, enough of that, now!), adding: "Each of us remains what nature made him and one cannot demand more from him!" In fact, Lezhnev did demand more of Rudin: earlier he had been sharply critical of the vaporous and destructive, above all falsifying nature of Rudin's rhetoric and verbosity.

Yet Rudin's final sober words, his sense of total failure, Turgenev indicates, also falsify the full truth of his botched life. ("A good word," Lezhnev remarks at one point, "is also a deed.") The call for "silence," on the symbolic plane of the narrative, brings us close to a more complete truth of Rudin, just as earlier Lezhnev's critique of Rudin's eloquence and verbosity was an effort to expose falsification of another sort. Yet Turgenev himself acknowledges the limits of limitation, of restraint, of measure—the limits, finally, to any attempt to "pin down" reality with words: "I fear, I avoid, phrases,"[40] he wrote in one of his aphoristic "poems in prose" (*Senilia*), "but the fear of phrases is also a pretension. Thus, between these two foreign words [*pretenzija, fraza*], between pretension and phrases, our complex life oscillates and hesitates." In *Rudin* Turgenev gives expression to that oscillation. In his novel, as in his work at large, Turgenev hesitates to "speak out," to make final distinctions, to *conclude*. In the end, the accent of his aesthetic of observation is upon complexity, a state of being or condition that words more often than not can only violate.

Not the flower but the root is the direct focus of Dostoevsky's "total realism." "They call me a psychologist," Dostoevsky observes in his notebook. "I am only a realist in the higher sense; that is, I depict all the depths of the human soul." [41] His realism, to borrow Turgenev's words, is loaded with a "wealth of veiled thoughts, secondary feelings and allusions"; it does not neglect surface, visible day-to-day reality, but it affirms, as in *Notes from the House of the Dead*, for example, that visible reality may be profoundly deceptive, at least as far as the everyday eye is concerned. One must penetrate through the "repulsive crust," through surface reality, Dostoevsky insisted, to arrive at the authentic core of human decency. To Turgenev's aesthetic of observation one may counterpose Dostoevsky's aesthetic of direct cognition. The artist must see, Dostoevsky believed, with the eyes of the soul. And he remained faithful to this image when he wrote elsewhere: "My critics understand only what goes on before their eyes, but because of nearsightedness they themselves are not only unable to look ahead, but cannot even understand how for another person the future results of present events can be crystal clear." [42] For Dostoevsky, art, vision is prophecy.

With respect to areas of psychological interest, scholars have noted that Dostoevsky and Turgenev often explore similar grounds. Turgenev's "Hamlet of Shchigrovo County" (1849), "The Diary of a Superfluous Man" (1849), *Rudin* (1855), and "A Correspondence" (1856) fully anticipate major psychological and philosophical emphases in Dostoevsky's *Notes from the Underground*. The Russian critic G. A. Byaly has even suggested that the notion of a radical opposition in psychological style between Dostoevsky and Turgenev has been "greatly exaggerated." There is some basis for this assertion, but largely, perhaps, with reference to some of Turgenev's writing in the 1850's. But even in his comparison of some of these works with *Notes from the Underground* Byaly underscores a crucial opposition. Thus the notion of "malice" in Turgenev's "Diary of a Superfluous Man" is manifested "within the limits of a psychological norm," whereas Dostoevsky consciously negates that norm, strives to violate it, intensifies the psychological situation to the "limits of the tragic, grotesque, fantasy, frenzy." [43]

Such hyperbole and straining of emotions were indeed uncharacteristic of Turgenev. The sense of a normative reality—aesthetically, a sense of measure—worked against this potential for hyperbole. For Dostoevsky, on the other hand, essential reality is revealed not in the ordinary moment, but in a moment of crisis, of rupture, of moral, spiritual, psychological breakdown. Psychology in Dostoevsky, eruptive, is typically "from the underground"; in *Notes from the Underground* that is almost the only perspective. Turgenev's distaste for this kind of psychologizing may be surmised from the outburst of one of Turgenev's characters in Turgenev's *Virgin Soil* (1876). Nezhdanov rails against "carrying on with one's own vile little thoughts and sensations, burrowing into all kinds of psychological ramifications and subtleties." He has no patience with the person who takes his own "sick, nervous irritability and caprice for courageous indignation, for the honest malice of a man of conviction! Oh, Hamlet, Hamlet, Danish prince, how does one escape from your shadow? How shall one cease imitating you in everything, even in ignominious enjoyment of self-laceration?"

In Dostoevsky's novelistic universe, the typical hero is very far from the "norm," or even a strong sense of the norm. He is far from that regulatory "nature" which provides Turgenev and the narrator of "A Journey to the Woodlands" with such a stable frame of reference, such a strong sense of inner order and equilibrium in the universe. Indeed, the whole quest of the Dostoevsky hero, consciously or unconsciously, is for the ethical and religious norm. "There's no order in me, no higher order," Dostoevsky's beloved Dmitry Karamazov exclaims in anguish as he thunders across the stage of Russian life. The principle of order which reasserts itself in the epilogues to Pushkin's "Queen of Spades," Turgenev's *Fathers and Sons*, or Tolstoy's *War and Peace* (the ordinary routine of work, the affairs of the family, marriage, reproduction) is generally absent in Dostoevsky's novelistic universe. Such epilogues, it is true, have a distinct middle-class flavor, but for Turgenev, middle-class values appear to be precisely those of nature.

Harmony, measure, equilibrium are key words in Turgenev's aesthetics of nature and in his vision of essential normative reality. This Turgenevian reality turns out to be full of cracks and fissures, contradictions and tragedy, for his heroes, yet like nature, it is self-restorative and hurls aside all those who like Bazarov in *Fathers and Sons* upset its equilibrium.

The Russian critic N. N. Strakhov, in an essay on *Fathers and Sons* in 1862, defined Turgenevian reality in the following way:

> If we look at the picture presented by the novel more calmly and at some distance, we readily note that though Bazarov stands head and shoulders above all the other characters, though he majestically crosses the stage, triumphant, worshiped, respected, loved and lamented, there is nonetheless something that as a whole is superior to Bazarov. What indeed is that something? If we closely attend the matter, we will find that that higher something is not any of the characters, but the *life* that inspires them. Higher than Bazarov is that fear, that love, those tears he inspires. Higher than Bazarov is that stage he crosses. The enchantment of nature, the charm of art, feminine love, family love, parents' love, *even* religion—all that, living, full, powerful, is the background against which Bazarov is drawn. That background is so clear, so sparkling, that the huge figure of Bazarov is etched upon it clearly, but at the same time somberly.[44]

These elements of Turgenevian reality may be found in Dostoevsky's novelistic universe, but they do not dominate. The world of Dostoevsky's major characters, their actions, their searing questions and their self-analyses, put this Turgenevian reality in question if they do not in fact rise out of a reality which is completely devoid of "background," or what Dostoevsky would call "foundations."

The notion of a higher order can also be found in Dostoevsky. If one concentrates attention, for example, on Father Zosima's vision in *The Brothers Karamazov* of ultimate reality in man and the universe, one might conclude that Dostoevsky conceives of nature and the cosmos in the aspect of world harmony, as a great ocean in a state of equilibrium wherein all flows and interacts. Certainly this vision is present and plays a structuring role in the Dostoevsky novel. It is the other dialectical pole of Dostoevsky's worldview—a primary vision of man and reality as turbulent, destructive, and contradictory—that is the real given and point of departure in Dostoevsky's novels. It is outside the monastery, outside Zosima's aesthetic and religious utopia, that one discovers the real material of Dostoevsky's "nature": the morally and aesthetically shapeless world of the Karamazovs, a world in which, in the somewhat sardonic language of the Russian writer V. V. Rozanov, "Russians have experienced a *fearful tragedy of the soul*, a tragedy precisely of world coldness, 'while the planet was flying from Hercules to Aries,' and nobody loved anybody, suffered because of this and still did not love. Of course, Dostoevsky's ascribing to the elder Zosima of 'such a love for all things,' for birds and the like, for children, etc., is very suspicious. Exactly so 'one blows into one's hands which have frozen stiff' or 'stamps with one's feet in freezing weather' to keep warm. Unfortunate ones. And we will pray for them."[45]

"Reality strives toward fragmentation," remarks the narrator of *Notes from the House of the Dead* in an extraordinary phrase apropos the impossibility of reducing or simplifying reality into categories or typologies. What is striking, of course, is the use of the verb *strive*, the conception of reality as active, dynamic, centrifugal in movement. The necessity of mastering this explosive force of "reality"—not only in the realm of sensuality (as in Turgenev's world as well), but in crucial moral, aesthetic, and even psychic areas—is a central problem in Dostoevsky's universe. The art of Dostoevsky, many of its unique and innovative features, is itself an expression of this striving to master centrifugal reality, chaos, in himself, in man, in history.

Harmony, measure, equilibrium, health, and *beauty* are, of course, decisive words and concepts in Dostoevsky's worldview. But these values are not to be found in man or nature as organic attributes; it is not "nature," not any "law of nature" or any unalterable law of earthly life, that introduces these elements into man or society. These are attributes, in Dostoevsky's view, of divinity and faith, of a lofty spirituality in a quest for form and faith. This lofty spirituality enables man to transcend pure "nature" in himself. What health, equilibrium, and happiness there is on earth is a function of man's tension toward the ethical and religious ideal. "Man strives on earth for an ideal which is *contrary* to his nature," Dostoevsky wrote in his notebook in 1864. "When man does not fulfill the law of striving for the ideal, that is, does not sacrifice his 'I' through love for people or another being . . . he experiences suffering and has called this condition sin. And thus man continually must experience suffering, which is balanced by the divine joy in fulfillment of the Law, i.e., sacrifice. Precisely here earthly equilibrium is to be found. Otherwise the earth would be senseless."[46] The pawnbroker's frightening vision in "A Gentle Creature" of "nature" and the "earth" as a stagnant, death-ridden wasteland is a direct projection of a life without love or sacrifice. Movement in Dostoevsky's universe is the illness and cure. Reality *strives* toward fragmentation, but man strives toward the ideal.

Turgenev's philosophical thought strangely parallels Dostoevsky's. Turgenev, too, sees in man's tension toward the ideal the most meaningful and creative stance of man as he faces his mortality. But here there is no religious faith, as in the case of Dostoevsky, no ecstatic religious optimism. The more purely aesthetic content of Turgenev's tension toward the ideal is suggested at the conclusion of his sketch "Enough," whereas its ethical emphasis, the idea of heroic self-sacrifice, is most clearly felt in Turgenev's concept of Don Quixote in his crucial essay "Hamlet and Don Quixote" (1860). "We are creators . . . for the hour," declares the artist-narrator of "Enough." Each of us is born with a destiny to fulfill. "Each of us more or less dimly understands his significance, feels his kinship to something lofty, eternal—and lives, must live, in the moment and for the moment. Sit in the mud, my good man, and strain for the heavens! The greatest among us are precisely those who more profoundly than others recognize this radical contradiction." Don Quixote, in Turgenev's view, embodies perfectly this contradiction, this striving for an ideal. To what does he give expression? "Faith first of all; faith in something eternal, unshakable, in truth, in a word, in a truth which lies *outside* the individual and which demands service and sacrifice."[47]

The concept of "radical contradiction" is a central one in Turgenev's artistic thought; yet the contradiction in Turgenev is less radical and, one may say, less tragic than it is in Dostoevsky. The cry of pain of Turgenev's dying artist ("Enough") before a nature that "knows no art as it knows no freedom, as it knows no good" is not as deep or authentic as the cry of the dying Ippolit Terentiev in *The Idiot* before the "dark, insolent and senselessly eternal force" of "nature." For the "nature" against which Turgenev rebels turns out to be his model as an artist. The "radical contradiction" is resolved, first of all, in aesthetic terms. In "Enough" the artist-narrator criticizes the finite character of art and beauty. But in the end he finds beauty justified in each of its separate, though finite, incarnations. The narrator sets forth what might be described as the aesthetic, and ultimately philosophical, canon of Turgenev's art:

> Only the transient is beautiful, said Schiller; and Nature herself, in the ceaseless play of her emerging and disappearing forms, is not hostile to beauty. Does she not bedeck the most evanescent of her offspring—the petals of flowers, wings of butterflies—with the most enchanting colors; it is not she who endows them with such refined contours? Beauty does not need to live endlessly in order to be eternal—one moment is enough for it.

And though the narrator goes on to express a typically Turgenevian ache, goes on to say that what he has said is true, "but only where there is no individual consciousness, no man, no freedom"; though he juxtaposes the endless reincarnations of the wing of a butterfly with the absolutely finite character of every individual and unique consciousness, yet in the end he finds man's destination in his creativity, however short-lived. Through our giving expression to the unique that lies within us, Turgenev seems to suggest, through our striving for the lofty, we make contact with the eternal. Turgenev the artist chooses finally to give himself over to the "moment" and to the creation of beauty in the moment, to the depiction of phenomena in their flowering and fading, to Nature and life in the "ceaseless play of her emerging and disappearing forms." In the end, art triumphs over philosophy by becoming its own justification.

"But what is this life?" Turgenev asks rhetorically in an early letter to Pauline Viardot in 1849 apropos of the life of the universe, of the world of plants or insects in a drop of water:

> Oh, I do not know anything about it, but I do know that for the moment it is everything, it is in full flowering, in full swing; I do not know if all this will last for a long time, but at least for the moment it exists, it makes my blood flow in my veins without my doing anything about it, and it makes the stars appear in the heavens like pimples on the skin, effortlessly and without its seeming a great merit. This thing that is indifferent, imperious, voracious, egoistic, encompassing, is life, nature, God; call it what you will. . . . All [this vitality in the world] is able to do nothing else but follow the Law of its existence which is Life.[48]

Here is the heart of Turgenev, the objective artist whose love of life expresses itself in a passion to reincarnate multiform reality. Yet side by side with this love of life, as we have seen, is a melancholy, a gnawing consciousness of the transiency of life, man, and happiness, which links him, perhaps, with his favorite philosophers, Schopenhauer and Pascal, a kind of despair before the infinite. "I can't bear the sky," Turgenev wrote to Pauline Viardot apropos the emotion aroused in him by the sight of a green branch covered with young green leaves etched against the blue sky. He is moved by the contrast between the little branch with its fragile stirring of life and the eternal and immense emptiness of the sky. "I can't bear the sky—but life, reality, its caprices, its accidentalities, its patterns, its fleeting beauty . . . all this I adore." [49]

Turgenev's love of life, his sense for the objective, concrete universal in life, dilutes his primordial dread of eternity. Indeed, his despair is never fully realized in the stern, tragic terms of Dostoevsky. Tragedy in Turgenev's universe is not seldom modified, mitigated, almost neutralized by the author's pantheistic sense of "life, nature, God." In this respect the concluding lines of *Fathers and Sons* provide eloquent testimony. Bazarov is dead: Bazarov, that protagonist who comes closest to giving really tragic embodiment to Turgenev's skepticism and despair. Bazarov's parents come to visit his grave. Is it possible that their tears and prayers are fruitless, that sacred love is impotent? asks the narrator. He replies: "Oh no! However passionate, sinful, rebellious the heart that is concealed in the grave, the flowers, growing on it, peacefully look at us with their innocent eyes: they speak to us not alone about eternal tranquility, about that great tranquility of 'indifferent' nature; they speak also about eternal reconciliation and about endless life."

Turgenev's hosanna to life, his ultimate faith in it, despite all his melancholy, his willingness in the end to accept the arbitration of nature, contrasts with Dostoevsky's tragic questioning precisely of life, nature, God. As is well known, Dostoevsky parodied Turgenev's sketch "Enough," along with several other works of Turgenev, in *The Devils*. Not the least irritant to Dostoevsky may have been Turgenev's concept of "radical contradiction" and (in "Enough" at least) his strongly esthetic and nonreligious resolution of the contradiction. For it is perhaps only in Dostoevsky's art that the radical contradiction may be said to be truly radical and unresolved, only in Dostoevsky that aesthetic and moral Don Quixotism acquires truly tragic character and serves to symbolize the human condition. The sense of "mud" and of "heaven," of disfiguration and opposing, perfect form; the despair over the evil in man, yet ecstatic faith in the transfiguring power of spiritual beauty—all this found supreme expression in Dostoevsky's art.

Beauty for Turgenev is tangible, real, however evanescent in life or nature. "The beautiful is the only thing that is immortal. . . . Nowhere does it shine more intensely than in the human personality." Few Russian writers equaled Turgenev in the perception of beauty and in the artistic crafting and modeling of the human physiognomy. For Dostoevsky, regardless of Ivan's delight in the "sticky little leaves," the highest beauty is not of this world. The beauty that in Turgenev's world conveys a poignant sense of vanished happiness, of man's incompleteness and yearning for some higher destiny, acquires philosophical and religious content in Dostoevsky's art. Beauty in the highest perception for Dostoevsky is linked with suffering and a sense of paradise lost. The motif of lost paradise is profoundly tragic not only because it expresses a deep yearning of man for an impossible return to innocence, but because it expresses his anguished quest for unity and balance. The classical harmonies, measure, and proportion, the beauty that Turgenev finds embodied in the living forms and processes of nature, in the play of character and human relations, Dostoevsky seeks finally in ecstatic aesthetic-religious experience. Turgenev, in his art and through his art, offers to man the epic vision of nature-divine; Dostoevsky holds out to man, tragic man, an aesthetic-spiritual transfiguration apocalyptic in character, inseparable from the Word of God.

The art of Dostoevsky, his vision of reality, challenges the very sense of unity and wholeness from which Turgenev's art emerges. When one imposes on this foundation the whole superstructure of social, psychological, and philosophical differences between these two writers, it is not difficult to understand Turgenev's deep-seated dislike of the art of Dostoevsky. Yet in turn, the art of Turgenev, quite apart from ideological differences, was part of the pathos of Dostoevsky's self-conception as an artist. Not without reason did Dostoevsky once refer to Turgenev as a "colossal artist," acknowledge in him (in *Crime and Punishment*) "the most artistic of all modern writers," and bracket him as pure artist with the writer he most revered in Russian literature—Alexander Pushkin.

The very values that are central in Dostoevsky's higher aesthetic— classical beauty, harmony, measure—are to be found embodied not only in Turgenev's art, but in his personality. Dostoevsky's early admiration, as a young writer, of Turgenev is undoubtedly linked with a longing for these values. It is noteworthy that one of his earliest responses to Turgenev projects a largely aesthetic, one might even say Apollonian, image. Not long after his first meeting with Turgenev, Dostoevsky wrote his brother in 1845: "But, brother, what sort of person is he? I too have almost fallen in love with him. A poet, a man of talent, an aristocrat, handsome, wealthy, intelligent, educated, twenty-five years old—I do not know what nature has denied him. Finally: an inexhaustibly straightforward, splendid personality, shaped in the best school."[50]

Joseph Conrad, who detested Dostoevsky, echoed this hymn to Apollo in a 1917 letter to Edward Garnett apropos of Turgenev:

> For only think! Every gift has been heaped on his cradle: absolute sanity and the deepest sensibility, the clearest vision and the quickest responsiveness, penetrating insight and unfailing generosity of judgement, an exquisite perception of the visible world and an unerring instinct for the significant, for the essential in the life of men and women, the clearest mind, the warmest heart, the largest sympathy—and all that in perfect measure. There's enough there to ruin the prospects of any writer.[51]

In conclusion, Conrad adds a line which almost certainly contains a reference to Dostoevsky: "For you know very well, my dear Edward, that if you had Antinous himself in a booth of the world's-fair, and killed yourself in protesting that his soul was as perfect as his body, you wouldn't get one per cent of the crowd struggling next door for a sight of the Double-headed Nightingale or of some weak-kneed giant grinning through a horse collar."[52]

It is remarkable how consistent the critics and commentators are in identifying the final statement of Turgenev's personality, art, and outlook not with "radical contradiction" or dissonances but with the attributes of his beloved nature: balance, measure, harmony. At the funeral of Turgenev, Ernest Renan stressed the "reconciling" character of Turgenev's art: "What in others produced discord in Turgenev became fundamental harmony"; in him contradictions were reconciled.[53] Renan is excessive, without doubt, in his emphasis upon the element of "harmony" in Turgenev. Yet one might say that Turgenev's artistic vision involves not a full resolution of conflicts but a recognition and toleration of the coexistence of contradictory elements in personal and social life. Harmony here is not the ironing out of all conflict but the open-ended approach to conflict, contradiction, error—everything implicit in what Conrad called Turgenev's "unfailing generosity of judgment," his instinct for the significant, his sympathy.

The qualities that Renan, Conrad, Virginia Woolf, Edmund Wilson, and others single out in Turgenev are not at all conspicuous in the art, personality, or outlook of Dostoevsky. "Everywhere and in everything, I go to the uttermost limits; all my life I have crossed the last line," Dostoevsky wrote Apollon Maikov apropos of his gambling mania.[54] As the Russian scholar Leonid Grossman has observed in connection with this remark, "This 'maximalism' of character, this surplus and extremity of feeling, this unrestraint in emotions, to a great extent defined his nature and lay at the foundation of his work."[55] There was very little leisure in Dostoevsky's life, the kind he envied in Turgenev, Goncharov, or Tolstoy. He was committed to deadlines almost all his life. No other Russian writer, Dostoevsky once wrote, ever worked in such difficult conditions. "Turgenev would die from the very thought."[56] Dostoevsky could be ecstatic or embittered, extraordinarily receptive and warm, or hostile and withdrawn, but moderation of judgment, magnanimity, equipoise, were not attributes of his personality, and his instinct was certainly not to see things in measure and proper proportion.

Yet the very absence of these attributes of "middle-of-the-road" culture is the virtue of his art, his radical, probing nature, his extraordinary responsiveness to suffering and injustice, his attention to the "radical contradictions" of man and history. "What a strange nature you have," writes the heroine of Dostoevsky's first novel, *Poor Folk*, to her friend and would-be benefactor Makar Devushkin. "You take everything to heart beyond measure . . . even now you live only by what I live: my joys, my sorrows, my heart! If you take everything that relates to other people so much to heart and if you sympathize so strongly in everything, then really you will turn out to be a most unhappy man." Here without doubt an aspect of Dostoevsky is reflected in Devushkin. Ivan Karamazov, at the other end of Dostoevsky's work, inherits, as it were, this trait of Devushkin's character. His inability to accept a world harmony that is based on a single child's unexpiated tears, his insistence on living with his own unsatisfied indignation, was precisely a failure to see things in their proper proportions. And indeed Dostoevsky criticizes Ivan for his "all-or-nothing" mentality, for his inflexible, rectilinear, moral logic, and his refusal to accept the reality of evil. Yet Ivan's rebellion, in the intensity of its response to suffering and the power of its moral protest, touches spiritual heights rarely reached in world literature. His rebellion is absurd in its moral logic, but as Ivan himself remarks, "Absurdities are only too necessary on earth. The world rests on absurdities, and without them, perhaps, nothing at all would have happened in it."

Dostoevsky, the Parisian critic Elie Halperine-Kaminsky wrote prophetically in 1894, "will only be truly understood when the mounting tension of our century has reached its climax."[57] The tension of the century, real or fancied, contributed powerfully to the near eclipse of Turgenev, at least among some of the elite reading public. Tolstoy and Dostoevsky were making their presence felt on the European scene. "No one, or hardly anyone, thinks of reading [Turgenev] at the moment," wrote another Parisian critic in 1894.[58] V. V. Rozanov dismissed Turgenev's work as topical in character and lacking in depth. Turgenev's characters, he wrote, "responded to the interests of their moment, were understood in their time, but now have left behind an exclusively artistic attractiveness."[59] "With that year [1899]," Conrad wrote Edward Garnett, "one may say, with some justice, that the age of Turgenev had come to an end too."[60] "The Russia which Turgenev represented is dead," wrote the German writer Paul Ernst in 1889; "the new young Russia is represented by people like Tolstoy and Dostoevsky."[61] "Long since, the issues that he fought out have ceased to be of any actual interest. . . . Turgenev is no longer a teacher or even a ferment. His work has become pure art," wrote Dmitry S. Mirsky in his *History of Russian Literature* in 1926.[62]

There were, of course, notable and stubborn holdouts against this new attitude, such as Joseph Conrad, W. D. Howells, or Henry James—James, who called Turgenev the "novelist's novelist—an artistic influence extraordinarily valuable and ineradicably established." He admired him for the "genial freedom" of his approach to the "innermost world, the world of our finer consciousness."[63] Then, too, there was Thomas Mann, who in 1914 remarked that he had just reread Turgenev with the "same zeal and rapture as twenty years before" and even entertained the idea of writing a major essay on him "chiefly because it seems to me that at the present time Turgenev has been underrated in favor of Dostoevsky in a most ungrateful and unseemly manner, indeed looked down upon. I shall be glad to speak out for him."[64] Louis Aragon expressed a great admiration for Turgenev. And Virginia Woolf admired Turgenev's rare art of combining the "photograph and the poem," the "fact and the vision." Overall, he gives us, in comparison with other novelists, "a generalized and harmonized picture of life . . . we are conscious of some further control and order."[65] Yet by the middle of the twentieth century, the very notions of balance and control seemed fanciful and unreal. The "mounting tension" of the century had reached its climax. Dostoevsky, among the Russians, seemed the only authoritative voice. Turgenev no longer seemed "relevant."

Such a view of Turgenev, of course, is entirely superficial. His art, with its aesthetic and ethical values of measure, moderation, and restraint, its accent on "middle culture," its acceptance of limitation, its open-ended view of human conflict, its profound understanding of human character, its realization of "seeing beautifully," and, last but not least, its tonic skepticism and principled war on rhetoric—all this is profoundly relevant to spirit, culture, and civilization.

Unbearable Questions

Two Views of Gogol and the Critical Synthesis

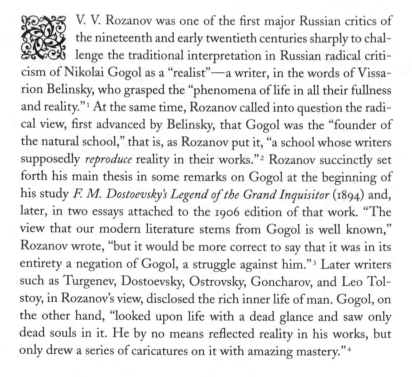V. V. Rozanov was one of the first major Russian critics of the nineteenth and early twentieth centuries sharply to challenge the traditional interpretation in Russian radical criticism of Nikolai Gogol as a "realist"—a writer, in the words of Vissarion Belinsky, who grasped the "phenomena of life in all their fullness and reality."[1] At the same time, Rozanov called into question the radical view, first advanced by Belinsky, that Gogol was the "founder of the natural school," that is, as Rozanov put it, "a school whose writers supposedly *reproduce* reality in their works."[2] Rozanov succinctly set forth his main thesis in some remarks on Gogol at the beginning of his study *F. M. Dostoevsky's Legend of the Grand Inquisitor* (1894) and, later, in two essays attached to the 1906 edition of that work. "The view that our modern literature stems from Gogol is well known," Rozanov wrote, "but it would be more correct to say that it was in its entirety a negation of Gogol, a struggle against him."[3] Later writers such as Turgenev, Dostoevsky, Ostrovsky, Goncharov, and Leo Tolstoy, in Rozanov's view, disclosed the rich inner life of man. Gogol, on the other hand, "looked upon life with a dead glance and saw only dead souls in it. He by no means reflected reality in his works, but only drew a series of caricatures on it with amazing mastery."[4]

Rozanov's indisputable contribution to the history of Gogol criticism was to redirect attention to the unique, stylistically distinct features of Gogol's art and the grotesque character of Gogol's vision; to subject the much abused words *realism* and *reality* in Russian radical criticism to sharp critical scrutiny; and finally to pose again the relation of the great Russian novelists to Gogol. At the same time, Rozanov, in his efforts to rescue Gogol criticism from radical oversimplification, drove the question of realism and the deception of reality in Gogol's works into the opposite corner: he denied that Gogol's art had any meaningful connection with Russian reality. The full import of this view will be lost on the reader who imagines that Rozanov was concerned alone with the purely literary or stylistic side of the matter, namely, the manner, "realistic" or caricatural, with which Gogol approaches reality. On close inspection, Rozanov's view that Gogol "by no means reflected reality in his works" may be seen as a final reaction—in Rozanov's case, a conservative one—on the part of nineteenth-century Russian literature and criticism to the grimness of Gogol's vision of man, in the first instance, Russian man and reality. What lies in the balance between the conception of Gogol as a depictor of reality on the one hand and a caricaturist or even pure inventor of reality on the other is the definition of Russian man and history, tragic questions of history and culture which have preoccupied Russian writers from Pushkin and Chaadaev to Gorky, Blok, and Mandelshtam. These questions, which of course were at the center of attention of social critics such as Belinsky and Herzen, are only very obliquely touched upon by Rozanov in his discussions of Gogol, although they are present in his discussion of Dostoevsky.

The great critical debate over Gogol's art, or over Gogolian "reality," it will be my contention, conceals a judgment of Russian man and reality, and, in turn a response to that judgment. In this debate (and we are concerned with it only at its highest levels) we shall find Belinsky and Rozanov, at least at first glance, occupying opposing points of view. In this same debate we shall find that Dostoevsky's views, as they may be discerned in his first novel, *Poor Folk* (1846), constitute a complex artistic synthesis of the opposing points of view of the debate. Belinsky, Rozanov, and Dostoevsky will be the three

points of reference in our discussion. All three writers were preoccupied with Gogol, or more accurately struggled with what appeared to
each of them a terrible judgment or prophecy concerning Russia. Belinsky built an imposing pediment of social criticism on Gogol's art,
though this criticism was by no means devoid of aesthetic insight.
Dostoevsky's view of Gogol was strongly influenced by Belinsky's, yet
it was free of the subterfuge and tendentiousness that characterized
much of Belinsky's public utterances. Rozanov's view of Gogol certainly rests heavily on an interpretation or, as I shall contend, a mis-
interpretation of Dostoevsky's position in *Poor Folk*. Subtly tendentious in its own way, despite its markedly aesthetic orientation, it
sought not only to refute Belinsky but to advance, half facetiously perhaps, a new idealist interpretation of Gogol's relation to Russian
reality.

Pushkin, not Gogol, insists Rozanov, is the real founder of the
natural school, always faithful to the nature of man, faithful also to his
fate. Pushkin, writes Rozanov in "Pushkin i Gogol," is the "symbol of
life: he is all movement."[5] His art "provides the norm for a correct
relation to reality" (*dlja pravil'-nogo otnošenija k dejstvitel'nosti*), constitutes "an ideal for normal healthy development."[6] "There is nothing
forced in him; there is no sick imagination or incorrect feeling. Hence
the individuality of his characters which are never reduced to general
types. A type in literature is already a shortcoming; it is a generalization; that is, a certain alteration of reality," writes Rozanov in a veiled
attack on much of Russian radical criticism.[7]

Gogol emerges in Rozanov's criticism as the antithesis to Pushkin.
In Gogol's art there are "absolutely no live people: only tiny wax figures artfully grimacing, seemingly moving but, in fact, motionless."[8]
We laugh at these figures, according to Rozanov, observe them as
though through a magnifying glass, "but we find nothing in common
with them; there is nothing that connects us with them."[9] Gogol is
the "progenitor of the ironic mood in our society and literature."[10] But
his "morbid imagination" often created "a second world above the real
one and then strove to adapt the first to the second." Gogol's art is the
antithesis, then, of Pushkin's art, which does not "alter, distort, deflect
from the tendency already embedded in the vital nature of man himself," which "does not hinder life."[11] Gogol's art moves in two direc-

tions only: "one of intense and aimless lyricism drawing upwards into lofty realms, and one of irony directed at everything that lies below." Both lyricism and irony in Gogol are essentially divorced from reality, but they are intimately related to each other. For the "lyricism in Gogol is always pity, sorrow, 'unseen tears through visible laughter' which somehow mixes with this laughter, but, remarkably, never precedes it but always follows it. What we have here is a great pity for man as he is depicted, a sorrow of an artist over the law of his own creation, his wail before the astounding picture which he cannot paint differently . . . but which, having sketched it that way, he nonetheless also despises and hates—though not without admiration."[12]

Rozanov no less than Gogol admires the artistry of the "astounding picture." Yet he, too, like the later Gogol (and, as we shall see, Dostoevsky's Devushkin) recoils from that picture as an authentic statement about man. Behind Rozanov's quite lucid efforts to distinguish Pushkin's representation of reality from Gogol's attitude toward reality, lies a deep mistrust of Gogol's vision of man, of his "imagination with its wrong relation to reality, its wrong relation to dreams"; nothing, Rozanov insists, can conceal "those everlasting corpses, and with them [Gogol's] truth that man can only despise man." In Gogol there is "an absence of confidence and respect for man."[13] Behind Gogol's literary method lies an incorrect view of life, or as Rozanov puts it, Gogol's "imagination with its wrong relation to reality, its wrong relation to dream." "Not only in our literature, but in all world literature [Gogol] stands the lonely genius, and his world is unlike any other world. He alone lived in it. But for us to enter this world, to connect him with our life and even to judge of it by the huge wax picture forged by this miraculous craftsman, would mean to lift a hand against ourselves."[14]

Rozanov's remarks leave little doubt of his sense of the shocking moral-spiritual and social implications of Gogol's art and universe. His Gogol criticism may rightly be viewed as a broadside attack on the radical critic Belinsky's interpretation of Gogol. In one of his early pieces on Gogol, "On the Russian Story and the Stories of Mr. Gogol" (1835), Belinsky declared that Gogol's special originality "lies in a comic inspiration always conquered by a deep feeling of sadness."[15] "Yes, Mr. Gogol does his playacting very nicely, and although one has to be obtuse in the extreme not to understand his irony, yet this irony suits him very well indeed. However, all this is only a device; Gogol's true humor springs from a correct view of life."[16] Rozanov, of course, completely reversed this emphasis of Belinsky. The radical critic notes the irony of Gogol, but what for him is playacting is for Rozanov the main center of gravity in Gogol. Belinsky "sees through" Gogol's irony to "a correct view of life," that is, a deeper and enlightened social apprehension of a negative Russian reality. Rozanov, on the other hand, finds that same irony opaque, perhaps even hallucinatory, and constituting in general a "wrong relation to reality," a gloomy distortion of reality as we know it. The unity of Gogol's style and content for Rozanov is to be found in the grotesque forms and figures of Gogol; lifeless, they reflect the unreal, fabulous world of Gogol's morbid imagination. Gogol's art, as Rozanov and others, such as A. L. Bem and Vladimir Nabokov, have conceived it is essentially theatre-for-itself; Gogol's characters, or puppets, relate only to this uniquely conceived theater. For Belinsky and many of his contemporaries, on the other hand, Russia itself was a theatre of the absurd. In this connection, we may recall Herzen's remark in *My Past and Thoughts* (1852–1868) apropos of one of his relatives: "He was one of those uniquely misshapen creatures who are only possible in Russia where life is so uniquely misshapen."[17]

Did Belinsky evade or suppress the question of the unity of form and content in his effort to harness Gogol's art to the task of radical social criticism and transformation? Was he unaware of what Rozanov accents as the grotesque, fantastic, even morbidly weird character of Gogol's artistic universe? Belinsky without question responded first of all to Gogol's art as exposé, as social criticism. He hailed the "social poet"[18] in Gogol, the "poet of real life"[19] who told the brutal truth about Russian life. "Is it surprising," he writes in "On the Russian Story and the Stories of Mr. Gogol," "that the distinguishing feature of recent works in general consists in a merciless frankness, in the fact that life in these works is, as it were, exposed to shame in all its nakedness, in all its frightful disfiguration (*bezobrazie*) and in all its solemn beauty, disclosed as though with an anatomical knife? We demand not an ideal of life but life itself as it is. Whether it be bad or good, yet we do not want to adorn it, because we believe that in poetic representation it is equally beautiful in the first or second case, precisely because it is truth; and where there is truth, there is also poetry." [20]

The link between the social importance, or message, of Gogol's art, and its aesthetic form for Belinsky lay precisely in the notion of "frightful disfiguration." The art of Gogol, he wrote in his famous "Letter to Gogol" (1847), had powerfully contributed to the "self-consciousness of Russia by giving it the possibility of looking at itself as it were in a mirror." [21] Belinsky well understood that Gogol's mirror was crooked. But Russian reality, Russian man, in Belinsky's view, was in the profoundest sense unformed, grotesque, disfigured. Literary types in his view conveyed the essence of this melancholy reality. Applicable to Gogol is "the definition of art as reproduction of reality in all its truth. Here the crux of the matter is in its *types*, while the *ideal* [here the Hegelian ideal] is to be understood not as the prettifying of reality and therefore as falsification but as the relations in which the author juxtaposes the types he has created in conformity with the idea which his work is intended to develop." [22] Authentic reproduction of reality, then, is not naive mimesis but reproduction of the essence or essential characteristic of reality; it is a generalization of reality in the Hegelian sense.

It was in his types, Belinsky wrote again in "A Reply to 'Moskvitjanin'" (1847), that Gogol emerged the "great painter of banality in life," an artist "who thoroughly grasps his subject in all its depth and breadth and grasps it in the fullness and unity of its reality." [23] But Belinsky insists that what comes through here is not merely "banal man, but man in general, as he is without prettifying or idealization." [24] Reality in type, moreover, has nothing to do with the humanistic outlook of the author. Indeed, as Belinsky points out, the author's spiritual idea may be alien to the heart of the reality he depicts. "The predominant character of Gogol's work," he writes in "A View of Russian Literature in 1847," "is negation; all negation, if it is to be alive and poetic, must be done in the name of an ideal; but this ideal is no more indigenous to him—that is, it is not native—than it is to other Russian poets, because our social life has still not acquired form and become sufficiently established to provide literature with this ideal." [25] The socially critical element in Gogol's art, then, the element of negation, comes not merely from the promptings of the author's social conscience or his moral-spiritual idealism, but also from the correct artistic perception of the truth of an unformed social life; that is, "life . . . in all its nakedness, in all its frightful disfiguration."[26] The grotesque Gogolian type is for Belinsky the perfect *aesthetic* embodiment of this disfiguration, this unformed personal and social life, this life without foundations. One cannot overstress the organic link between Belinsky's somber assessment of Russian man and reality and his aesthetics of the Gogolian type.

Herzen had apprehended the chief meaning of *Dead Souls* (1842) in its types. Recoiling before the "horror" of a "disgusting reality," Herzen wrote gloomily that "we encounter [these dead souls] at every step . . . in one way or another we lead one of the lives of Gogol's heroes."[27] He wrote again of the "universal inexorable character of these types because there can be no others in Russia." Belinsky fully shared Herzen's pessimistic point of view. In his important letter to K. D. Kavelin on November 22, 1847, the Russian critic, nearing the end of his short life, touched directly on the question which lay at the heart of his Gogol criticism, or at least of his understanding of the unity of form and content in Gogol's art: the question of "form," of the development of the personal element in Russian man and life. In an extensive essay on the ancient Slavs,[28] Kavelin had affirmed that in the social organization of the ancient Slavs, one based on blood ties, the element of personality did not exist. "Family life and relationships did not cultivate in the Russian Slav that feeling of separateness, of concentrated oneness that compels a man to draw a sharp line between himself and another, to distinguish himself from others in all respects and at all times."[29] The development of the Russian people, Kavelin believed, consisted in the gradual development and appearance in them of the "element of personality,"[30] of the idea of the person (*lico*), an idea, introduced by Christianity, of the dignity of man and of his many-sided development.[31]

Belinsky responded to Kavelin's theory skeptically and pessimistically:

> You have launched the idea of the development of the personal element as the content of the history of the Russian people. You and I have a short

time to live, while Russia has centuries, perhaps thousands of years. We want to hurry things up, but it is in no hurry. The concept of personality among us is only just taking shape and therefore the Gogolian types are *for the time being* [Belinsky's emphasis] the most authentic Russian types. This is as plain and simple as $2 \times 2 = 4$.[32]

One would be hard put to find in Russian social-cultural criticism, except in Chaadaev's *Philosophical Letters* (1829), a more dismal statement about Russian man and history. The Gogolian grotesque, here the Gogolian type, emerges as the tragic truth of Russian life and history, witness to its deepest distress, namely the failure to produce the phenomenon of personality (*lichnost*), in all its dignity and development. In this perspective Gogolian grotesque is not a distortion of Russian life, as Rozanov insisted; it is as real as Plyushkin's epic chaos in *Dead Souls*; it constitutes in itself an integral unity of form and content.

Belinsky's theory of Gogolian type, therefore, embodies a tragic judgment of Russian man and history; here aesthetic and social-historical interpretation are closely interwoven. It follows that a refutation of Belinsky's Gogol criticism (or of the somber implications of Gogol's art) would necessarily have to involve a challenge of a historical judgment, in the broadest sense, a challenge of the judgment of Russian history, of Russian environment, of Belinsky's $2 \times 2 = 4$. If Russian history and environment had in a manner of speaking overcome man, one would have to reverse this process and in art at least overcome history, environment, and fate as they manifested themselves in Russian man and society.

But one would have to overcome history in a way which simultaneously acknowledged the terrible historical truth of Russian life, in a way which did not divorce Gogol from Russian reality; that is, overcome Russian history in a way that did not deny the authenticity of the problem posed by Gogol's art.

What is suggested here is not only the painful complexity and gravity of the so-called Gogol question for the great writers and critics of the 1840's, in particular Turgenev and Dostoevsky, but their paradoxical manner of resolving the question. In *Poor Folk* Dostoevsky succeeded in overcoming congealed Gogolian "environment," but without wholly denying Gogol. True to the injunction of his great mentor, Friedrich Schiller, Dostoevsky posited art, indeed aesthetic consciousness, not only as the great transformer of inert conscious-ness (Gogol had already moved in this direction in his "Overcoat"), but as the creator of a reality which had as much legitimacy as inert environment.

I shall return to Dostoevsky and *Poor Folk*. Let me note at this point that Belinsky, though he expressed his thought in the language of literary criticism, sought the redemption of Russian reality neither in literature nor in criticism. He conceived the role of the artist and critic of his time largely in terms of disclosing and diagnosing social disease; little or no place was given to the disclosure of an ideal or the depiction of "positive" heroes. Belinsky's hopes for the redemption of Russian reality lay in social change, in the first instance in an active relation to Russian life. In the letter to Kavelin quoted above, Belinsky qualifies his pessimism over Russian life. He identifies his whole out-look on Russian man and Russia with Peter the Great and Peter's love-hatred for Russia. He writes:

> Hatred sometimes is only a special form of love . . . Love often errs, seeing in the beloved something that is not there; that is true; but sometimes only love reveals in [the beloved] that beautiful and great element which is inaccessible to observation and the mind. Peter the Great would have had more right than anybody to despise Russia, but he "did not despise his native land. He knew its destiny" [Pushkin, "Stanzas," 1826]. Peter for me is my philosophy, my religion, my revelation in everything that con-cerns Russia. He is the example for the great and small who want to do something, to be useful in some way. Without the direct element every-thing is rotten, abstract and lifeless, just as with only the direct element all is wild and absurd.[33]

Belinsky would seem to have identified Gogol's art—an art, he admitted, unconscious of its basic impulses—with Peter the Great's activism, with this special kind of love-hatred of Russia. Gogol's art in this sense was as devastating as Peter the Great's savage blows at the status quo of his time. Gogol's work, his grotesque types, his phantasmagoria conveyed to the contemporary Russian mind (what-ever Gogol's conscious intentions) the same message as Chaadaev's *Philosophical Letters*, a document which presents a bleak and, to some, grotesque picture of Russian history and culture, yet a document which objectively was an integral part of a vast renascence of Russian culture in the first half of the nineteenth century. But Gogol's art and Chaadaev's *Philosophical Letters* played this role largely because they aroused a storm in Russian cultural consciousness, a furious and at the same time poignant desire to negate the alarming "truth" of these writers, a desire to bring to full intensity those flickering lights which here and there illuminate the somber landscape of even Gogol's art.

It was clear to Belinsky, of course, that the statement of Gogol's art was by no means limited to its immediate social statement or even to Russian reality, that indeed it differed vastly from the new literature of the so-called natural school. Gogol depicts not just "scoundrels," Belinsky wrote, but "man in general . . . He is just as much a tragedian as a comic writer," Belinsky wrote to Kavelin December 7, 1847. Apropos of Gogol's *The Inspector General* (*Revisor*, 1836), Belinsky insisted that "the best of us are not alien to the shortcomings of these monsters, but, on the other hand, these monsters are not cannibals either."[34] At the same time, Belinsky recognized in Gogol's art the presence of an element which defied simple social or moral definition, something that lay uncannily beyond good and evil, for he adds in this same letter to Kavelin: "But you are right, strictly speaking there are neither vices nor virtues in them."[35] At this point in his letter Belinsky, clearly meditating on the strangeness of Gogol's art, goes on to say: "That is why I feel anguish in advance at the thought that I will probably have to write more than one article about Gogol in order to express my last word about him. One would have to say much that would be unexpected to you." And as though responding to an inner thought, Belinsky goes on to make this startling though confidential admission:

A whole abyss lies between Gogol and our school, a whole abyss; but still it takes its point of departure from him, he is its father, he not only gave it form, but pointed to its content. [The natural school] made use of this [content] no better than he did (indeed, how was it to struggle against him in this area!) but more consciously. That he functioned unconsciously—that is obvious.[36]

Belinsky did not write his "last word" on Gogol. He carried much to his grave that might have been unexpected to posterity, much perhaps that would have given more balance to subsequent Russian radical criticism. Yet in his letters to Kavelin, he hinted at enough to make it clear that his understanding of Gogol was as profound as Dostoevsky's and certainly as canny as that of Rozanov. Why had he not spoken more fully in his public writings? As he wrote Kavelin in his letter of November 22, 1847, to have expressed himself fully in public on Gogol would have meant "leading the wolves to the sheep,"[37] leading Gogol's critics to Gogol himself.

Belinsky's reticence to reveal the abyss separating Gogol from the natural school was understandable in the narrow context of his polemics: in the earliest period of the reception of Gogol's art, he was battling against critics, in social viewpoint often conservative, who often saw only the superficial and narrowly comic in Gogol and who denied any connection between Gogol's art and Russian reality. To have acknowledged the abyss separating Gogol from the natural school, to have dwelled at that point upon the idiosyncratic character, the peculiarities and paradoxes, of Gogol's art, its curious manner of simultaneously penetrating and yet eluding reality, would have weakened Belinsky's publicistic version of the social significance of Gogol's art. What is more, it might have forced into the open his own pessimistic judgment of Russian man and historical reality, his view that "Gogolian types are *for the time being* the most authentic Russian types."

In his letter to Belinsky, Kavelin had raised a question that was to become increasingly important to the young generation of writers such as Dostoevsky and Turgenev, a question which had already been introduced in the debate over Gogol's art and in Gogol's writings. Was there another side of Russian reality than that represented by the Sobakeviches, Nozdryovs, Chichikovs, and other Gogolian types? Do these types give expression to the whole truth? In Kavelin's own words, cited by Belinsky, "Is there *another* side to contemporary Russian life which, if artistically reproduced, would present to us the positive side of our national physiognomy?"[38]

Belinsky is cautious in answering these questions. He makes some concessions, but he holds to his basic position in the end. Belinsky agrees that there are many "good people" in Russian life. "Russia is chiefly a land of extremes, of wonderful, strange and incomprehensible exceptions." But he insists that literature "cannot use good people without falling into idealization, into rhetoric and melodrama; it cannot present them realistically as they are in reality."[39] Is there a passing allusion here to Devushkin in Dostoevsky's *Poor Folk*, a work which had been published early in 1846 and had been hailed by Belinsky? Did he find more historical truth and realism in Gogol's Akaky Akakievich than he did in the half-sentimentalized version of Devushkin and in the generally melodramatic portrayal of "poor folk" in Dostoevsky's first novel? In any case, Belinsky falls back in his argument upon the pervasiveness of the negative Gogolian type and the oppressive fatality of Russian environment. "A good person in Russia can be a hero of good sometimes, in the full sense of the word," he concedes, "but this does not prevent him from being a Gogolian character either; though honorable and truthful, he may yet beat his wife. Good in him is a 'gift of nature,'" Belinsky suggests in a somewhat Rousseauesque vein. But one must contend with environment in him. "There is no ground beneath his feet, as you rightly put it. Here we have to do not with a heaving sea, but a huge piece of glass."[40] In this brilliant image Belinsky again reveals his preoccupation with what he had described as a social life that had still not acquired form, a life marked by the absence of the element or concept of personality (*lichnost*). Gogol in his view vividly gave expression to this morally and socially unformed element in Russian life; or, put another way, he gave expression to the near triumph in Russian man of congealed environment. Certainly Gogol himself dreamed of transcending this environment, of illuminating this trivial landscape with an ideal. But his genius, Belinsky believed, did not lie in this direction. But what of other writers in the 1840's?

Belinsky, obviously, was suspicious of contemporary literature that sought to strike too far above the level of a realism of negation, an art that sought out too much of an ideal in the Russian landscape. Yet some of Belinsky's remarks to Kavelin suggest the transitional character of his criticism. Belinsky died at a moment when Russian literature had just begun to take up the pessimistic challenge of Gogol's types, to scrutinize the notion of a sterile, congealed Russian environment. Belinsky had conceived of Gogol's art as a frontal attack on this environment, a purely negative exposé of it. But in the late 1840's the attack on Gogolian environment also came, in part at least, in the form of a negation of the Gogolian vision itself, in the form of a negation of the negation. At the very moment Belinsky was declaring that Gogol's types were the authentic Russian types *for the time being*, the supremacy, or accuracy, of this type was being challenged in literature. Turgenev was beginning work on *A Sportsman's Notebook* (1847–1852), a brilliant series of sketches revolutionary in form and content that would evoke the deeply poetic, transcendental element in Russian man. Turgenev did not abandon the "critical tendency" that Belinsky had found in Gogol, but he moved along lines of distinct idealization: beneath the disfiguration (*bezobrazie*) of Russian man, he discerned life and form (*obraz*), authentic aesthetic and spiritual beauty. *A Sportsman's Notebook*, one of the greatest works in Russian literature, struck at congealed Russian environment from within as well as from without.

In *Poor Folk*, in his creation of Devushkin and other little men, Dostoevsky had already challenged the hegemony of the grotesque, albeit pathetic Gogolian urban type, Akaky Akakievich. Yet Devushkin's polemic with Gogol, his personal rejection of "The Overcoat," cannot be wholly identified with Dostoevsky's point of view. Dostoevsky struggles with environment in Gogol's art with a deep sense of the inner realism of Gogol's apprehension of Russian reality. Gogol's *Dead Souls* and his play *The Marriage*, Dostoevsky wrote many years later in his *Diary of a Writer* (1876), were "the profoundest of works, richest in inner content precisely through the artistic types delineated in them."[41] Dostoevsky's views here provide a sharp contrast to Rozanov's denigration later on of the Gogolian type as well as of the phenomenon of literary type itself. "The whole depth, the whole content of an artistic work . . . consists only in types and characters," Dostoevsky observes.[42] And in this connection, seemingly echoing Belinsky's melancholy reflections in his letter to Kavelin, Dostoevsky remarks: "Gogol's artistic types almost oppress the mind with the most profound and unbearable questions, evoke in the Russian mind the most disturbing thoughts, with which—one feels this—it may be possible to cope only in some far-off distant time; indeed, will we ever cope with them?"[43]

Poor Folk, of course, was written precisely with these unbearable questions and disturbing thoughts in mind. There can be no doubt, too, that Dostoevsky shared Belinsky's view of Gogol as a "poet of real life," a writer whose types exposed Russian life "in all its frightful disfiguration." Yet like Turgenev, Dostoevsky saw other elements in the Russian environment.

In one of his encounters with the higher bureaucratic world Devushkin has occasion to see himself reflected in the mirror in the anteroom of a government office. "I looked into the mirror on the right," he remarks, "and simply could have gone crazy over what I saw." The remark could easily symbolize the response of the Russian intellectual to Gogol's art. But Devushkin's remark is a significant one when examined in the light of the novel's aesthetic concerns. The mirror stands as a brilliant image, an ironic commentary on the aesthetic "theory" of Devushkin. The naive but sensitive Devushkin accepts the dictum that "literature is a picture . . . and a mirror . . . really subtle criticism, instructions for edification." But his reading of Gogol's "Overcoat" (his friend Varvara presents him with a copy of this story as well as Pushkin's "The Station Master") deals a stunning blow to his aesthetic notions. Gogol's mirror, hailed by Belinsky for its merciless frankness, only fills Devushkin with disbelief and horror. He recoils from the image of the little man Akaky Akakievich as he recoils from his own mirror image. "The Overcoat," he concedes, is a faithful surface description of reality. "It is correctly described"; nevertheless, he finds it intrusive and disrespectful in the way it exposes to light the private world of little people like himself. The subtle criticism of literature, it turns out, is not so subtle after all; it is neither comforting nor edifying. Devushkin, in short, views "The Overcoat" as a "caricature," a "slander" on the poor clerk. In the end, he rejects Gogol's story because it is "simply lacking in truth, because it simply could not happen that there could be such a clerk."

In the spirit of Rozanov's Gogol criticism, Devushkin rebukes Gogol for a *wrong attitude toward reality*, for concentrating on the typical rather than on the individual in man. Indeed, Rozanov's own critique of Akaky Akakievich is a sophisticated reformulation of some of Devushkin's responses. In his essay "On the Development of Akaky Akakievich as a Type," Rozanov insists that the creative formation of the hero of "The Overcoat" in Gogol's artistic imagination did not involve a deepening of his character or inner being but rather a reverse movement, "a narrowing, simplifying, impoverishing of reality."[44] Rozanov singles out a sentence that appears in an early draft of "The

Overcoat": "In essence he [Akaky Akakievich] is a very kindly animal." Gogol removed that sentence from the final text of his story.
But in Rozanov's view, that sentence "establishes for us the point of
view from which the portrait was drawn"; "an animal, an unthinking
and unfeeling animal: such was its theme," concludes Rozanov.[45] It is,
of course, precisely what Rozanov, rightly or wrongly, calls Gogol's
narrowing and abasement of man that Devushkin reacts against in
"The Overcoat." What Devushkin misses in the depiction of Akaky
Akakievich is what he finds in Pushkin's portrayal of Samson Vyrin: a
warmth and sympathy that not only humanizes the hero, but makes it
possible for the reader, while empathizing with him, to reconcile himself to his fate. All that Devushkin finds in "The Station Master," in
contrast to "The Overcoat," is "natural" and true to life as he knows it
in the perspective of his inner feelings and rationalization of his
experience.

But Devushkin's inability to find any "verisimilitude" in "The
Overcoat," though it attests to an acute awareness of his own inner
human image, is nonetheless deceptive; it by no means reflects Dostoevsky's entire point of view. Dostoevsky found a profound and tragic
truth in "The Overcoat," and his description of Devushkin's response
to Gogol is evidence of this fact. The mirror image in *Poor Folk*
is ambiguous in its meaning: on the one hand, it reveals none of
Devushkin's inner world; on the other hand, it points with terrible
truthfulness to an objective condition of despair and degradation, to a
self-alienation that borders almost on a pathological ambivalence. Devushkin does not recognize himself. The truth is so terrible that the
individual, precisely because he retains an inner purified image of his
self, refuses to recognize his own negation, his objective alienation
from his own self-image.

The rigid, dogmatic character of Devushkin's rejection of his image in Gogol's mirror is clear evidence of how deeply "The Overcoat"
threatens his internal stability. Gogol's story certainly evokes in Devushkin, as it does in Dostoevsky, "most disturbing thoughts," "the
most profound and unbearable questions." The radical social implications of Gogol's story, it would appear, are uppermost in Devushkin's mind. Even before he mentions "The Overcoat" in his letter to
Varvara, Devushkin gives expression to his anxieties: "To one person

it is given to wear a general's epaulettes; to another—to serve as a titulary councillor; to one person it is given to command, and to another to obey timidly and in fear. All this is based on the abilities of a person . . . and abilities are arranged by God himself."

Devushkin clearly senses the revolutionary social implications of "The Overcoat." At issue here, however, is more than a response to the rampaging ghost of Akaky Akakievich, who terrorizes the comfortable citizens of Petersburg. "The Overcoat" raises not only questions of social inequality; it is more than social protest; it raises Dostoevskian issues: the question of an unjust, arbitrary fate, of an unjust universal order in which man's place may be no more permanent or dignified than that of a transient fly, a world in which human existence may be essentially without meaning. Devushkin clings desperately to the concept of a meaningful social and world order "arranged by God himself." But the stubbornness with which he clings to his belief is in inverse relation to his nagging doubts.

The motif of a senseless universe echoes in his letters. "Why does it always happen," he writes Varvara, "that a good man is left in a state of desolation while others have happiness thrust upon them?" Such thinking, he admits, smacks of "free thinking," but "in all frankness, to be quite truthful, why does the raven Fate croak happiness to one person who is still in his mother's womb, while another goes out into the world from an orphanage?" Devushkin, to be sure, reluctantly gives expression to such thoughts. He represses the disturbing speculations and impulses aroused by a reading of "The Overcoat," for Gogol's story strikes a blow at his whole adaptive, rationalizing psychology and at the fragile structure of his worldview. In its deeply pessimistic portrayal of the human condition (enslaved and degraded by environment, a victim of chance, accident, fate), Gogol's story threatens to undermine his confidence in the world's meaning. It leaves no middle ground for man to stand on. One is driven to one of two extremes: either to despairing revolt, which is thinkable but completely unacceptable to Devushkin ("Really, now, after this it would be impossible to live peacefully!") or to a passive, self-annihilating despair. The psychological drama of Devushkin moves precariously along the knife edge of these two possibilities, ones that are curiously reflected in the responses of Belinsky and Rozanov to Gogol: either

Petrine activism, a terrifying and crushing assault on the "huge piece of glass" of Russian life (Belinsky), or despair and suicide: "to connect [Gogol] with our life . . . would mean to lift a hand against ourselves" (Rozanov).

The critical positions of Belinsky and Rozanov are both reflected in Dostoevsky's complex image of Devushkin. Both of these positions constitute a paradoxical unity of opposites. Both critics recognize Gogol's artistic vision as grotesque, and both affirm the tragic character of that vision as it pertains to Russian life (the one approvingly, the other disapprovingly). Belinsky's social aims and ideology shaped his Gogol criticism; it determined his emphasis upon the ethical significance or revolutionary potential of Gogol's so-called art of negation. His social criticism expressed what many contemporaries felt: that after a reading of Gogol, in the words of Devushkin, "it is impossible to live peacefully."

Yet Belinsky's preoccupation with the social function of literature, with literature as an adjunct to social change, led him to understate, at least in his public writing, the role of the autonomous artist in creating his own fantastic world; it certainly led him to underestimate the importance, and even deny the place, of a literature concerned with the "positive" or "ideal" in Russian life. His radical position led him finally to camouflage the abyss that lay between Gogol and the newly emerging school of realistic writers and in this sense to do violence to his deeper and more complex understanding of Gogol. Belinsky in this sense anticipated, and contributed to, a tendency in later radical criticism to divorce social and aesthetic analysis, and more broadly to manipulate artistic truth in the name of an ideological or social cause. Nonetheless, Belinsky's Gogol criticism, taken in its totality, reveals an extraordinarily perceptive, if not profound critic.

Rozanov's criticism was an effort to redress the balance that was lost in radical criticism, to restore the aesthetic element to Gogol criticism, to bring criticism back to its central concern—the work of art. He recognized with the comfortable retrospective glance denied to Belinsky that the development of the new realistic school of writers involved a recoil from Gogol, a struggle with Gogolian pessimism and a search for embodied moral and spiritual reality in Russian man and history.

Yet one detects in Rozanov's effort to disconnect Gogol's art from any roots in Russian life a tendentious one-sidedness quite as damaging as Belinsky's troublesome insistence on seeing in Gogol's art a "full representation of reality." The mark of the conservative is as apparent in Rozanov's criticism as the mark of the radical is in Belinsky's. Near the end of his essay "Pushkin and Gogol," Rozanov exclaims, somewhat in the spirit of Arkady Dolgoruky's mentor in *The Raw Youth*: "*Tranquility*—that is what we need most of all." And he expounds on the absence of "clarity in our consciousness," "naturalness in the expression of our feelings," any "simplicity in our relation to reality." But a handful of years before the Russian Revolution of 1917, Rozanov complains: "We are excited, alarmed, and this excitement, this alarm is betrayed by the convulsivenss of our actions and the disorder of our thoughts." Gogol, the vision of Gogol, according to Rozanov, lies across the path leading to a "normal, healthy" and "natural development"; he bars the way "not so much by his irony, by the absence of confidence and respect for man, as by the whole cast of his genius, which became the cast of our souls and our history."[46] Hence Rozanov's criticism not of Gogol's brilliant art but of his "imagination with its wrong relation to reality, its wrong relation to dream"; his criticism of an imagination which has "*corrupted* our souls and undermined life, after filling both the former and the latter with the deepest sufferings."[47]

When we examine Rozanov's thought closely, here, we discern an ingenious but ultimately weak design. Radical materialist aesthetics had viewed Gogol as the founder of the natural school, a school whose writers supposedly transmit reality in their works. "My negative remarks," Rozanov observes at this point, "apply only to this naive assertion."[48] This assertion is indeed naive. We have seen, however, that Belinsky's understanding of Gogol's artistic representation of reality was more complex than Rozanov assumes. Rozanov's trick, on the other hand, was to turn radical materialist aesthetics on its head; philosophically speaking, he *idealizes* it: he depicts Russian man and cultural consciousness *after* Gogol as a reproduction of Gogolian artistic reality.

While in no way denying a reciprocal relationship between Gogol's art and Russian reality, it must be said that Rozanov here succumbs to the blandishments of paradox and play. For his clever parody of radical aesthetics constitutes a disaster for his Gogol criticism. It closed the door to what might have been the most incisive and comprehensive Gogol criticism of the nineteenth and twentieth centuries, namely, a criticism which embraced the full dialectic of Gogol as it finds expression in Dostoevsky's *Poor Folk*—the most brilliant "embodied" commentary on Gogol's "The Overcoat" in all Russian literature and criticism.

Gogol's art clearly troubled Rozanov quite as much as it troubled Belinsky and Dostoevsky. But in his criticism he essentially seeks to evade or mute the seriousness of the Gogol question. If Gogol found an intimate place in nineteenth-century Russian consciousness (and of this there cannot be the slightest doubt), it was not only because the soil was congenial but because Gogol in the first instance had peered deeply into the "huge piece of glass" of Russian life—peered deeply and discovered something profoundly Russian as well as universal. But Rozanov, carried away by his effort to discredit a moribund tradition of antiaesthetic utilitarian and civic criticism, seeking not revolution but "tranquility," denies the possibility of any organic connection between Russian reality and Gogol's terrible vision, denies it, one feels, with the same rigidity and transparent camouflage that characterizes Devushkin's response to "The Overcoat."

Rozanov grasped much of the literary-historical significance of Devushkin's indignant rejection of "The Overcoat"; indeed, he is deeply indebted to Devushkin (significantly he makes no mention of *Poor Folk* in his Gogol criticism); but he grasped only one part of Dostoevsky's dialectic. He approaches Gogol in the conservative spirit of Devushkin, a person who wanted, in spite of all his doubts and experience, to view Russian reality in a more hopeful light. Like Devushkin, Rozanov wants to affirm the existence of an embodied spiritual reality. But Devushkin's denial of Gogolian grotesque affirms a new dimension of reality only in the context of Dostoevsky's deep recognition of the troubling authenticity of the Gogol question. Devushkin is not Dostoevsky. "There is no instinct in our public, as in every crowd," Dostoevsky wrote February 1, 1846 to his brother. "They do not understand how one can write in such a style. They are accustomed to see the mug of the author in everything; but I didn't show mine. They don't seem to guess that it is Devushkin who is speaking and not I."[49] Dostoevsky's remarks are equally applicable where Devushkin's literary judgments are concerned.

It is in *Poor Folk* that one must seek the complex interweaving of points of view which find articulation in the widely separated criticism of Belinsky and Rozanov. The great Russian realists, as Rozanov suggests, put a soul into Russian man and humanized Gogol's stark landscape. To react against Gogol's grim and grotesque vision of life, however, was not necessarily to deny the components of reality in that vision; it was an attempt in aesthetic terms to redeem that reality, to shape it, to seek out its inner spirit. The double movement or dialectic here goes beyond simple negation. Dostoevsky in *Poor Folk* recognizes the bitter truth of Gogol's art in Devushkin's traumatic response to "The Overcoat," in his hero's feverish efforts to deny all but the surface realities in Gogol's story. Yet at the same time, Devushkin's denial of reality was in itself an existential affirmation of the supremacy of the transcendent human element over inert environment, over the morally and socially frozen landscape of Russian life.

No other Russian writer so deeply embodied in his art the curse of Russian history as Gogol. No other writer awaited with greater pain or impatience in his own art the appearance of that inspiration which would give the fullness of human dimensions to the amazing creatures of his art. In the history of Russian literature's response to Gogol, Dostoevsky's *Poor Folk* takes its place as a colossal act of aesthetic necromancy. Devushkin's indignant refusal to recognize the tattered puppet in the mirror was an earthquake in Gogol's Russian universe, one of the first cracks in the huge piece of glass of Russian life.

11   *In the Darkness of the Night*

Tolstoy's *Kreutzer Sonata* and Dostoevsky's
Notes from the Underground

> "Do you agree with Pozdnyshev when he says that doctors have ruined
> and are ruining thousands and hundreds of thousands of people?"
> "Are you really interested in knowing?"
> "Very much."
> "Then I won't tell you!" And he laughed, twirling the thumbs of his
> hands.
>
>   Maxim Gorky, *Reminiscences of Tolstoy*

I

At the end of the third chapter of *The Kreutzer Sonata*
(1891), the nervous, exasperated and shrill Pozdnyshev—
"landowner, university graduate and a marshal of the nobility"—begins his account of a "critical episode" in his life, the drama
surrounding his murder of his wife, with a definition of depravity.
Addressing the first or frame narrator of *The Kreutzer Sonata*, Pozdnyshev observes:

> "Depravity really doesn't lie in anything physical; indeed, no physical out-
> rage can be called depravity. Depravity, real depravity, consists precisely
> in freeing oneself from moral relations with a woman with whom you
> enter into physical relations. And precisely this kind of liberation I set
> down for myself as meritorious. I remember how I was once terribly upset
> when I did not manage to pay a woman who, after apparently falling in
> love with me, had given herself to me; and I regained my peace of mind
> only after I had sent her money, showing in this way that I did not con-
> sider myself bound to her in any way... Now don't shake your head as
> though you agreed with me," he suddenly shouted at me. "I really know
> what I'm talking about. All of us, and you too, at your best, unless you are
> a rare exception, share the same views that I did. Well, it makes no differ-
> ence, forgive me," he continued, "but the fact is that this is terrible, ter-
> rible, terrible!" "What is terrible?" I asked. "The whole abyss of error in
> which we live concerning women and our relations to them. Yes, I cannot
> speak calmly about it, and not because of this 'episode' [of the murder] as

[the lawyer] just put it, but because ever since that episode occurred, my eyes have been opened and I have come to see everything in quite a different light. Exactly the opposite, exactly the opposite!" He lit up a cigarette and resting his elbows on his knees, went on talking. I could not see his face in the darkness.

Pozdnyshev's recollection of how he literally settled accounts with his mistress recalls the climax of the Underground Man's second meeting with the prostitute Liza in his flat. After a moment of reconciliation and catharsis, a moment in which he sobs hysterically in the arms of Liza, the Underground Man is overtaken by a feeling of "domination and possession," of alternating attraction and hatred. "One feeling intensified the other. This was almost like vengeance!" The moment of sex that follows is an utterly loveless act. His "outburst of passion," as the Underground Man describes it, "was precisely revenge, a further humiliation of her," a confession not only that he was "incapable of loving" Lisa, but that for him, "love meant to tyrannize and be morally superior. . . . Even in my underground dreams I could not imagine love except as a struggle, beginning always with hatred and ending with moral subjugation."

After the moment of sex, the Underground Man is furious with impatience for Liza to leave. "Suddenly I ran up to her, seized her hand, opened it, put something in it, and then closed it again." This cruel gesture, the Underground Man admits, was "so insincere, so deliberately invented, so bookish" that even he could barely stand it. But the gesture nonetheless signals his "depravity"—in Pozdnyshev's sense of the word—his freedom from moral relations with Liza.

More than a gesture draws the attention of the reader of *The Kreutzer Sonata* to Dostoevsky's *Notes from the Underground*.[1] Tolstoy's classic work devoted to the theme of sexuality, marriage, and the family is singularly "Dostoevskian" in its focus on the exceptional and catastrophic, its dramatic whirlwind development of its story within a story, its exploration of a pathological state of mind, and finally its use of an anti-hero to conduct polemics and to illustrate in his character the predicament of his thought.[2] Whether or not Dostoevsky's attempt at fusing polemics and fiction drew Tolstoy's special attention at the time he wrote *The Kreutzer Sonata*, the tasks he set himself in this work certainly led him to solutions that bear comparison with *Notes*.

2

Pozdnyshev tells his story to the frame narrator in a railway compartment illuminated by a single candle. The time of the narration is between twilight and dawn. The end of his narration at eight o'clock the next morning merges with the end of his story, a tale that itself ends with a journey: Pozdnyshev's return home by railroad from a trip in autumn. Real time and story time end together. The line of narration and the line of action are apocalyptic in character: Poznyshev's discourse on social, marital, and sexual relations concludes with a call for an *end to procreation*. The story of his sexual and marital life ends in *murder*. The idea of grand apocalypse which is projected as an ideal is realized in a little apocalypse.

The train that carries Pozdnyshev is itself an embodiment of apocalypse: as in *Anna Karenina*, the train thunders about the dislocation of values in modern civilization. "People have grown cultured," an old merchant remarks bitingly apropos of the phenomenon of divorce. The narrator adds: "The train, moving along more and more rapidly, thundered so loudly I could hardly hear." Like a thundering chorus, the railroad is accomplice, if not instigator, in the actual crime of murder. "This eight-hour journey by rail had something horrible about it for me, something that I shall never forget in my life," recalls Pozdnyshev of his journey home. "Either because I vividly imagined myself upon entering the carriage as having reached the end or because railroad travel has an agitating effect on people—in any case, as soon as I took my seat, I could no longer control my imagination, which ceaselessly, with extraordinary vividness, began to bring up before me pictures kindling my jealousy."

Pozdnyshev's whole confession is permeated by ideas of an "end" to lying and deceit. "They keep on lying," mutters Pozdnyshev early in the story. He proclaims the lie of relations between the sexes, "the abyss of error in which we live regarding women and our relations with them." Pozdnyshev quickly emerges in his confession not only as a person who is in a position to expose all this lying, but as a kind of prophet of the approaching end to the whole disorder of human relations. After speaking of girls "whom their parents enthusiastically gave in marriage to men suffering from a certain disease," Pozdnyshev cries out: "Oh! oh the abomination of it! But a time will come when this abomination and lie will be exposed!" And again: "'Yes, you laugh!' he shouted at me, 'but this is by no means a joke. I am certain that a time will come, and, perhaps, very soon, when people will understand this and will be amazed that a society could exist in which such acts could be permitted which violated the public peace.'" "Oh, when will these magi with their deceits be uncrowned? It is time!"

Pozdnyshev's story of his marriage and disillusionments, his social critique of the marriage market and the reprehensible role played by both men and women in it, his observations on the nature of his sexual relations with his wife, lead him to see things in a "new light." "Yes, only after having fearfully suffered, only thanks to that have I understood where the root of it all lies, understood what must be, and therefore perceived the horror of all that is." The root of evil, he maintains, lies in the "unnatural" animal character of sexual relations between men and women. What "must be" is abstention from sexual relations. To the question asked by the first narrator of *The Kreutzer Sonata*—how would the human race be perpetuated through abstention from sexual relations?—Pozdnyshev replies with irony:

> "And wouldn't it be a terrible thing if the human race perished! . . . Why should it be continued—this human race? . . . If there is no goal, if life is given to us for life, there is no reason to live. . . . But if there is a goal of life, then it is clear that life must come to an end when the goal is achieved. . . . If the goal of mankind is well-being, goodness, love, if you wish; if the goal of mankind is what is said in the prophecies, that all men will be united in the universal love . . . then what stands in the way of attaining this goal? Human passions. Of all the passions, the most powerful and vicious and stubborn is sexual, carnal love. And therefore if the passions are annihilated and with them the most powerful—carnal love—then the prophecy will be fulfilled, men will be united, the goal of mankind will have been achieved, and there will no longer be any reason for existence."

All this, Pozdnyshev recognizes, is only an "ideal." "So long as mankind lives, the ideal will stand before it": not the piggish ideal of propagation of the species or enjoying the refined pleasures of sexual passion, "but the ideal of good, achieved by abstention and purity. Toward this people have always striven and are striving now." Abstention and purity, however, have been impossible for Pozdnyshev; his

"fall" (Pozdnyshev refers to his "first fall" as a young man as "the ru-
ination of innocence"), like that of the heroes of Tolstoy's "Father Sergius" and "The Devil," is marked by anger, hatred, and feelings of
impurity. His murder of his wife, giving embodiment to his own concept of sexuality as crime and arising at the same time from a striving
for self-purification, far from attaining the biblical goal of "universal
love," locks him into an eternal prison of alternating hatred and
remorse.

3

Some of the questions raised by Tolstoy through the medium of
the emotionally distraught and disturbed Pozdnyshev were by no
means unfamiliar to Dostoevsky or the inhabitants of his novelistic
universe. Unlike Tolstoy, Dostoevsky never wrote explicitly on the
subjects of marriage, women, or sexuality. The problem of sexuality in
the life of the individual and society, however, concerned him deeply.
As with everything else in his writing and thought, his feelings here
seem to have been ambivalent. There are motifs in his writings that
parallel those Tolstoy expresses in *The Kreutzer Sonata* and some other
works.

"Swinish sensuality with all its consequences, sensuality to the
point of cruelty, crime, the marquis de Sade," Dostoevsky had written
synoptically in his notebook for *The Brothers Karamazov*.[3] In the majority of his novels, "swinish sensuality," whether manifested directly
in the form of the sexual activity or the experience of inflicting violence on others, is seen as posing a mortal threat to the welfare and
spiritual health of both individual and society. Apropos of the depraved nobleman-convict Aristov's "insatiable thirst for the coarsest,
most animal physical pleasures," the narrator of *Notes from the House
of the Dead* writes: "No, better fire, better plague and hunger, than
such a being in society." Variants of this amoral type appear in Dostoevsky's novels. The unbridled sensualist (Bykov, Svidrigailov, Versilov, Stavrogin, and others) preys upon women and children. Dostoevsky's Ridiculous Man insists that "sensuality" is "the sole source of
almost all sins of our mankind." His dream of beatitude ends with his
"corrupting" everyone. The dream of paradise turns into a nightmare
of human history: "Sensuality was soon born; sensuality begot jeal-

ousy, jealousy—cruelty." In the moral and social chaos that ensues over the centuries, "proud men and sensualists" appear "who boldly demanded all or nothing."

For the most part, sexuality in Dostoevsky's novelistic universe is disclosed in its negative, or destructive, manifestations. In *The Brothers Karamazov*, Dostoevsky, while indicting Fyodor Karamazov for his unbridled sensuality, at the same time discovers in the "earthly Karamazov" force a deep vitality, a "thirst for life," a guarantee of spiritual rebirth. Yet the formulation is abstract and is not exemplified in human relations (though one may perhaps assume that the future relationship between Dmitry and Grushenka will be characterized by a union of carnal and spiritual elements). In any case, Dostoevsky tends to identify the highest moral and spiritual virtues with personalities in whom the sexual instinct is sublimated, crippled, or dormant (Zosima, Myshkin, Alyosha). Yet Dostoevsky never presents sexuality in the human being as a phenomenon isolated from other aspects of personality. Cruel or violent sexuality, Dostoevsky suggests in *The Gambler*, is the correlative of moral, social, and spiritual imbalance. The only real surcease in Dostoevsky's world from the tyranny of sexual tensions lies in spiritual and religious sublimation of the sexual impulse.

In the final analysis, duality defines Dostoevsky's attitude toward sexuality and marriage, as it does Tolstoy's. This is apparent in Dostoevsky's treatment of this theme in his notebook in 1863. Here Dostoevsky speaks of marriage and sexuality as a manifestation of egoism and alien to the highest spiritual ideal. "[For in the resurrection] they neither marry nor seek to possess, but live as divine angels (Matthew 22:30). "A profoundly significant trait [in the future nature of the future being]," observes Dostoevsky. He offers the following reflections on this theme:

(1) They do not *get married* and do not *seek to possess*—because there is no reason to; to develop, achieve one's goal by means of changing generations, is no longer necessary, and (2) marriage and seeking to possess women is as it were the greatest deviation from humanism, the complete isolation of the pair from *everyone* (little remains for everyone). The family, that is the law of nature, but still an abnormal, an egotistical state in the full sense, coming from man. The family—the most sacred thing

of man on earth, for by means of this law of nature man achieves the goal through development (that is, through the change of generations). But at the same time, also according to same law of nature, in the name of the final ideal of his goal, man must continuously deny it. (Duality.)[4]

Dostoevsky's ideas at essential points coincide with those to which Pozdnyshev gives exaggerated expression in *The Kreutzer Sonata*. Both Pozdnyshev and Dostoevsky acknowledge the biblical "goal" in which men will be united in "universal love" (as Dostoevsky puts it, citing Matthew, in the Resurrection, men will live as "divine angels"). Both view marriage and sexuality as something that "stands in the way of attaining that goal" (for Dostoevsky, this is "the greatest deviation from humanism"); both recognize the goal as an "ideal" toward which men will strive. Pozdnyshev speaks directly of the need for "abstention and purity," the striving for an "ideal," and Dostoevsky speaks of man's need, in part, "continuously to deny" the procreative "law of nature."

Yet fundamental differences separate Dostoevsky's position from that of Tolstoy's anti-hero. Pozdnyshev's mind is not merely focused abstractly on matters pertaining to the end of the world; he directly poses, with savage irony, the question "Why should it be continued— this human race?" He is disillusioned with marriage and overcome by a loathing for everything pertaining to sexuality. He is overcome by the apocalyptic impulses of his mind and emotions. For him, time has collapsed. His murder of his wife constitutes a perverse fulfillment of the "prophecies." In his self-centered egotism he has lost all connection with the living life. In moral-psychological terms, the narrator whose voice we hear and the person who emerges in his account of his life is "possessed"—a helpless bearer, like the Underground Man, of the principle of destruction and self-destruction. Like the Underground Man, he has carried to an extreme what others carry only halfway.

Dostoevsky's central thought in his notebook in 1864 is upon "development." For him, the whole history of humanity is a striving for a state of universality in which the "law of the 'I' [will] merge with law of humanism" and the individual will attain his highest development, "the paradise of Christ. The whole history both of mankind and in part of every person separately is only development, struggle, striving and achievement of this goal."[5] But "man on earth is in a transitory

state," and "Christ himself preached his teaching only as an ideal."[6]
Dostoevsky therefore insists that man must maintain a delicate balance where family and sexuality, the "change of generations," are concerned. His final statement is "duality"; that is, man must live with
opposing truths or realities in his movement toward the ideal.

Pozdnyshev is not Tolstoy, just as the Underground Man is not
Dostoevsky. Tolstoy's thoughts on the family, marriage, and sexuality—if we examine them in the broad spectrum of his nonfictional
writings—disclose different emphases, indeed "duality." Even in his
"Afterword" Tolstoy sets forth "chastity" not as "a rule or prescrip-
tion," but

> as an ideal or rather one of its conditions. But an ideal is only an ideal
> when its realization is possible only in the idea, in thought. . . . Such is
> the ideal of Christ. . . . The whole meaning of human life consists in
> moving in the direction of this ideal [of Christian love], and therefore the
> striving for the Christian ideal in all its aggregate and for chastity as one
> of the conditions of this ideal not only does not exclude the possibility of
> life, but, to the contrary, the absence of this Christian ideal would anni-
> hilate the movement forward and, therefore, the possibility of life.[7]

In his didactic "Walk While You Have Light (A Tale from the
Times of the Ancient Christians)," written a few years before *The
Kreutzer Sonata*, Tolstoy struggles to validate "special [carnal] love for
woman" in "Christian marriage." In the story, a pagan asks: How can
there be a violation of the will of God in marriage? His Christian
interlocutor responds:

> "The violation occurs when a man loves in a woman his pleasure in sexual
> union with her and not a person like himself, and therefore enters into
> marriage for the sake of his pleasure. Christian marriage is possible only
> when a person has a love for people and when the object of carnal love
> already is the object of brotherly love of one person for another. Just as
> it is possible to build a house rationally and solidly only when there
> is a foundation . . . so carnal love becomes right, reasonable and stable
> only when respect and love of one person for the other lies at its foun-
> dation. . . . The best example of how . . . so-called love-eros becomes
> savage when it is not based on brotherly love for all people is the case of
> violence perpetrated on a woman who supposedly likes the violator who
> is compelling her to suffer and who is ravaging her. This concealed vio-
> lence is often to be found in non-Christian marriage."[8]

4

The state of being free from moral relations with women with whom one enters into physical relations defines at root not only Pozdnyshev's relations with his casual female acquaintances in his premarital days, but his sexual relations with his wife, a woman whom he claimed to know "only as an animal." The ultimate freedom from moral relations is murder; murder, in the case of Pozdnyshev, is the direct outcome of a relationship (as he conceives it) based on "swinishness," upon "crime." The "mutual hatred" that Pozdnyshev and his wife had for each other was that of "accomplices in a crime."

Pozdnyshev's murder of his wife was a crime of passion in more than one sense. The murder is not simply the result of jealousy; it is the displaced fulfillment of the frustrated sexual impulse. "In court I was asked: why, how did I kill my wife? Fools! They think that I killed her with a dagger on the fifth of October. I didn't kill her then, but much earlier. In exactly the same way that men are all killing their wives now, all, all." "But how [*da chem zhe*]?" asks the narrator. Pozdnyshev answers by pointing to the crime of his sexual relations with his wife during her pregnancies. But the allusion to the phallic organ as a murder weapon is unmistakable; it underscores Pozdnyshev's central notion that sexual intercourse, by the very nature of the animal instincts it arouses, is incompatible with moral relations or spiritual communion.

The concept of the sexual act as a form of murder, or of the dagger thrust as a surrogate for the sexual act, lies at the psychological core of Pozdnyshev's crime. The playing of the first presto movement of Beethoven's *Kreutzer Sonata,* or more specifically, the playing of some unnamed "passionate" and "obscenely sensual" piece of music, serves first, in Pozdnyshev's view, to break down the moral "barrier" between his wife and her musical partner, Trukhachevsky. But what is less apparent, but equally important, is that the same music which breaks down this barrier and opens the way (at least in Pozdnyshev's conjecture) for a "swinish" adulterous embrace ("was it not clear that everything was accomplished that evening?") also has a "fearful impact" on Pozdnyshev. This music aroused in him "quite new feelings, so it seemed to me, new possibilities of which I had been hitherto unaware," a strange sense of "joy" in which he saw everything "in quite a different light." The motif of "joy" (like "light") in *The Kreutzer Sonata* is apocalyptic in its content. The word itself is linked persistently with Pozdnyshev's feelings of underground spite, his exultation in his "mad" and murderous feelings, his uncontrolled outbursts of "animal" rage and violence against his wife (a person who characteristically remains unnamed), and these feelings have their source in his animal jealousy, his frustrated sexual impulses, his "swinishness." Music, "the most subtle lust of the senses," is perceived by Pozdnyshev to be the precipitant in a drama that ends with adultery and murder. It breaks down the moral and aesthetic barriers to the adulterous embrace and the murderous dagger thrust, two actions which in Tolstoy's presentation are psychologically related.

5

In form, design, and tone, *The Kreutzer Sonata* and *Notes from the Underground* bear some striking resemblances. The use of first-person narration in both works allows the protagonists the maximum freedom to create their own worlds and to give free play to their paradoxical and contradiction-ridden discourse.[9] Both works take the form of a confession. In both works, polemics—a hard core of ideological, social, and philosophical discussion—are interwoven with personal narrative. *Notes from the Underground* divides into polemics (part 1) and personal reminiscences (part 2), though the division between polemics and reminiscences is not absolute. *The Kreutzer Sonata*, originally conceived as a personal drama of a man betrayed by his wife, gradually evolved into a work in which polemical issues of broad social content involving marriage, family, and sex occupy almost equal space with personal history. The division between polemics and personal confession is less defined in *The Kreutzer Sonata* than in *Notes from the Underground*. A consistent thread of story, or personal drama, runs from the beginning to the end of the work. Nonetheless, as in *Notes from the Underground*, the first part of the confession (chapters 3–17) tends to concentrate on polemical issues, while the last part (chapters 18–28) is devoted by and large to the tragic denouement of Pozdnyshev's relations with his wife.

What is important, however, is not the formal distinction between polemics and story but the integral relation of these elements to the development of the whole work, to the unfolding of the dramas of Pozdnyshev and the Underground Man. In both works the polemical issues lie at the core of the tragic personal dramas of the heroes. The Underground Man's irrational-will philosophy—polemically directed in part 1 at his invisible interlocutors, the rationalists, utilitarians, and utopian socialists—is disclosed in part 2, on the psychological plane, as the engine driving him into deepening humiliation, destruction, and self-destruction. Pozdnyshev's theories pertaining to sexual relations, marriage, and women serve in the course of his narrative to provide the ideological basis for his deteriorating relations with his wife. For both the Underground Man and Pozdnyshev, ideological justification or explanation for behavior is a product of reflection *after* catastrophe.

The psychological motivation for the reminiscences, or confessions, of both men is a crime that weighs heavily on their consciences: Pozdnyshev's actual murder of his wife and the Underground Man's spiritual murder of Liza. The Underground Man looks back on the Liza episode after sixteen years of remorse, of suffering with a "crime" on his conscience. "I was angry with myself, but of course it was she who would suffer for it," he recalls. "A terrible malice against her suddenly blazed up in my heart. I think I could almost have killed her."

The confessions of Pozdnyshev and of the Underground Man are outpourings of men who, though conscience-stricken, are bent on justifying themselves. Self-justification, however, leads finally to self-indictment and involves a broad critique of social relations. "I am a sick man," the Underground Man declares in the opening words of his notes. In his concluding words, he observes to his unseen interlocutors: "I have merely carried to an extreme in my life what you have not dared to carry through even halfway." "All the features for the anti-hero have been gathered here deliberately and, chiefly, all this creates a most unpleasant impression because we are all divorced from life, all crippled, each of us more or less." Pozdnyshev describes himself as ill, a "kind of insane man." "I am a wreck, a cripple. But one thing I have: I know. Yes, it is clear that I know what the rest of the world does not yet know." Like Eugene Irtenev in Tolstoy's "Devil," Pozdnyshev finds the same indications of insanity in the so-called normal bourgeois men and women of his social class. Putting it another way, he notes that the French psychologist Charcot would probably have pronounced his wife a victim of hysteria and would have said that he, Pozdnyshev, was abnormal, "and he probably would have tried to cure us. But there was no disease to cure."

The essence of Pozdnyshev's rationalizations for his crime is that his murder of his wife simply represented an extreme manifestation of a moral and social calamity afflicting the entire upper class in society. "The slavery of woman consists in precisely this, that men choose to take advantage of her as an instrument of enjoyment and consider it right to do so." Such slavery is compared to social systems in which "people, just the same as ever, like to profit by the labors of others." Woman, Pozdnyshev insists, remains "the same depraved slave as before and her husband the same depraved slave owner."

The protagonists of Tolstoy and Dostoevsky at the moment of confession live at the periphery of society. Both present themselves to their interlocutors as people who have gained a special knowledge of the world that is contrary to what the majority thinks or wants to know. In their suffering and accumulated spite, both are intent on revealing the "bare" disgusting truth about themselves and their contemporaries. Theirs is the spite and anguish of disillusioned romantics, victims of romantic illusions and spurious ideals. The Underground Man sarcastically expatiates on his infatuation in the 1840's with the "beautiful and the sublime." "In the very moments when I was most capable of knowing all the gradations of 'the beautiful and the sublime' . . . I happened not only to know but to carry out the most indecent actions." Banality, egotism, vice, lie beneath the show of idealism. Pozdnyshev tirelessly heaps scorn upon the notions of ideal good, Platonic love, or beauty. "It is a remarkable thing how full of illusion is the notion that beauty is good." He points to the contiguity of beauty and vice. Man—at least upper-class man—finds room for Sodom in his idealism. A woman knows that "our kind lies when he talks about lofty feelings—what he wants is only the body." The romantic is deluded. "I was soiled with lewdness and yet at the same time I was looking for a girl whose purity would meet my standards." Love masks vice. "Every man feels for every pretty woman what you call love." The Underground Man also is ambivalent in his attitude toward love. Apropos his first encounter with Liza in the brothel, he recalls that in the course of two hours he did not exchange a word with this "creature" and did not consider it necessary. "Now, however, I suddenly realized clearly how absurd, repulsive like a spider, was the idea of vice which, without love, coarsely and shamelessly begins precisely where real love finds its consummation." Yet this awareness does not stop the Underground Man from preaching his lofty idealism to Liza; it fuels his cynical "game" with her; one which ends with him taking out on her all the humiliations he has experienced. Disillusioned in his idealism, the Underground Man, like Pozdnyshev, turns on others with a terrible vengeance.

The confessions of both anti-heroes are carried on in "darkness" (the "underground," the brothel, and the night train). The light they bring to themselves, their partners, and the world is apocalyptic. They destabilize the ideals and social codes of their society and demonstrate in their behavior and thought their emptiness. Their message about man and human relations is one of tragic discord, the wide gap between illusion and reality, ideal and nature.

Both men evidence in their behavior the triumph of biological, instinctual man over rational, social man. Man is irrational. This disaster is evident first in the permanently angry, disturbed, and agitated manner in which both the Underground Man and Pozdnyshev discuss their lives and ideas. But it is in their reminiscences of the past that both emerge as incarnations of the uncontrollable, the irrational. Like the man with toothache who delights in his groans and pain, the Underground Man reaches the pitch of delight, despair, and madness in his encounters with Apollon and Liza at the climax of part 2 of *Notes from the Underground.* He dissolves in the fury of his tormenting anguish, his destructive and self-destructive spite. In his effort to assert his authority over his suave servant, the Underground Man becomes more and more insensate. "Go at once! now, this minute, go, go, or you can't dream of what will happen!" the Underground Man screams at Apollon. "I'll murder him, I'll murder him," he shouts later on, pounding the table in a towering rage. The Underground man's terrible, tyrannical debauch of emotions in his final encounter a few moments later with Liza is well known. "And what do I give a damn whether you understand anything of this! And really, what do I give a damn, a damn for you and for whether you perish there or not?" And after his cruel tirade in which he verbally tramples upon the feelings of trust that he had awakened in her, after he cruelly exposes to her the psychological motives that underlay his sentimental behavior toward her in the brothel, he recalls: "She turned white as a sheet, wanted to say something, her lips painfully twisted; but she collapsed in a chair as though she had been cut down by an ax."

Pozdnyshev's excited, shrill voice, his odd physical behavior, his abrupt, near-hysterical utterances, recall the Underground Man. His behavior in the days and hours leading up to the murder seems wholly out of the "underground." Deliberately spiteful, full of mingled self-pity and hatred, he encourages the meeting between his wife and Trukhachevsky. "But, strange as it may seem, some strange, fateful force induced me not to repel him, to keep him at a distance, but on the contrary, to bring him closer." "I smiled pleasantly [at my wife] pretending that I was very pleased." After the concert, the brooding Pozdnyshev is filled, perversely, with "genuine pleasure." In spite of his suffering and wild jealousy, some "strange feeling" compelled him to be "all the more affectionate," the more Trukhachevsky's presence tormented him. But behind all the courteousness is a burning hatred and malice. "And the chief feeling, as always in all spite, was self-pity." "I must do something to make her suffer," he recalls thinking at the time, "so that she may appreciate that I have suffered." Precisely this syndrome of self-pity, resentment, and revenge characterizes the Underground Man's behavior with Liza in his final encounter with her. Indeed, we are in the realm of typical "underground" psychology as we encounter it everywhere in Dostoevsky's works.

"Madness has its own laws," remarks Pozdnyshev as he recalls the fatal momentum of his self-induced spite and rage. Only in *Notes from the Underground* and *The Kreutzer Sonata* do we find classical examples of what might be called the self-orchestrated progressively gathering momentum of spite. As his rage bursts out into the open, Pozdnyshev rouses himself to ever-greater frenzy:

> "For the first time, I wanted to express this spite physically. I leaped up and moved toward her, but at the moment I leaped up, I remember, I was conscious of my spite and asked myself whether it was a good thing to give way to this feeling, and immediately answered that it was good, that

it would frighten her, and immediately, instead of resisting this malice, I began to fan it in myself even more and to rejoice because it grew more and more intense. 'Get the hell out, or I will kill you!' I shouted, approaching her and seizing her by the hand. I consciously intensified the tones of malice in my voice as I spoke these words. And probably I must have been terrifying, because she suddenly quailed. . . . 'Go,' I roared even more loudly. 'Only you can drive me to madness. I won't answer for myself!' Having thus given reign to my madness, I delighted in it, and I wanted to do something extraordinary, to show the full extent of my madness. I terribly wanted to beat and kill her, but I knew that this was not to be had."

On arriving home the evening of the murder, Pozdnyshev is overcome by the same "need for destruction, violence, and the delight of madness and yielded to it." The expression on the faces of his wife and Trukhachevsky when he first spies upon them arouses in him a sense of "agonizing joy." As he rushes at them, he feels that he is "completely mad and must be terrible, and rejoiced in this." The rising crescendo of Pozdnyshev's madness, his "joy," his "ecstasy of destruction," recalls the Underground Man's verbal duel with Apollon, and later, with Liza. The sequel to the Underground Man's madness, if we disregard the important but transient moment of spiritual communication with Liza, is the loveless act of sex. The paying of money—the formal cash nexus defining relations between buyer and seller—is but the Underground Man's final signature to a relationship that for him was almost totally lacking in moral and spiritual foundations. In the case of Pozdnyshev, the order of murder and sex is reversed. Animal sex, identified by Pozdnyshev with market relations and the master-slave relationship, always in his view characterized his relationship with his wife. The real physical murder which brings to a close his tragic bedroom history is a surrogate for the frustrated sexual act, an act which Pozdnyshev perceives, in retrospect at least, as depravity, crime, murder.

The fantastic stories that the Underground Man and Pozdnyshev tell—stories that lead to catastrophes—end in moments of bitter reflection. "Never before did I experience such suffering and remorse." "Even now, after all these years, I recall all this with a particularly *bad* feeling." Pozdnyshev is racked by alternating feelings of rage and remorse. At the very end of his story, after he has related how he had murdered his wife, there is an abatement in his narrative frenzy. He speaks of his eleven months of prison as a period in which he reflected on himself and his past and came to an understanding of it. "I began to understand on the third day" [the day of the funeral]. "Only then, when I saw her dead face, I understood everything that I had done. I understood that I, I had killed her, that I was responsible for her—living, moving, warm—now becoming immobile, waxen, cold, that it was impossible ever, anywhere, in any way to rectify this. He who has not experienced this cannot understand it."

Here there is "understanding," but no love or compassion. His "understanding," however, is ambiguous. In those eleven months he discovered his remorse and angry apocalyptic truth, the truth that perversely justifies his crime. It is significant that his understanding begins, symbolically, on the "third day" after his wife's death. The Easter symbolism here is unmistakable. Yet only love, or at least a recognition of his wife as another human being, can bring spiritual renewal. It is noteworthy that Pozdnyshev words center on the *body* of his wife: before she was "living, moving, warm"; now she is "immobile, waxen, cold." It is the body (he knew her only as an "animal"), not the person (he never names her), that is in the background of his mind. Here there is a recognition of bankruptcy (much as occurs with Raskolnikov at the end of *Crime and Punishment*) but not a deep and transforming *feeling* of remorse. There is no hint of spiritual renewal. Has Pozdnyshev's remorse come too late? It is noteworthy that the name Pozdnyshev is formed on the root of the Russian word *podznij* (late). The story ends on a point of nonending: Pozdnyshev continues on his railroad journey. The end of his story is not the end of his journey. So, too, the Underground Man remains locked in his "underground."

A consideration of *The Kreutzer Sonata* against the background of Dostoevsky and *Notes from the Underground* usefully foregrounds the artistic complexities of a work that for the most part has received little attention as a novel. *The Kreutzer Sonata*, like *Notes from the Underground*, whatever "ideas" it seeks to promote, is a work of fiction. Pozdnyshev is not Tolstoy any more than the Underground Man is Dostoevsky. Without question, Tolstoy uses his second narrator, Pozdnyshev, to set forth his ideas on the relationship between the sexes, advance his notion of celibacy, and so on. Polemical arguments thread their way through Pozdnyshev's narrative; these ideas find expression in an afterword that Tolstoy later (and, it appears, somewhat reluctantly) appended to *The Kreutzer Sonata*. Yet Tolstoy's ideas on sex and marriage, once launched in his narrative, lead a life of their own; they become the property of Pozdnyshev. His frenzied and lopsided mental state, his extremism, his catastrophic story, as with the Underground Man, do not serve in the end to validate his ideas but to make a question of them.

Chekhov—who reproached Tolstoy for "the audacity with which [he] discusses things which he knows nothing about, and which out of stubborness he does not want to know anything" (syphillis, foundling homes, women's [supposed] aversion to intercourse)—nonetheless insisted that "these defects are scattered like feathers in the wind; because of the quality of the story, one simply does not notice them, or if you do notice them, then it is only to regret that the story did not escape the fate of all human work which is imperfect and not free of blemishes." "Apart from its artistic merits, which in places are staggering, we should give thanks alone for the way the story stimulates thought to the extreme. Reading it, you can barely restrain from shouting out: 'this is true!' or 'this is absurd!'" [10] *The Kreutzer Sonata*, in the final analysis, is a *story*, one that lives a life of its own in spite of Tolstoy's deeply personal relation to the hero and his efforts to use him as a mouthpiece for his ideas.

The tortuous, often baffled way Tolstoy related to *The Kreutzer Sonata* at the time of its writing strongly suggests that the theme of the work not only aroused deep and troubled feelings within him, but brought the artist in him into sharp conflict with the polemicist. "I never expected that my train of thought would lead me where it did," Tolstoy wrote in his afterword to *The Kreutzer Sonata*. "I was horrified at my own conclusions, wanted not to believe them, but it was impossible not to." [11] Tolstoy's convoluted way of expressing his thought ("I never expected . . . wanted not to believe . . . impossible not to") causes the reader to wonder whether it was really his conclusions that horrified him or the blind alley into which he led his hero. In the course of the two years during which he worked on *The Kreutzer Sonata* (it went through nine major variants), Tolstoy continually oscillated between expressions of satisfaction over the "useful" quality of the book and dissatisfaction with the story's artistic rendering. "I have been thinking that I've been fussing over the writing of *The Kreutzer Sonata* out of vanity," he wrote in his notebook August 29, 1889. "One doesn't want it to appear before the public without a fine finish, unshapely, even poor. And what we have here is dreadful. If there's something useful, necessary for people, they will get it even from something that is poor. A refined, perfected story will not make my conclusions more convincing. One has to be a *yurodivy* [holy simpleton] in writing."[12]

Tolstoy, however, continues to struggle with the artistic side of his work; the idea of the artistic inadequacy of the work continues to bother him. Responding to N. N. Strakhov's critical comments on the work, Tolstoy in a reply of November 17, 1889, humbly acknowledges artistic flaws in the work but maintains that he "can't go on revising it." The work as it stands is not only "not without usefulness, but of a certainty very useful to people and new in part. If one were to write in an artistic way—something which I do not renounce—then one would have to begin anew and right away."[13] Tolstoy goes on revising and polishing his work. Yet the work has become a "fearful bore," he confides to his notebook on December 6, 1889. "Chiefly because of the fact that there's something artistically not right about it, false."[14] Nonetheless, Tolstoy continues to put the finishing touches on this "useful" work and continues to express satisfaction over its usefulness. Yet on April 15, 1891, responding negatively to news (subsequently proven wrong) that the emperor had promised to allow the official publication of *The Kreutzer Sonata*, Tolstoy wrote: "I am by no means happy about this. For there was something nasty [*durnoe*] in *The Kreutzer Sonata*. I have found it terribly repugnant, every recollection of it. There was something nasty in the motives that guided me as I wrote, it evoked such malice. I even see this nastiness."[15] The reader also sees and feels that "nastiness," but not in a way that undermines his sense of the artistic integrity of the work.

Dostoevsky, like Tolstoy with respect to *The Kreutzer Sonata*, seems to have related to his *Notes from the Underground* in an ambivalent way. He wrote the work at a time of great emotional and physical stress: "My nerves are disordered. . . . My torments *of all sorts* now are so painful that I cannot even mention them," he wrote to his brother

Mikhail while at work on *Notes*. "My wife is dying, *literally*."[16] He views his writing of *Notes from the Underground* as a race with death, his wife's.[17] His physical ailments[18] and emotional tensions add up to a kind of "external fatalism"[19]—a fatalism that may explain in part at least the sense of ineluctable fate that rules the Underground Man. Dostoevsky found the work "far more difficult to write" than he had anticipated, he wrote again in this period to his brother. "And yet it is absolutely necessary that it be good; *for me myself* this is necessary. In its tone it is too strange, and the tone is harsh and wild."[20] Yet he nonetheless speaks of the work as "strong and frank; it will be the truth."[21] Years later, Dostoevsky again reflected ambivalently on his work. Responding with a broad smile to a reader's compliments about *Notes from the Underground*, he went on to say that *Notes* "is really too gloomy. Es ist schon ein überwundener Standpunkt. Nowadays I can write in a more serene, conciliatory way."[22] Clearly, *Notes from the Underground* lacked the element of transcension for Dostoevsky. The dialectic of freedom that the Underground Man embodies and that serves as a bulwark against forces assaulting the individual is fundamentally tragic in its development, ultimately destructive of both individual and society. The Underground Man, like the protagonist of *The Kreutzer Sonata*, for all the moral-philosophical truth to which he gives expression, is bankrupt. Dostoevsky, like Tolstoy, seems to have recoiled from the "underground" he explored, an "underground" in which he leaves his anti-hero and, in a certain sense, his reader.

There is nothing decisive, though there may be something valuable, in an author's opinion of his own work. He stands before his finished work like any other critic. The observations of Tolstoy and Dostoevsky on *The Kreutzer Sonata* and *Notes from the Underground*, viewed in the context of all we know about their history and writing, attest to the special place these works occupy in their authors' oeuvres. Tolstoy's nagging self-criticism points to his massive struggle to cope simultaneously with the conflicting demands of art and polemic and with his own "malice." Malice was also a strong component in Dostoevsky's ideological polemics in *Notes from the Underground*, polemics that reached deeply into his own experience in prison. "Malice," indeed, masters both the authors and the protagonists of these works and results in works in which the tragic element is expressed in the form of unmitigated catastrophe. Both *Notes from the Underground* and *The Kreutzer Sonata*, finally, are profoundly disturbing, even disorienting works. Dostoevsky and Tolstoy are rightly wary of their products and, as it were, warn against them even as they vouch for their truth and the authenticity of their conclusions.

With good reason. There is a pervasive sense in these works not merely of broken crockery, but permanently botched human endeavor. They are in this sense singularly modern works; their strength and appeal lie not in any resolution to the problems raised but in the courage with which the authors face the intractable questions of human nature. *Notes from the Underground* and *The Kreutzer Sonata* are, indeed, very gloomy and nasty works. Yet as Franz Kafka once observed, "We must have those books that come upon us like ill-fortune, and distress us deeply, like the death of one we love better than ourselves, like suicide. A book must be an ice-ax to break the sea frozen within us."

12   *States of Ambiguity*
Early Shakespeare and Late Dostoevsky,
the Two Ivans

How can I tell the many thousand ways
By which one heart another heart divines?
How can I tell the many thousand ways
By which it keeps the secret it betrays?

Longfellow, *Emma and Eginhard*

 Every reader of *The Brothers Karamazov* remembers how, after the murder of his father, Ivan makes three visits to Smerdyakov. Each visit brings this nineteenth-century Oedipus closer to the truth about the murder, closer to the realization of his complicity in the crime. The process of probing and self-disclosure continues until, in the last visit, Smerdyakov boldly declares: "You murdered him, you are precisely the chief murderer; I was only your instrument, your faithful servant Licharda, and it was following your words that I carried through your business." "Carried it through?" Ivan stammers. "Why, did you murder him?" Ivan, the narrator writes, turned cold. "Something seemed to give way in his brain."

The drama for the reader in these scenes lies not so much in the revelation of the truth about Smerdyakov's role in the crime as in the psychological self-unravelling of Ivan, a process that is dialectical and involves Ivan's relation to himself and his alter ego, Smerdyakov. Ivan had sought to mask his complicity. Guilt drives him toward self-disclosure.

Guilt and knowledge of complicity in one sense mark all of Ivan's conversations with Smerdyakov in the novel. The important conversations between Ivan and Smerdyakov on the eve and morning of

Ivan's departure from his father's house reveal how Smerdyakov, sensing Ivan's wishes, obliquely conveys to him his vile intentions. Ivan seems to grasp Smerdyakov's intentions; indeed, on a certain level of his consciousness, he does comprehend them ("I remember my im pressions," he remarks later on). But he suppresses his rage and does not strike Smerdyakov. He fails to realize, however, that by suppressing his rage he is signaling his consent to crime. When Ivan finally agrees to go to Chermashnya—"you see . . . I am going to Chermashnya" suddenly broke from his lips—Smerdyakov remarks: "It's a true saying, then, that 'it's always worthwhile speaking to a clever man.'" Ivan suddenly laughs. His is the sick laughter of complicity and imbalance.

When Ivan finally ferrets out the truth in his conversations with Smerdyakov, the latter vigorously defends himself. He insists that he was not "playing" with Ivan in the conversations before the murder; he had put his whole trust in him as "in God Almighty." Smerdyakov maintains that Ivan had "guessed" why he wanted him to go to Chermashnya: to be away from the house when the crime took place; "I thought you were [a coward] like me." Smerdyakov thought that Ivan knew beforehand of the murder and had left Fyodor to his fate. Indeed, Smerdyakov insists that Ivan was "very desirous" of his father's death. Ivan, he argues, had a foreboding about him, and yet went away. "You as good as said: 'You can murder my parent, and I won't hinder you,'" "and by your consent you silently sanctioned my doing this business."

Let us turn to another Ivan, another work, another time. I have in mind Shakespeare's play *King John*. The play was probably written in the early 1590's. A long and elaborate play, it contains two episodes which are of particular interest to analysts of the Ivan-Smerdyakov relationship. In the first episode (at the end of scene 2, act 3), King John, a usurper on the English throne, instigates Hubert, a citizen of Angers, to kill young Arthur, duke of Brittainy and legitimate claimant to the English throne. In the second episode (at the end of scene 2, act 4) King John, believing the murder to have been accomplished but now fearing the consequences for himself, accuses Hubert of provoking him, King John, to crime.

These episodes are closely related to each other; in fact, they may be said to form a single unit in the dramatic and psychological sense. It is these two episodes that I shall discuss; in the process, I wish to show their affinities with the corresponding, though more elaborate scenes in *The Brothers Karamazov* dealing with Ivan and Smerdyakov. What concerns us here is not the very problematic question of influence (always of minor importance where great works of art are concerned) but the similar ways two great artists approached the problem of moral duplicity in the criminal compact.[1]

King John wishes to put Prince Arthur, rightful heir to the throne of Richard Coeur de Lion, out of the way. Taking his chamberlain Hubert aside, he raises the subject of murder indirectly, through hints, allusions, imagery. His language gives expression to his duplicity: he wishes to express his vile purposes, but without words; he wishes his purposes to be heeded, but silently. "I had a thing to say, but let it go," he says twice, but without letting go. He wishes to be seen, as he puts it, "without eyes / Hear me without thine ears, and make reply / Without a tongue, using conceit alone / Without eyes, ears, and harmful sound of words." "I would into thy bosom pour my thoughts: But, ah, I will not. Yet I love thee well."

King John, like the tempter, wraps his purposes in a confusion of words and flattery. Finally he reveals his identity, but perversely in reverse perspective: he calls Arthur a *serpent*. "Dost thou understand me? Thou art his keeper," he says to Hubert. Hubert grasps John's intentions at once and promises to "keep him so well that he shall not offend your majesty." At this point there follows a brilliant exchange of words whose very brevity speaks of the evil that weighs them down:

King John: Death.
Hubert: My lord?
King John: A grave.
Hubert: He shall not live.
King John: Enough.

"I could be merry now," King John adds with the same nervous levity that afflicts Ivan when his compact with Smerdyakov is made.

William Hazlitt called this scene "a masterpiece of dramatic skill." One might add that the extraordinary compression and terseness of language at its conclusion anticipates Pushkin in his *Little Tragedies*, particularly in the complicity scene between Albert and his servant Ivan in "The Covetous Knight."

King John seems fully conscious of his vile purposes, though he prefers, significantly, to let Hubert draw the conclusions so as morally to implicate him in the crime. Yet John, like Ivan Karamazov and, as we shall see, Smerdyakov, is not prepared in the end to accept responsibility for the crime.

In the episode I have discussed, King John and Hubert agree, almost tacitly, that Arthur shall be murdered: his eyes put out (the metaphor of sight and blindness is central in *King John*). But Hubert, despite his verbal readiness to accomplish John's wishes, at the last moment decides to release Arthur. He is incapable, it seems, of matching his purpose with the actual deed.

In act 4, scene 2, King John and Hubert meet again. Hubert warns John that a rumor of the death of Arthur is rousing the populace. Alarmed, John's first response is to blame Hubert for urging Arthur's death, an accusation that is without foundation.

> Why urgest thou so oft young Arthur's death?
> Thy hand hath murdered him: I had a mighty cause
> to wish him dead, but thou hadst none to kill him.

We may recall at this point Ivan's remarks to Smerdyakov: "Perhaps I really had a secret desire for . . . my father's death, but I swear I was not as guilty as you think, and perhaps I didn't urge you [*podbivat'*] at all." Like John, Ivan does not comprehend, or wish to comprehend, the link between wishes and the hand that commits the crime.

King John, then, insists that Hubert had no cause to kill Arthur. Hubert, taken aback by John's refusal to recognize his culpability, retorts that John was the person who instigated him to kill Arthur. At this point John adopts an astounding and subtle line of defense, one he sums up later with these words: "How oft the sight of means to do ill deeds, make deeds ill done." But John remarks at this point:

> It is the curse of kings to be attended
> By slaves that take their humours for a warrant
> To break within the bloody house of life,

And on the winking of authority
To understand a law, to know the meaning
Of dangerous majesty, when perchance it frowns
More upon humour than advis'd respect.

Not the king, then, with his "winking of authority," but the slave who follows up the hint, or "winking of authority," is to blame!

At this point Hubert presents John with proof of the king's complicity in the proposed crime. "Here is your hand and seal for what I did." But John is not abashed. For a moment he admits his complicity but then falls back on his defense, blaming both the king's seal and Hubert:

O, when the last accompt 'twixt heaven and earth
Is to be made, then shall this hand and seal
Witness against us to damnation!
How oft the sight of means to do ill deeds
Make deeds ill done! Hadst not thou been by,
A fellow by the hand of nature mark'd
Quoted and signed to do a deed of shame,
This murther had not come into my mind;
But taking note of thy abhorr'd aspect,
Finding thee fit for bloody villainy,
Apt, liable to be employ'd in danger,
I faintly broke with thee of Arthur's death;
And thou, to be endeared to a king,
Made it no conscience to destroy a prince.

The brazen and bland evasiveness and posture of innocence of John is striking. For a moment John seems to admit his complicity, but only indirectly: it is, he suggests, the "hand and seal," the concrete embodiment of the king's authority, of power, that is somehow to blame. But it is not merely the sight of the seal, the visible sanction of authority, that instigates men to commit a crime; according to John, the very sight of men who are prepared to commit vile deeds draws men of power, like him, into crime. In short, if kings were not surrounded by slaves, sycophants, and vile example, they would not be tempted to tempt others into crime. It is the presence of slavish people of "abhorr'd aspect," of vile appearance and demeanor, that makes possible evil deeds. The sight of Hubert, "by the hand of nature marked," John insists, seduced John into crime. "I faintly broke with thee of Arthur's death; and thou, to be endeared to a king, made it no conscience to destroy a prince."

There is much Shakespearean wisdom in King John's words, though he fails to grasp their application to himself. The existence of men of "abhorr'd aspect," of men "fit for villainy," is indeed an inducement to crime. And it is precisely this truth that Dostoevsky explores in *The Brothers Karamazov*. Smerdyakov, an illegitimate creature of "nature," a man of vile aspect, is indeed a temptation to crime. But at the same time we recognize in Smerdyakov the concentrated expression, or projection, of the vile side of Ivan's character. It is noteworthy, too, that Ivan, like John, views his coconspirator as a lower being. Smerdyakov, Ivan contemptuously declares, is "first-rate material" for crude insurrection. In turn, the lackey Smerdyakov, idolizing Ivan, carries out his wishes and murders Fyodor. John's rebuke to Hubert—"and thou, to be endeared to a king, made it no conscience to kill"—would seem appropriate here.

Whatever the general applicability of John's words, they impute to Hubert a villainy that more properly fits John himself. We shall see in a moment that John's defense, his refusal to recognize his responsibility, anticipates on the moral-psychological plane Smerdyakov's defense before Ivan. Let us first, however, listen to the final words of John's defense. They lead us into the heart of that type of complicity or moral duplicity that Dostoevsky explores in *The Brothers Karamazov*.

King John, as I have noted, gave Hubert the wink of authority, or signal to commit a crime. In his final words to Hubert, John blames Hubert for signaling back to him his willingness to commit the crime.

> Hadst thou but shook thy head or made a pause
> When I spake darkly what I purposed,
> Or turn'd an eye of doubt upon my face,
> As bid me tell my tale in express words,
> Deep shame had struck me dumb, made me break off,
> And those thy fears might have wrought fears in me:
> But thou didst understand me by my signs
> And didst in signs again parley with sin;
> Yes, without stop, didst let thy heart consent,
> And consequently thy rude hand to act

The deed, which both our tongues held vile to name.
Out of my sight, and never see me more!

John's words once again testify to his shameless refusal to accept responsibility for the crime. Yet at the same time these words contain a superior awareness: when men conspire to commit crime in the ambiguous and morally duplicitous manner of John and Hubert, and even more of Ivan and Smerdyakov, the criminal compact depends as much upon the response of the person to whom one signals as one's signals. Responsibility is mutual in this game.

An ambiguous game of signs and signals is at the heart of the conspiracy of Ivan and Smerdyakov to commit crime. In the middle of his conversation with Ivan at the gateway to Fyodor's house, Smerdyakov informs Ivan that he has conveyed to Dmitry the "signals" for gaining entrance to Fyodor's house. With the knowledge of these signals, Dmitry could make his way into the house and murder his father. But in telling Ivan that he had disclosed to Dmitry the signals for entering the house, Smerdyakov in effect makes the first signal to Ivan of his intention to aid and abet any action that might result in Fyodor's death. Ivan, as we know, signals back his consent in ways that contradict his words. He participates in a game of signs and signals.

In the two conversations between Ivan and Smerdyakov on the eve and morning of Ivan's departure, language loses its function as a direct communicator of thought and is transformed into a series of signs and signals whose function is not to convey thought clearly but to obfuscate or mask it. This corruption of language, this shortcircuiting of the sign and the signified, is the concomitant in the linguistic realm of the breakdown of those moral and social "connections" which distinguish the functioning social organism from an arbitrary collection of disconnected happenings. It is no accident that the words *sin* and *sign* are punned upon in *King John*, are identified with one another on the semantic plane.

We are confronted by a paradox: the very same play with language that is the life of art (as in *King John* or *The Brothers Karamazov*) in the sphere of human relations signals disintegration in life. In the breakdown of the individual or society, language is the first victim. Dostoevsky understood this very well.

Let me bring my brief discussion to a conclusion. King John blames Hubert for understanding him "by his signs," and in turn for parleying in sin by means of signs. Here we must note that John's defense essentially parallels Smerdyakov's defense before Ivan. Ivan, Smerdyakov insists, understood his hints and signals. "By your consent you silently sanctioned my doing this business." In other words, Ivan, in Shakespeare's words, "didst in signs again parley with sin." When Smerdyakov finally realizes that Ivan was at least partially unaware of his complicity in the crime, when his idol crumbles, he bids him "farewell" much as John, confronted by the reality of his image in Hubert, banishes Hubert from his sight forever.

John insists that had Hubert shaken his head "or made a pause," he, John, would have been struck by "deep shame." But there is nothing in John's character to suggest that he is any more capable of feeling deep shame than Smerdyakov. Like Smerdyakov, John is first cowardly, devious, and in his relations at least with Hubert, a master of sophistry. William Hazlitt rightly observed that "there are few characters on the stage that excite more disgust and loathing" than King John. We might say the same of Smerdyakov. Now, if we look at John more closely, we recognize that he is a king in name but a Smerdyakov in soul. A "usurper" on the throne, he is, to use Shakespeare's word, "unnatural" in his person. His defense of his actions is marked by singular insight, but it is an insight that serves to mask him from himself. Insight here, paradoxically, is blindness; it conceals a character of "abhorr'd aspect." John attributes to Hubert the vileness and cowardice of his own nature, his own "abhorr'd aspect," much as Smerdyakov mistakenly sees in Ivan a mirror image of himself. "I thought you were like me." Smerdyakov, of course, is wrong, just as John is wrong in seeing in Hubert a person of "abhorr'd aspect." "You have slandered nature in my form," Hubert with considerable truth remarks later to John.

I began by calling attention to certain parallels between the two Ivans, Ivan Karamazov and King John. But I close with the suggestion that on the moral, or moral-psychological, plane, John more closely resembles Smerdyakov. John, not Hubert, has the soul of a slave. In turn, Hubert, though obviously capable of crime, would appear, like

Ivan, to be endowed with a certain irreducible nobility and conscience; he is unwilling or unable, in the last analysis, to match his criminal intent with the criminal deed. In his general predisposition toward self-division, at least, Hubert resembles Ivan.

What links John and Smerdyakov, finally, is a kind of bland insularity or sense of innocence in the midst of evil. And there is no more terrifying evil than that which wraps itself in the bland innocence of an inert soul.

13 *Counterpoint*
Nietzsche and Dostoevsky

 The Russian philosopher Nicholas Berdyaev once maintained that Dostoevsky knew everything Nietzsche knew
and something more.[1] I should like to reply with a similar
turn of phrase: Nietzsche knew everything Dostoevsky knew and
something more. There is no real paradox here: both of these statements are true. Nietzsche and Dostoevsky share a vast field of insights
into the nature of man. They differ not so much in their fundamental
tragic perception of man—what they *know*—as in the form, the shape
they give as artist-philosophers to the dialectic of life as they know it.
The "something more" was what each asked of man—asked contrary
to what each in his own way knew to be the truth. The secret of
Dostoevsky and Nietzsche is that both desperately wanted to create
truth: the one in the affirmation of an unattainable ideal of love and
self-sacrifice; the other in the affirmation of a heroic, Promethean
conception of human potential. Especially noteworthy here is not only
the opposing character of these two ideals, but the way each ideal
emerges from a shared tragic vision.

At the outset I should like to single out and contrast in the work
of Nietzsche[2] and Dostoevsky two crises leading to two very opposite
kinds of revelation or truths. My first example is from *Thus Spoke
Zarathustra,* and my second is from Dostoevsky's short sketch "The

Peasant Marey." In the prologue to *Thus Spoke Zarathustra*, Nietzsche depicts a momentous crisis in the life of its godlike hero, a crisis which Zarathustra himself later sums up ironically: "God too has his hell: that is his love of man."[3] As the work opens, Zarathustra, overflowing with wisdom, descends from his mountain retreat in search of followers. "I love man," he declares to an old hermit he encounters in the woods. But the hermit who had gone into the forest in disillusionment because he had once loved man all too much, replies: "Now I love God; man I love not. Man is for me too imperfect a thing. Love of man would kill me."[4] And he advises Zarathustra—much in the spirit of Dostoevsky's Grand Inquisitor—not to bring men gifts but to take part of their load.

But Zarathustra wishes to distribute the honey of his wisdom, and he wants followers. He goes to the marketplace in town, where a tightrope-walking act is in progress, and preaches the *overman* (the *Übermensch*). Using the tightrope act as a metaphor, he preaches that "man is a rope, tied between beast and overman—a rope over an abyss. A dangerous across, a dangerous on-the-way, a dangerous looking-back, a dangerous shuddering and stopping. What is great in man," Zarathustra continues, "is that he is a bridge and not an end: what can be loved in man is that he is an *overture* and a *going under*."[5] Zarathustra pleads that man "remain faithful to the earth"[6]—a core idea of Nietzsche—that as a first step he become conscious of himself as a polluted stream. He preaches self-overcoming and exposes the wasteland of the gregarious, self-oriented, banal existence of the "last man."

But the people on the square remain dumb to Zarathustra's pleas; they laugh at his idealism and shout: "Turn us into those last men! Then we shall make you a gift of the overman!"[7] Zarathustra, like Jesus, though with a different message, is rejected.

The tightrope walker falls and is mortally injured. Zarathustra comforts the dying man: he is but a symbol to Zarathustra of man's dangerous crossing over and going under; his death is a fulfillment of man's vocation—a perpetual confrontation with the giant accident, with the intrinsic meaninglessness of existence.

Zarathustra, forced to leave town, is sad, and his dark night of the soul begins. He carries the dead man into the mythic forest, puts him

into the hollow of a tree, and falls asleep. The next morning he awakens, refreshed, a renewed man (like Faust at the beginning of part 2 in
Goeth's drama); he awakens joyously; "for he saw a new truth," he tells
us; he will no longer "seek corpses, herds and believers," no longer
speak to the people, but only to a few select disciples. "Never again
shall I speak to the people: for the last time I have spoken to the
dead."[8]

Zarathustra's first great crisis is resolved. On the ideological and
social plane, it involves a turning away from the "people" and the
"herd," a rejection, ultimately, of all Christian, socialist, eudaemonis-
tic ideas and solutions; a rejection of compassionate ministering to the
philistine herd. Zarathustra chooses what the Danish critic Georg
Brandes later termed "aristocratic radicalism." What is involved here,
on the social plane at least, is a despairingly pessimistic view of contemporary man, of the people—*das Volk*: for Nietzsche, as for Ibsen,
simply a term for petit bourgeois, philistine man. Zarathustra will
hold out for the absolute: "What is great in man is that he is a bridge,
not an end."[9] He will teach the beautiful ideal of the overman, the
ideal of future man, what man must become. For with the death of
God, man as he exists must die, and the overman must follow. The
paradox of Zarathustra's aristocratic rejection of the people, yet his
general solicitude for man's fate, is perhaps best summed up in one of
Nietzsche's notes dated 1886: "The *artist*-philosopher. Higher concept
of art. Whether a man can place himself so far distant from other men
that he can form them?"[10]

Let us now turn to another significant sleep and awakening, and
an equally astounding one. I have in mind the sketch in Dostoevsky's
Diary of a Writer of February 1876 entitled "The Peasant Marey," a
work in which Dostoevsky takes us back to his days as a convict in
prison, and, beyond that to his childhood.[11] We are witness to an il-
lumination in which the artist-convict Dostoevsky discovers the truth
about the Russian people. At the outset of his sketch, Dostoevsky recalls his first Easter Monday in prison in 1850. He accents the terrible
degradation of the whole environment, the disgusting violence and
brutality of the convicts. "I was never able to endure without revulsion
the drunken orgies of the people, and here in this place in particular."
Dostoevsky recalls how in the midst of this barracks nightmare he lay

down on his bunk and began to daydream about his childhood; how once, overcome by a fear of wolves in the country, he had rushed into the arms of the benevolent and kindly peasant Marey. In his dream recollection, the convict Dostoevsky recalled the "gentle motherly smile" of the poor serf, the way Marey signed him with the cross and comforted him. The memory of this episode has a powerful impact on Dostoevsky the convict; as Dostoevsky the writer recalls it, he arose from his daydream a changed man, the possessor, like Zarathustra, of a new truth:

> And so when I got off the bunk and looked around, I remember, I sud-
> denly felt that I could look at these unhappy creatures with quite a differ-
> ent glance, and that suddenly, as though by some miracle, all hatred and
> anger vanished from my heart. I went about looking into the faces of
> people I encountered. This rascal of a peasant with shaven head and
> branded face, intoxicated, bawling out his drunken hoarse song—why, he
> too may be the very same Marey: after all, I really can't look into his heart.

After reading "The Peasant Marey," we are inclined to think of the title of Goethe's autobiography: "From My Life. Poetry and Truth." Here in "The Peasant Marey" there is the repulsive earthly truth about the convicts, but then "suddenly" as the result of an intervening daydream there is poetry, the revelation of another, spiritual truth. Suddenly Dostoevsky the convict looks at the people with different eyes.

"The Peasant Marey" illustrates a striking feature in Dostoevsky's art and outlook: the permanent and creative interaction of poetry, the fictive art, on the one hand, and the reality of truth, or truth of reality on the other. Reality for Dostoevsky always is pregnant with an inner truth, a poetry that can at any moment suddenly make itself felt (and *suddenly* is one of his favorite words); a poetry that in spiritual-religious terms is revelation but in purely aesthetic terms for Dostoevsky means a triumph over naturalistic surface reality, a disclosure of the rich but usually masked interiority of man and human reality. "One need only remove the outer, superficial crust and examine more attentively the kernel itself, more closely and without prejudice," Dostoevsky writes in *Notes from the House of the Dead* "and some of us will see things in the people that we never expected." And in a casual aside at the outset of the work—one which might almost pass unnoticed were it not for "The Peasant Marey" fifteen years later—the narrator of *House of the Dead* remarks, "I see it all now almost as in a dream."

We may recapitulate at this point and draw the first threads of our discussion together. Zarathustra and the narrator of "The Peasant Marey" endure severe crises involving the question of love or esteem of the people; both pass through a dark night of the soul, and both awake with a renewed sense of truth; but that truth takes a different form for each of them. Both Nietzsche and Dostoevsky—I think we can substitute their names here—recoil from direct contact with the people; each seeks refuge in poetry: Nietzsche in a poetry of transcendence, an ecstatic ideal of aesthetic individualism; Dostoevsky in a poetics of insight and transfiguration and a poetry of an ecstatic populism.

Nietzsche turns away from the herd in the name of the future overman. Dostoevsky, whose contact with the convicts sent him in anguish and despair to the sick ward of the prison hospital, affirms through memory another reality beneath the repulsive crust. Both Nietzsche and Dostoevsky in fact recoil from the nature of man as they find him in everyday reality. Dostoevsky (to borrow some phrases from the early Nietzsche) affirms the "redeeming vision," "redemption through illusion,"[12] the "joyous necessity of the dream experience,"[13] he envisages redemption ultimately through man's acknowledgement of the humble virtues and through the action upon man of higher spiritual beauty and man's striving for that beauty. Nietzsche, on the other hand, in his disgust and despair calls upon man to make way for the overman, calls upon man-in-transition, or an elite core of men, to overcome themselves, to become their own reality; in the face of an indifferent universe to make of themselves and their life a living art form. "Everything has become," Nietzsche repeats in his writings, everything is open to man in his striving to become himself.

In *Birth of Tragedy* Nietzsche posits art as the only thing that gives meaning to existence: "only as an *aesthetic phenomenon* is existence and the world . . . eternally justified."[14] In his later work this passionate reliance upon art expresses itself in a demand that man make an art form of himself, that he "give style" to his character, comprehend his "strengths and weaknesses" "in an artistic plan."[15] In the words of Zarathustra, man must "create and carry together into One what is fragment, and riddle and dreadful accident."[16] "To become master of the chaos one is," Nietzsche insisted, "to compel one's chaos to become form"—that, in art, is the "grand style."[17] The core of Nietzsche's aesthetic individualism rests, perhaps, on this belief in self-creation, a belief not in contemporary man but in the greatness of human resources.

The idea of aesthetic self-creation is a strong, though ultimately ambivalent motif in Dostoevsky's art and outlook. "Man does not live his whole life, but *composes himself*," Dostoevsky wrote in his notebook toward the end of his life.[18] Life is a whole art, he liked to emphasize, and to live means to make a work of art of oneself. In his great works, of course, such as *The Devils* or "A Gentle Creature," the impulse to self-creation is often presented by Dostoevsky in the corrupted and evil forms of a striving to become the man-god. Self-creation becomes an aspect of pride, of demonic temptation. But the impulse toward self-creation in Dostoevsky is also full of anxiety. For Dostoevsky and for some of his heroes, the quest for form is inseparable from a feeling of inadequacy (Ordynov, Myshkin). This quest is the concomitant of a profound doubt in those very elements and resources in man which Nietzsche draws upon to create his ideal overman. Dostoevsky's quest for form, finally, is not only a search for unity in self-creation but also a craving for self-sublimation, for mystically ecstatic union with God or the universe. Prince Myshkin's experience of world harmony in the moments before his epileptic fit is a good example of the fantastic and extremely problematic character of self-creation in Dostoevsky's art and outlook. Myshkin's experience of world harmony is a moment of "beauty and prayer," an experience of classical form itself, an experience of perfect measure and proportion. But it is a moment of blinding light followed instantly by a profound darkness and chaos.

The search for form, ultimately for religious beatitude, is linked in Dostoevsky not with the exaltation of man and his rational powers but with the fall of man; it is inseparable from a recognition of the reality of original sin, of man's primal guilt, but it is also inseparable from a recognition of man's freedom of will in a moral universe. "By making man responsible," Dostoevsky wrote in his *Diary of a Writer* in 1873. "Christianity in this way also recognizes his freedom."[19]

For Nietzsche, on the other hand, the quest for self-creation can be based only on the renunciation of the "error of accountability," which in turn rests on the "error of freedom of will."[20] It is not immoralism, of course, that Nietzsche preaches. One may recall here Nietzsche's observation about Lou Andreas-Salomé in a draft of a letter to Dr. Paul Rée in 1882. "She herself told me she has no morality—and I thought she, like me, had a stricter morality than anyone else, and brought to it frequently, daily and hourly, some personal sacrifice, and had a right to think about morality."[21] It is not immoralism that Nietzsche preaches: both art and overman attain their maximum freedom through conscious subordination to the laws of necessity. But we are free, Nietzsche believes, only to the degree that we dispense with a priori "illusions" of realities, only when we cease believing in realities which are no realities. The categories of "aim," "unity," or the concept of "truth," Nietzsche insists, "*refer to a purely fictitious world.*"[22] The most pernicious illusion is the one that makes us happy.[23]

We are at the crossroads of Nietzsche and Dostoevsky. The latter affirms not only the reality but the necessity of illusion: the necessity of faith in something beyond and above man, something that man ceaselessly strives for and even worships but can never attain on earth. If we would comprehend Dostoevsky's outlook fully, we must recall the melancholy words he put down in his notebook in 1864: "Man strives on earth for an ideal that is *contrary* to his nature. . . . When man does not fulfill the law of striving for the ideal . . . he experiences suffering and he calls this sin. And thus man continually must experience suffering, which is balanced by the divine pleasure in fulfillment of the Law, i.e., sacrifice. Precisely here, then, is earthly equilibrium. Otherwise the earth would be senseless."

Dostoevsky found his ideal expressed most vividly in the image and example of Christ, an aesthetic, perhaps Hellenized image; he found it in the classical art of antiquity—the Apollo of Belvedere and the Venus of Milo; in the paintings of Raphael and Correggio; in the dream of a golden age, such as he read into one of Claude Lorraine's famous paintings, *Acis and Galatea*. With Dostoevsky, especially where his higher aesthetic is concerned, we are in the presence of a cult of classical form, a religious worship of an art, a seeking for legendary moral and spiritual values, for the good, the true and the beautiful.

There is no doubt that the philosopher Nietzsche found this side of Dostoevsky suspect. He writes in *Beyond Good and Evil* of the "impassioned and exaggerated worship of 'pure forms' among philosophers and artists: let nobody doubt that whoever stands that much in *need* of the cult of surfaces must at some time have reached *beneath* them with disastrous results." [24] The remark could easily apply to Dostoevsky.

Yet paradoxically nobody more than Nietzsche recognized the profound role that art, illusion, myth, and dream play in the life of man. Had he not in his earliest work accented the "joyous necessity of the dream experience," the "radiant dream-birth of the Olympians," "redemption through illusion," and the "redeeming vision"? Nietzsche, it is true, came to see man's salvation only in the event of his full recognition that "there is no reality for us," [25] only in man's stripping from himself all illusions and confronting—that is, shaping—his own reality. Yet this same Nietzsche also propounded and accepted to the end of his days the counterthought that "we possess *art* lest *we perish of the truth*." [26] "There is only *one* world," he insists in 1886 in a draft preface for a new edition of *The Birth of Tragedy*, "and this is false, cruel, contradictory, seductive, without meaning." And he adds:

> *We have need of lies* in order to conquer this reality, this "truth," that is, in order to *live*—That lies are necessary in order to live is itself part of the terrifying and questionable character of existence. . . . "Life *ought* to inspire confidence": the task thus imposed is tremendous. To solve it, man must be a liar by nature, he must be above all an *artist*. . . . That the character of existence is to be misunderstood—profoundest and supreme secret motive behind all that is virtue, science, piety, artistry.[27]

One is astounded here by Nietzsche's readiness to acknowledge the necessity of illusion in the face of his striving to provide the philosophical foundations for a life without illusions. Dostoevsky, we cannot doubt, survived his terrible confrontations with death and imprisonment only through the dream and illusion, only through an act of art and faith, one which enabled him, in the language of Nietzsche, "to conquer this reality, this 'truth,' " "this terrifying and questionable character of existence." Such was the triumph of Greek art, in the view of Nietzsche; such was the accomplishment of Dostoevsky's tragic art.

We have found the point of convergence between Nietzsche and

Dostoevsky in their common recognition of the terrifying and questionable character of existence. Where, then, do they diverge from one another? Fundamentally, Nietzsche, the later Nietzsche, for all his recognition of illusion and its place in life ("all of life is based on semblance, art, deception, points of view, and the necessity of perspectives and error")[28] *does not want to live with illusion.* The secret motive of artistry is that "the character of existence is to be misunderstood." Yet Nietzsche himself, above all, did not want to misunderstand the terrifying character of existence. In *Human, All-Too-Human,* he confesses that "it is not without profound sorrow that one admits to oneself that in their highest flights the artists of all ages have raised to heavenly transfiguration precisely those conceptions which we now recognize as false: they are the glorifiers of the religious and philosophical errors of mankind."[29]

Nietzsche, of course, wished to make, and wanted man to make, a heroic break with these errors through acknowledging them to be errors. With a terrifying lucidity, he insisted that one had to come to terms with an objectively indifferent, purposeless world, to face necessity and, through that confrontation to rediscover or create meaning and authentic freedom. "My formula for greatness in a human being is *amor fati,* that one wants nothing to be different, not forward, not backward, not in all eternity. Not merely bear what is necessary, still less conceal it—all idealism is mendaciousness in the face of what is necessary—but *love* it."[30]

But in contrast to Nietzsche, yet with the same tragic vision of life, Dostoevsky the artist *did not want to remain with earthly truth.* No other Russian writer, unless it be Gogol, had more of a craving than Dostoevsky for what Nietzsche called religious and philosophical errors. One must go back to those fearful Siberian years when he was as though "buried alive and closed up in a coffin"[31] to realize why such a man might come to believe more fervently than ever in the raising of Lazarus. "I turned my will to health, to *life,* into a philosophy," Nietzsche wrote in *Ecce Homo.*[32] Sickness, he maintained, brought him to reason. Dostoevsky, physically sick and depressed in prison, turned his will to health into an art of aesthetic and spiritual transfiguration. Sickness and adversity strengthened religious convictions in him that alone made life on earth meaningful to him. He was terribly far from Nietzsche's *amor fati.* His choice *not* to remain with earthly truth was nowhere more vividly and poignantly expressed than in a letter he wrote to N. D. Fonvizina immediately on his release from prison. In this letter he speaks of his terrible "thirst to believe," one which is "all the stronger in my soul the more there are opposite proofs in me." Dostoevsky concludes that even "if somebody proved to me that Christ was outside the truth, and it *really* were so that the truth was outside of Christ, then I would rather remain with Christ than with the truth."[33] Such was the paradoxical triumph of illusion, of the aesthetic-religious image, of Christ in the heart of Dostoevsky: a triumph of illusion, of faith, in the face of "opposite proofs." And this paradox remains central to Dostoevsky's artistic philosophy throughout his life. The paradox found its final formulation in the legend of the Grand Inquisitor in the dialectical opposition of two truths: the truth of the Grand Inquisitor, the earthly truth, the truth of man's weaknesses and evasiveness, and the truth of Christ, the truth that man will *instinctively* strive for spiritual beauty and the ideal. The appearance of Christ before the Seville cathedral, Ivan observes apropos of the beginning of his "poem," "might be one of the best parts of the poem, that is, precisely why the people recognize Him. The people strive toward Him [*stremitsja k Nemu*] with unconquerable force, surround Him, flock about Him, follow Him."

As we have seen, Nietzsche clearly recognized the role of illusion in every aspect and form of life: but just as Dostoevsky's leap into faith, his existential choice of illusion, was contrary to "opposite proofs," the proofs of reason, so Nietzsche's *amor fati,* his will to "see how reality is constituted fundamentally," his heroic confrontation with the harsh earthly truth of man's existence, was in its own way also a leap, one made in full recognition of the opposite proofs of man's tragic need for illusion. I can think of no other formation than this to encompass the contradictions in the creative thought of Nietzsche and Dostoevsky, the manner in which these philosophies differ in their movement, yet the way they concur at their point of departure: a tragic vision of man. The thought of both Nietzsche and Dostoevsky, taken separately, can be apprehended only in movement. When we juxtapose them, then, we can speak not of a correlation between two fixed points but a kind of philosophical rhythm which allows for the most antithetical movements, one which in itself constitutes a unified, coherent design or dialectic.

Nietzsche and Dostoevsky, then, take separate paths at the crossroads of illusion. But both understood reality in the same way; both faced reality with the "courage of despair," to use a phrase of Nietzsche's.[34] But survival for one meant the embracing of illusion; survival for the other meant ultimately the rejection of illusion. Each in his own way explored the path of the other, acknowledged it, but in the end rejected it.

Let me take one remarkable illustration from Dostoevsky. I have in mind a passage from his novel *The Raw Youth* in which the enigmatic Versilov imagines a world in which the great idea of immortality has vanished and men are alone with themselves. Versilov calls this vision "a fantasy and a most improbable one," but, he tells us, he has pictured it often: "All my life I could not have lived without it."

> "I picture to myself, my dear," he began with a pensive smile, "that war has now ended and the battle has subsided. After the curses, the mud balls, the hisses has come a lull, and people are left *alone*, as they had wished: the great idea of old has left them; the great source of strength that till then had nourished and heartened them was departing like that majestic beckoning sun in Claude Lorrain's painting, but it was somehow the last day of humanity. And people suddenly understood that they had been left quite alone, and at once felt profoundly orphaned. My dear boy, I have never been able to imagine people ungrateful and grown foolish. People left orphaned would immediately begin to press together more closely and more lovingly; they would grasp each other's hands, now understanding that they alone were all that they had left for each other. The great idea of immortality would have vanished, and one would have to replace it; and all that great abundance of former love for Him who was immortal, would be directed to nature, to the world, to people, to every blade of grass. They would come to love the earth and life passionately and increasingly with their gradual awareness of their own transient and finite existence, and now with a special love, unlike the former one. They would begin to notice and discover in nature phenomena and mysteries that they had never dreamed of before, because they would be looking at nature with new eyes, with the look of a lover looking on his beloved. They would awaken and hurry to kiss one another, hastening to love, realizing that their days were numbered, and that these were all that were left to them. They would work for one another, and each would give his own to everybody, and with this alone would be happy. Each child would

know and would feel that every person on earth was a mother and father to him. 'Let tomorrow be my last day,' each one would think, looking on the setting sun, 'yet all the same, I will not die, but all of them will remain, and after them their children'—and this thought that they would remain, in the same way loving and solicitous for each other, would replace the idea of a meeting beyond the grave. O, they would hasten to love in order to stifle the great sadness in their hearts. They would be proud and courageous for themselves, but would become timid with each other; each person would tremble for the life and happiness of the other. They would become tender with each other and would not be ashamed of it, as now, and would caress each other as children do. Meeting each other, they would look at one another with a deep and knowing glance, and in their glances would be love and sadness."

Such is the lofty vision of Versilov, a kind of melancholy-tragic heroism, the closest Dostoevsky ever came in a positive sense to the Nietzschean *amor fati*, to a vision of man without God, man drawing upon his own spiritual resources, man remaining faithful to the earth; but it is a vision in which (quite uncharacteristic of Nietzsche) love plays an overwhelming role. What is noteworthy, furthermore, is that this vision of Versilov does not contain the slightest trace of irony on Dostoevsky's part. Versilov's painting, as he calls it, is not the innocent beatitude of a golden age, nor is it the beatific, though terrible, anti-utopia of the Grand Inquisitor. It is a picture of humanity lucidly resolute without God; it is, one might say, a pure unclouded fragment of that atheistic humanism which Dostoevsky imbibed in his youth but against which he struggled all his life, and, we shall have to acknowledge, against which he struggles even here.

For Versilov's painting is not complete. Versilov surprises us with a last stroke of the brush, as it were, one of those unexpected revelations that tell us so much about Dostoevsky. He tells us that he always finished his picture, his portrait of humanity without God, with a vision such as that to be found in Heinrich Heine's vision of Christ.[35] "I could not do without Him, I could not but imagine Him, finally, among his orphaned people," says Versilov. "He would come to them, extend his arms, and say: 'How could you forget Him?' And there and then the veil, as it were, would fall from their eyes and there would ring out a great exultant hymn of a new and final resurrection."

Such is Versilov's epilogue: poetry, miracle, revelation—a revelation as miraculous, in its own way, as Dostoevsky's final vision of Marey in prison.

In Versilov's vision we find all of Dostoevsky: his profound humanism, his realism, and his craving for an all-reconciling moment in which anguish and anxiety would find some grand resolution and transfiguration.

Of course, precisely this little epilogue, this rapturous apocalypse, this concept of an harmonious, all-reconciling end, this plunging of man back into the womb of dependence and illusion was repugnant to Nietzsche. And I think just at this point we can understand what Nietzsche meant when, after praising Dostoevsky to Georg Brandes "as the most valuable psychological material known to me," he added: "I am grateful to him in a remarkable way, however much he goes against my deepest instincts."[36] What are these instincts and where are they most vividly and poetically expressed? I think we can locate them in Zarathustra's dramatic plea to his disciples in the finale of part I of *Thus Spoke Zarathustra*. What we have here is almost a prayer in its rhythms and spirit; and I think Thomas Mann was absolutely correct in speaking of its "spiritual materialism":[37]

> Remain faithful to the earth, my brothers, with the power of your virtue. Let your gift-giving love and your knowledge serve the meaning of the earth. Thus I beg and beseech you. Do not let them fly away from earthly things and beat with their wings against eternal walls. Alas, there has always been so much virtue that has flown away. Lead back to the earth the virtue that flew away, as I do—back to the body, back to life, that it may give the earth a meaning, a human meaning.[38]

Nietzsche and Dostoevsky were artists with a tragic view of human existence. They were despairing creators who, unable to reconcile themselves to the face of the world as they saw it, were similarly unable to renounce their high idealism, an idealism which expressed itself, however, in radically different approaches to the place of illusion in human existence. Dostoevsky had deep doubts about human nature; his compromise with it, his view of fractured man striving toward an unattainable ideal, was in the end more realistic than Nietzsche's uncompromising demands upon man and human nature. For this reason the artist-philosopher Dostoevsky is more comforting than the philosopher-artist Nietzsche. Yet there is in Nietzsche something monumental and Promethean, a vigor and unexampled courage, an epic burst of energy and faith in man's potential as a builder that we do not find in Dostoevsky and perhaps in no other modern thinker except Marx.

"The central fact," Karl Jaspers observed, "is that Nietzsche makes man depend upon himself alone."[39] In all his contempt for the "herd," for mass man, Nietzsche has seemed to remain faithful to a Renaissance vision of man: man as an individual, man at the center of the universe, man as an explorer, man as creator. Reading Zarathustra, listening to him summon man to overcome himself, one involuntarily thinks of those great uncompleted sculptures of Michelangelo; those extraordinary images of stone figures emerging from stone, half hewn, struggling to life against the giant weight of time; looking at these figures, one wonders: are they testimony to some extraordinary liberation that occurred in the past or of one that will occur in the future; or are they simply dumb witness to a stupendous failure? Here is where we are left with Nietzsche. But here is where we are left by man.

14 *Vision in His Soul*

Vyacheslav I. Ivanov's Dostoevsky

> Finally, it must be asked concerning every artist how he is in relation
> to the highest knowledge and to those laws which do not take holiday
> because men and times forget them.
>
> James Joyce

 Vyacheslav Ivanov's study *Dostoevsky* (1932), a composite of
writings extending over twenty years, is one of the few significant literary-philosophical studies in the twentieth century on the great Russian novelist. Written in the majestic prose of
one of Russia's great poets, it is perhaps the finest example of the ontological and metaphysical school of Dostoevsky criticism that flour-
ished in Russian writing at the end of the nineteenth century and the
beginning of the twentieth, a body of writing that includes the work
of such thinkers as Vasily Rozanov, Dmitry Merezhkovsky, Nicholas
Berdyaev, and Leo Shestov. At the same time, Ivanov's study stands
on the threshold of modern Dostoevsky criticism. The appearance of
Ivanov's *Dostoevsky* in German translation in 1932,[1] nearly coinciding
with the publication of M. M. Bakhtin's rigorously formal *Problems of
Dostoevsky's Art* in 1929,[2] might indeed be regarded as symbolic of the
meeting and parting of ways of the old and new. Ivanov himself took
note of the new prevailing critical directions: "In our modern and
more sober times, investigation is directed almost exclusively towards
matter of fact problems of form; that is to say, on the one hand towards biography, and on the other hand towards the technique of
narration, towards questions of style, subject, artistic methods and
literary-historical derivations. The investigation of Dostoevsky's religious philosophy remains as a serious task for the future."[3]

Yet if Ivanov's work with its interest in the ethical and religious dimensions of Dostoevsky's novels may be considered characteristic of the "old criticism," it also anticipated the new criticism of Bakhtin, Leonid Grossman, and others in its concern with the form of Dostoevsky's novels and their roots in tragedy and myth. It is no surprise that Bakhtin, then a relatively unknown author, placed Ivanov at the head of a list of writers in whose critical works "attempts are made at a more objective approach to Dostoevsky's works—not only to the ideas in and of themselves, but also to the works as artistic entities."[4] Indeed, a perusal of Ivanov's *Dostoevsky* suggests that he anticipated the concept of the polyphonic novel of Dostoevsky. Further, with his conception of the "thou art" principle as central to Dostoevsky's worldview, Ivanov laid a foundation upon which Bakhtin would construct his fine model of Dostoevsky's poetics.

Vyacheslav Ivanovich Ivanov was born in Moscow February 16/28, 1866, and died in Rome July 16, 1949. Major Russian poet, theoretician of the Russian symbolist movement, classical philologist, historian, and translator—a veritable Renaissance figure—Ivanov was also a religious thinker who in the last decades of his life in Rome embraced Roman Catholicism (though he continued to observe the Eastern rites). Referring to the general condition of Europe and Russia, he wrote in his well-known "Lettre à Charles Du Bos" in 1930: "In this atmosphere where the spiritual torpor of the bourgeois world corresponded by some sort of diabolical counterpoint with the revolutionary fever [in Russia], that familiar call sounded again imperiously in my soul; it was the persistent call which, ever since my youthful contact with that great and saintly man who was Vladimir Solovyov, had led me slowly but inexorably towards joining the Roman Catholic church."[5]

Ivanov studied Roman history for five years with the renowned Theodor Mommsen in Berlin in the late 1880's and early 1890's, working at the same time in his favorite area of classical philology. Nietzsche soon engaged his attention, but Ivanov quickly struck out on his own path away from him, particularly where matters of religious consciousness were concerned. Yet later, in *A Correspondence from Two Corners* (1922), he could still write of Nietzsche as "one who joins the company of the great modelers of the ideal; from an iconoclast he turns into an icon painter."[6] Ivanov wrote again in the same work: "It is most doubtful whether in today's cultural milieu any personal initiation can take place without the initiate . . . meeting [Nietzsche] as the 'guardian of the threshold.' Nietzsche has said: 'Man is something that must be overcome'—thereby testifying once more that the way of personal emancipation is a path up to the heights and down into the depths, a vertical movement."[7]

Ivanov's deep involvement with all aspects of European culture, history, and literature, particularly the Hellenistic period, continued throughout his life (he spent forty-four years of his life abroad, living and traveling in Germany, Italy, France, England, Greece, Egypt, and Palestine, even though during these years he made frequent trips to Russia). A signal example of this concern for European culture was his *Correspondence from Two Corners*, a work which the German cultural historian Ernst Robert Curtius referred to as "the most important statement about humanism since Nietzsche."[8] In this unique epistolary dialogue with the distinguished literary and cultural historian M. O. Gershenzon (each exchanged six letters with the other) Ivanov set forth his views on the nature of culture and tradition and on the questions of decline and continuity in Western culture:

> What is "decadence"? It is a feeling of the most refined organic bond with the grand tradition of a past high culture together with a painful and proud consciousness that one is the last of a line. In other words, decadence is memory benumbed, its promotive capacity gone, not allowing us to participate in our fathers' initiations, no longer providing impulses for any real creativity. It is the knowledge that prophecy has ceased, as, indeed, the decadent Plutarch suggests in the title of one of his works, "The Cessation of the Oracles."[9]

Ivanov's work—his poetry, criticism, and literary-philosophical writings—is itself deeply situated in, and conscious of, cultural tradition; it is in its own way "oracular" in spirit and deeply concerned with the problem of memory and oblivion. "Memory is a dynamic principle," Ivanov observes in his *Correspondence from Two Corners*, "oblivion is weariness and the interruption of movement, decadence and a return to a state of relative stagnation."[10] Looking back into the past, Ivanov wrote in an essay, "On the Law and Connections" (1908), the man who has lost touch with life "encounters at its end a gloom and vainly tries to distinguish in that gloom forms resembling recollection." Then he experiences that "impotence of exhausted thought that we call oblivion. Nonbeing is directly disclosed to [his] consciousness in the form of oblivion which negates it." This tragedy is the direct result, Ivanov believes, of not recognizing that life is "embodiment," that "man lives for those who have passed and for the future, for ancestors and descendants alike. . . . Every moment changes everything preceding him in time. Hence the obligation *to live* is the only obligation. Because 'obligation' is 'connection.'"[11] The ethical idea expressed here was to remain a constant in Ivanov's writing and lies at the center of his fundamentally religious understanding of Dostoevsky. Bakhtin, it may be noted, echoes some of these same ideas of Ivanov's in his perception of Dostoevsky. "[The Russian novelist]," he wrote in 1961 in "Toward a Reworking of the Dostoevsky Book," "asserts the impossibility of solitude, the illusory nature of solitude. The very being of man (both external and internal) is the *deepest communion. To be* means to *communicate*. Absolute death (nonbeing) is the state of being unheard, unrecognized, unremembered."[12]

Not everything that is new is innovatory. Innovation for Ivanov, as he demonstrates in his examination of myth in his Dostoevsky book, is rooted always in a profound cultural memory, a sense of history and tradition. Ivanov was fond of citing Goethe's words: "The truth has been found long ago; it unites the august company of spiritual minds. Grasp it, the age-old truth" (Vermächtnis).

Ivanov first emerged as a poet with the publication of two collections of poetry in 1904 and 1905. In the same period, he took up the study of the history of religion, in particular the Dionysian cults, publishing in 1904 *The Hellenic Religion of the Suffering God*. Ivanov's most important work on Greek religion and myth was his *Dionysus and the Origin of his Worship* (1924). His preoccupation with Hellenistic religion, culture, and myth also found direct expression in his three early essays on Dostoevsky and his Dostoevsky book.

The first part of his book, "Tragedic Aspect," remains, with some additions, changes, and excisions, the brilliant excursus on Dostoevsky's "novel-tragedy" that dates back to 1911 (the original essay was divided into two sections entitled "The Principle of Form" and "The

Principle of World View"). In it Ivanov discusses the form and dynamics of Dostoevsky's "novel-tragedy": "Each cell carries within it the germ of an agonistic development; and, if the whole is catastrophic, so then is each synapse of the particular. This is the explanation of Dostoevsky's law of epic rhythm, which exactly accords with the essential nature of tragedy: the law of the progressively gathering momentum of events."[13]

The thematic structure of Ivanov's book has a rhythm that gives expression to his conception of Dostoevsky's art and his notion of "realistic symbolism." In art this type of symbolism "leads the soul of the spectator *a realibus ad realiora* . . . from reality on the lower plane, a reality of lesser ontological value, to the more real reality."[14] Thus in his book there is the movement *from tragedy*, with its "liberating final convulsion of the spirit" (pt. 1, "Tragedic Aspect"), *through myth*, where mythic archetypes emerge as patterns of the human spirit disclosing a higher reality (pt. 2, "Mythological Aspect"), *to theology* (pt. 3, "Theological Aspect")—that is, to a moment of the highest knowledge. Ivanov signals this moment with a line from Dante: "Reader, sharpen here your vision of truth, for the veil is now so fine that indeed it is easy to pierce"[15] (*Purgatory*, 8, 19). Here Ivanov's own deep commitment to Christianity takes center stage. This is a book about Dostoevsky. It also represents in important respects a crystallization of Ivanov's spiritual and religious ascent.

What is noteworthy about Ivanov's book is its holistic approach to Dostoevsky. It combines philosophical, biographical, and formalistic analysis. Throughout, Ivanov posits the unity of the man, artist, and thinker. "[Dostoevsky's] work," Ivanov writes early in the book, "is the most striking example we know of the identity of form and content—in so far as by content we mean the original intuitive perception of life, and by form the means of transmuting this by art into the flesh and blood of a new world of living entities."[16] Toward the end of his study, Ivanov speaks of the "infallible criterion" for his interpretation of Dostoevsky's religious thought: "the accord between what Dostoevsky had to teach [*der didaktischen Formel*] and the living artistic imagery in which he clothed it."[17] For Ivanov, Dostoevsky is a fundamentally religious writer, but one whose religiosity emerged as much from the fundamentally tragic nature of his art as from the depths of his experience and being. "Art once served religion and wholly rested on it," Ivanov wrote in his first Dostoevsky study, *Dostoevsky and the Novel-Tragedy*. "'If it were possible to tear art from religion, it would perish because it would be torn from its roots,' say the defenders of a connection between art and religion . . . [But] is such a disengagement itself possible? Here the decisive voice belongs to tragedy. It says, no: it is impossible."[18] Ivanov's thought leads him to a consideration of "tragic guilt"—a theme that enters into Ivanov's discussion of *Crime and Punishment*.

Ivanov's early preoccupation with Nietzsche yielded, partly under the influence of the religious philosopher Vladimir Solovyov, to a literary and ethical outlook based on the principles of *sobornost'*—the idea of ecumenicity. In "The Crisis of Individualism" (1905), he argues that "individualism, in its contemporary, involuntary and unconscious metamorphosis, is acquiring features of spiritual union or ecumenicity."[19] "Serve the spirit, or the true 'I' in you," he writes, "with the same faithfulness that you would wish from every person in his service to the spirit inhabiting him."[20] A year later, in "Presentiments and Portents," he welcomes the arrival of "a new organic epoch and theater of the future," one that would foreground the choral and ecumenical element.[21]

"The one through the other we found ourselves—each found himself and more than only self: I would say we found God," Ivanov wrote in his "Autobiographical Letter" (1917) about his relationship with Lydia Dmitrievna Zinovieva.[22] Ivanov's central metaphysical theme, at once personal, aesthetic, and religious, emerges in this simple line as it does in more complex ways in his poetic and philosophical writings (for example, in "Thou art" [*Ty esi*] in Ivanov's long poem "Man" [Chelovek, 1915–1919] and in an article, "Thou Art" [1907]). Thus, too, in his Dostoevsky book the idea of "the one through the other we found ourselves" is embodied in the concept of Dostoevsky's realism as based on the notion of "Thou art." Ivanov maintains that Dostoevsky's "higher realism" is based not upon theoretical cognition, with its constant antithesis of subject and object but upon an act of will and faith approximately corresponding to the Augustinian *transcende te ipsum*. Ivanov likens this process to the idea conveyed by a Russian word, a favorite of Dostoevsky's, *proniknovenie* (penetration, perception, discernment, sagacity), a word which for Ivanov is conveyed to some extent by the German word *Sicheinsetzen*.

> *Proniknovenie* is a transcension of the subject. In this state of mind we recognize the other Ego not as our object, but as another subject. It is therefore not a mere peripheral extension of the bounds of individual consciousness, but a complete inversion of its normal system of coordinates. The authenticity of this transvaluation is demonstrated primarily in one's inner life: in the experience of true love. . . . The spiritual penetration finds expression in the unconditional acceptance with our full will and thought of the other-existence—in "Thou art." If this acceptance of the other-existence is complete; if, with and in this acceptance, the whole substance of my own existence is rendered null and void (exinanitio, kenosis), then the other-existence ceases to be an alien "Thou"; instead, the "Thou" becomes another description of my "Ego." "Thou art" then no longer means "Thou art recognized by me as existing," but "I experience thy existence as my own, and in thy existence I again find myself existing." *Es, ergo sum.*[23]

In his essay "The Religious Work of Vladimir Solovyov" (1911), Ivanov expresses his idea through the example of an individual observing the reflection of himself through two mirrors:

> The individual looking into a mirror finds a true reflection of himself only when a reflection in a second image is created. It is this second mirror, correcting the first—speculum speculi—that is "the other" for the man who wants to know. Truth is only authenticated if it is seen in another. Where two or three are together in the name of Christ, there among them is Christ Himself. Thus an adequate cognition of the secret of being is possible only in mystical communion, that is, in the Church.[24]

Ivanov, one might say, in certain respects anticipates Bakhtin's later theory of the polyphonic perception of the human image. In his notes "Toward a Reworking of the Dostoevsky Book," discussing the "impossibility of the existence of a single consciousness," Bakhtin writes: "I am conscious of myself and become myself only while revealing myself for another, through another, and with the help of another. . . . I cannot manage without another, I cannot become myself without another; I must find myself in another by finding another in myself (in mutual reflection and mutual acceptance)."[25]

Dostoevsky himself, Ivanov believes, arrived at "transcension" through his personal experience. His "realism was his faith, which he received after he had lost his 'soul', that is to say, his selfhood." Ivanov alludes to Dostoevsky's experience just before he expected to be executed.

It is only through the realism founded on "Thou art," through the affirmation of the consciousness of "the other," Ivanov believes, not as object but as subject—in a word, through love—that the individual can overcome solipsism.

Ivanov posits a direct authorial presence in Dostoevsky's novelistic universe, one in which literary form is a function of an ethical-religious worldview. This is evident in the way Ivanov understands the artist Dostoevsky's polyphonic interrelations with the world. In a passage in *Dostoevsky and the Novel-Tragedy*, one that was later omitted from his 1932 study, Ivanov, contrasting the creative methods of Tolstoy and Dostoevsky, writes that Tolstoy

> placed himself like a mirror before the world, and everything that entered the mirror entered into him: thus he wants to fill himself up with the world, absorb it, make it his own through appropriating it, and after having overcome [the world] in consciousness, return to people both the world that passed through him and that which he learned while it was passing through—the norms of relating to the world. This act of return is the second act, an act of concern for the world and love for people, understood as service; but the first act of return was pure observation and contemplation. Dostoevsky's path was a different one. His whole striving was not to absorb the given world and life around him, but on coming out of himself, to *penetrate* and *enter into the multitudes of life* around him; he does not need to fill himself up, but *to lose himself.* Living beings, access to whom was immediately opened up to him, are not things of the world, but people—human personalities; because they are really of the same nature as he. Here the energy of the centrifugal movements of the human "I" which make up the Dionysian pathos of character evoke in the soul of the genius a realization of self that reaches into the uttermost depths, into deposits inherited from ancient times; as a result the *soul seems to itself like a many-stringed instrument*, wondrous and all-accommodating; to all the experiences of the other's "I" it seems to find in itself a corresponding echo and on the basis of these similarities and features of a kindred likeness, *can create in itself any state of the other's soul.* The spirit, listening with strained attention to how the prisoner in the next room lives and moves

about, demands of his neighbor but a few slight signals in order to divine the unexpressed, the unsaid.[26] [Italics mine]

Ivanov perceives Tolstoy's creative process as consisting of two separate acts or actions: the first, aesthetic, consists of "pure observation and contemplation"; the second, ethical, is one of love. Dostoevsky's *penetration* of reality, by contrast, is one in which the aesthetic and ethical impulses are joined into one. Important in this connection is Ivanov's formal representation of Dostoevsky's muse as a "many-stringed instrument" capable of sounding out, and responding to, many and diverse voices. The artist, indeed, can incarnate any state of "the other's soul." He does not reach out coldly as if "to things of the world" (objects); he reaches out to "people—human personalities." Ivanov's idea is clear: where Dostoevsky is concerned, *the creative act is a human or humanizing act.* The aesthetic impulse is indistinguishable from the ethical impulse. The artist is not aloof from his creations: rather he loses himself in them.

The concept of Dostoevsky's artistic muse as "many-stringed," or multivoiced, and of his world as polyphonic is also expressed in another way in Ivanov's first Dostoevsky essay and later in his book. Ivanov represents Dostoevsky as the union of an empirical or external self, one prey to worldly sin and error, and a new inwardly free and transcendent self. He goes on to define the relation between these selves on the one hand and that existing, on the other, between Dostoevsky's new self, or artistic muse, and his creations:

> Not only did Dostoevsky give his double, who faced the outer world, full freedom to live as he chose, or as he was compelled, to live: we actually find the artist ever busy creating new doubles for himself, all of them contained behind the polymorphous masks of his own many-faced and all-human Ego, which is no more bound to *one* face. For the more the inner Ego is freed from the outer, the more closely it feels itself allied to all humanity; since, in the boundless wealth of individual differences, it recognizes only variously conditioned forms of its own subjection to the law of separate existence. The expression: "Nothing that is human is alien to me" becomes a complete truth only when a new Ego, free from all taint of human limitations, is brought to birth.[27]

Dostoevsky lets his "double"—in this case, his outer, empirical self which faces the external world—live its own life. Duality here is not evidence of a pathological state of being but a manifestation of a hard-won freedom of the spirit; "the inner Ego" has been freed from the outer external or empirical self. The artist Dostoevsky can now give himself over to multiplication of his "doubles" under the "polymorphous masks" of his many-faced, all-human Ego, or "I"— one that can now identify with *all* humanity, whether good or evil ("Nothing that is human is alien to me"). Thus Dostoevsky has the ability to project himself into other beings and personalities while at the same time maintaining his essential spiritual integrity; in other words, his point of view.

Dostoevsky's "doubles" exist independently of him, live their own life in accord with the "law of separate existence." Yet Dostoevsky's "all-human Ego" stands in an active ethical relation to "the other," to his "doubles": the interweaving threads of their free lives fulfill *his* ultimate design—to make manifest ultimate spiritual truth. Thus Ivanov writes:

> It is true that Dostoevsky's work gives evidence of violent spiritual strug-
> gles, which provide this mighty dialectician with abundant material for
> the creation of those tragedies of the spirit in which the metaphysical
> tumult proclaims itself in many a different guise; but these gigantically
> sprouting antitheses are so balanced that—far from effacing the basic
> knowledge already won, and branded on the soul—they actually widen
> and deepen it.[28]

The effect of the convulsed and warring consciousnesses in Dostoevsky's polyphonic world, the clash of "independent" voices speaking their own truth, the impression created by "doubles" living their
own lives, is for Ivanov ultimately a sense of "a deepening and wid-
ening" of the way. The reader of a Dostoevsky novel, if he has read
deeply and well, is left with a "basic knowledge already won"; he is
left, as Ivanov puts it, with the "religious truth of society . . . [Dos-
toevsky's] truth that relations between the personality and society
must be founded on mutual love."[29]

Ivanov's view of the Dostoevsky novel as a type, then, would seem
to fall somewhere between the polyphonic and monological models of
Bakhtin. Likewise, Ivanov's Dostoevsky, though a "many-stringed instrument," is a musician who orchestrates his strings to express a very
definite worldview. They are wrong, Ivanov writes of certain inter-

preters of Dostoevsky who "by listing contradictory statements that
he has put into the mouth of his seekers and deniers of God," seek "to
convict him of disbelief" or "radical skepticism and despair."

> This theory is tenable on grounds neither of biography, nor of psy-
> chology . . . nor yet of logic; and it can be equally well refuted by a study
> either of the context of the particular passages in which the negative atti-
> tude is expressed, or of the great organic unity of Dostoevsky's work as a
> whole. Indeed, all parts of his "doctrine" have such an inwardly funda-
> mental and living relationship—his ethics, psychology, metaphysic, an-
> thropology, sociology and eschatology so utterly determine and comple-
> ment each other—that the deeper we penetrate into the nature of the
> connection between them, the more certain must we come to realize that
> for Dostoevsky the creation of literary form was only a medium for the
> polymorphous development of a synthetic idea of the universe, which
> from the outset he had carried within him as a comprehensive vision and
> a morphological principle of his spiritual growth.[30]

These final lines admirably sum up Ivanov's view of the organic unity
of Dostoevsky the man, thinker, and artist.

Midway on the path to his exposition of Dostoevsky's "doctrine,"
in part 2, "Mythological Aspect," Ivanov examines those areas of Dostoevsky's work where higher truth is "refracted in the coloured in-
termediate plane of myth and imagination."[31] Ivanov elaborates his
theory of "realistic symbolism" according to which "a nucleus [of the
epic tragedy] contains from the beginning the full symbolic force of
the whole work, its entire 'higher realism'; that is to say, the original
intuition of a transcendental reality. . . . To describe this nucleus of
symbolic creation, we use the word 'myth.'"[32]

Ivanov focuses upon *The Devils, Crime and Punishment*, and *The
Idiot*. As always, Ivanov works toward a disclosure of the fundamental
ethical and religious content of Dostoevsky's work. Taking as his point
of departure the biblical concept of the people as a "personality," and
conceiving the people as a unity of two principles, feminine and mas-
culine, Ivanov, in the chapter "The Enchanted Bride" locates the basic
theme of *The Devils* in the "symbolism of the relationship between
Earth's soul, the daring, erring human spirit and the Powers of Evil";[33]
he analyzes the triangular relationship between the cripple, Maria Ti-
mofeyevna, perceived as a figure of Mother Earth, or symbolic virgin,
the satanic Peter Verkhovensky, and the would-be savior, Stavrogin,

the "Russian Faust: but in a negative version."[34] In general, Ivanov signals the strong presence of Goethe's *Faust* in Dostoevsky's work.

At the opening of his book, one may note here, Ivanov draws Goethe's *Faust* into his discussion of the metaphysical dimension of Dostoevsky's art:

> Not in the earthly stage of being lie the roots of that intellectual and spiritual substance, clothed in flesh, which is known as man, but in an existence beyond this world; and each individual destiny has its "Prologue in Heaven." In that transcendent sphere where God and Devil do battle over the fate of the creature—and "their battlefield is in the hearts of men"—here *incipit tragoedia*.[35]

Yet man is free. Without free self-determination, Ivanov insists, the word *tragic* cannot properly be used. "Thus it comes about that Dostoevsky sets the real key-point of the tragic tangle in the realm of metaphysics; for only here we are allowed to premise the pure activity of the free will and have an insight into it through the prism of art."[36]

Ivanov's "Prologue in Heaven," of course, is a direct allusion to Goethe's "Prolog im Himmel" in *Faust* (and beyond that to the Book of Job), the scene in which God and the devil debate the uprightness of the "little earth god" Faust. In this scene the Lord maintains that "a good man in his dark strivings is conscious of the right way." "The Legend of the Grand Inquisitor" in *The Brothers Karamazov* serves the same function as the "Prologue in Heaven" in *Faust*. In the confrontation between the Grand Inquisitor and his prisoner Jesus, the question of man's capacity to be free and responsible is posed—a question that is lived out in the dramas of the heroes of the novel. Dmitry Karamazov serves Ivanov as an illustration of a person in whom spiritual struggle ends (at least as far as his relations with his father are concerned) with a choice of the "right way." He cites Dmitry: "'Well, it was like this: whether it was someone's tears, or my mother prayed to God, or a good angel kissed me at that instant, I don't know. But the devil was conquered.'" Ivanov links the "angel's kiss" with the memory of Zosima's genuflexion before Dmitry in the cell, "the genuflexion that foretold to Dmitry the expiatory suffering in store for him." What is central for Dostoevsky, according to Ivanov, is that man lives not in solipsistic isolation but in a unified spiritual field in which all actions and happenings, past and present, are united through memory. Thus man is ever in communion with "countless spirits," with the living and the dead. Ivanov cites Father Zosima: "What grows lives and is alive only through the feeling of its contact with other mysterious worlds."

Ivanov considers *Crime and Punishment* (in the chapter "The Revolt against Mother Earth," pt. 2) "Dostoevsky's first great revelation to the world, and the main pillar of his subsequent philosophy of life."[37] It is significant that Ivanov discusses *Notes from the Underground* only very briefly, and then in a later chapter given over to "Daemonology." Leo Shestov, in *Dostoevsky and Nietzsche* (1903), had seen in *Notes from the Underground* "a public, albeit a veiled, renunciation of [Dostoevsky's] past."[38] Ivanov not only speaks of *Notes* as "a devastating criticism of present-day social relations," but observes that "the author has no objection to uttering through the character's mouth the religious truth concerning society in its elementary form: the truth that relations between the personality and society must be found on mutual love."[39] The Underground Man certainly does not give verbal expression to this religious truth, at least not in the version of the work that has come down to us (it is possible that Ivanov had in mind Dostoevsky's letter to his brother Mikhail in which the novelist declares that the censor had eliminated passages from the novel [chap. 10, pt. 1] where "I deduce . . . the need for faith and Christ").[40] Yet Ivanov correctly deduces from the text Dostoevsky's basic ethical-religious intention. This idea finds dramatic expression in the pietà episode (chap. 11, pt. 2), the moment when, sobbing, the Underground Man falls into Liza's arms. Clearly the censored passages in chapter 10, part 1, of the original version of *Notes* gave verbal expression to the idea of the pietà episode.

In "The Revolt Against Mother Earth," Ivanov suggests that *Crime and Punishment* and Pushkin's "Queen of Spades" are united not only on the grounds of plot but on the basis of "shared mythical conceptions": "Both [protagonists] incur the guilt of killing the Parca, and must suffer her posthumous revenge." Ivanov links both the countess and the pawnbroker with the theme of the "female avenger . . . emissary of Mother Earth, rising in wrathful resistance."[41] It is in this connection that Ivanov discusses the problematic of guilt and its roots in Aeschylus and Sophocles. In general, the questions raised by Ivanov on the relationship of Dostoevsky's novels to classical tragedy, for example to *Oedipus*, deserve more attention.

Goethe's *Faust* and Sophocles' *Oedipus* serve Ivanov as valuable points of comparison for discussion of *The Possessed* and *Crime and Punishment*, respectively. Cervantes' *Don Quixote*, a favorite work of Dostoevsky's, leads Ivanov to a consideration of Myshkin in *The Idiot*. Yet Ivanov more centrally locates Myshkin in the "poor fool" of medieval legend, the Ivan-Tsarevich of the old Russian tale, "the simple and true-hearted one." Myshkin is "above all, the type of a spirituality that descends, that seeks the Earth: rather a spirit that assumes flesh than a man who rises to the spiritual. . . . [The] preponderance of the Platonic *anamnesis* over the sense of reality is just what makes him at once a fool and a wise seer amongst men." [42] In a provocative essay on Ivanov's literary criticism, René Wellek has found in Ivanov's mythopoetic interpretation of *The Idiot* (and of other works of Dostoevsky) an example of "the dangers of arbitrary allegorizing." "One has to conclude that Ivanov is expounding a book which he would have wanted Dostoevsky to have written, rather than the one he actually wrote." [43]

Wellek's criticism seems unduly harsh. There is no question that Ivanov mythopoeticizes Myshkin, that is, suggests a mythic derivation that Dostoevsky does not literally advance with respect to Myshkin. Yet that derivation, however fanciful from one point of view, does accord with Dostoevsky's highly allegorical representation of Myshkin as a Christ figure, albeit a failed one. Where Ivanov seems to have fallen short in his analysis of *The Idiot* is not in his search for myth in Dostoevsky but in his general unwillingness or hesitation to come to grips with the problem of Myshkin as a Christ figure. Christ, of course, is *not* a mythic figure for Ivanov—and this is probably the nub of the matter. He is not a mythic figure for Dostoevsky, either; yet Dostoevsky the artist has certainly turned Myshkin into a mythic Christ figure, or has woven Christ, or aspects of him, into myth, and this issue must be faced directly in any analysis of Myshkin or interpretation of the novel. Here Wellek's observation that Ivanov "ignores the description of 'the complete breakdown of [Myshkin's] mental faculties,' his imbecility," is very much to the point. [44] The idea of a crippled or failed Christ must have been inconceivable to Ivanov. The very idea that a fictional character could be a Christ figure may also have bothered him.

In the final section of his book, "Theological Aspect," Ivanov focuses directly on the basic assumption of his entire book: Dostoevsky's commitment as man, thinker, and artist to a Christian religious outlook. The two chapters of part 3, "Daemonology" and "Hagiography," are largely given over to a discussion of the symbolic presence of Lucifer and Ahriman in Dostoevsky's works on the one hand and *The Brothers Karamazov* on the other. Ivanov develops a rich discussion of the problem of evil in Dostoevsky's novelistic universe around the ideas associated with Lucifer and Ahriman (though Dostoevsky himself does not use the second, Zoroastrian term).

If the names of Goethe, Byron, Pushkin, Sophocles, or Aeschylus appear with frequency in the first two parts of Ivanov's book, it is Dante, along with Dostoevsky, who occupies the center of the stage in the third and final part. In a provocative introduction to part 3 entitled "Theological Aspect" (the essay does not appear in any of the earlier Dostoevsky pieces), Ivanov insists that "we are . . . entitled to speak—*mutatis mutandis*—of a 'doctrine' propounded by Dostoevsky."[45] He acknowledges that Dostoevsky can comprehend the "inner form and true essence" of his doctrine only "when it is mirrored in myth: [in this he is] like all artists whose task it is, in the words of Plato, to create myths (μυθουϛ) and not doctrines (λογουϛ)."[46] Yet with this qualification in mind, Ivanov argues that both Dostoevsky and Dante "see the way to this end [i.e., leading mankind to a state of bliss] in religious truth. Both have taken the veil of poetry from the hand of truth; . . . both alike are teachers of the Faith; both peer down into the deepest chasms of evil; both accompany the sinful and redemption-seeking soul along the difficult paths of its ascent." In contrast, however, to Dante's teaching—"rigid as the order of Hell"— "Dostoevsky's apologetics . . . are essentially dynamic and tragic."[47] Yet Dostoevsky's works, from *Crime and Punishment* to *The Brothers Karamazov*, when considered in terms of the movement of living thought within them, form "the links of a dialectical chain, of theses and antitheses, the ladder of one continual ascent of the self-perceiving idea."[48] That idea, according to Ivanov, finds its supreme embodiment in Christ.

Ivanov's concept of Dostoevsky's art as Greek in its roots and Christian in its flowering is a rich one. In the more than half century since Ivanov's book was written, critical scholarship has disclosed the multiple ways Dostoevsky's ethical-religious thought has entered into the conception and design of his art. Ivanov, however, posits a religious "doctrine" directly binding all aspects of Dostoevsky's work and providing the key to its architectonics. There is, without doubt, a rigidity to this formula, one that transforms the artist into a teacher of the faith and his art into an unambiguous fulfillment of intentional design. Ivanov speaks convincingly about the religious foundations of Dostoevsky's artistic thought but for the most part discounts the moral-philosophical pressures and tensions, or "contradictions," that also manifest themselves in his novels. Dostoevsky himself, it is interesting to note, in spite of the Christian character of his higher aesthetics and worldview, rejected the notion that he was "one of those people who save souls, settle spiritual problems [*razreshit' dushi*], put grief to flight. Sometimes people write this about me," he wrote in a letter to A. L. Ozhigina February 28, 1878, "but I know *for certain* that I am capable of instilling disillusionment and revulsion. I am not skilled in writing lullabies, though I have occasionally had a go at it. And, of course, many people demand nothing more than that they be lulled."[49]

Dostoevsky of course is not addressing the question of deep Christian design in his work, but he is surely suggesting the complexity of his work *as art*, the central concern of his novels with raising and exploring questions as opposed to resolving them in some didactic way. He is certainly recognizing that his works deal with a disturbing or disturbed reality and may in turn have disturbing and unanticipated effects on the reader. Though we are under no obligation to accept Dostoevsky's view of the potential for the negative impact of his work, the history of the reception of Dostoevsky suggests that more than misunderstanding is at the root of the wide and passionate diversity of opinions on him. Even the philosopher Nicholas Berdyaev, one of the great religious interpreters of Dostoevsky, recognizes the unpredictable nature of Dostoevsky when he warns that one must read him "in an atmosphere of spiritual emancipation."[50] Berdyaev's remark leaves open the door to the view that misunderstandings of Dostoevsky are simply misreadings: the more emancipated we are, the less likely we are to draw misleading conclusions. Yet even among emancipated readers there has been no consensus about Dostoevsky. Nor should there be.

Ivanov, to be sure, was fully aware of the problematic side of Dostoevsky's work. In the introduction to his 1916 study, *Dostoevsky and the Novel-Tragedy*, he emphasizes the complex character of Dostoevsky's art and the way it not only gives expression to, but creates and shapes, the Russian mind and spirit.

> He dwells in our midst, because from him or through him comes everything that we are living through—both our light and our underground. He is the great founder and definer of our cultural complexity. Before him, everything in Russian life, in Russian thought, was simple. He made complex our soul, our faith, our art; he invented, just as "Turner invented the London fog," that is, he discovered, disclosed, realized in form, our developing and still unrecognized complexity.[51]

Ivanov revised this passage in his introduction to his 1932 Dostoevsky book. Viewing Dostoevsky in a universal rather than specifically Russian context, he writes more broadly of Dostoevsky's contribution to contemporary "intellectual and spiritual complexity." He notes the "peculiar effects of the ferment he induced, which had the power to stir up all the depths of our conscious and subconscious existence," but drops the reference to the "underground."[52] Ivanov in the late 1920's seems increasingly drawn to aspects of Dostoevsky that concord with his own spiritual and religious development. At the same time, his view of our understanding of Dostoevsky is a dynamic one. "Dostoevsky dwells in our midst," he writes as he did in 1916, but this time adds, "and changes as we do."[53] "An author," Bakhtin wrote in his "Answer to a Question from the Editorial Board of *Novy Mir*" (1970), "is a prisoner of his epoch, of the world about him. Subsequent times liberate him from the imprisonment, and literary scholarship is called upon to assist in this liberation."[54] Ivanov had a profound appreciation of this truth. He recognized, too, that Dostoevsky was not merely a prisoner awaiting liberation in this or that time dimension, but liberated his liberators.

Whether all of Dostoevsky—the explosive and antinomian character of his artistic thought and creation—can be encompassed by

Ivanov's thesis on the role of religious doctrine in his art is a question. Indeed, all of Dostoevsky's work is a question. What is certain, however, is that Vyacheslav Ivanov's book remains one of the great entrances to Dostoevsky's artistic and spiritual universe. "Beside it," Isaiah Berlin has rightly observed, "Gide's famous study as well as all the well-meaning essays of the interpreters of the Russian soul, seems trivial and shallow." Ivanov's study has widened and deepened our understanding of the tragic foundations of Dostoevsky's art, the universal language and symbolic forms that give it shape, and the ethical-religious principle that informs it. Profound and provocative, Ivanov's book has opened the way to new insights into old truths. Few are the works that attain these goals. More than this we cannot ask.

15   *Bakhtin's Poetics of Dostoevsky and Dostoevsky's 'Declaration of Religious Faith'*

"God can get along without man," Mikhail M. Bakhtin wrote in *Toward a Reworking of the Dostoevsky Book* in 1961, "but man cannot get along without Him."[1] How does Dostoevsky get along with God? Vyacheslav Ivanov directly addresses this question in his Dostoevsky book (1932) and directly answers: "Dostoevsky has long since made his choice: his surety and pledge for it is the figure of Christ shining upon his path."[2] The "infallible criterion" for this claim, Ivanov insists, is "the accord between what Dostoevsky had to teach and the living artistic imagery in which he clothed it."[3] For Ivanov, "the investigation of Dostoevsky's religious philosophy remains as a serious task for the future."[4] Bakhtin began writing his book in the immediate postrevolutionary period in Russia, but a few years after Ivanov's early Dostoevsky studies (1914, 1916, 1917); he published it in 1929, shortly before the appearance of Ivanov's book in 1932, a work in which Ivanov consolidated his ideas and writings on Dostoevsky.[5] A revised and expanded edition of Bakhtin's work appeared in 1963. On the surface, Bakhtin has very little to say about Dostoevsky's religious philosophy per se. Yet a close reading of Bakhtin's study suggests that Dostoevsky's poetics, as Bakhtin understands it, does address the religious question in fundamental ways, and is organic to Dostoevsky's declared religious outlook.[6]

Bakhtin's ground-breaking study—a work proclaiming Dostoevsky "creator of the polyphonic novel,"[7] architect of "a polyphonic world," and destroyer of the "established forms of the fundamentally monologic (homophonic) European novel"[8]—relegates the religious question, among other broadly ideological matters pertaining to Dostoevsky, to the back shelf of his concerns. "The present book is devoted to problems of Dostoevsky's *poetics* and surveys his work from that viewpoint *only*" (Bakhtin's italics), Bakhtin wrote emphatically in the opening line of his preface to his revised *Problems of Dostoevsky's Poetics* in 1963.[9] "The fundamental innovation that this poetics represents, its organic unity within the whole of Dostoevsky's work," Bakhtin adds, "has received far too little elucidation in the scholarship. Literature on Dostoevsky has focused primarily on the ideological problems raised by his work." In the foreword to the original edition of his Dostoevsky book in 1929, Bakhtin put the matter in slightly different words:

> The present book is limited solely to theoretical problems of Dostoevsky's art. We have had to exclude all historical problems. . . . Dostoevsky's work has been, up to now, the object of a narrowly ideological approach and treatment. Of greatest interest has been the ideology that found its direct expression in the pronouncements of Dostoevsky (or more precisely of his characters). The ideology that determined his artistic form, his extraordinarily complex and completely new novelistic construction, has remained to this day almost completely unexamined.[10]

The "ideology that determined [Dostoevsky's] artistic form" is distinguished from Dostoevsky's "pronouncements," many of which, of course, expressed his religious point of view. The qualification—"more precisely [those] of his characters"—is a noteworthy one. Though Dostoevsky in general shares the religious convictions of some of his characters, these characters for the most part do not give expression to the philosophical ambience and complexity of his religious outlook. Bakhtin's qualification may suggest that he did not wish to place Dostoevsky's pronouncements on religion at a distance from "the ideology that determined his artistic form." At the very outset of his 1929 book, then, Bakhtin leaves the door open for a relationship between Dostoevsky's religious outlook and his poetics, although he narrows his focus to a discussion of Dostoevsky's poetics.

Bakhtin's book, begun in the early years of the Russian Revolution and published at a time of increasingly heated rhetoric of revolution, was essentially an attempt to lift the question of ideology or worldview above the conventional attempts in Western as well as Russian criticism to identify Dostoevsky with this or that character, this or that idea or ideology. It was an effort to transcend these efforts and to locate Dostoevsky and his ultimate statement in the "higher unity" of the so-called polyphonic novel.[11] For Bakhtin, the real message of the Dostoevsky novel is the author's means of representing the multileveled, multivoiced, nonfinalized, dialogical nature of all character, idea, human experience, life itself. It is in Dostoevsky's *way* of looking at the world, in the artist's "completely new type of artistic thinking,"[12] his "new form of artistic visualization" of the world,[13] and the "objectivism" of that visualization,"[14] rather than in any formal or conventional authorial affirmation of his Christian faith through one or another character, that Bakhtin finds Dostoevsky's ultimate statement on man's relation to God and to the universe.

When Bakhtin says that "one should learn not from Raskolnikov or Sonya, Ivan or Zosima (thereby ripping their voices out of the polyphonic whole and by that act alone distorting the novels)," that one should rather "learn from Dostoevsky himself as a creator of the polyphonic novel,"[15] he in no way denies the importance of what he calls "Dostoevskian ideas,"[16] Dostoevsky's "pronouncements," or the presence of a personal authorial ideology or point of view in his creative works. "A novel without an authorial position . . . is in general impossible," Bakhtin readily concedes.[17] He does not deny, further, that some of Dostoevsky's novels have "conventionally literary, conventionally monologic" endings,[18] that is, definitive or "finalizing" resolutions that give expression to a monological viewpoint. What Bakhtin denies is that these conclusions retain their absolute hegemony in the body of the artistic work or form a basis upon which to judge the author's deepest artistic statement. "The ideas of Dostoevsky the thinker upon entering his polyphonic novel change the very form of their existence, they are transformed into artistic images of ideas."[19] What is involved in the Dostoevsky polyphonic novel is "not an absence but a radical change in the author's position." Dostoevsky's "radically new authorial position" led to the discovery of a "new integral view on the person," one that offers "a new form for visualizing a human being in art."[20]

The new authorial position in the polyphonic novel, Bakhtin maintains, is "located above the monological position."[21] The entire realm of the artist's "creative subjectivity" has been objectified in his characters' voices. It follows from this new position that the unity of a Dostoevsky novel as a whole is "above personal style and above personal tone."[22] We are involved, then, not with two Dostoevskys—author-ideologist and artist-philosopher—but with a new positioning of the author-ideologist in the multivoiced world created by the artist, one in which the ideologist participates on equal terms with other voices. It is on this plane of relationships between voices that Bakhtin will find the value orientation of the Dostoevsky novel. The nature of authorial participation in the Dostoevsky novel and the form in which Dostoevsky's point of view manifests itself is crucial to Bakhtin's thinking on Dostoevsky's poetics.

Dostoevsky emerges in his creative work, in Bakhtin's conception, as the creator of the "free people, capable of standing alongside their creator, capable of not agreeing with him and even of rebelling against him." "A plurality of independent and unmerged voices and consciousnesses, a genuine polyphony of fully valid voices is in fact the chief characteristic of Dostoevsky's novels."[23] The author's "word" or "voice" is but one of a number of voices, none of which are reduced to a single ideological common denominator.[24] Here, too, there is no thought of an ultimate synthesis, of contradictions and bifurcations becoming dialectical and "moving along a temporal path or in an evolving sequence; they were rather spread out in one plane . . . as constant but not merging or as hopelessly contradictory . . . as an eternal harmony of unmerged voices." Not evolution toward some grand synthesis but "coexistence and interaction . . . space, not time" constitute the fundamental category in Dostoevsky's mode of artistic visualization.[25]

In chapter 1 of his revised Dostoevsky book, "Dostoevsky's Polyphonic Novel and Its Treatment in Critical Literature," Bakhtin to one degree or another faults almost the entire body of critical literature on Dostoevsky before and after his 1929 book for attempting to "monologize" Dostoevsky's "multivoiced world." He directs his attention, first, to Vyacheslav I. Ivanov, a writer, he acknowledges, who nonetheless pointed to the active "fundamental principle at work in Dostoevsky's art."[26] Ivanov, he writes approvingly, defined Dostoevsky's realism "as a realism based not on cognition (objectified cognition) but on 'penetration.'" As Bakhtin formulates Ivanov's position, "The affirmation of someone else's consciousness ["Thou art"]—as an autonomous subject and not as an object—is the ethico-religious postulate determining the *content* of the novel."[27] When Bakhtin later sums up his own theory of the way the "larger sense of [Dostoevsky's] artistic form . . . liberates and de-reifies the human being," he will return to Ivanov's basic "Thou art" formulation: "Thus the new artistic position of the author with regard to the hero in Dostoevsky's polyphonic novel is a fully realized and thoroughly consistent dialogic position, one that affirms the independence, internal unfinalizability, and indeterminacy of the hero. For the author the hero is not 'he' and not 'I' but a fully valid 'Thou,' that is, another and other autonomous 'I' ('Thou art')."[28]

Bakhtin, however, complains that Ivanov, "having arrived at a profound and correct definition of Dostoevsky's fundamental principle . . . proceeded to monologize this principle, that is, he incorporated it into a monologically formulated authorial worldview and perceived it as merely one of the interesting themes in a world represented from the point of view of a monologic authorial consciousness."[29] Bakhtin, I think, understates the importance Ivanov attributes to the "Thou art" principle in Dostoevsky's novel; it is considerably more than a "theme." The core of Bakhtin's criticism, however, is that Ivanov committed "a typical methodological error: he moves *directly* from the author's worldview to the content of the author's works, *passing over the form*. In other instances Ivanov more correctly understands the interrelationship between worldview and form (my italics)."[30] Bakhtin writes:

> Vyacheslav Ivanov did not show how this principle of Dostoevsky's worldview becomes the principle behind Dostoevsky's *artistic* visualization of the world, the principle behind his artistic structuring of a *verbal* whole, the novel. But it is only in this form, as a principle governing concrete literary construction and not as the ethico-religious principle behind an abstract worldview, that it is essential for the literary scholar.[31]

Bakhtin, then, does not differ with Ivanov on the centrality of the "Thou art" principle in Dostoevsky's art—for Ivanov, the core of Dostoevsky's ethical-religious point of view. His main criticism is that Ivanov did not disclose the pervasive, informing, and structuring role of the "Thou art" principle in the Dostoevsky's *artistic-philosophical* rendering of his novelistic universe, that he did not follow through on his initial insight. On this point Bakhtin is certainly correct. Yet as I have noted in my discussion of Ivanov's Dostoevsky book, the Russian philosopher, like Bakhtin, clearly affirms "the great organic unity of Dostoevsky's work as a whole." Ivanov continues:

> Indeed, all parts of his "doctrine" have such an inwardly fundamental and living relationship—his ethics, psychology, metaphysic, anthropology, sociology and eschatology so utterly determine and complement each other—that the deeper we penetrate into the nature of the connection between them, the more certain we come to realize that for Dostoevsky the creation of literary form was only a medium for the polymorphous development of a synthetic idea of the universe, which from the outset he had carried within him as a comprehensive vision and a morphological principle of his spiritual growth.[32]

Dostoevsky's "literary form" for Ivanov is an integral part and expression of the novelist's "doctrine," his concept of the "polymorphous development of a synthetic idea of the universe." Ivanov puts the word *doctrine* in quotation marks: he fully recognizes that Dostoevsky's art does not emerge literally from a doctrine. He might have used the word *poetics*—a word which in Bakhtin's usage embraces problems of "literary form" and addresses the whole question of Dostoevsky's fundamental innovation: his artistic construction of "a new artistic model of the world," "a polyphonic world."[33]

In his remarks on Ivanov, Bakhtin uses the notion of *worldview* somewhat ambiguously. He uses this term in the first instance to designate Dostoevsky's ethical-religious outlook, that position ("the author's worldview" [*mirovozzrenie*]) from which Ivanov, erroneously in Bakhtin's view, "moves directly . . . to the content of the author's work, passing over the form." In Bakhtin's view, however, the underlying ethico-religious *principle* of this worldview—"Dostoevsky's fundamental principle"—lies at the heart of "Dostoevsky's artistic visualization of the world," his artistic worldview. At root, then, Dostoevsky's "abstract worldview" and his "artistic visualization of the world" bear a close resemblance to each other.

Bakhtin's distinction between an "abstract worldview" and a higher worldview, or "artistic visualization" (*khudozhestvennoe videnie*) of the world, nonetheless remains crucial to his understanding of Dostoevsky's poetics. Noteworthy is Bakhtin's consistent use of the noun *videnie* (vision, visualization, or seeing), with its root in the Russian word *videt'* (to see) when speaking of Dostoevsky's artistic worldview.[34] Active or artistic seeing, the creation of images in words, on the one hand and making abstract ideological pronouncements (such as might constitute a worldview in the conventional use of the term) on the other are two different things. Thus apropos of Dostoevsky's capacity to "see and represent the world" only in the "category of co-existence," Bakhtin cautions: "The characteristic of Dostoevsky we offer here is not, of course, a trait of his worldview [*mirovozzrenie*] *in the ordinary sense of the word. It is a trait of his artistic perception of the world*" (my italics).[35] Bakhtin's qualification—"in the ordinary sense of the word"—leaves open precisely the possibility of using the term *worldview* in the higher sense of the word, as he uses it to a large extent in his discussion of Dostoevsky's poetics. Yet Bakhtin implicitly contrasts *worldview* in the ordinary sense of the word with *visualization* when he juxtaposes Dostoevsky's religious views—in particular as they take shape in the mouths of his characters—with Dostoevsky's "artistic cognition of the human world."[36]

To provide another example: when discussing Dostoevsky's notion of the being of man (in Bakhtin's words, "*to be* means *to communicate*"), Bakhtin cautions that "all this is no philosophical theory of Dostoevsky's—it is the way he artistically visualized the life of human consciousness, a visualization embodied in the form of a content."[37] Bakhtin, it should be noted, is careful in his formulation to avoid the "methodological error" he attributes to Ivanov; that is, he does not directly "pass over form" to content but speaks of "a visualization embodied *in the form* of a content" (my italics). Bakhtin's notion of visualization in the form of a content is important in another respect: it implies that visualization is never passive but always forming, shaping, image producing. Thus, for example, he refers to "Dostoevsky's visualizing power [*videnie Dostoevskogo*] . . . organizing and shaping this diversity [of unmerged voices] in the cross-section of a given moment."[38] Dostoevsky's "new form of visualization," Bakhtin suggests, is also a kind of unveiling. The polyphonic novel, he writes, contributed to the "seeing and discovery of something new in life."[39] "Artistic form or vision, correctly understood, does not shape already prepared and found content, but rather permits content to be found and seen for the first time."[40] Dostoevsky himself repeatedly stressed the special unveiling character of artistic vision. "Really, examine some fact of real life, even one which at first glance is not very striking," Dostoevsky wrote in his *Diary of a Writer* in October 1876, "and if only you are able and have the eyes, you will discover in it a depth such as is not to be found in Shakespeare. But really here is just the whole point: *whose eyes and who is able?* Indeed, not only to create and write artistic works, but even just to note a fact, something in the way of an artist is also needed."[41] The artistic visualization of reality here, as Bakhtin recognized, is of a different order than a realism based on cognition.

The words of the critic (or of the author, outside the work of art) may violate the organic form-content unity that emerges from genuine artistic visualization. Expository language or discourse, however subtle, is not the same as the language of artistic visualization. At one point Bakhtin himself apologetically speaks of translating "into the language of an abstract worldview that which was the object [for Dostoevsky] of concrete and living artistic visualization and which then became a principle of form."[42] Bakhtin's comment serves to remind the reader that he is not concerned with Dostoevsky's worldview "in the ordinary sense of the word," that is, with abstract pronouncements, but with a mode of expression in which words are used not to preach or teach directly but to create or form images. Thus Bakhtin emphasizes: "As an artist, Dostoevsky did not create his ideas in the same way philosophers or scholars create theirs—he created images of ideas found, heard, sometimes divined by him *in reality itself,* that is, ideas already living or entering life as idea-forces."[43] "For Dostoevsky, there are no ideas, no thoughts, no positions which belong to no one, which exist 'in themselves.' Even 'truth in itself' he presents in the spirit of Christian ideology, as incarnated in Christ; that is, he presents it as a personality entering into relationships with other personalities."[44] Yet for all the limitations of the "language of an abstract worldview," it may convey accurately, albeit in a cumbersome way (as is often the case in Bakhtin's study), the truths of the language of imagery, the language of artistic visualization. The point is an important one: the essence and dynamic of Dostoevsky's artistic visualization of reality find subtle expression in some of his religious "pronouncements," in his abstract "ideology."

At the beginning of his third chapter, "The Idea in Dostoevsky," a section concerned with the "positioning of the idea in Dostoevsky's artistic world," Bakhtin stresses that in his analysis he will "avoid matters of content in the ideas introduced by Dostoevsky—what is important for us here is their artistic function in the work."[45] At the end of this same chapter, after citing a passage from Dostoevsky's notebook in which the Russian novelist affirms his personal faith in Christ, Bakhtin writes: "In these thoughts the important thing for us is not Dostoevsky's Christian declaration of faith in itself, but those living *forms* of his artistic and ideological thinking that are here so lucidly realized and expressed."[46] Bakhtin, however, all but directly affirms an organic relationship between Dostoevsky's declaration of faith and the "living forms" of his thinking. He simply insists that "Dostoevskian ideas" "enter the great dialogue of the [Dostoevsky] novel on *completely equal terms* with other idea-images."[47]

Yet how do "Dostoevsky ideas" fare, ultimately, in the great dialogue? Bakhtin speaks not of a definitive or "finalizing" triumph of Dostoevsky ideas or worldview. With respect to his understanding of "worldview" in general, Bakhtin follows Dostoevsky closely: "Dostoevsky understands worldview not as an abstract unity and sequence in a system of thoughts and positions, but as an ultimate position in the world in relation to higher values," Bakhtin observes in "Toward a Reworking of the Dostoevsky Book." "Worldviews embodied in voices. A dialogue among such embodied worldviews, in which he himself participated."[48] In some important lines in the same notes, Bakhtin provides an important clue to the form Dostoevsky's "ultimate position" takes in his novels, to the way it is manifested. "Not faith (in the sense of a specific faith in orthodoxy, in progress, in man, in revolution, etc.) but a *sense of faith*, that is, an integral attitude (by means of the whole person) toward a higher and ultimate value."[49] In this definition of faith there is no final victory; there is only a tension, or movement, of the whole being toward higher value. Man cannot wholly know or appropriate "higher values," ultimate value, truth, or God, but he can with his whole being sense it, lean toward it, stand in a positive relationship to it. Such is the essence of Luke 12:30: "And thou shalt love the Lord thy God with all thy heart, and with all thy soul, and with all thy mind, and with all thy strength." Here there is a tension toward God, not a merging with, or appropriation of, God. When the scribe repeats with some elaboration on this notion (12:33), Jesus replies: "Thou art not far from the kingdom of God" (12:34).

This sense of "an integral attitude . . . toward a higher and ulti-mate value," manifested in the tension of unfinalized dialogue within the self, objectified in the clash of voices on the novelistic plane or plane of life, is well illustrated by one of Dostoevsky's central obser-vations in his notebook: "Man strives on earth for an ideal that is *contrary* to his nature."[50] The idea of permanent striving for value, for the ideal, for God, is central to Bakhtin's understanding of the authorial position in a Dostoevsky novel.

Bakhtin recognizes the centrality of the question of Dostoevsky's authorial position in his novel. In a letter to the Russian scholar Vadim V. Kozhinov in 1961, Bakhtin notes that his discussion on the position of the author in the polyphonic novel "has more than anything else given rise to objections and misunderstanding."[51] In his notes "To-ward a Reworking of the Dostoevsky Book," Bakhtin seeks to address this misunderstanding:

> Our point of view in no way assumes a passivity on the part of the author, who would then merely assemble others' point of view, others' truths, completely denying his own point of view, his own truth. This is not the case at all; the case is rather a completely new and special interrelationship between the author's and the other's truth. The author is profoundly *active*, but his activity is of a special *dialogic* sort. It is one thing to be active in relation to a dead thing, to voiceless material that can be molded and formed as one wishes, and another thing to be active *in relation to someone else's living, autonomous consciousness*. This is a questioning, provoking, an-swering, agreeing, objecting activity; that is, it is dialogic activity no less active than the activity that finalizes materializes, explains, and kills caus-ally, that drowns out the other's voice with nonsemantic arguments. Dos-toevsky frequently interrupts, but he never drowns out the other's voice, never finishes it off "from himself," that is, out of his own and alien con-

sciousness. This is, so to speak, the activity of God in His relation to man, a relation allowing man to reveal himself utterly (in his immanent development), to judge himself, to refute himself. This is activity of a higher quality. It surmounts [*preodolevaet*: surmounts, overcomes, prevails over] not the resistance of dead material but the resistance of another's consciousness, another's truth.[52]

Bakhtin does not provide any concrete illustrations of how dialogic "activity" "surmounts" or overcomes the "resistance . . . of another's consciousness" while at the same time remaining open-ended. What does it mean to "surmount . . . the resistance of another's consciousness, another's truth"? Dostoevsky's "sense of faith," his "ultimate position in relation to higher values," his tension toward the ideal, finds expression in the *continuous* and *continuing process* of surmounting another truth, or surmounting the resistance of another truth. Bakhtin for this reason rejects as inauthentic and "monological" the conclusions of some of Dostoevsky's novels (as, for example, the epilogue in *Crime and Punishment*); typical of Dostoevsky's abstract ideology, they contradict, in Bakhtin's view, the novelist's polyphonic artistic stance. As opposed to the idea of a finalizing monological conclusion, the concept of "surmounting" may suggest, however, a *permanent tendency* toward such a conclusion. The "conclusion" is never reached, and it may certainly be challenged, even mocked by other voices, but in the overall configuration of voices, there is always a felt tendency toward it; or, in Bakhtin's words, "a sense of faith," an "integral attitude . . . toward a higher and ultimate value."

In general, there is a close connection between the idea of a permanent process of open-ended surmounting or overcoming another's truth in Dostoevsky's novelistic universe and Dostoevsky's ethical religious thinking in his notebooks. A consideration of Bakhtin's analogy between Dostoevsky's artistic activity and the "activity of God in His relation to man" will serve to open up this question.

Frequent are the comparisons in critical literature between Leo Tolstoy and God (Gorky, Thomas Mann, and others have drawn this analogy). Dostoevsky himself once referred to Tolstoy as "a god of art." Only Bakhtin among the major critical thinkers, it would seem, has drawn an analogy between Dostoevsky the artist and God. In this comparison, simultaneously aesthetic and theological, Dostoevsky emerges in his novelistic activity as God-Creator, but above all as God "in His relation to man, a relation allowing man to reveal himself utterly (in his immanent development)."[53] What is at issue is God's grand design with respect to the salvation of man. The artist-god here is not the monologically oriented personal god of the Old Testament who is always interfering with the destinies of his people—now threatening them, now punishing them, now rewarding them, and always laying out their destiny—but the God of the New Testament who leaves man free to decide for himself, free "to judge himself, to refute himself" in self-regulating dialogical processes.

If Dostoevsky's relation to his multivoiced world may be compared to the activity of God in his relation to man, then the "divine" principle behind Dostoevsky's activity is freedom—open-ended dialogue, interchange, struggle, continual movement, or nonfinalized striving. In this sense, the "new artistic model of the world" that Dostoevsky created is the *world as it is*, the world that God created: a world of endless struggle between good and evil, of many competing truths, autonomous tendencies; a world in which men are in turmoil and "argument" has not ceased; a world, above all, in which "the end is not by and by" (Luke 21:8–9).

"As major heroes," Bakhtin writes, "Dostoevsky portrays only those people in his work with whom argument has not yet ended (for indeed it is not yet ended in the world)."[54] An element of unfinalizability defines the strivings of Dostoevsky's heroes. Bakhtin, in this connection, cites Alyosha on his brother Ivan in *The Brothers Karamazov*: "Oh, his soul is a stormy one. His mind is a prisoner of it. There is a great and unresolved thought in him. He is one of those who don't need millions, they just need to get a thought straight [*nadobno mysl' razreshit'*; literally, they need to resolve a thought]." "It is given to all of Dostoevsky's characters to 'think and seek higher things,'" comments Bakhtin; "in each of them there is a 'great and unresolved thought'; all of them must, before all else, 'resolve a thought.' And in this resolution of a thought (an idea) lies their entire real life and their own personal unfinalizability."[55]

Indeed, Dostoevsky's heroes are endlessly trying to resolve the unresolvable, to solve the insoluble, to cross uncrossable boundaries. Ivan's supreme effort to reach a "resolve a thought"—the problem of freedom itself—is his "Legend of the Grand Inquisitor," a "poem" that sets forth "the unsolved historical contradictions of human nature." Ivan's quest for resolution of this question remains, like the historical contradictions of human nature, unsolved in the legend. It is in the novel as a whole, however, in the developing drama of Ivan and other characters, that one observes a tendency toward a resolution; a point of view emerges out of the configuration of these struggles that gives embodiment to "Dostoevsky ideas."

The artistic position of Dostoevsky as "God" is eminently an ethical position but one that does not involve direct action in the form of "an externalizing and finalizing approach" to his characters.[56] Dostoevsky does not overwhelm his characters, in Bakhtin's view, with his supreme power and knowledge. He respects "that internally unfinalizable something in man," their intrinsic freedom and independence as human beings, their essential unfinalizable character. "In Dostoevsky's subsequent works [after *Poor Folk* and other early works], the characters . . . all do furious battle with such [finalizing secondhand] definitions in the mouths of other people."[57]

Dostoevsky's open-ended godlike approach to his characters may be compared to that of the Lord in the Book of Job or Goethe's *Faust*. The supreme *finalizing* approach to, and definitive definition of, man, however, surely belongs to Satan and the Grand Inquisitor—demonic entities who stress the idea of the limited and defective nature of human beings, man's inability to bear the burden of freedom, his negative drive toward self-limitation and self-destruction—toward an *end*. The devil in *Faust* asks only that God allow him to go to work on the "little earth god" Faust to demonstrate the truth of the devil's tragic definition. God grants the devil's request; he is confident of his creation and leaves it to Faust to discover the truth: "A good man in his dark striving is conscious of the right way." It is in *The Brothers Karamazov* that the Joban and Faustian design finds most dramatic embodiment. The Grand Inquisitor's definition of man—"I swear, man is weaker and baser by nature than Thou hast believed him"—is tested in the dramas of the Karamazov brothers, in particular in the drama of Dmitry Karamazov.[58] Dmitry spends the two days before the murder of his father "literally casting himself in all directions, 'struggling with his fate and saving himself,' as he himself put it later." Characteristically, the quoted words are spoken by Dmitry, not by the omniscient narrator. Dmitry recognizes his struggle to be a universal one. "God and the devil are fighting there and the battlefield is the heart of man." "Struggling with his fate and saving himself" speak of Dmitry's salvation as something in process. Dmitry does "save himself" from killing his father with his own hand (though he contributes to the murder of his father), but his struggle is still going on at the end of the novel. What is important is that he has become conscious of his inner struggle, of the task, endless for him as for humanity, of continuously striving, of continuously trying to "save himself." Dmitry rejects—and then not so much in thought as in action, in the drama of his life—the Grand Inquisitor's humiliating definition of man. In seeking to define himself, in his furious and ever-continuing internal dialogue ("unknown ideas are storming within me," "various philosophies are tormenting me"), Dmitry *tends* (in spite of all backslidings and opposite movements) in the direction of a lofty ideal. His ecstasy over the poetry of Schiller serves both to signal these higher ideals and his own inner striving toward them.

It is significant that Dmitry speaks of the birth of a "new man" within himself. Yet even such a happening appears utopian. "You wanted through suffering to be reborn into another man," Alyosha says to his brother. "In my opinion, remember only and always through your life . . . this other man—and that will be enough for you." Memory here serves to foreground the purity of intention, the point of light toward which Dmitry can strive. Ethical behavior in Dostoevsky's artistic universe, in the language of Russian grammar, is in the imperfective or durative aspect, not perfective or punctual. One cannot speak in any sense of a resolution of Dmitry's conflicts; one cannot speak of a new formed outlook or faith in any specific sense. Yet one may speak of a "sense of faith . . . an integral attitude (by means of the whole person) toward a higher and ultimate value." Dostoevsky's representation of the dynamic, ongoing drama of Dmitry validates Bakhtin's view of the Russian novelist's work as "the activity of God in His relation to man, a relation allowing man to reveal himself utterly (in his immanent development), to judge himself, to refute himself."

Bakhtin provides no illustrations of how Dostoevsky's "point of view" manifests itself in his work or in the lives of his heroes; he rigorously excludes from his circle of concerns precisely concrete and rounded discussions of the ideological dramas of Dostoevsky's characters. He does indicate, however, that in the realm of competing consciousnesses, truths, voices, *some* voices, *some* truths that sound out are more "authoritative." After characterizing Dostoevsky's "method of integral juxtapositions,"[59] his "form-shaping ideology," Bakhtin observes:

> As a result of such an ideological approach, what unfolds before Dostoevsky is not a world of objects, illuminated and ordered by his monologic thought, but a world of consciousnesses mutually illuminating one another, a world of yoked-together semantic human orientations. Among them Dostoevsky seeks the highest and most authoritative orientation, and he perceives it not as his own true thought, but as another authentic human being and his discourse. The image of the ideal human being or the image of Christ represents for him the resolution of ideological quests. This image or this highest voice must crown the world of voices, must organize and subdue it. Precisely the image of a human being and his voice, a voice not the author's own, was the ultimate artistic criterion for Dostoevsky: not fidelity to his own convictions and not fidelity to convictions themselves taken abstractly, but precisely a fidelity to the authoritative image of a human being.[60]

These lines are among the most important in Bakhtin's study; they deserve the most careful attention. Bakhtin projects, as it were, a horizontal plane to the Dostoevsky novel on which coexist multiple "consciousnesses"—separate, albeit "yoked together" "semantic human orientations," "voices," each jostling one another, each bearing its own truths. At the same time he suggests what we may term a vertical dimension in Dostoevsky's novelistic universe, a hierarchy of voices, orientations, or truths arising out of this sea of autonomous jostling truths. This hierarchy of orientations results from the special activity of the author. "Among [these orientations] Dostoevsky seeks the highest and most authoritative orientation." The highest orientation is the voice of Christ and his "discourse." The highest word, in short, is the word of Christ, and "his voice must crown the world of voices, must organize and subdue it."

One point deserves emphasis here: Dostoevsky, in Bakhtin's view, characteristically *seeks* the "highest and most authoritative orientation;

he perceives it not as his own thought"; the image of Christ represents for him "the resolution of ideological quests," a resolution, however, that is clearly not at hand. There is a paradox here. Christ's voice or word is one among many voices or "words" on the horizontal, egalitarian plane of the novel's life and work, as on the stage of life. Yet because of Dostoevsky's seeking—the correlative of the seeking of all characters in his novels ("It is given to all of Dostoevsky's characters to 'think and seek higher things'")—Christ's "word" (in the figurative sense, above all) acquires a privileged, though not uncontested, status as an "authoritative orientation" or ideal.

The concept of Dostoevsky seeking the highest truth within a world of competing truths is a crucial one in Bakhtin's understanding of Dostoevsky's relation to his novelistic universe. Dostoevsky the seeker plays no didactic role on the stage of his novel's activity (such a role, for example, is played by Father Zosima in *The Brothers Karamazov*); he does not impose his point of view through authorial pronouncement. It is Christ's voice, Christ's *image*, not Dostoevsky's opinions, that must "crown the world of voices, must organize and subdue it" at the end of time—though not at the end of the novel! The final goal toward which Dostoevsky and his characters strive in light or darkness, consciously or unconsciously, may be previsioned, anticipated, even symbolized in memory, dream, or art, but it cannot be achieved in the novel, as it cannot be achieved in life. All that can be done is to seek; all that can be achieved in the social, ethical, and spiritual realm is "an integral attitude toward a higher and ultimate value." "Do not lose touch with life, preserve your soul, believe in the truth," Dostoevsky wrote Nadezhda P. Suslova on April 19, 1865. "But *seek* it *intently* all life long, or else it is terribly easy to go astray."[61] Dostoevsky's words admirably give expression to his "abstract worldview" and his "artistic visualization" of reality.

Dostoevsky's relation to his novelistic world, then, is a double one: as ideologist, as a man with a point of view, it is that of any character in his novel seeking truth, striving not to go astray in a world where the end is not yet in sight; as artist, it is that of the grand architect who "allows man freely to reveal himself utterly (in his immanent development), to judge himself, to refute himself." In both roles Dostoevsky acknowledges the unfinished or unfinalized nature of human experience and striving, the permanent reality of freedom and uncertainty, dialogue and dilemma, in this world. For both writer and seeker, the voice of Christ has a privileged place as "the highest voice," or truth, but it is a truth that one can only stand *in relation* to, a truth to which one can only relate imperfectly and, at best, with a sense of faith or fidelity.

The distinction between "fidelity" to an authoritative image as opposed to fidelity to one's own convictions or convictions taken abstractly is important to Bakhtin's understanding of the relation of Dostoevsky or his characters to an ideal or ultimate value. In his effort to clarify the distinction between these two types of fidelity—and so establish more clearly Dostoevsky's special position in relation to his universe of voices—Bakhtin cites the Russian novelist's response in his notebook (1881) to some remarks by the Russian historian K. D. Kavelin:

> It is not enough to define morality as fidelity to one's own convictions. Even more one must endlessly stimulate within oneself the question: are my convictions true? Only one verification of them exists—Christ. But this is no longer philosophy, it is faith, and this faith is a red color. . . .
>
> I cannot recognize one who burns heretics as a moral man, because I do not accept your thesis that morality is an agreement with internal convictions. That is merely *honesty* (the Russian language is rich), but not morality. I have one moral model and an ideal, Christ. I ask: would he have burned heretics?—no. Well, that means the burning of heretics is an immoral act. . . .
>
> Christ was mistaken—it's been proved! A scorching feeling tells me: better that I remain with a mistake, with Christ, than with you. . . .
>
> Living life has fled you, only the formulas and categories remain, and that, it seems, makes you happy. You say there's more peace and quiet (laziness) that way. . . .
>
> You say that to be moral one need only act according to conviction. But just where do you get your convictions? I simply do not believe you and say that on the contrary it is immoral to act according to one's convictions. And you, of course, cannot find a way to prove me wrong.[62]

At the heart of Dostoevsky's comments is his conviction summed up in his observation "better that I remain with a mistake, with Christ." That is, even if Christ were wrong, I would rather remain with him. Bakhtin prefaces his observations on this passage with the remark that "in these thoughts the important thing for us is not Dostoevsky's Christian declaration of faith in itself but those living *forms* of his artistic and ideological thinking."[63] "Declaration of faith" and "living forms" of artistic thought (like the opposition of "worldview," "in the ordinary sense of the word," to "artistic visualization") seem to emerge here as antithetical categories. Yet it is clear that Dostoevsky's "Christian declaration of faith" not only sums up his religious worldview, but precisely gives expression, albeit "in the language of an abstract worldview," to the "living forms" of his "artistic and ideological thinking." Bakhtin, indeed, seems fully conscious of this fact. In his discussion of Dostoevsky's response to Kavelin, Bakhtin centers on what is the very dynamic character of Dostoevsky's religious outlook. "Formulas and categories" are alien to Dostoevsky's thinking, Bakhtin writes:

> [Dostoevsky] prefers to *remain with the mistake but with Christ*, that is, without truth in the theoretical sense of the word, without truth-as-formula, truth-as-proposition. . . . A distrust of convictions and their usual monologic function, *a quest for truth* not as the deduction of one's own consciousness, in fact not in the monologic context of an individual consciousness at all, but rather in the ideal authoritative image of another human being, *an orientation toward the other's voice*, the other's word: all this is characteristic of Dostoevsky's form-shaping ideology. An authorial idea or thought must not perform in the work the function of totally illuminating the represented world, but *must rather enter into that world as an image of a human being, as one orientation among other orientations, as one word among many words. This ideal orientation (the true word) and its potential must never be lost sight of* [literally, must be before the eyes], but it must not color the work with the personal ideological tone of the author.[64] [My italics]

Dostoevsky's stress, in the conception of Bakhtin, upon the "quest for truth" as something disclosed not in "the deduction of one's own consciousness" (that is, merely in words, ratiocination, abstract philosophy) but "rather in the ideal authoritative image of another human being" and in an "orientation" toward that voice; his notion that in Dostoevsky's work the "ideal orientation (the true word) and its possibility" must remain before the eyes; fully concords with Dostoevsky's conception of the appearance of Christ and man's relation to him in the design of divine salvation. "Christ," Dostoevsky wrote in his notebook, "is the ideal of man *in the flesh*."[65] Renan and others consider

Christ an ordinary man and criticize the teachings of Christ as inappropriate for our times, Dostoevsky observes in his notebook for *The Devils*, "But here there are not even any teachings, only occasional words, while the main thing is the image of Christ from which comes all teaching."[66] "Not Christ's morality, not the teaching of Christ will save the world, but precisely faith that the Word became flesh. This faith is not just intellectual recognition of the superiority of His teachings, but direct attraction."[67] One must believe that "the word was flesh, i.e. that the ideal was in flesh, and therefore the ideal is not impossible, [but] is attainable by mankind."[68] Jesus, the Grand Inquisitor notes, declared that "man must hereafter with free heart decide for himself what is good and what is evil, having only Thy image before him as his guide." The hero of the "Dream of a Ridiculous Man" experiences in his dream "real images and forms" of higher beauty. "I saw, I saw," he declares, "and the living image filled my soul forever . . . the living image of what I saw will always be with me and always correct and guide me." The ridiculous man relates directly to the *image* of beauty; characteristically he has difficulty formulating his vision in *words*. "After my dream I lost the knack of putting things into words. At least, into the most necessary and most important words." What is important now is his organic relationship to his vision: "I have indeed beheld it [heaven on earth] with my own eyes, though I cannot describe what I saw." Verbal descriptions or affirmations of faith ("the most necessary and most important words") cannot substitute for, or convey, the image of beauty itself. One can only *see* the "living image," be drawn toward it, follow it: "The living image . . . will always be with me and always correct and guide me."

Dostoevsky relates to the image of Christ much as the Ridiculous Man relates to his "living image" of beauty and truth: in his *Diary of a Writer* Dostoevsky, like the Ridiculous Man after his dream, sets out at times directly to preach his religious idea. In the artistic universe of his novels, however, Dostoevsky, as it were, preaches his idea in imagery.[69] Bakhtin speaks of Dostoevsky's images of ideas. "The idea—as it was *seen* by Dostoevsky the artist—is not a subjective individual-psychological formation with 'permanent resident rights' in a person's head. . . . The idea is a *live event* . . . the idea is similar to the *word* . . . like the word, the idea wants to be heard, understood, and 'answered' by other voices from other positions."[70] Similarly the embodied "idea" of Christ, this "ideal authoritative image," also wants to be heard, understood, and "answered." And indeed, the power and presence of Jesus is felt most strongly in *The Brothers Karamazov* precisely in a moment of dialogue when he is "answered" by the Grand Inquisitor.

What is important in man's orientation toward the "ideal authoritative image"—whether he be the Ridiculous Man, Dmitry Karamazov, or the crowd of people in front of the cathedral in Seville who "strive toward" Jesus[71]—is the fact that he continue to strive toward it. The ideal orientation (the true word) and its possibility must always be before the eyes. Man must freely discover Christ, "the ideal authoritative image," "as one orientation among other orientations, as one word among many words." Christ, the idea-image of Christ, emerges as the supreme embodiment of man's never-ending "quest for truth" or, in the aesthetic and spiritual terms of "artistic visualization," as the supreme ideal of man in his *quest for form.*[72]

The idea of a permanent quest for form, for absolute spiritual beauty and truth, is embodied in Dostoevsky's readiness to "remain with a mistake," that is, with Christ. The thought that Dostoevsky expresses here—Bakhtin was surely familiar with it—found expression in a letter Dostoevsky wrote to Mme N. D. Fonvizina immediately on his release from prison in 1854. In that letter Dostoevsky speaks of his religious beliefs:

> I am a child of the age, a child of lack of faith and doubt till now, and (this I know) this will be true till the coffin closes over. What frightful torments this thirst to believe has cost and costs me now, one which is all the stronger in my soul the more there are opposite proofs in me. And yet God sometimes sends me moments in which I am perfectly tranquil; in these moments I love and find that I am loved by others, and in such moments I have formed in myself a symbol of faith in which everything is clear and sacred for me. This symbol is very simple; here it is: to believe that there is nothing more beautiful, profound, sympathetic, intelligent, manly, and perfect than Christ, and not only is not but, with jealous love I say to myself, cannot be. Even more, if somebody proved to me that Christ was outside the truth, and it *really* were so that the truth were outside of Christ, then I would rather remain with Christ than with the truth.[73]

Dostoevsky, in short, is prepared to "remain with a mistake," with Christ. He allows for the existence of a negative truth—"opposite proofs"—a truth that *logically* denies the divinity of Christ. Yet in the face of that truth, he makes a leap of faith that places Christ back into the circle of revealed truth. The paradoxical formulation of faith here is central both to Dostoevsky's "artistic visualization of the world, the principle behind his artistic structuring of a verbal whole, the novel"[74] and to his Christian ethical-religious outlook. Dostoevsky's "even if," his choice to remain with Christ even if he were outside the truth, is that of a man who will remain "a child of the century, a child of disbelief and doubt" until his grave closes over. This spiritual condition Dostoevsky describes in these lines is that of a person in a permanent state of spiritual tension in which the "thirst to believe" is *continually overcoming* the "opposite proofs," doubt, the negative truth. What defines this condition in him is not a definitive triumph of Christ's truth but a continual "quest for truth," a continual and agonizing quest for form, a continual positing of an ideal authoritative image.

Dostoevsky's letter to Fonvizina in 1854 contains the earliest extant formulation of what Bakhtin in his *Poetics* calls Dostoevsky's "Christian declaration of faith," his philosophical-religious outlook. Bakhtin makes no reference to this letter, nor does he refer to the most definitive reformulation of this declaration of faith, one that may be found in Dostoevsky's notebook April 17, 1864. On the occasion of the death of his first wife and at the time of writing *Notes from the Underground*, Dostoevsky put down some thoughts that constitute the core of his worldview. He posits Christ as the "everlasting ideal since the beginning of time, towards whom man aspires. . . . The entire history of mankind, and partly that of each individual, is only the development, the struggle, the striving, and the achievement of this goal."

Central to Dostoevsky's entire view of man and history is the idea of permanent movement, development, transition. "Man on this earth is only a developing creature." His life is a permanent process of "achieving, struggling and, through all defeats, refocusing on the ideal [Christ] and struggling for it." Dostoevsky posits this process as a "law of nature," the "law of striving for the ideal," the law that gives spiritual life through setting into creative movement or tension the opposing truths or realities of human existence. "Man strives on earth for an ideal that is contrary to his nature." Spiritual health for Dostoevsky is not in stasis, not in utopia, and certainly not in anti-utopia, not in any definitive perfection of personality or society, but in movement, movement toward an ideal—ultimately, the religious ideal. "The teaching of the materialists is universal stagnation and the mechanism of substance, that is, death. The teaching of true philosophy is the destruction of inertia, that is, thought . . . i.e., God, i.e., endless life."[75]

Bakhtin deduces from Dostoevsky's decision to "remain with a mistake, with Christ" Dostoevsky's fundamental understanding of the protean, indeed "unfinalizable" character of truth—truth as movement, truth as something alien to formula, categories, inertia. It is precisely man's endless quest for higher truth, for an authoritative voice, for the ideal—one never to be attained on earth—that distinguishes Dostoevsky's concept of the "teachings of true philosophy," indeed his philosophical outlook, from the tragic *perpetuum mobile* of the Underground Man. This denizen of the underworld also prefers to remain with the mistake—with the irrational leap, with his formula $2 + 2 = 5$—but his is a course of action that excludes Christ. In chapter 11, the Underground Man confesses that he is lying when he celebrates the "underground": "I am lying, because I know, as twice two is four, that it is not at all the underground which is better, but something else, quite different, for which I thirst but which I can in no way find!" In the uncensored but no longer extant manuscript of *Notes from the Underground*, Dostoevsky indicated that this "something else," the "different ideal" that the Underground Man sought, the ideal that would indeed give meaning to his own and mankind's seemingly meaningless endless motion, is Christ. Thus in a letter to his brother Mikhail March 26, 1864, a letter written but a few weeks before his jottings in his notebook of April 16, Dostoevsky complains of "horrible excisions" of his manuscript by the censor:

> It really would have been better not to have printed the penultimate chapter (the main one where the very idea is expressed) [chap. 10 in pt. 1] than to have printed it as it is, that is, with sentences thrown together and contradicting each other. But what is to be done! The swinish censors let pass those places where I ridiculed everything and blasphemed *for show*—that is allowed, but where I deduce from all this the need for faith

and Christ—that is forbidden. Really, are these censors in a conspiracy against the government or something?[76]

Dostoevsky uses the pronoun *I*—"where I deduce from all this"— yet it was of course not through his own pronouncements or intervention but through the discourse, the internal dialogue of the Underground Man, that Dostoevsky in the original text disclosed the Underground Man's religious ideal. In some oblique or paradoxical way, the Underground Man, in the uncensored edition of *Notes*, must have given expression to thoughts that Dostoevsky set down in his April 1864 notations in his notebook: "the law of striving for the ideal," the ideal of Christ. The Underground Man is not a believer.[77] Yet it is only a step 'from the meaningless and rebellious $2 + 2 = 5$ of the Underground Man to the meaningful and spiritually productive $2 + 2 = 5$ of the Ridiculous Man, to the $2 + 2 = 5$ of Dostoevsky, the novelist's "readiness to remain with a mistake, with Christ" in spite of all "opposite proofs."[78] The Underground Man could have had only a glimpse of "the need for faith and Christ." That glimpse would not have transformed him or altered the dark ambiguities of the text, but it would have signaled more clearly to the reader what we might today call Dostoevsky's Christian existential design. It might have clearly disclosed, in short, the religious-philosophical foundations—that veritable religious credo—that underlies his notion of the "unfinalizable" character of truth, the notion of truth as movement, truth as something alien to formula, categories, inertia. What is certain is that Dostoevsky's "Christian declaration of faith" in his letter to Fonvizina in 1854, his private thoughts in his notebook in 1864, and his remarks about Kavelin in his notebook in 1881, that is, his abstract philosophical-religious worldview, is integral to his poetics and in full harmony with what Bakhtin calls the "living forms of [Dostoevsky's] artistic and ideological thinking," his "completely new kind of artistic thinking."

Bakhtin clearly recognized this direct relationship between Dostoevsky's religious thought, his "pronouncements," on the one hand and his artistic worldview on the other. Indeed, his book may be viewed precisely as an effort to do what he believed Vyacheslav Ivanov did not do: "show how this [ethico-religious] principle of Dostoevsky's worldview becomes the principle behind Dostoevsky's artistic visualization of the world" and is not merely "the ethico-religious principle behind an abstract worldview."[79] His desire to demonstrate that "Dostoevsky is first and foremost an artist"[80] goes a long way to explain his principled avoidance of direct discussion of Dostoevsky's religious beliefs. Yet it is obvious that the times in which Bakhtin worked on his book and published it (the 1920's and early 1960's) were not propitious to the appearance of a book in which the author would not only more fully acknowledge his indebtedness to the religious philosopher, poet, and thinker Vyacheslav I. Ivanov, but would bring to the foreground the Christian foundations of Dostoevsky's poetics.

In his introduction to Caryl Emerson's fine scholarly edition and translation of Bakhtin's study of Dostoevsky, Wayne C. Booth, after justly praising Bakhtin's high achievements, goes on to complain about Bakhtin's "failure to settle into sustained study of any one of Dostoevsky's works. . . . Whenever an author dwells at great length on general theories about huge lumps of literature called 'the novel' or even about smaller piles called 'Dostoevsky's works,' without settling into detailed efforts at exemplification, I grow restless."[81] More than one reader has experienced this kind of restlessness with Bakhtin's book. Yet those same readers will also forgive Bakhtin for his omissions: he was obliged to work in conditions of "restlessness" that Russians will long remember.

Bakhtin clearly did not leave us the kind of sustained study of Dostoevsky's works that many of us in the more comfortable quarters of the world might have wished for. Such a study might have done much to clarify Bakhtin's view on the authorial position in the Dostoevsky text, among other matters. What Bakhtin did leave, however, is a stunning work, one which indeed is "devoted to the problems of Dostoevsky's poetics and [which] surveys his work from that viewpoint *only*," but one which in the depth of its treatment of its theme goes a long way toward meeting Vyacheslav I. Ivanov's appeal for "an investigation of Dostoevsky's religious philosophy" and toward validating what Ivanov considered "the accord between what Dostoevsky had to teach and the living images in which he clothed it."

16 *Last Stop*

Virtue and Immortality in *The Brothers Karamazov*

Und ein Gott ist, ein heiliger Wille lebt,
  Wie auch der menschliche wanke;
Hoch über der Zeit und dem Raume webt
  Lebendig der höchste Gedanke,
Und ob Alles in ewigem Wechsel kreis't,
Es beharret im Wechsel ein ruhiger Geist.

  Schiller, *Die Worte des Glaubens*

 Writers and scholars have more than once noted the absolute character of oppositions in Dostoevsky. Thus Ivan Karamazov in his "rebellion" forces his audience to choose between future world harmony and attention to the tears of a child. Fyodor Karamazov asks, "Is there a God or is there no God?" If God exists, asks Ivan, why so much misfortune? If God does not exist, reflects Dmitry, does that mean all is permissible?

The Russian scholar Leonid Dolgopolov, reflecting on Dostoevsky, writes: "Dostoevsky's pictures of the world are antithetical in their essence." Contrasting the Russian novelist with Chekhov, he adds: "Chekhov overcomes precisely this antithetical, absolute character of Dostoevsky's ideas."[1] There is no question that the kinds of radical oppositions in characters and ideas that one encounters in Dostoevsky's novelistic universe are not only untypical in Chekhov's artistic universe but uncongenial to his way of thinking. Yet the radical oppositions we encounter in Dostoevsky's novels were not wholly congenial to Dostoevsky either, at least as he reflected on them. Quite clearly, he pondered on the dangers of the "either-or" mentality of many of his characters. This was particularly true in *The Brothers Karamazov* where the question of the relationship between faith and virtue is in the foreground.

The question of man's capacity to love his neighbor, indeed the question of his essential nature, is raised early in *The Brothers Karamazov* in the important discussion of Ivan's article on church jurisdiction. Ivan, according to Miusov (who reports Ivan's ideas), insists that

> "there is absolutely nothing on earth that could compel people to love each other, that a law of nature saying that man must love mankind simply does not exist, and that if there is and ever has been any love on earth, this is not from any natural law but simply because people believed in immortality. Ivan added, parenthetically, in this connection, that precisely in this consists the whole natural law, so that if you destroy humanity's faith in immortality, there will immediately dry up in it not only love, but also every living force necessary to perpetuate life on earth. Even more: there will no longer be anything immoral, everything will be permissible, even cannibalism."

Ivan himself adds on the occasion of Miusov's recollection, "There is no virtue if there is no immortality." The question which I would address briefly is simply posed but not so easily answered: Does Dostoevsky agree with Ivan's view that "there is no virtue if there is no immortality?" My answer will be that in *The Brothers Karamazov* Dostoevsky finds Ivan's statement acceptable only as a theological truism, as an affirmation of the divine unity of all aspects of God's world, but that as a guide to action, he finds Ivan's proposition limited, dogmatic, and dangerous.

If we turn, however, to the December 1876 issue of Dostoevsky's *Diary of a Writer*, we find these words blazing forth at us:

> I declare (once again *for the time being*) without proof that love for humanity is even quite unthinkable, incomprehensible and *quite impossible without concurrent faith in the immortality of the human soul.*[2] [Dostoevsky's italics]

It is significant that Dostoevsky's remarks are made in an article entitled "Arbitrary Assertions" and that he prefaces his remarks by saying that he intends to "amuse" those "gentlemen of ironclad ideas" who believe that love for humanity and its happiness is all set, comes about cheaply and without a thought. Dostoevsky's above-cited remark is provocative and ironical, and directed against interlocutors who have never really confronted or deeply responded to real suffering.

We may note, too, in this connection that Ivan's comments on the interdependence of love for humanity and faith in immortality are uttered before a group of provincial ladies (hardly a forum for the serious discussion of morality and religion) and, most likely, uttered with the purpose of amusing them, shocking them out of their easygoing and simplistic notions about love for humanity.

In Dostoevsky in the *Diary of a Writer* and Ivan Karamazov, then, we are dealing with authors who are speaking polemically and teasing their audience with a blunt and difficult truth; we are concerned precisely with "arbitrary assertions," not the ambience of art or the dialectical thinking of an artist-philosopher.

If we wish to find out Dostoevsky's views on these complex questions, we must turn to his art, and first to *The Brothers Karamazov*, a work which provides us with a broad context for evaluating Ivan's remarks. Here we discover that Dostoevsky subjects to critical scrutiny Ivan's—and his own—unambiguously stated assumptions, or "arbitrary assertions," about the fateful interdependence of love for humanity and faith in immortality.

"There is no virtue if there is no immortality": from one point of view, there is nothing at all problematic about this statement. Thomas Aquinas, for example, recognized an "inclination to good" in man but went on to say that "the natural law is nothing else than the participation of the eternal law in the mind of a rational creature." God, in short, makes himself or his will felt in us. Aquinas might easily have said, "There is no virtue if there is no immortality." But he did not question God, and the question of the possibility of virtue without faith—a question only raised seriously in the positivistic environment of the nineteenth century—was one that he simply would not entertain. It is a question that Dostoevsky too, as a believer, refuses to entertain; it is one, however, with which he as artist deals very seriously and sensitively in *The Brothers Karamazov* and elsewhere in his work.

The torment of Ivan Karamazov as God-struggler is that he allows for the existence of a religious moral law but does not believe in the immortality of his soul or the goodness of man. He is a victim, finally, of the fatal logic of his position: believing absolutely in the concrete, as it were, day-to-day interdependence of virtue and faith but lacking personal belief in immortality, he arrives at the intellectual position that "all is permissible." His moral nature will not permit him openly to sanction the death of his father, but his ideas are picked up by his disciple Smerdyakov, who implements them with a ruthless logic.

The practical implications of Ivan's proposition—"There is no virtue if there is no immortality"—for an unbeliever are grasped immediately by Dmitry Karamazov: "Excuse me . . . have I heard things right? 'Villainy must not only be permitted but even recognized as the inevitable and even rational outcome of his position for every atheist'! Is that so or not?" "Precisely," says Father Paissy. "I'll remember that," says Dmitry. Dmitry draws these conclusions; in the end, however, he does not act upon them. Smerdyakov, however, whose intellectual processes resemble the rigid rules of grammar, draws these conclusions and acts upon them. "If there is no eternal God, then there is no virtue," he reminds Ivan in his last meeting with him, adding, "And, indeed, there's really no necessity for it."

It is this final conclusion, this simplistic deduction, this intoxicated leap into crime and chaos—"And, indeed, there's really no necessity for it"—that lies hidden in Ivan's speculations and deeply troubles Dostoevsky. How is one to surmount the fatal logic of either-or: either faith or cannibalism, either beatitude or nihilistic despair? Such are the extreme choices that inhere in Ivan's notion that "there is no virtue if there is no immortality." "You are blessed in believing that, or else most unhappy," Zosima remarks perceptively to Ivan. "Why unhappy?" Ivan asks, smiling. "Because in all probability you don't believe yourself in the immortality of your soul." Ivan has left himself, and mankind, little room for maneuver or morality.

It is not only Ivan who is subject to the dangers implicit in a dogmatic formulation of faith, but his brother Alyosha as well. He stands for the moment, it is true, at the opposite pole from Ivan, at the pole of faith. Yet we remark in him at the opening of the novel the same Karamazov mind-set, the same inclination toward extreme and dogmatic formulations, we find in Ivan. Alyosha has chosen a different road than the majority, but

> with the same thirst for swift achievement. He had no sooner, after serious thought, been struck by the conviction that immortality and God exist, than he naturally said at once to himself: "I want to live for immortality, but I accept no halfway compromise!" Similarly, if he had decided that there was no immortality and God, then he would have joined the

atheists and socialists because socialism is not only the labor question or the so-called fourth estate, but chiefly the atheistic question, the question of the modern embodiment of atheism, the question of the Tower of Babel, built precisely without God.

"Halfway compromise," Dostoevsky believes, is necessary, not in love, the surest path to faith, but in the realm of "serious thought" and "decisions" about the existence of immortality and God, a realm where there are no "proofs." Alyosha, of course, is blessed and happy in the certainty of his faith in the immortality of his soul, but his peculiarly Karamazov mind-set—either-or, no "halfway compromise"—provides a weak foundation for future tests of faith, tests, if we are to believe the sketchy evidence with respect to Dostoevsky's projected continuation of his novel, lay directly ahead of Alyosha.

Ivan, as we have noted, recognizes the existence of morality that derives its strength from faith, but he sees no inclination to good in man. His remedy, as he outlines it in his article on church jurisdiction, somewhat resembles the ideas of the seventeenth-century English philosopher Thomas Hobbes. The English philosopher recognized the existence of a moral law found in God. Yet this law appeared to him so contrary to human passions, to man's "savage state of nature" ("man is a wolf to man") that he saw no possibility of morality without the absolute power of the state to enforce it. Ivan's notions of enforcement, however, lie in the direction of the theological state. He proposes a theological order that would combine civic and church jurisdiction. In present circumstances, according to Ivan, a Russian who commits a crime can excuse himself by saying that he has only broken a civil law. In Ivan's theological church-state, however, the criminal would be instantly cut off from Christ if he committed a crime.

Ivan finds nothing in man, no action of the eternal law in man's consciousness, to counteract his criminal tendencies or guide him toward salvation. Hence his reliance on an authoritarian church-state. The position of Father Zosima is quite different. Like Ivan, he believes in a universal church "at the end of the ages." In the meanwhile, however, he does not despair. While Ivan places his hope in social-religious compulsion and excommunication, Zosima believes in a divine law acting in man and in "the law of Christ expressing itself in the recognition of one's own conscience." Zosima essentially affirms a faith in man's conscience, in the possibility of man freely arriving at a sense of truth and goodness through his own conscience. His position is radically different from that of Ivan, who lacks any faith in human nature and whose faith in God at the very least is badly shaken.

Placed in the framework of the Augustinian and Pelagian theological controversy, it may be noted, Ivan's position would seem to gravitate toward radical Augustinian doctrine, or Jansenism, according to which post-Fall man lacks the power to abstain from sin and can be saved only by virtue of God's grace. Zosima's thought, with its emphasis on man's freedom of conscience and its faith in man, would seem to gravitate in the direction of Pelagian doctrine, which placed less emphasis on original sin and affirmed man's perfect freedom to do right and wrong and, in the end, to discover his path of salvation. Pelagian doctrine finds direct expression in Goethe's *Faust*, where it is summed up in the words of the Lord in the Prologue: "A good man in his dark striving is conscious of the right way." It is certainly Dmitry Karamazov who most directly embodies this truth. The range of Dostoevsky's thought would appear to be expressed in the polarities of Augustinian and Pelagian doctrine, but as an artist-thinker, he decisively leaned in the direction of Pelagian doctrine, with its great trust in man.

This trust is reflected in the subtlety with which Dostoevsky approaches Ivan's and his own didactic notion that love for humanity is impossible without concurrent faith in the immortality of the human soul. Ivan does not express the matter as bluntly as Dostoevsky. His statement "there is no virtue if there is no immortality," as we have noted, is ambiguous and taken by itself is subject to varying interpretations. Ivan, however, comes close to Dostoevsky's blunt statement in *Diary of a Writer* when he affirms that "if you destroy in humanity its faith in immortality, there will immediately dry up in it not only love, but also every living force necessary to perpetuate life on earth." The key word here is *if*.

We must ask this question: is faith here to be understood narrowly as active, conscious, articulated, and unwavering belief in God and immortality? Or does Dostoevsky give a broader construction to the notion of faith? The evidence of *The Brothers Karamazov* and other works suggests a more liberal construction. Through Ivan, Dostoevsky suggests the dire consequences for mankind that might follow the destruction of its faith in immortality. In "The Verdict" (October 1876, *Diary of a Writer*), Dostoevsky presents to the reader an example of a suicide that proceeds logically from the deductions of a logic-dominated mind. But how typical is this example in Dostoevsky's novelistic universe? The self-proclaimed atheist, in Dostoevsky's eyes, was not necessarily a pure atheist. Those who lose faith under the influence of reading, like Kolya Krassotkin for example, do not immediately accept in their soul the logical consequences and conclusions of atheism. Atheism for Dostoevsky is not so much an ideology as a state of behavior and consciousness. When the hero of *A Raw Youth* declares that he is not a believer, his father remarks: "No, you are not an atheist, you are a cheerful person."[3] Cheerfulness as an attribute of character, then, excludes the possibility of real atheism, an ideology that in Dostoevsky's view finds its emotional concomitant in dark despair.

Despair itself, however, is often qualified by the despairing person's "unconscious longing" for the idea of immortality that has been obscured in the soul, for life itself. The desire of people to kill themselves, Dostoevsky writes in "Something About Youth" in the December 1876 issue of *Diary of a Writer*, is an impulse of "anguish, unconscious perhaps, for the sublime significance of life which they have found nowhere."[4] Such is the case with the Ridiculous Man in "The Dream of a Ridiculous Man." Belief in immortality, the very idea of immortality, is linked with life itself. Dostoevsky's argument is of a circular, self-proving nature. "'If the conviction in immortality is so necessary for human existence,'" he writes in "Arbitrary Assertions" in the December 1876 issue of *Diary of a Writer* (Dostoevsky cites his own words in the October issue of his *Diary*), "'it follows then that [this conviction] is the normal state of humanity, and if this is so, then the immortality of the human soul *exists without question.*' In a word, the idea of immortality is life itself, the living life, its final formula and the chief source of truth and correct consciousness for mankind."[5]

Dostoevsky's point, at least as far as the vast majority of people is concerned, is that man at root is not a creature of reason or logic, that even when he strives to be most logical, he does not know himself; ultimately he comes up against the limitations of reason itself. "Le coeur a ses raisons que la raison ne connaît pas," as Pascal puts it. One may declare oneself an atheist and yet not be one because of one's love of, or longing for, life.

In this connection, Dostoevsky insists that there are some convictions that secretly everybody shares but is ashamed to admit. One may have faith, or yearn for it, but not reveal it to others or even to oneself. Dostoevsky maintained that the Russian people were religious at heart, though their knowledge of Christian dogma and their morality left much to be desired. "They know Christ and have been carrying Him in their hearts from time immemorial," Dostoevsky wrote in his article "Vlas" in *Diary of a Writer* (1873). "Much may not be consciously conceived, but only felt. One may know a very great deal unconsciously."[6]

Finally, we may note, Dostoevsky recognized that in everyday life virtue was possible without a concomitant belief in God. The socialist and atheist Belinsky, Dostoevsky observed in "Old People" (*Diary of a Writer*, 1873), valued "reason, science, and realism above all." Yet this same person, Dostoevsky acknowledged, knew that these principles could produce nothing but an anthill. Belinsky knew that "the moral principle is at the root of everything." Finally, this man who did everything to "depose Christianity, the religion from which emerged the moral principles of the society he negated," nonetheless, like Herzen, "was himself a good husband and a good father."[7]

In the final analysis, Dostoevsky approaches the question of the interdependence of virtue and faith in a radically different way than Ivan. Ivan insists that love and virtue can come only through faith. Zosima, however, believes that belief in God and faith in immortality are inseparable from love. Hell is the "suffering over the impossibility of loving," observes Zosima. "Try to love your neighbors actively and ceaselessly," Zosima counsels Mrs. Khokhlakova. "To the extent that you succeed in love, you will become convinced in the existence of God and in the immortality of your soul. But if you reach the point of total self-renunciation in love for your neighbor, then without question you will believe, and no doubt will be able to enter your soul." Zosima's thought echoes here Goethe's *Faust*: "Es reget sich die Menschenliebe, die Liebe Gottes regt sich nun." More importantly however, Zosima's remarks echo the First Epistle of John: "We know that we have passed out of death into life, because we love the breth-

ren. He who does not love remains in death." "God is love." "If a man
say, 'I love God' and hateth his brother, he is a liar" (3:14; 4:16–20).
These lines, it may be noted, were marked in Dostoevsky's personal
Bible. They convey most exactly Dostoevsky's thought in *The Brothers
Karamazov.*

Dostoevsky, then, affirms the interdependence of virtue and faith
in the most fundamental sense, but he recognizes, as does Friedrich
Schiller in his poem "Resignation," that the individual cannot approach the interrelationship of virtue and faith in abstract rationalistic
or contractual terms without thereby fracturing the organic unity of
that relationship, without replacing the whole with a lifeless relationship of parts, with an uncompromising, dogmatic proposition: either
faith and immortality—and then virtue; or, if no faith, then no virtue
at all—everything is permissible.

It is no surprise that Ivan, in his great peroration at the end of the
chapter "Rebellion," awakens the metaphor of redemption and with
savage irony compares the dynamics of Christian salvation to a commercial transaction with God as the supreme merchant. For all his
genuine distress over suffering, his own as well as that of children,
Ivan projects on the universe his own Euclidean mind and mentality.
He confronts God and demands, in effect, a balancing of the scales of
justice.

The drama in Schiller's poem "Resignation" is not the same as that
in *The Brothers Karamazov*, but the problem content of the poem and
the mentality of the poem's protagonist are singularly Dostoevskian
and bear close resemblance to Ivan's ideological drama of faith and
despair. The protagonist of Schiller's philosophical poem, after a virtuous life, holds out his "letter of credit on happiness" (*Vollmachtbrief
zum Glücke*) to the great "remunerator" who holds the "scales of justice." A conventionally religious and virtuous person, the narrator of
the poem now, at the end of his life, demands his "salary." His language is studded with words of a commercial character, much like the
language of Ivan in his peroration at the end of "Rebellion." Schiller's
thought in his poem—and *The Brothers Karamazov* provides evidence
that Dostoevsky subscribed to this point of view—is that sacrifice
cannot be made with a view toward payment in an afterlife. "Our
moral obligations," Schiller wrote in a comment on his poem, "bind
us unconditionally and not contractually. The virtues that one prac-

tices only on the legal assurance of future good have no value. Virtue carries in itself a character of *inner* necessity, even if there is no immortality."[8] An echo of Schiller's "even if" is to be found in another variant in Dostoevsky's credo in his letter to Natalya Fonvizina in 1854: "[Even] if somebody proved to me that Christ was outside the truth, and it *really* were so that the truth was outside of Christ, then I would rather remain with Christ than with the truth."[9]

Dostoevsky believed in immortality, but he recognized that proofs were impossible,[10] that man must live and act in the ambience of uncertainty, must continue to act and live virtuously in the absence of rational proofs and even in the absence of conscious conviction in immortality. Not virtue through faith but faith through love is Dostoevsky's response to Ivan.

"I have never yet allowed myself in my writings to follow *some* of my convictions to the end, to say the *very last* word," Dostoevsky wrote in a letter to Vsevolod Solovyov in July 1876. "On the whole," he writes later in the letter, "man somehow in no way likes the last word of a 'spoken' thought, [and] says that 'the thought spoken is a lie [*mysl' izrechennaja est' lozh'*].'"[11] The propositions of Dostoevsky (in his *Diary of a Writer*) and Ivan on the interdependence of virtue and faith lie in Tyutchev's paradoxical category of the "lie." And not because these comments are lacking in truth for Dostoevsky but because as *final spoken words* they finalize (in the Bakhtinian sense of this word) this truth, limit the possibility of its qualification or development and lend themselves, in the all-too-human conditions of human existence, to dogmatic interpretation, to falsification.

Dostoevsky in *The Brothers Karamazov*, I conclude, does not so much resolve the problem posed by Ivan in his formula "There is no virtue if there is no immortality" as discover its limitations. The problem is not solved but (in the Jungian sense) "outgrown." Not either-or, not virtue or cannibalism, but the dissolution of the problem in the felt realization that "God is love." The boys in the epilogue of the novel experience precisely this epiphany at the funeral of Ilyusha as they gather about the "stone"—that symbol of the tomb and immortality—and listen to Alyosha speak first not of God but of the binding act of remembering, of brotherhood and love.

Notes

Notes

The abbreviation *PSS* is used in citations of the following works: F. M. Dostoevsky, *Polnoe sobranie sochinenij v tridtsati tomakh* (Leningrad, 1972–90); Leo Tolstoy, *Polnoe sobranie sochinenij (Jubilejnoe izdanie)* (Moscow-Leningrad, 1928–58); and Ivan Turgenev, *Polnoe sobranie sochinenij i pisem v dvadtsati vos'mi tomakh* (28 vols.: works, 15 vols.; letters [*pis'ma*], 13 vols.) (Moscow-Leningrad, 1960–68). Since the volumes of the works of Turgenev containing Turgenev's letters are numbered separately, references to his letters are "Turgenev, *PSS: Pis'ma*."

Introduction

1. V. V. Rozanov, *Legenda o velikom inkvizitore* (Berlin, 1924), pp. 40–41.

2. Vjacheslav I. Ivanov, *Dostoevskij i roman-tragedija* (1916), in *Sobranie sochinenij* (Brussels, 1986), vol. 4, p. 52.

3. Georgij V. Adamovich, "Kommentarii," in *Opyty* (New York, 1953), vol. 1, pp. 98–99.

4. Dostoevsky, *PSS*, vol. 23, p. 31. Schiller, Dostoevsky believed, was more native and meaningful to Russia than to any other nation outside of Germany.

5. M. E. Saltykov-Shchedrin, "Svetlov, ego vzgljady, kharakter i dejatel'nost'," in A. A. Belkin, ed., *F. M. Dostoevskij v russkoj kritike* (Moscow, 1956), p. 231.

6. Mikhail M. Bakhtin, *Problems of Dostoevsky's Poetics*, ed., trans. Caryl Emerson (Minneapolis, Minn., 1984), vol. 8, p. 88.

7. Dostoevsky, *PSS*, vol. 29, bk. 1, pp. 128–29.

8. Ibid., vol. 22, p. 28–29.

9. It should be noted, of course, that Turgenev also deeply experienced the violence of Russian life. As a child, he grew up on the estate of his despotic mother surrounded by the physical and social brutalities of serfdom. These experiences left a deep imprint upon him: not only a hatred for serfdom, but without question deep psychological wounds. One can only speculate to what extent Turgenev's personal experiences with violence were a factor in making him shudder over all that "lies hidden there" in the souls of the men and women watching the execution of Tropmann. It is certain, in any case, that he internalized the experience of violence in very different ways than Dostoevsky.

10. Anton P. Chekhov, *Polnoe sobranie sochinenij i pisem v tridtsati tomakh: Pis'ma v dvenadtsati tomakh,* vol. 4 of *Pis'ma* (Moscow, 1976), p. 32.

11. See Chekhov's story "Three Years" (1894).

12. Tolstoy, *PSS,* vol. 66, p. 254.

13. Ibid., pp. 253–54.

14. M. Gorky, *Materialy i issledovanija,* ed. S. D. Balukhaty and V. A. Desnitsky (Moscow-Leningrad, 1941), vol. 3, pp. 135–36.

15. Dostoevsky, *PSS,* vol. 28, bk. 1, p. 229.

16. *Oeuvres complètes de M. le Vicompte de Chateaubriand* (Paris, 1826–28), vol. 11, p. 288.

17. Dmitry Merezhkovsky, "Turgenev," in *Polnoe sobranie sochinenij* (Moscow, 1914), vol. 18, p. 58.

18. Dostoevsky, *PSS,* vol. 27, p. 65.

19. Turgenev's stories "The Inn," "A Correspondence," and "Diary of a Superfluous Man," for example, anticipate emphases in Dostoevsky's *Notes from the Underground* and later works. See my article "Turgenev's 'The Inn': A Philosophical Novella," *Russian Literature* 16 (1984): 411–20, where I discuss Turgenev's posing of the problem of theodicy, a major emphasis in *The Brothers Karamazov.*

20. Dostoevsky, *PSS,* vol. 22, p. 106.

21. V. I. Belinsky, *Polnoe sobranie sochinenij* (Moscow, 1956), vol. 12, p. 433.

22. Cited by N. K. Gudzij, "Tolstoy and Dostoevsky," *Jasnopoljanskij sbornik: Stat'i i materialy. God 1960* (Tula, 1960), p. 114.

23. *Perepiska L. N. Tolstogo s N. N. Strakhovym. 1870–1894* (St. Petersburg, 1914), p. 117.

24. "The artistry of Tolstoy, perhaps, is more perfected than the artistry of Dostoevsky—his novels are the best novels in the world. Dostoevsky is a more powerful thinker than Tolstoy." Nikolai Berdyaev, *Mirosozertsanie Dostoevskogo* (Paris, 1968 [1921]), p. 19.

25. Tolstoy, *PSS,* vol. 63, p. 142.

26. See Chapter 11, note 9, where I cite Strakhov's criticism.

27. George Steiner, *Tolstoy or Dostoevsky: An Essay in the Old Criticism* (New York, 1959), p. 283.

28. See Davie's "Tolstoy, Lermontov, and Others," in *Russian Literature and Modern English Fiction: A Collection of Critical Essays*, ed. Donald Davie (Chicago, 1965), pp. 164, 169.

29. Ibid., p. 169.   30. Steiner, p. 283.

31. On the question of the poetics of "didactic fiction" in general, see Gary Saul Morson's important article "The Reader as Voyeur: Tolstoi and the Poetics of Didactic Fiction," Special Issue: L. N. Tolstoi 1828–1910–1978, *Canadian-American Slavic Studies* 12, no. 4 (Winter 1978): 465–80. Morson rightly argues that "these fictions [didactic literature] do not ignore literary conventions, they defy them" (p. 467).

32. It is perhaps noteworthy that *Ivan* in Russian is one variant of *John*.

33. Letter to Georg Brandes, November 20, 1888, in *Selected Letters of Friedrich Nietzsche*, ed. and trans. Christopher Middleton (Chicago, 1969), p. 327.

34. Nietzsche, *The Will to Power*, trans. Walter Kaufmann and R. J. Hollingdale (New York, 1968), pp. 434–35.

35. Letter to Franz Overbeck, February 23, 1887, *Letters of Nietzsche*, pp. 260–61.

36. Berdyaev, p. 59.

37. Ivanov, *Freedom and the Tragic Life: A Study in Dostoevsky*, trans. Norman Cameron, ed. S. Konovalov (Oxford), foreword by Sir Maurice Bowra (London, 1952; repr. Wolfeboro, N.H., 1989, with new introduction by Robert Louis Jackson). See note 1, Chapter 14, for a discussion of the complicated history of Ivanov's original (now lost) Russian text.

38. Ibid., pp. 109–10.   39. Ibid., p. 110.

40. Ibid., p. 112.   41. Bakhtin, p. 11.

42. Dostoevsky, *PSS*, vol. 28, bk. 1, p. 176.

43. Ibid., vol. 20, pp. 172–75.   44. Bakhtin, p. 18.

45. Ibid., p. 87.   46. Ibid., p. 98.

47. Ibid., p. 294.   48. Ibid., p. 4.

49. Ibid., pp. 91–92.   50. Ibid.

51. Bakhtin, p. 92.   52. Dostoevsky, *PSS*, vol. 24, p. 49.

Chapter 1

1. I avail myself here of *The Republic of Plato*, trans. with Notes and an Interpretive Essay, Allan Bloom (New York, 1968), p. 119.

2. The responses of Turgenev, Dostoevsky, and Tolstoy to looking at executions and the problem of capital punishment in general are relatively late additions to a controversy that had engaged society in England and the Continent in the nineteenth century. The question of looking at executions—that is, the moral and social meaning of public executions—was a matter of special concern to Charles Dickens. He noted in 1845 the "horrible fascination," the "strange fascination," that executions and all that is connected with them have for people. "I should have deemed it impossible that I could have ever felt any

large assemblage of my fellow creatures to be so odious," he wrote of the 40,000 crowd—ribald, debauched, drunken, and "flaunting vice in fifty other shapes"—that attended the execution of Courvoisier. Dickens frequently attended executions at home and abroad, observing carefully both victim and spectator. He spoke out strongly against public executions and capital punishment, though on the question of the latter his position shifted toward the end of his life. Thackery, who had far less stomach than Dickens for executions, wrote at the conclusion of his account, "Going to See a Man Hanged," in 1840: "I am not ashamed to say that I could look no more, but shut my eyes as the last dreadful act was going on." See David D. Cooper, *The Lesson of the Scaffold: The Public Execution Controversy in Victorian England* (Athens, Ohio, 1974), pp. 77, 80, 90. Victor Hugo was a lifelong opponent of capital punishment, public or behind walls. "On voit le soleil!" This exclamation of the condemned man in Hugo's *Le dernier jour d'un condamné* (1829) Dostoevsky quotes from memory in his letter to his brother Mikhail on December 22, 1849, right after his mock execution staged by Nicholas I. Dostoevsky refers to Hugo's "masterpiece" in his preface to his story "A Gentle Creature" (1877).

3. "The Execution of Tropmann" was first published in the journal *Vestnik Evropy* no. 6 (1870): 872–90.

4. For Dostoevsky's entire letter to Strakhov, see Dostoevsky, *PSS*, vol. 29, bk. 1, pp. 127–29. The links between Dostoevsky's parody in *The Devils* and Turgenev's "The Execution of Tropmann" were first explored by Ju. A. Nikol'skij in his monograph *Turgenev i Dostoevskij* (Sofia, 1920), pp. 67–71, and by A. S. Dolinin in his article "Turgenev v *Besakh*," in *Dostoevskij: Stat'i i materialy*, ed. A. S. Dolinin (Leningrad, 1925), vol. 2, pp. 119–36. Two recent articles on Turgenev's "Execution of Tropmann" deserve to be mentioned: William C. Brumfield, "Invitation to a Beheading: Turgenev and Tropmann," *Canadian-American Slavic Studies* 17, no. 1 (Spring 1983): 79–88; A. B. Muratov, "Ocherk I. S. Turgeneva 'Kazn' Tropmana,'" in *Khudozhestvenno-dokumental'naja literatura*, ed. L. A. Rozanova (Ivanovo, 1984), pp. 75–88.

5. In this discussion I make use of David Magarshack's translation of "The Execution of Tropmann" in Ivan Turgenev, *Literary Reminiscences and Autobiographical Fragments* (New York, 1958). In places I have amended the translation for stylistic reasons.

6. Compare with the narrartor in Turgenev's "The Jew" (1846) who, after vividly recalling the last terrifying moments of a man about to be hanged, concludes: "They put the noose on the Jew... I closed my eyes and rushed off." The gesture of *turning away* expresses here not only horror but a latent sympathy with the Jew.

7. "Sight is the coldest of the senses, whereas hearing acts immediately on the soul." Johann Gottfried Herder, *Sämtliche Werke*, ed. B. Suphan (Berlin, 1878), vol. 4, p. 44.

8. Cf. *Hamlet* (act 3, scene 4) and Hamlet's reproach to his mother: "What devil was't / That hath cozened you at hoodman-blind? / Eyes without feel-

ing, feeling without sight, / Ears without hands or eyes, smelling sans all, / Or but a sickly part of one true sense / Could not so mope."

9. Hugo's aphorism appears in bk. 3, "William Shakespeare," in *Oeuvres complètes*, ed. Jean Massin (Paris, 1967–70), vol. 12, p. 314.

10. *Obraz* in Russian may stand for "form," "shape," "image," but it also may mean "icon." *Obraz* as image or form carries with it a spiritual or religious meaning. Ippolit's question, then, conceals another question that involves in Russian a contradiction in terms: Can one conceive a beautiful or spiritual image that is ugly or lacking in spirituality?

11. The expression appears first in Terence's play *The Self-Tormenter (Heauton timorumenos)*: "Homo sum: humani nil a me alienun puta" (I am a man: nothing human is alien to me). The line, which also has an ironical twist in Terence's play, became famous and was often alluded to by Cicero, Seneca, and others. Dostoevsky's formulation of the phrase is not literally Terence's.

12. Dostoevsky, *PSS*, vol. 29, bk. 1, pp. 128–29.

13. See Ivan Turgenev, *Nouvelle correspondance inédite*, ed. A. Zviguilsky (Paris, 1971), vol. 1, pp. 252–53. A. Zviguilsky, who compiled the letters, was the first to call attention to this letter in his paper "Ivan Tourguénev et la peine de mort," in *Actes du Colloque sur la peine de mort dans la pensée philosophique et littéraire: Autour de L'exécution de Troppmann d'Ivan Tourguéniev* (Paris, 1980), p. 68.

14. See Zviguilsky's introduction to *Nouvelle correspondance inédite*, vol. I, pp. xxxviii–xliii, for a discussion of Turgenev's special relationship with Claudie, daughter of Pauline Viardot, and his correspondence with her. Turgenev could compose in his letters, as he did in some of his fables, strange surrealistic tales interwoven with grotesque, erotic, and scatological imagery. An astounding example of one of Turgenev's grotesque fables may be found in his letter to Claudie of April 1, 1877 (ibid., pp. 278–80).

15. *Macbeth*, act 5, scene 5. Macbeth's exact words are "I have supp'd full with horrors."

16. Turgenev, *PSS: Pis'ma*, vol. 8, pp. 168–69.

17. See Chapter 9 of this study.

18. It is of symbolic significance that the train carrying Myshkin enters Petersburg in a fog so thick that "it was difficult to see anything."

19. Adelaida, the narrator writes at the beginning of *The Idiot*, "was a remarkable painter; but for many years almost nobody knew this, and it was discovered only lately, and then accidentally."

20. Editor's commentary to *Republic of Plato*, p. 377.

21. Dostoevsky, *PSS*, vol. 28, bk. 2, p. 160.

Chapter 2

1. Tolstoy, *PSS*, vol. 23, p. 8.   2. Ibid., vol. 47, p. 118.

3. Ibid., p. 121. "I began to experience without any reason an inexplicable

anguish," Tolstoy recalled, after leaving Paris, in a letter of April 11 to his aunt Ergolskaya. Quoted by N. N. Gusev in *Lev Nikolaevich Tolstoy: Materialy k biografii s 1855 po 1869* (Moscow, 1957), p. 190.

4. In her memoirs A. A. Tolstaya recalled that Tolstoy had told her: "I wanted to test myself and went to a guillotining of a criminal, after which I couldn't sleep I was so distraught." *Perepiska L. N. Tolstogo s gr. A. A. Tolstoj* (St. Petersburg, 1911), p. 4; cited by Gusev, p. 196.

5. Tolstoy, *PSS*, vol. 47, pp. 121–22.

6. This is what Tolstoy told the writer I. N. Zakharin-Yakunin April 26, 1899. Zakharin-Yakunin, *Vstrechi i vospominanija* (St. Petersburg, 1903), p. 225; quoted by Gusev, p. 194.

7. Tolstoy, *PPS*, vol. 60, pp. 167–68.

8. Ibid., vol. 47, p. 122.

9. Dostoevsky, *PSS*, vol. 20, p. 192.

10. This is certainly true of the initial encounter between Makovkina and Father Sergius in Tolstoy's "Father Sergius": "He pressed his face to the glass. The little icon lamp was reflected by it and shone on the whole glass. . . . Their eyes met and they recognized each other." This "recognition" scene goes beyond the instinctual acknowledgement of a common chemistry. The looking through the "glass" echoes 1 Corinthians 13:12: "For now we see through a glass, darkly; but then face to face: now I know in part; but then shall I know even as also I am known." Tolstoy's poetics of eye-to-eye contact is rich and diverse in content.

11. A whole series of verbs in the final part of the execution scene convey the idea of descent downward: *opustiv, spustilos', opuskalos', spustiv, padajush-chee, s opushchennymi golovami*, etc. (sank, fell, falling, lowered, etc.).

12. For a discussion of Pierre's renewal, see my essay "The Second Birth of Pierre Bezukhov," *Canadian-American Slavic Studies* 12, no. 4 (Winter 1978): 534–42.

13. E. F. F. Hill, *Apocalypse and Other Essays (The Crisis of Spirit in a Demonic Age)*, introduction by D. S. Savage (Mevagissey, England, 1989), pp. 74–75.

14. See Charles S. Singleton in Dante Alighieri, *The Divine Comedy: Inferno* 2, Commentary, Bollingen Series LXXX (Princeton, N.J., 1970), p. 9.

Chapter 3

1. Derzhimorda is the vulgar police captain in Gogol's *The Inspector General [Revizor]*.

2. For a general and detailed discussion of *Notes from the House of the Dead*, see my *The Art of Dostoevsky: Deliriums and Nocturnes* (Princeton, N.J., 1981), esp. chaps. 2–5.

3. See Chapter 8, p. 148–49, where this passage is cited in full from *Notes from the House of the Dead*.

4. See my article "The Bathhouse Scene in *Notes from the House of the Dead*," Literature, Culture, and Society in the Modern Age: In Honor of Joseph Frank, Part I, *Stanford Slavic Studies* 4, no. 1 (1991): 260–68.

5. "la mia mente fu percossa da un fulgore" (*Paradiso*, 33: 140–41).

Chapter 4

1. In his use of the device of an unfinished story, Chekhov here anticipates the use of a similar device in the "play within the play" in *The Seagull*. In this play, Konstantin Gavrilovich fabricates a legend not too different from a fairy tale, with its demons and embattled knights. But the play ends abortively, with the hero in his empty "well" postponing his triumph over the devil. The dramatic movement within the "play within the play," and the abortive ending of that play itself, prefigures the fate of Konstantin Gavrilovich in the larger play of his life. See my article "The Seagull: The Empty Well, the Dry Lake, and the Cold Cave," in Jean-Barricelli, ed., *Chekhov's Great Plays, A Critical Anthology* (New York, 1981), pp. 3–17.

2. On this question, see my chapter "The Sentencing of Fedor Karamazov" in *The Art of Dostoevsky* (Princeton, N.J., 1981), pp. 304–18.

3. Another suggestive detail indicating the link of Chekhov's story with *The Brothers Karamazov* is the name Karp. Grigory maintains that the seducer of Smerdyakov's mother, Lizaveta, is not Fyodor Pavlovich but "Karp, a dangerous convict, who had escaped from prison and whose name was well known to us, as he had hidden in our town."

4. I have translated the word *besedka* here as "arbor." *Besedka* may also be translated as "summerhouse." The action of the story, however, takes place around Christmas. The narrator is not likely to be resting in a summerhouse near the main house. What we are involved with here is undoubtedly an indoor arbor or bower, a small structure covered with ivy. Dostoevsky refers to such an arbor in the discarded variant of *Netochka Nezvanova*: "I entered a room," Netochka recalls, "where there were a great many flowers; an entire arbor [*tselaja besedka*] had been constructed by the window out of the rarest plants" (Dostoevsky, *PSS*, vol. 2, p. 440).

Chapter 5

1. Strakhov joined the staff of the Dostoevsky brothers' journal *Vremja* in 1861. He cooled toward Dostoevsky in the middle of the 1870's and gravitated toward Tolstoy.

2. See *Perepiska L. N. Tolstogo s N. N. Strakhovym, 1870–1894*, vol. 2 of *Tolstovskij Muzej*, ed. B. L. Modzalevsky (St. Petersburg, 1914), p. 308.

3. See O. Miller and N. N. Strakhov, *Biografija, pis'ma i zametki iz zapisnoj knizhki F. M. Dostoevskogo* (St. Petersburg, 1883). Strakhov's memoir of Dos-

toevsky, "Vospominanija o Fedore Mikhajloviche Dostoevskom," included in this volume, has been republished in *F. M. Dostoevskij v vospominanijakh sovremennikov* (Moscow, 1990), vol. 1, pp. 375–532; citations from Strakhov's memoir refer to this edition.

4. Strakhov, "Vospominanija o Dostoevskom," pp. 425, 426.

5. Cited in *Istoriko-kriticheskij kommentarii k sochinenijam F. M. Dostoevskogo*, ed. V. Zelinskij (Moscow, 1885), vol. 1, p. 91.

6. The words in brackets, omitted from the 1914 edition of the Tolstoy-Strakhov correspondence, appear in the manuscript of Strakhov's letter and have been widely cited.

7. *Tolstovskij Muzej*, pp. 307–10. Dostoevsky's widow, Anna Grigorievna, cites the letter in full in her memoirs. See *Vospominanija A. G. Dostoevskoj*, ed. L. P. Grossman (Moscow-Leningrad, 1925), pp. 285–86. The letter is also cited in a later edition of Anna Grigorievna's memoirs, *A. G. Dostoevskaja, Vospominanija*, ed. S. V. Belov and V. A. Tunimanov (Moscow, 1971), pp. 396–97.

8. Quoted by L. P. Grossman in his introduction to *Vospominanija A. G. Dostoevskoj*, p. 15.

9. See Anna Grigorievna's "Answer to Strakhov" in her *Vospominanija* (1971), pp. 395–406. For a thorough discussion and strong refutation of the rumor that Dostoevsky had raped a young girl, see V. N. Zakharov, "Fakty protiv legendy," in his *Problemy izuchenija Dostoevskogo* (Petrozavodsk, 1978), pp. 75–109. Zakharov links the rumor with discussions among the intelligentsia that focused on the censored chapter of *The Devils*, the one in which Stavrogin tells of how he raped a young girl. Zakharov points out, too, that remarks made by Turgenev and D. V. Grigorovich in the late 1870's and early 1880's served to perpetuate this baseless rumor.

10. "A. G. Dostoevskaja i ee vospominanija," in *Vospominanija A. G. Dostoevskoj* (1925), p. 15. Anna Grigorievna's characterization of her husband may be found in her "Conversation with Tolstoy," *Vospominanija* (1971), pp. 391–95.

11. In this connection, see Lija Mikhailovna Rozenbljum's discussion of Dostoevsky's literary relationship with Strakhov in her study of Dostoevsky's notebooks, *Tvorcheskie dnevniki Dostoevskogo* (Moscow, 1981), pp. 30–45.

12. Dostoevsky, *PSS*, vol. 24, p. 240. In her discussion of the context of these remarks, Rozenbljum (p. 44) writes: "If Dostoevsky happened to know (and this might really have been the case) that Strakhov, his recent friend, had participated in discussions about [Dostoevsky's so-called] 'filthy behavior,' then the angry words of the writer—'he himself does vile things; in spite of his strict moral air . . .'—would be understandable."

13. See Dostoevsky's letter to N. D. Fonvizina after being released from prison in February 1854; Dostoevsky, *PSS*, vol. 28, bk. 1, p. 177.

14. Tolstoy, *PSS*, vol. 63, p. 142.

15. See *L. N. Tolstoj v vospominanijakh sovremennikov* (Moscow, 1978), vol. 2, p. 495.

16. Ibid. It is noteworthy that Gorky repeatedly parodied Dostoevsky's characters by reducing them to what he considered lifelike, realistic equivalents. The Dostoevskian characters in Gorky's writings do indeed turn out to be "much simpler, more understandable." Gorky may well have been selective in conveying Tolstoy's views on Dostoevsky.

17. Tolstoy, *PSS*, vol. 63, p. 43.

18. *A. G. Dostoevskaja, Vospominanija* (1971), p. 393.

19. D. P. Makovitskij, unpublished "Jasnopoljanskie zapiski," note of May 12, 1909; quoted by N. N. Gusev, *Lev Nikolaevich Tolstoj: Materialy k biografii s 1881 po 1885* (Moscow, 1970), p. 222.

20. See Tolstoy's letter to A. K. Chertkova, October 23, 1910. Tolstoy, *PSS*, vols. 88–89, p. 229.

21. Ibid., vol. 63, p. 24.

22. *L. N. Tolstoj v vospominanijakh sovremennikov* (Moscow, 1978), vol. 2, p. 120. (P. A. Sergeenko recalls that Tolstoy also "regarded as amazing" particularly *Crime and Punishment* and the first part of *The Idiot.*) Ibid., p. 146. *Notes from the House of the Dead* has always attracted attention as a work of autobiographical interest. Tolstoy was one of the first who also commented on it from a specifically artistic point of view.

23. Ibid., vol. 1, p. 351.   24. Ibid., vol. 2, p. 181.

25. Cited in N. N. Gudzy, "Tolstoj i Dostoevskij," in *Jasnopoljanskij sbornik: Stat'i i materialy: God 1960* (Tula, 1960), p. 127.

26. *L. N. Tolstoj v vospominanijakh sovremennikov*, Vol. 2, p. 67.

27. Ibid., p. 146.   28. Ibid., p. 263.

29. See chapter xvi of *What Is Art?* Along with Dostoevsky, Tolstoy also names Dickens.

30. See *L. N. Tolstoj v vospominanijakh sovremennikov*, vol. 2, p. 146.

31. There are many short studies but few book-length works that deal in a comparative way with the writings of Tolstoy and Dostoevsky. The best-known studies are D. M. Merezhkovsky, *L. Tolstoj i Dostoevskij* (1900), and George Steiner, *Tolstoy or Dostoevsky: An Essay in the Old Criticism* (New York, 1959). Valuable as these works are in initiating comparative study of Dostoevsky and Tolstoy, they only begin to explore and evaluate the extensive literary, social, historical, and philosophical interchange between the two writers in their fictional work.

32. Tolstoy, *PSS*, vol. 63, p. 142.

33. See *Pushkin-kritik* (Moscow, 1978), p. 121. Pushkin's notation is dated November 1825.

34. In some recollections of her meeting with Tolstoy in 1885, written after she had read Strakhov's letter attacking Dostoevsky, Anna Grigorievna recalls her words to Tolstoy praising her husband for his goodness, magnanimity,

truthfulness, delicacy, and compassion. At the end of her remarks, she records Tolstoy's remark: "'I always thought this about him,' he said somehow thoughtfully and with conviction. 'Dostoevsky always seemed to me a man in whom there was much truly Christian feeling'" (*Vospominanija* [1971], p. 394).

35. Tolstoy had used Pressensé's books; for example, *Histoire des trois premiers siècles de l'eglise chrétienne* (1856–1859), *Jésus Christ, ses temps, sa vie* (1865). It is not clear, however, what book Strakhov had sent him.

36. Turgenev died in 1883.   37. Tolstoy, *PSS*, vol. 63.

38. In a letter of January 10, 1884, to A. N. Pypin, Tolstoy set down some of his views on Turgenev's art. "I was always fond of [Turgenev]," Tolstoy writes, "but it was only after his death that I properly appreciated him." Of central importance in Turgenev was his "truthfulness." Turgenev was a "splendid person (not very profound, very weak, but a kind, good man) who says well and always exactly what he thinks and feels. . . . He lived, sought and in his works expressed what he found—everything he found. He did not use his talent (the ability to depict well) to hide his soul, as writers have done and continue to do, but to disclose everything" (Tolstoy, *PSS*, vol. 63, pp. 149–50).

39. Mikhail Bakhtin, *Problems of Dostoevsky's Poetics*, vol. 8 of *Theory and History of Literature*, ed. Caryl Emerson (Minneapolis, 1984), p. 39.

40. Ibid., p. 38. Shklovsky's comment may be found in his *Za i protiv: Zametki o Dostoevskom* (Moscow, 1957), p. 258.

41. Bakhtin, p. 38.

42. See Chapter 12, pp. 271, 274–77, where I discuss Bakhtin's view of the principle behind Dostoevsky's artistic visualization of the world.

43. Bakhtin, pp. 39–40.

44. See my discussion of this problem, "Aristotelian Movement and Design in Part Two of *Notes from the Underground*," in my *The Art of Dostoevsky: Deliriums and Nocturnes* (Princeton, N.J., 1981), pp. 171–88.

45. Bakhtin, p. 227.   46. Ibid., pp. 229–30.

47. Ibid., p. 230.

48. See Dostoevsky's letter to his brother Mikhail, March 26, 1864, where he complains that the censor excised those parts of chapter 10, part 1—the "most central one, where the very idea [of the work] is expressed, where I deduced the need for faith and Christ" (Dostoevsky, *PSS*, vol. 28, bk. 2, p. 73). The original manuscript has not been preserved, and the omissions were never restored. Dostoevsky maintains in his letter that the chapter had to be printed with "sentences thrown together and contradicting itself." I cite this portion of Dostoevsky's letter in Chapter 15, p. 290–91.

49. See note 77 of Chapter 15, where I discuss this point.

50. Cited by V. V. Timofeeva (O. Pochinkovskaja) in her memoir of Dostoevsky, "God raboty s znamenitym pisatelem," in *F. M. Dostoevskij v vospominanijakh sovremennikov* (Moscow, 1990), vol. 2, p. 186.

51. Dostoevsky, *PSS*, vol. 16, p. 329.

52. Steiner, pp. 74–75.

53. Ibid., p. 74.
54. Georgy Adamovich, "Kommentarii," in *Opyty* (New York, 1953), bk. 1, p. 99.

Chapter 6

1. M. Gorky, *Novaja zhizn'*, no. 5, April 23, 1917, in M. Gorky, *Nesvoevremennye mysli. Stat'i 1917–1918 gg.*, ed. G. Ermolaev (Paris, 1971), p. 29 (hereafter, *Nesvoevremennye mysli*).
2. Dostoevsky, *PSS*, vol. 25, p. 201.
3. Gorky, *Istorija russkoj literatury* (Moscow, 1939), p. 276.
4. Cited by the editors in their commentary on Gorky's "O 'karamazovshchine,'" in Gorky, *O literature. Literaturno-kriticheskie stat'i*, ed. N. P. Zhdanovskij and A. I. Ovcharenko (Moscow, 1953), p. 836 (references to Gorky's two articles on "Karamazovism" will refer to *O literature*).

5. Ibid., p. 151.   6. Ibid.
7. Ibid., p. 155.   8. Ibid., p. 156.
9. Ibid., p. 154.   10. Ibid., p. 153.
11. Ibid., p. 154.   12. Ibid.
13. Ibid., p. 156.   14. Ibid.
15. Ibid., p. 158.   16. Ibid.

17. Quoted by B. A. Bjalik in "Dostoevskij i dostoevshchina v otsenkakh Gor'kogo," in *Tvorchestvo Dostoevskogo*, ed. M. L. Stepanov et al. (Moscow, 1959), p. 68.
18. Gorky, *Sobranie sochinenij v vosemnadtsati tomakh* (Moscow, 1962), vol. 12, p. 256.
19. Gorky, "Sovetskaja literatura. Doklad na Pervom vsesojuznom s'ezde sovetskikh pisatelej 17 avgusta 1934 goda," in *O literature*, p. 705.
20. Quoted by Bjalik, p. 90.
21. Gorky, *Materialy i issledovanija*, ed. S. D. Balukhatyj and V. A. Desnitskyj (Moscow-Leningrad, 1941), vol. 3, pp. 135–36.
22. *O literature*, p. 152.
23. See Nikolai K. Mikhailovsky, *A Cruel Talent*, trans. Spencer V. Cadmus, Jr. (Ann Arbor, Mich., 1978).
24. *O literature*, p. 152.   25. Ibid.
26. Ibid. "Karataevism": Gorky refers here to Tolstoy's Platon Karataev in *War and Peace*, a peasant who has traditionally been viewed as a fatalistic type.
27. Ibid., p. 158.   28. Ibid., p. 159.
29. Ibid., p. 158.
30. Gorky, *Sobranie sochinenij*, vol. 12, p. 256.
31. Gorky, *O russkom krest'janstve* (Berlin, 1922), p. 23.
32. *O literature*, p. 159.
33. Ibid., p. 152.   34. Ibid., p. 159.
35. Ibid., p. 135.   36. Ibid., pp. 159, 160.

37. *Nesvoevremennye mysli*, pp. 29–30.

38. Ibid., p. 56.   39. Ibid., p. 55.

40. Ibid., p. 118.   41. Ibid., p. 120.

42. Ibid., p. 141.   43. Ibid., p. 144.

44. Ibid., p. 198.

45. For a discussion of "Karamora" in the context of Gorky's polemic with Dostoevsky, see the chapter "Maksim Gorky and *Notes from the Underground*" in my *Dostoevsky's Underground Man in Russian Literature* (The Hague, 1958; repr. Westport, Conn., 1981), pp. 127–46. See also Edward J. Brown's article "The Symbolist Contamination of Gor'kij's 'Realistic' Style" for an analysis of one of Gorky's outstanding stories in this period (*Russian Literature* 14–15 [Nov. 1988]: 465–81).

46. *Nesvoevremennye mysli*, p. 46.

47. Gorky, "Sovetskaja literatura," p. 705.

48. Ibid., p. 705.

49. See *Letters of Gorky and Andreev 1899–1912*, ed. Peter Yershov, trans. Lydia Weston (New York, 1958), p. 88.

50. Ibid., p. 37.

51. V. Bryusov, *Dnevniki: 1890–1910* (Moscow, 1927), p. 94.

52. Gorky, *Istorija russkoj literatury*, p. 63.

53. *Letters of Gorky and Andreev*, p. 130. In a letter to Andreyev, Gorky referred to Dostoevsky as "our evil genius." (Ibid., p. 120.)

Chapter 7

1. Leonid Grossman, "Russkij Kandid," *Vestnik Evropy* (May 1914): 194.

2. *Oeuvres complètes de M. le vicomte de Chateaubriand* (Paris, 1826–28), vol. 14, p. 249 (hereinafter, *Oeuvres*).

3. Ibid., vol. 9, p. 19.   4. Ibid., vol. 14, p. 261.

5. Ibid., vol 11, p. 7.   6. Ibid., vol. 11, pp. 21–22.

7. Ibid., vol. 14, p. 234.

8. "The Christian education I received," Chateaubriand writes in the preface to *Essai sur les révolutions*, "left deep traces in my heart, but my head was troubled by books that I had read, the gatherings I had attended. I resembled almost all the men of this period: I was a child of my century" (*Oeuvres*, vol. 1, p. xxiii). Dostoevsky's spiritual and intellectual development in the 1830's and 1840's was marked by this same duality: an early religious faith and a deep philosophical idealism mixed with ideas of the French Enlightenment, the French utopian socialists, and radical social thinkers like the Russian critic Vissarion Belinsky.

9. *Oeuvres*, vol. 14, pp. 284–85.

10. Dostoevsky, *PSS*, vol. 28, bk. 2, p. 176.

11. Cited by Victor Giraud in *Le christianisme de Chateaubriand* (Paris, 1928), vol. 2, p. 149.

12. Cited by A. Maurois in *Chateaubriand* (Paris, 1938), p. 447.

13. Dostoevsky, *PSS*, vol. 28, bk. 2, *op. cit.*, p. 176.

14. *Oeuvres*, vol. 11, pp. 278–79.

15. Ibid., vol. 11, p. 286. "If you could kill a man in China only by wishing it," asks Chateaubriand, "and inherit his fortune in Europe with the supernatural conviction that nobody would ever know anything about it, would you consent to give expression to this desire?" At the bottom of his heart, Chateaubriand hears "a voice that cries loudly against the very idea of such a supposition, so that I cannot doubt for an instant the reality of conscience." Chateaubriand traces the example he uses to Rousseau. The example appears later in Balzac's *Père Goriot* and Dostoevsky's *Crime and Punishment*.

16. *Oeuvres*, vol. 14, p. 199.   17. Ibid., vol. 11, pp. 278–79.

18. All citations from *The Brothers Karamazov* are translated from the Russian.

19. Quoted by Maurois, *Chateaubriand*, p. 107.

20. *Oeuvres*, vol. 2, p. 393.   21. Ibid., vol. 14, p. 228.

22. Ibid., vol. 14, p. 227.   23. Ibid., vol. 11, p. 285.

24. Ibid., vol. 2, p. 287.   25. Ibid., vol. 11, p. 290.

26. Ibid., vol. 13, p. 197.

27. See Leonid Grossman, *Biblioteka Dostoevskago* (Odessa, 1919), p. 139.

28. Dostoevsky, *PSS*, vol. 28, bk. 1, p. 108. "The fate of works is always such—one reworks them endlessly," Dostoevsky writes his brother. "I do not know if Chateaubriand's Atala was his first work, but he reworked it seventeen times, you will remember."

29. Ibid., p. 55.

30. Ibid., p. 229. Letter to A. E. Vrangel, April 13, 1856.

31. The question of the influence of *The Genius of Christianity* upon Dostoevsky's aesthetics was raised by the Russian scholar A. S. Dolinin in notes to vol. 1 of Dostoevsky's letters; Dostoevsky, *Pis'ma* (Moscow, 1928), vol. 1, p. 469.

32. Grossman, "Russkij Kandid," p. 197.

33. *Oeuvres*, vol. 11, p. 300.

Chapter 8

1. Letter to M. E. Saltykov-Shchedrin, September 24, 1882; Turgenev, *PSS: Pis'ma*, vol. 13, bk. 2, p. 49.

2. Letter to P. Annenkov, September 25, 1882; ibid., p. 51.

3. I have been unable to locate this particular title in Sade's works. Possibly *Les 120 journées de Sodome* or another work of Sade's had been published under a spurious title.

4. Letter to Saltykov-Shchedrin, p. 49.

5. One may note that it is only in recent times that serious attention has been given to the philosophical and historical content of Sade's work. The

general view of Sade in the nineteenth and early twentieth centuries in Russia at least was that of a mere pornographer. F. Kautman makes this point in his essay "Dostojevskij a Markyz de Sade," *Filosofický časopis* 3 (Prague, 1968): 384–86. Turgenev's view of Sade, at least as it is reflected in his letters to Annenkov and Mikhailovsky, was not exceptional.

6. Dostoevsky, *PSS*, vol. 19, p. 135. Dostoevsky clearly puts Sade here in the realm of pornographic literature, although he understands the significance of Sade's writings in a much deeper way. In general, Dostoevsky believed that the impression of pornography was in the mind of the viewer. In the same article I have cited, he suggests that had the Venuses of Medici and Milo been exhibited in Moscow in the seventeenth century, they would have been perceived by the general populace in a coarse and salacious way. Dostoevsky adds that "one must be pure to the extreme, moral and properly developed to look on this divine beauty without confusion. The *chastity* of an image will not save one from a crude and even, perhaps, filthy thought. No, these images produce a lofty, divine impression of art precisely because they are themselves a work of art. Here reality has been transformed, *passing through art*, passing through the fire of a pure, chaste inspiration and through the artistic thought of the poet. This is the secret of art, and every artist knows about it. Even art, however, will not have its effect on an unprepared, undeveloped nature, or on a coarse, debauched person. The more developed, the better the soul of a person, the fuller and more authentic will be the impression of art on it" (ibid., p. 134).

7. In his study *The Romantic Agony*, 2d ed. (New York, 1970), Mario Praz devotes a whole chapter to the pervasive influence of Sade's work on European literature. He also raises the question of Sade's impact on Dostoevsky but gives little attention to the philosophical dimension of Dostoevsky's concern with "sadism." Much the same may be said of P. M. Bicilli's brief mention of Sade and Dostoevsky at the end of his article "O vnutrennej forme romana Dostoevskogo," first published in Bulgaria in 1945–46 and reprinted in the United States in 1966 (*O Dostoevskom, Stat'i*, ed. Donald Fanger, Brown University Slavic Reprint IV [Providence, R.I., 1966]). F. Kautman, to my knowledge, was the first to pose the question of Sade and Dostoevsky in an in-depth manner.

8. *Cf.* D. S. Savage, "The Idea of *The Gambler*," in *Twentieth Century Views: Dostoevsky (New Perspectives)*, ed. Robert Louis Jackson (Englewood Cliffs, N.J., 1984), p. 122.

9. A. G. Dostoevsky, *Vospominanija*, ed. S. V. Belov and V. A. Tunimanov (Leningrad, 1971), p. 100.

10. Ibid.

11. See my discussion of Strakhov's observations on Dostoevsky on pp. 106–9.

12. Where looks are concerned, one is stuck by a certain resemblance between Dostoevsky's general portrait of Stavrogin and Sade's depiction of

Dolmance in *Philosophy in the Bedroom.* "Dolmance, my dear sister, has just turned thirty-six; he is tall, extremely handsome, eyes very alive and very intelligent, but all the same there is some suspicion of hardness and a trace of wickedness in his features; he has the whitest teeth in the world, a shade of softness about his figure and in his attitude, doubtless owing to his habit of taking on effeminate airs so often; he is extremely elegant, has a pretty voice, many talents, and above all else an exceedingly philosophic bent to his mind. . . . He is the most notorious atheist, the most immoral fellow. . . . His is the most complete and thoroughgoing corruption, and he the most evil individual, the greatest scoundrel in the world." See Sade, *Justine,* in *Philosophy in the Bedroom and Other Writings,* comp., trans. Richard Seaver and Austryn Wainhouse, introductions by Jean Paulhan and Maurice Blanchot (New York, 1965), pp. 187–88.

13. Dostoevsky, *PSS,* vol. 19, pp. 135–36.

14. For a more extended discussion of this theme, see "The Nethermost Pit and the Outer Darkness: 'Akulka's Husband: A Story,'" in my *The Art of Dostoevsky: Deliriums and Nocturnes* (Princeton, N.J., 1981), pp. 70–114.

15. "There are no *foundations* to our society, no principles of conduct that have been lived through, because there have been none in life, even," Dostoevsky wrote in his notebook in 1875. "A colossal eruption, and all is crumbling, being negated, as though it had not even existed. And not only externally, as in the West, but internally, morally." Dostoevsky, *PSS,* vol. 16, p. 329.

16. Ibid., vol. 20, p. 191.   17. Ibid., vol. 15, pp. 228–29.

18. For a discussion of this moment in "Over the Brandy" in *The Brothers Karamazov,* see my *The Art of Dostoevsky* (Princeton, N.J., 1981), pp. 304–18.

19. Dostoevsky, *PSS,* vol. 27, p. 56.

20. Albert Camus, *The Rebel,* trans. Albert Bower (New York, 1956), p. 36.

21. Sade, *Juliette,* trans. Austryn Wainhouse (New York, 1968), p. 175.

22. Sade, *Justine,* in *Philosophy in the Bedroom,* p. 495.

23. Ibid., pp. 237–38.   24. Ibid., p. 360–61.

25. Sade, *Juliette,* p. 580.

26. Sade, *Justine,* in *Philosophy in the Bedroom,* p. 217.

27. Ibid., p. 609.   28. Ibid., p. 695.

29. *Juliette,* p. 13.   30. *Justine,* p. 317.

31. Ibid., p. 253.   32. Ibid., p. 286.

33. Ibid., p. 304.   34. Ibid., p. 297.

35. Ibid., p. 301.

36. Pierre Klossowski, "Nature as a Destructive Principle," in *The Marquis de Sade: "120 Days of Sodom" and Other Writings,* comp., trans. Austryn Wainhouse and Richard Seaver, introductions by Simone de Beauvoir and Pierre Klossowski (New York, 1966), p. 65.

37. For a discussion of "Bobok," see "The Ridiculous Man—Beyond Don Quixote" and "Some Considerations on 'The Dream of a Ridiculous Man' and 'Bobok' from the Esthetic Point of View," in my *The Art of Dostoevsky.*

38. Dostoevsky, *PSS*, vol. 20, p. 172.

39. Ibid., p. 173.

40. Throughout his work, Dostoevsky stresses this "aesthetic" dimension to human cruelty and sensuality. "An animal could never be so cruel, as man, so artistically, so aesthetically cruel," Ivan says to Alyosha. The guard Zherebyatnikov, in *Notes from the House of the Dead*, passionately loved the "art of execution, and loved it solely for the art."

41. *Literaturnoe nasledstvo: F. M. Dostoevskij: Novye materialy i issledovanija*, vol. 86, pp. 79–80.

42. Sade, *Justine*, p. 608.

43. It is noteworthy that Dostoevsky included *Thérèse philosophe* (1749) in the reading destined to influence the fall of his hero in his projected *Life of a Great Sinner*. This work, subtitled *ou Mémoires pour servir à l'histoire des P. Dirrag et de Mademoiselle Eradice*, has been attributed to Jean-Baptiste de Boyer, marquis d'Argens, as well as to Darles de Montigny. *Thérèse philosophe*, in its erotic content, its critique of conventional ethical attitudes, and its attitude toward "nature," anticipated Sade. "*Thérèse philosophe* was there, a charming performance from the pen of the Marquis d'Argens," wrote Sade in *Juliette*, "alone to have discerned the possibilities of the genre, though only partially realizing them; alone to have achieved happy results from the combining of lust and impiety. These, speedily placed before the public, and in the shape the author had initially conceived them, finally gave us an idea of what an immoral book could be" (p. 462). For *Thérèse philosophe* and Dostoevsky, see William C. Brumfield, "*Thérèse philosophe* and Dostoevsky's Great Sinner," *Comparative Literature* 323, no. 3 (Summer 1980): 238–52.

44. Kautman, "Dostojevskij a Markyz de Sade," p. 398.

Chapter 9

1. V. V. Vereshchagin, *Ocherki, nasbroski, vospominanija* (St. Petersburg, 1883), p. 141.

2. Nikolai Berdyaev, *Mirosozertsanie Dostoevskogo* (Paris, 1968 [1921]), pp. 235, 233, 234. "Culture with all its great values is middle course [seredina]," Berdyaev argues. "There is no environment of culture, no middle culture and almost no cultural tradition in Russia." In Berdyaev's view, the "dionysian" and "apocalyptic" elements in Dostoevsky's novelistic universe have the potential for undermining middle culture—in the Russian case what Berdyaev finds lacking in the Russian people: strongly developed traditions of responsibility, self-discipline, and spiritual independence. Dostoevsky dramatized the "crisis of humanism, materialistic and idealistic"; he prophesied the disaster of two Russian revolutions; he set before all people the future triumph of the "religion of freedom and love." He was "not a teacher of life, in the strict sense of the word," however. "He does not set forth that maturity of spirit that is

manifested when the spirit masters the chaotic spiritual element, disciplines it and subjects it to a higher goal"; "he does not show the paths of self-discipline of the spirit" (Ibid., pp. 233, 14, 233, 224, 227, 236, 230, 232, 231).

3. Dmitry Merezhkovsky, "Turgenev," in *Polnoe sobranie sochinenij* (Moscow, 1914), vol. 18, p. 58.

4. Ibid., pp. 59, 66.

5. Joseph Conrad, foreword to Edward Garnett, *Turgenev* (London, 1927), p. x.

6. Paul Bourget, "Ivan Tourguéniev," in *Essais de psychologie contemporaine: Oeuvres complètes de Paul Bourget* (Paris, 1899), pp. 424–32. Bourget's article on Turgenev first appeared in *Nouvelle Revue*, May 15, 1885.

7. Letter to K. S. Aksakov, October 16, 1852; *PSS: Pis'ma*, vol. 2, p. 71.

8. The appeal to nature's simplicity and humility is a constant in Turgenev's writing. See, for example, his letter to Countess Lambert June 10, 1856: "One must learn from nature's correct and tranquil movement, from her humility"; *PSS: Pis'ma*, vol. 2, p. 365.

9. Letter to P. V. Annenkov, February 24, 1853; *PSS: Pis'ma*, vol. 2, p. 128. See also Turgenev's unpublished review of S. T. Aksakov's *Zapiski ruzhejnogo okhotnika Orenburgskoj gubernii*, where he speaks of man as nature's "son" and stresses the unity of all parts of nature—a unity, however, in which every "separate unit . . . exists exclusively for itself, conceives itself as the center of the universe." In this same review, Turgenev cites several lines from Goethe's fragment "Die Natur" (1782–83); *PSS: Pis'ma*, vol. 5, pp. 414, 415, 416.

10. Letter of January 3, 1857; *PSS: Pis'ma*, vol. 3, p. 76.

11. Speech about Shakespeare in Turgenev, *PSS*, vol. 15, p. 51.

12. Speech on the opening of the Pushkin monument, 1880; Turgenev, *PSS*, vol. 15, p. 73.

13. Ibid., p. 71.   14. Ibid., p. 73.

15. Ibid., p. 72.

16. Ibid., p. 75. The idea of a return to Pushkin was not a new one for Turgenev. In a letter to A. V. Druzhinin November 11, 1856, he wrote: "You remember that I, a champion and devoted follower of Gogol, once held forth to you on the necessity to a return to the Pushkin element as a counterweight to that of Gogol? A striving for objectivity and for whole Truth is one of the few good qualities for which I am grateful that nature has given me"; *PSS: Pis'ma*, vol. 3, p. 30.

17. Turgenev, *PSS*, vol. 15, p. 74.

18. F. M. Dostoevsky, *V vospominanijakh sovremennikov* (Moscow, 1990), vol. 2, p. 244.

19. Turgenev later included "Live Relics" in his *A Sportsman's Notebook* (*Zapiski okhotnika*, 1852); the vast majority of these sketches belong to the late 1840's and early 1850's.

20. See Turgenev, *PSS*, vol. 4, pp. 513–14.

21. Letter of June 16, 1876, in Turgenev, *PSS: Pis'ma*, vol. 11, p. 279–80.

22. Ibid., vol. 3, p. 354. Turgenev's concept of the tragedy of everyday life, one may note in passing, anticipates Maeterlinck's concept of "*le tragique du quotidien*" (Maurice Maeterlinck, "Le tragique quotidien," in *Les trésor des humbles* [Paris, 1898], pp. 179–201) and Chekhov's conception of the relation of everyday actions to tragedy. "Let everything on the stage be as complex and at the same time as simple as in life. People dine, only dine, but at that time their happiness is taking shape or their life is being smashed." "Vospominanija Ars. G. (I. Ja. Gurljand)," in *Teatr i iskusstvo* no. 364 (1904); quoted by A. Skaftymov in "K voprosu o printsipakh postroenija p'es A. P. Chekhova," *Stat'i o russkoj literature* (Saratov, 1958), p. 317.

23. Turgenev, *PSS*, vol. 12, p. 310.   24. Ibid., vol. 5, p. 391.

25. Letter of October 3, 1860; *PSS: Pis'ma*, vol. 4, p. 135.

26. Letter of June 16, 1876 to V. L. Kign; *PSS: Pis'ma*, vol. 11, p. 280.

27. Letter to L. Ja. Stechkina, April 25, 1878; *PSS: Pis'ma*, vol. 12, bk. 1, p. 317.

28. Letter of February 11, 1855; *PSS: Pis'ma*, vol. 2, p. 259.

29. Letter to L. Ja. Stechkina, April 25, 1878; *PSS: Pis'ma*, vol. 12, bk. 1, p. 318.

30. Letter to Ja. P. Polonsky, January 2, 1868; *PSS: Pis'ma*, vol. 7, p. 26: "Truth is air, without which it is impossible to breath; but art is a plant, sometimes a rather fantastic one, which matures and develops in this air. But these gentlemen ["the Sleptsovs, the Reshetnikovs and the Uspenskys"] are *seedless* and have nothing to *sow*."

31. Letter to P. V. Annensky, February 14, 1868; *PSS: Pis'ma*, vol. 7, p. 65. See also Turgenev's letter to I. P. Borisov, March 16, 1865 (*PSS: Pis'ma*, vol. 5, p. 364) where Turgenev, with *War and Peace* in mind, castigates Tolstoy for his "cleverly noted and preciously expressed, petty psychological observations which, under the pretext of 'truth,' he hunts out from the armpits and other dark places of his heroes—how wretched all this is on the broad canvas of an historical novel."

32. Letter of November 25, 1875; *PSS: Pis'ma*, vol. 11, p. 164.

33. Letter to Leo Tolstoy, June 29, 1883; *PSS: Pis'ma*, vol. 13, bk. 2, p. 180.

34. Letter to I. P. Borisov, January 12, 1869, *PSS: Pis'ma*, vol. 12, p. 279.

35. George Moore, "Turgueneff," in *Impressions and Opinions* (New York, 1891), pp. 70–71.

36. A. Clutton-Brock, "Turgenev," in *Essays on Books* (London, 1920), p. 160.

37. For a discussion on the questions of Turgenev's attitude toward "rhetoric" in *Rudin* as well as a view of his "poetics of silence," see Jane T. Costlow, *World Within Worlds: The Novels of Ivan Turgenev* (Princeton, N.J., 1990), in particular Chap. 1, "Rhetoric and Sincerity: Turgenev and the Poetics of Silence." See also Costlow, "The Death of Rhetoric in *Rudin*," *Russian Litera-*

ture 16 (1984): 375–84. See also Elizabeth Cheresh Allen's discussion of Turgenev's silences and use of language in her *Beyond Realism: Turgenev's Poetics of Secular Salvation* (Stanford, Calif., 1992), pp. 100–135. Allen's and Costlow's outstanding studies of Turgenev are dramatic evidence of the rediscovery and revaluation of Turgenev that have marked the last decades of the twentieth century. Both works provide new insights into the aesthetic and ethical dimensions of Turgenev's work.

38. Letter of October 30, 1856; *PSS: Pis'ma*, vol. 3, p. 29. "For you," Turgenev writes, "this whole trend is a delusion which has to be rooted out; for me it is partial Truth which always will find (and must find) followers at that stage of human life when full Truth is still inaccessible." "Try to tell young people you can't give them the full truth because you yourself don't possess it," Lezhnev remarks in *Rudin*.

39. Letter of November 25, 1857; *PSS: Pis'ma*, vol. 3, p. 169.

40. *Fraza* (phase), as Turgenev uses the word here, implies in this context a high-flown, florid expression lacking in inner content or concealing the falseness of its content.

41. Dostoevsky, *PSS*, vol. 27, p.65.

42. Cited by V. V. Vinogradov in *Problema avtorstva i teorija stilej* (Moscow, 1961), p. 535. See also Dostoevsky's remark in his notebook in the mid-1860's: "Realism is the mind of the crowd, of the majority, who do not see farther than their nose, but it is cunning and keen, quite adequate for the present moment" (Dostoevsky, *PSS*, vol. 20, p. 182).

43. G. A. Byaly, "Dve shkoly psikhologicheskogo realizma (Turgenev i Dostoevskij)," in *Russkij realizm kontsa XIX veka* (Leningrad, 1973), pp. 32, 36.

44. N. N. Strakhov, in *Vremja* (1862); quoted in *Sobranie kriticheskikh materialov dlja izuchenija proizvedenij I. S. Turgeneva*, ed. V. Zelinskij, 2d ed. (Moscow, 1895), p. 234.

45. See Rozanov's footnote to a letter of Strakhov in V. V. Rozanov, "Pis'ma N. N. Strakhova k V. V. Rozanovu," in *Literaturnye izgnanniki* (St. Petersburg, 1913), vol. 1, p. 252.

46. Dostoevsky, *PSS*, vol. 20, p. 175.

47. "Gamlet i Don-Kikhot," Turgenev, *PSS*, vol. 8, p. 173.

48. Letter of July 16–19, 1849; *PSS: Pis'ma*, vol. 1, pp. 350–51.

49. Letter of May 1, 1848; *PSS: Pis'ma*, vol. 1, p. 297.

50. Dostoevsky, *PSS*, vol. 28, bk. 1, p. 115.

51. Conrad, foreword, p. ix.

52. Ibid., pp. ix–x.

53. "Adieu à Tourguéneff," in *Oeuvres complètes de Ernest Renan* (Paris, 1947), vol. 1, p. 870.

54. Letter of August 16, 1867; Dostoevsky, *PSS*, vol. 28, bk. 2, p. 297.

55. Leonid Grossman, *Dostoevskij* (Moscow, 1965), p. 48.

56. Letter to A. V. Korvin-Krukovskaya, June 17, 1866; Dostoevsky, *PSS*, vol. 28, bk. 2, p. 160.

57. E. Halperine-Kaminsky, "'La Puissance des ténèbres' sur la scène française," *La Nouvelle Revue*, February 1, 1888, p. 629.

58. T. de Wyzewa, "Revue russes," *Revue des deux mondes*, May 15, 1894, p. 458.

59. Rozanov, p. 40. The elevation of Turgenev's "form" over his content, an implicit separation of form from content, was to characterize a whole category of Turgenev criticism, especially in the West. "Does not life come before form? . . . If this be so, and who shall say it is not so, then Balzac is the greatest," George Moore remarks in a discussion of Balzac and Turgenev in *Avowals*. But Moore valiantly defends Turgenev. "In a tale by Turgenev we are with life as it exists in our own hearts. . . . Balzac is more astonishing, more complete, but not so beautiful; he is not so perfect; and in the same way Turgenev, though not so astonishing or so complete as Balzac, is more beautiful and more perfect." Moore, *Avowals*, in *The Collected Works of George Moore* (the Carra ed.) (New York, 1923), vol. 9, pp. 133–34.

60. Conrad, pp. v–vi.

61. Quoted by Peter Brang in "Ist Turgenjew veraltet," *Neue Zürcher Zeitung* no. 205, September 3–4, 1983, p. 65.

62. D. S. Mirsky, *A History of Russian Literature*, ed. Francis J. Whitfield (New York, 1958 [1926]), p. 207.

63. "Turgenev and Tolstoy" (1897), in Henry James, *The Future of the Novel*, ed. Leon Edel (New York, 1956), pp. 228, 233.

64. Letter to Alexander Eliaberg, June 5, 1914; Thomas Mann, *Briefe 1889–1936* (Frankfurt am Main, 1961), p. 109.

65. Virginia Woolf, "The Novels of Turgenev," in *Collected Essays* (New York, 1967 [1933]), pp. 249, 250.

Chapter 10

1. "Otvet 'Moskvitjaninu,'" in *Belinskij o Gogole: Stat'i i retsenzii, pis'ma*, ed. S. Mashinskij (Moscow, 1949), p. 374 (references to this edition, Belinsky).

2. "Pushkin i Gogol'," in appendix to Rozanov, *Legenda o velikom inkvisitore F. M. Dostoevskogo: Opyt kriticheskogo kommentarija: S prilozheniem dvukh etjudov o Gogole*, 3d ed. (Petersburg, 1906), p. 260 (references to this edition, Rozanov).

3. Rozanov, p. 15.

4. Ibid., p. 18. Rozanov, of course, was not the first critic to view Gogol's characters as distortions or caricatures. For a history of the term *caricature* as applied to Gogol in the nineteenth century, see Vasily Gippius' chapter "Sborishche urodov [An Assemblage of Freaks]" in his *Gogol'* (Leningrad, 1924), pp. 153–68.

5. Rozanov, p. 255.   6. Ibid., p. 256.

7. Ibid., p. 255.

8. Ibid., p. 261.

9. Ibid., p. 262.

10. Ibid., p. 254.

11. Ibid., p. 256.

12. Ibid., p. 278.

13. Ibid., p. 263.

14. Ibid., p. 261.

15. Belinsky, p. 77.

16. Ibid., p. 78.

17. A. I. Gertsen, *Byloe i dumy* (Leningrad, 1946), pt. 1, ch. 1, p. 13.

18. Belinsky, p. 183.

19. Ibid., p. 62.

20. Ibid., p. 42.

21. Ibid., p. 360.

22. Ibid., p. 405.

23. Ibid., p. 372.

24. Ibid., p. 374.

25. Ibid., p. 404.

26. Ibid., p. 42.

27. Gertsen, *Sobranie sochinenij v tridtsati tomakh* (Moscow-Leningrad, 1954), vol. 2, p. 220.

28. K. D. Kavelin, "Vzgljad na juridicheskij byt drevnej Rossii," in *Sovremennik* (Petersburg, 1847), vol. 1, pt. 11, pp. 1–52.30.

29. Ibid., p. 11.

30. Ibid., p. 12.

31. Ibid., p. 10.

32. Letter to K. D. Kavelin, Nov. 22, 1847; V. G. Belinsky, *Polnoe sobranie sochinenij* (Moscow, 1956), vol. 12, p. 433.

33. Ibid.

34. Ibid., p. 461.

35. Ibid.

36. Ibid.

37. Ibid., p. 432.

38. Ibid., p. 459.

39. Ibid., p. 460.

40. Ibid.

41. Dostoevsky, *PSS*, vol. 22, p. 106.

42. Ibid., pp. 106–7.

43. Ibid., p. 106.

44. Rozanov, p. 274.

45. Ibid., p. 276.

46. Ibid., p. 264.

47. Ibid., pp. 264–65.

48. Ibid., p. 260.

49. Dostoevsky, *PSS*, vol. 28, bk. 1, p. 117.

Chapter 11

1. George Steiner has compared *Notes from the Underground* with *The Death of Ivan Ilych*. He juxtaposes Dostoevsky's descent "into the dark places of the soul" with Tolstoy's descent "into the dark places of the body." With respect to the relation of *The Kreutzer Sonata* to *Notes from the Underground*, Steiner observes only that Tolstoy's "non-heroes" (among whom he includes the narrator of *The Kreutzer Sonata*) have "a humaneness in suffering and a moral assertiveness which set them worlds apart from the bilious masochism of the underground man" (*Tolstoy or Dostoevsky: An Essay in the Old Criticism* [New York, 1959], pp. 228–29). Steiner does not address the question of the affinities between these two men or the question of similarities in design between *Notes from the Underground* or *The Kreutzer Sonata*.

2. In many of its features, of course, *The Kreutzer Sonata* resembles major

works of Tolstoy in the 1880's and 1890's, as Lydia Opulskaya notes in her discussion of *The Kreutzer Sonata* (Opul'skaja, *Lev Nikolaevich Tolstoj: Materialy k biografii s 1886 po 1892 god* [Moscow, 1979], p. 177). It is also true that *War and Peace* provides an early example of Tolstoy's fusion of the artistic and the publicistic elements. *The Kreutzer Sonata* and its anti-hero nonetheless are marked by a distinct "underground" ethos.

3. Dostoevsky, *PSS*, vol. 15, p. 228.

4. Ibid., vol. 20, p. 173. It should be noted that Dostoevsky's text from Matthew—"ne zhenjatsja i ne posjagajut, a zhivut, kak angely bozhii"—derives from the old Slavonic Bible, which uses the verb *posjagat'* (from *sjagat'*, to reach out for, take hold of, seize) instead of the modern Russian phrase *vykhodit' zamuzh* (to marry or get married [of a woman]). In one of its meanings, *posjagat'* means "to take a wife," that is, to marry; it also may mean "to impose upon," infringe upon, to attempt to possess, or to attack. I have translated *ne posjagajut'* more literally as "they do not seek to possess" since Dostoevsky's use of the phrase—*posjagnovenie na zhenshchinu* (seeking to possess a woman)—in the text cited clearly suggests that he understood the verb *posjagat'* in the literal sense of "possessing," or taking possession of a wife, as well as in its ritualized meaning of getting married.

5. Ibid., p. 172.   6. Ibid., p. 173.

7. Tolstoy, *PSS*, vol. 27, p. 84.

8. Tolstoy, *PSS*, vol. 26, pp. 269, 270. Tolstoy's story "Khodite v svete, poka est' svet (Povest' iz vremen drevnikh khristian)" was written in the late 1880's. It was first published in English in the October 1890 issue of the *Fortnightly Review* and in Russian in Geneva in 1892. The story was printed in Russia in 1893. Tolstoy was clearly dissatisfied with this work. "There are good thoughts in it," he wrote to V. G. Chertkov on April 25, 1887, "but it is written inartistically—coldly." "In form it is all very bad—very [bad]," he wrote again to Chertkov on June 21, clearly reluctant to have anything more to do with the story (Ibid., pp. 739, 740).

9. "You have written nothing *stronger* than this, and what is more, nothing more *somber*," N. N. Strakhov wrote Tolstoy on November 6, 1889, apropos of *The Kreutzer Sonata*. "There are many comments and descriptions that are amazing in the deep way they penetrate the spirit, and terrible in their truth. And it is all told and grasped so simply and clearly!" Strakhov then offered some critical comments: "You took the form of narration in the person of the hero, a form which very much hampered you, and the readers began asking: 'who is the interlocutor [*sobesednik*, the frame narrator]?' Why does the narrator take so long in getting down to business, and instead carry on discussions on general questions? Moreover it seems to me there is one main bit of haziness: in what spirit does he tell his story? In some places one might think that his egotism has been crushed and that he already sees his actions in their true significance; in other places it seems that he is ready again to go on killing his wife and that there is not a trace of repentance in him. Moreover, the

denouement comes about too rapidly, i.e., little is said up to the moment when the musician appears. Therefore it seems that the hero is not a completely normal man, [he is] excessively jealous and nervous." Quoted by Opul'skaja, pp. 176–77; see also *Perepiska L. N. Tolstogo s N. N. Strakhovym: 1870–1894* (St. Petersburg, 1914), p. 395. There is nothing unclear or cloudy about Tolstoy's use of first-person narration. Strakhov, as Opulskaya suggests, seems not at all to have grasped the stylistic features of Tolstoy's later work. He certainly did not recognize that Pozdnyshev's constant shifting of positions (so typical also of the Underground Man) precisely characterizes his inner conflict—a conflict that is part of Tolstoy's ideological design.

10. See Chekhov's letter to A. N. Pleshcheyev, February 15, 1890; Chekhov, *Polnoe sobranie sochinenij i pisem v tridtsati tomakh: Pis'ma*, (Moscow, 1976), vol. 4, p. 18.

11. L. N. Tolstoy, "Posleslovie k 'Krejtserovoj sonate," in *PSS*, vol. 27, p. 88.

12. Tolstoy, *PSS*, vol. 27, p. 580.   13. Ibid., vol. 64, p. 334.

14. Ibid., vol. 50, p. 189.   15. Ibid., vol. 87, p. 83.

16. Dostoevsky, *PSS*, vol. 28, bk. 2, p. 75.

17. "She hasn't the *slightest chance* of living beyond two weeks. I'm trying to finish the story as soon as possible, but judge for yourself—is this a good time for writing?" (ibid., p. 73). And again, a few days later: "I fear that the death of my wife will be soon, and here there will *necessarily* be an interruption in my work. If there weren't this interruption then, perhaps, I'd finish" (ibid., p. 75).

18. With respect to his ailments, Dostoevsky writes his brother on March 5, 1864: "I am now *physically* unable to write anything now. . . . I am ill, Marya Dmitrievna is terribly ill" (ibid., pp. 68, 69).

19. "All this is an external fatalism; all this does not depend on me" (ibid., p. 84).

20. Ibid., p. 70.   21. Ibid., p. 82.

22. See the memoirs of V. V. Timofeeva (O. Pochinkovskaya), "God raboty s znamenitym pisatelem," in *F. M. Dostoevskij v vospominaniyakh sovremennikov* (Moscow, 1964), vol. 2, p. 176. The German phrase is in the original text.

Chapter 12

1. It is certainly possible, of course, that Dostoevsky had read *King John* in one of several Russian (or even French) translations. His deep lifelong appreciation of Shakespeare is well known. References and allusions to Shakespeare abound in Dostoevsky's fiction, notebooks, and letters. For a recent discussion of Dostoevsky and Shakespeare, see Ju. D. Levin, "Dostoevskii i Shekspir," in *Dostoevsky: materialy i issledovaniia* (Leningrad, 1974), vol. 1, 108–34. Dostoevsky, however, makes no direct references to *King John*. That play may be

found in Russian translation in *Polnoe sobranie dramaticheskikh proizvedenij Shekspira*, which first appeared in 1865–68 and was edited by N. A. Nekrasov and N. V. Gerbel' (a second and third edition appeared in 1876 and 1880, respectively). The 1876 edition was in Dostoevsky's library at the time of his death (L. Grossman, *Biblioteka Dostoevskogo* [Odessa, 1919], p. 137). A. V. Druzhinin's translation of *King John*, which appears in the Nekrasov-Gerbel' edition of Shakespeare's work, was first published separately in the journal *Sovremennik* in 1860, a journal which Dostoevsky certainly followed closely. An excellent, very accurate prose translation of *King John* by the well-known Shakespeare translator, N. Kh. Ketcher (1806?–1886) was first published, along with other chronicle plays of Shakespeare, in 1841 (the title of the play was translated as *Korol' Ioann*). Ketcher's works were very popular in the 1840's. Mikhail Dostoevsky, Dostoevsky's brother, sent him precisely Ketcher's prose translations of Shakespeare at the time Dostoevsky was imprisoned in the Petropavlovsk fortress in 1849. (See M. M. Dostoevsky's letter of September 10, 1849, in *Iskusstvo (1927)*, vol. 3, vyp. 1, p. 114). We do not know, however, which issues of the Ketcher translations Dostoevsky received. A second edition of Ketcher's complete works of Shakespeare was published again in 1879 at the time Dostoevsky was at work on *The Brothers Karamazov*. For a detailed account of Shakespeare in Russia (translations, theater productions, criticism, etc.), see *Shekspir i russkaia kul'tura*, ed. M. P. Alekseev (Moscow-Leningrad, 1965).

Apropos of Dostoevsky's possible interest in *King John*, it should be noted that the story of John was familiar in Shakespeare's time as a parallel to Queen Elizabeth's. For a consideration of the parallels between John's order to murder Arthur and Elizabeth's treatment of Secretary Davison (Elizabeth asked Davison to have Mary Queen of Scots murdered and later he was made the Queen's scapegoat), see E. A. J. Honigmann's introduction to *King John*, in *The Arden Edition of the Works of William Shakespeare*, ed. E. A. J. Honigmann (London, 1967), pp. xxvii–xxix. Dostoevsky's interest in the complicity themes of *King John* would certainly have been stimulated by Schiller's treatment of the same themes in *Maria Stuart*, a work that Dostoevsky read avidly as a young man.

Chapter 13

1. "Dostoevsky knew everything that Nietzsche knew," Berdyaev wrote in his study of Dostoevsky, "but he also knew something that Nietzsche did not know." N. Berdyaev, *Mirosozertsanie Dostoevskogo* (Paris, 1968 [1921]), p. 59.

2. All citations from Nietzsche, unless otherwise noted, refer to the following editions in English (I indicate in parentheses the letter symbols used to refer to these works in the notes): *Beyond Good and Evil (BGE)*, trans. Walter Kaufmann (New York, 1966); *The Birth of Tragedy (BT)* trans. Walter Kauf-

mann (New York, 1967); *The Gay Science* (*GS*), trans. Walter Kaufmann (New York, 1974); *On the Genealogy of Morals* (*GM*), trans. Walter Kaufmann and R. J. Hollingdale, *Ecce Homo* (*EH*), trans. Walter Kaufmann (New York, 1967); *Thus Spoke Zarathustra* (*Z*), in *The Portable Nietzsche*, ed., trans. Walter Kaufmann (New York, 1954); *The Will to Power* (*WP*), ed. Walter Kaufmann, trans. Walter Kaufmann and R. J. Hollingdale (New York, 1968).

3. *Z*, p. 203.   4. Ibid., p. 123.
5. Ibid., pp. 126–27.   6. Ibid., p. 125.
7. Ibid., p. 130.   8. Ibid., pp. 135, 136.
9. Ibid., p. 127.   10. *WP*, p. 419.

11. Unless otherwise noted, translations from Dostoevsky's works are my own.

12. *BT*, p. 45.   13. Ibid., p. 35.
14. Ibid., p. 15.   15. *GS*, p. 290.
16. *Z*, p. 251.   17. *WP*, p. 842.

18. *F. M. Dostoevskij ob isskusstve*, ed. S. Aleksandrov (Moscow, 1973), p. 461.

19. Dostoevsky, *PSS*, vol. 21, p. 16.

20. "The history of the moral sensations," Nietzsche writes in *Human, All-Too-Human*, "is the history of an error, the error of accountability, which rests on the error of freedom of will." See *A Nietzsche Reader*, trans. R. J. Hollingdale (Middlesex, England, 1977), pp. 71–72.

21. Cited by Rudolph Binion in *Frau Lou, Nietzsche's Wayward Disciple* (Princeton, N.J., 1968), p. 544. Karl Jaspers stresses Nietzsche's explicit demand for the preservation of traditional morality. See Jaspers, *Nietzsche: An Introduction to the Understanding of his Philosophical Activity*, trans. Charles F. Wallraff and Frederick J. Schmitz (Chicago, 1965), p. 153.

22. *WP*, p. 13.   23. Ibid., p. 249.
24. *BGE*, p. 71.   25. *GS*, p. 121.
26. *WP*, p. 435.   27. Ibid., pp. 451–52.
28. *BT*, p. 22.   29. *Nietzsche Reader*, p. 129.
30. *EH*, p. 258.

31. "Those four years," Dostoevsky wrote his brother Andrey on his release from prison, November 6, 1854, "I consider a time in which I was buried alive and closed up in a coffin." Dostoevsky, *PSS*, vol. 28, bk. 1, p. 181.

32. *EH*, p. 224.

33. Dostoevsky, *PSS*, vol. 28, bk. 1, p. 176.

34. *WP*, p. 443.

35. The poem referred to here is "Frieden" from Heine's cycle *Die Nordsee*.

36. Letter to Georg Brandes, November 20, 1888; *Selected Letters of Friedrich Nietzsche*, p. 327.

37. "This is the urge to permeate material things with human spirit," Mann writes apropos of Zarathustra's plea. "It is spiritual materialism—which is socialism"; see Mann's essay "Nietzsche's Philosophy in the Light of Recent

History," in *Last Essays*, trans. Richard and Clara Winston et al. (New York, 1959), p. 169.

38. Z, p. 138.

39. Karl Jaspers, *Nietzsche and Christianity*, trans. E. B. Ashton (New York, 1961), p. 64.

Chapter 14

1. The history of Ivanov's Dostoevsky study is a complicated one. *Freedom and the Tragic Life: A Study in Dostoevsky*, first published in 1952 by Noonday Press, is an *English* translation of a *German* translation (Wjatscheslaw Iwanow, *Dostojewskij, Tragödie—Mythos—Mystik*, autorisierte Übersetzung von Alexander Kresling, J. C. B. Mohr [Tübingen, 1932]) of Ivanov's original *Russian* text. The main title of the English translation, *Freedom and the Tragic Life*, is not Ivanov's; it was added by the English translator or editor. Ivanov, who had a perfect command of German, supervised the German translation. Unfortunately, the original Russian manuscript used by the German translator has *disappeared*. The German text, therefore, remains the canonic text, at least as far as the English translation is concerned. The question of the canonic text, however, is complicated by the fact that in writing and preparing his 1932 book, Ivanov incorporated—with many cuts, additions, and changes—three earlier essays he had written in Russian on Dostoevsky and published in Russia before the revolution: a long essay on Dostoevsky (*Dostoevsky and the Novel-Tragedy*) dating back to 1911; a short piece on *The Devils (Excursus: The Basic Myth of "The Possessed")* dating back to 1914; these two essays were published in the collection *Furrows and Boundaries (Borozdy i mezhi)* in 1916; finally, an essay on *The Brothers Karamazov* (*Faces and Masks of Russia: A Study of Dostoevsky's Ideology*), written in 1916 and published in the collection *Matters Native and Universal* (*Rodnoe i vselenskoe*) in 1917. Recently, a new *Russian* translation has been made of the German text, using wherever possible Ivanov's *earlier* Dostoevsky essays. This new Russian translation-restoration, along with Ivanov's three earlier essays, appears in vol. 4 of Vyacheslav Ivanov, *Sobranie Sochinenij [Collected Works]*, ed. D. V. Ivanov and Olga Deschartes (Brussels, 1986). In the absence of the original Russian manuscript of Ivanov's 1932 Dostoevsky book, the German translation Ivanov supervised must be regarded as the canonic text.

My citations from Ivanov's 1932 book are taken from the English edition of Ivanov's *Freedom and the Tragic Life: A Study in Dostoevsky*, tr. Norman Cameron, ed. S. Konovalov (Oxford), foreword by Sir Maurice Bowra, new introduction by Robert Louis Jackson (repr. Longwood Academic, Wolfeboro, N.H., 1989); the translation is referred to simply as *Dostoevsky* (1932). All *other* citations from Ivanov's *earlier* Dostoevsky essays, as well as to his other writings, are taken from his Russian original and refer to the *Sobranie sochinenij*, vols. 1–4 (cited as *SS*).

2. A much expanded second edition of Bakhtin's study appeared in 1963 under the title *Problemy poetiki Dostoevskogo* (*Problems of Dostoevsky's Poetics*). See Caryl Emerson's translation and scholarly edition, Mikhail Bakhtin, *Problems of Dostoevsky's Poetics*, vol. 8 of *Theory and History of Literature* (Minneapolis, 1984). Citations from Bakhtin's study and from his notes "Toward a Reworking of the Dostoevsky Book" (included as an appendix to the English translation of *Problems of Dostoevsky's Poetics*) are taken from the Emerson edition.

3. *Dostoevsky* (1932), p. 118.

4. Bakhtin, *Problems of Dostoevsky's Poetics*, p. 10.

5. Ivanov, *SS*, vol. 3, p. 424.   6. Ibid., *SS*, vol. 3, p. 403.

7. Ibid., p. 402.

8. Ernst Robert Curtius, *Deutscher Geist in Gefahr* (Stuttgart, 1932), p. 116.

9. Ivanov, *SS*, vol. 3, p. 396.

10. Ibid.   11. Ibid., pp. 128–29.

12. Bakhtin, *Poetics*, p. 287.   13. Ivanov, *Dostoevsky* (1932), p. 11.

14. Ibid., p. 49.   15. Ibid., p. 109.

16. Ibid., p. 7.   17. Ibid., p. 119.

18. *Dostoevskij i roman-tragedija* (1916), *SS*, vol. 4, pp. 426–27.

19. Ivanov, *SS*, vol. 1, p. 839.   20. Ibid., p. 833.

21. Ibid., vol. 2, p. 86.   22. Ibid., p. 20.

23. Ivanov, *Dostoevsky* (1932), p. 27.

24. Ivanov, *SS*, vol. 3, p. 303.

25. Bakhtin, *Poetics*, p. 287. In his study "The Author and Hero in Aesthetic Reality," Bakhtin speaks of the intrinsic falsification involved in looking into a mirror or at a photograph of oneself, or of painting one's self-portrait: "In this sense one could speak of the absolute aesthetic need of a person for another, for the looking, remembering, gathering, and uniting activity of the other, which alone can create his externally complete personality; this personality will not exist if another does not create it." Bakhtin, "Avtor i geroj v estetičeskoj dejatel'nosti," in *Estetika slovesnogo tvorchestva*, 2d ed. (Moscow, 1986), p. 37.

26. *Dostoevskij i roman-tragedija*, pp. 416–17.

27. Ivanov, *Dostoevsky* (1932), p. 36.

28. Ibid., p. 34.   29. Ibid., p. 134.

30. Ibid., p. 116.   31. Ibid., p. 71.

32. Ibid., p. 50.   33. Ibid., pp. 57, 60.

34. Ibid., p. 61.   35. Ibid., p. 15.

36. Ibid., p. 16.   37. Ibid., p. 78.

38. Leo Shestov, *Dostoevsky and Nietzsche: The Philosophy of Tragedy*, trans. Spencer Roberts, in *Dostoevsky, Tolstoy and Nietzsche* (Ohio, 1969), p. 170.

39. *Dostoevsky* (1932), p. 134.

40. Dostoevsky, *PSS*, vol. 28, bk. 2, p. 73.

41. *Dostoevsky* (1932), p. 76.   42. Ibid., pp. 89, 90.

43. René Wellek, "The Literary Criticism of Vyacheslav Ivanov," in *Vyacheslav Ivanov: Poet, Critic and Philosopher*, ed. Robert Louis Jackson and Lowry Nelson, Jr. (New Haven, 1986), pp. 232, 233. Wellek's article on Ivanov's criticism is a valuable introduction to a generally unexamined area of Ivanov's work.

44. Ibid., p. 232.   45. Ibid., p. 109.
46. Ibid., p. 118.   47. Ibid., p. 110.
48. Ibid., p. 115.

49. Dostoevsky, *PSS*, vol. 30, bk. 1, p. 9.

50. Nikolai Berdyaev, *Mirosozertsanie Dostoevskogo* (Paris, 1968 [1921]), p. 92.

51. *Dostoevskij i roman-tragedija*, p. 402.

52. *Dostoevsky* (1932), p. 4.

53. Ibid., p. 3. The German text: "Er weilt in unserer Mitte und wandelt mit uns."

54. "Otvet na vopros redaktsii 'Novogo mira'," in *Estetika slovesnogo tvorchestva*, p. 352.

Chapter 15

1. Mikhail Bakhtin, *Problems of Dostoevsky's Poetics*, ed., trans. Caryl Emerson, vol. 8 of *Theory and History of Literature* (Minneapolis, 1984), p. 285.

2. Vyacheslav Ivanov, *Freedom and the Tragic Life: A Study in Dostoevsky*, foreword by Sir Maurice Bowra, new introduction by Robert Louis Jackson (Wolfeboro, N.H., 1989), pp. 111–12.

3. Ibid., p. 119.   4. Ibid., p. 118.

5. See Chapter 14, note 1, for my discussion of the composite character of Ivanov's 1932 Dostoevsky book.

6. Katerina Clark and Michael Holquist discuss this question in their *Mikhail Bakhtin* (Cambridge, Mass., 1984), pp. 248–52. See also Gary Saul Morson and Caryl Emerson, *Mikhail Bakhtin: Creation of a Prosaics* (Stanford, Calif., 1990), for a discussion of Bakhtin and Dostoevsky among other questions.

7. Bakhtin, *Poetics*, p. 7.   8. Ibid., p. 8.
9. Ibid., p. 3.   10. Ibid., pp. 275, 276.
11. Ibid., p. 17.   12. Ibid., p. 3.
13. Ibid., p. 38.   14. Ibid., p. 278.
15. Ibid., p. 36.   16. Ibid., p. 92.
17. Ibid., p. 67.   18. Ibid., p. 39.
19. Ibid., p. 92.   20. Ibid., pp. 57, 58.
21. Ibid., p. 18.   22. Ibid., p. 15.
23. Ibid., p. 6.   24. Ibid., p. 17.
25. Ibid., pp. 30, 28.

26. Ibid., p. 11. For a general discussion of Bakhtin and Ivanov, see Nikolai Kotrelev, "K probleme dialogischeskogo personazha (M. M. Bakhtin i Vjach.

Ivanov," in *Cultura e Memoria: Atti del terzo Simposio Internazionale dedicato a Viaceslav Ivanov*, vol. 2: *Testi in russo*, ed. Fausto Malcovati (Florence, 1988), pp. 93–103.

27. Ibid., p. 10. See pp. 256–57 in the essay on Ivanov for a discussion of Ivanov's "Thou art" concept.

28. Ibid., p. 63. Or, as Bakhtin articulates Dostoevsky's artistic position in his notes "Toward a Reworking of the Dostoevsky Book": "I cannot manage without another. I cannot become myself without another; I must find myself in another by finding another in myself (in mutual reflection and mutual acceptance)" (ibid., app. 2, p. 287).

29. Ibid., p. 11.   30. Ibid., p. 44.

31. Ibid., p. 11.

32. Ivanov, *Dostoevsky* (1932), p. 116. There is no evidence that Ivanov read Bakhtin's study of Dostoevsky when he was preparing his 1932 Dostoevsky book. Bakhtin could have had no knowledge of these particular observations of Ivanov, since they do not appear in his earlier essays on Dostoevsky.

33. Bakhtin, *Poetics*, pp. 3, 8.

34. *Videt', videnie*—words etymologically linked with "knowing" (as in the German *wissen*). The Russian word *videnie* is uncommonly rich in meanings and connotations: it means literally "the capacity or possibility of seeing"; it may be "sight" or "eyes"; "vision" (prophetic); or "face" or "image."

35. Bakhtin, *Poetics*, p. 29.   36. Ibid., p. 285.

37. Ibid., p. 287.   38. Ibid., p. 30.

39. Ibid.   40. Ibid., p. 43.

41. Dostoevsky, *PSS*, vol. 23, p. 144.   42. Bakhtin, *Poetics*, p. 288.

43. Ibid., p. 90.

44. Ibid., pp. 31–32. See also "It is characteristic that in Dostoevsky's works there are absolutely no *separate* thoughts, propositions, or formulations such as maxims, sayings, aphorisms which, when removed from their context and detached from their voice, would retain their semantic meaning in an impersonal form" (ibid., p. 95).

45. Ibid., p. 78.   46. Ibid., p. 98.

47. Ibid., p. 92.   48. Ibid., p. 296.

49. Ibid., p. 294.

50. Dostoevsky, *PSS*, vol. 20, p. 175.

51. See notes to app. 2, *Toward a Reworking of the Dostoevsky Book* (Bakhtin, *Poetics*, p. 283).

52. Ibid., p. 285.

53. There is an analogy here with Bakhtin's whole understanding of form: "Artistic form, correctly understood, does not shape already prepared and found content, but rather permits content to be found and seen for the first time" (*Poetics*, p. 43).

54. Ibid., p. 284.   55. Ibid., p. 87.

56. Ibid., p. 58.   57. Ibid., p. 59.

58. For a more extensive discussion of some of the ideas set forth here on

Dmitry Karamazov, see my chapter "Dmitri Karamazov and the Legend," in my *The Art of Dostoevsky: Deliriums and Nocturnes* (Princeton, N.J., 1981), pp. 335–46.

59. Bakhtin, *Poetics*, p. 97.   60. Ibid., p. 97.

61. Dostoevsky, *PSS*, vol. 28, bk. 2, p. 123.

62. Cited in Bakhtin, *Poetics*, pp. 97–98. See Dostoevsky's observations in *PSS*, vol. 27, pp. 56, 57, 58, 85.

63. Bakhtin, *Poetics*, p. 98.   64. Ibid.

65. Dostoevsky, *PSS*, vol. 20, p. 172.

66. Ibid., vol. 11, p. 192.

67. Ibid., pp. 187–88.   68. Ibid., p. 112.

69. Dostoevsky's tendency to conflate the roles of artist and preacher is strikingly evident in the *Diary of a Writer*. "Bobok" and "The Dream of a Ridiculous Man," belletristic works that appear in the *Diary*, clearly call for interpretation in the context of Dostoevsky's discussions and polemics in his *Diary*. For a broad and detailed discussion of *Diary of a Writer* as a "boundary genre," see Gary Saul Morson's important *The Boundaries of Genre: Dostoevsky's "Diary of a Writer" and the Traditions of Literary Utopia* (Austin, Tex., 1981).

70. Ibid., p. 88.

71. In the opening scene of Ivan's "poem," the people in front of the cathedral in Seville recognize the silent Christ and freely "strive toward" him. "That might be one of the best passages in the poem," Ivan remarks, "I mean, why they recognize Him. The people are irresistibly drawn to Him, they surround Him, they flock about Him. follow Him."

72. For a discussion of Dostoevsky's higher aesthetic, see my *Dostoevsky's Quest for Form: A Study of His Philosophy of Art* (New Haven, 1966; 2d ed., Physsardt, 1978).

73. Dostoevsky, *PSS*, vol. 28, bk. 1, p. 176.

74. Bakhtin, *Poetics*, p. 11.

75. Dostoevsky, *PSS*, vol. 20, pp. 172, 173, 174, 175.

76. *PSS: Pis'ma*, vol. 28, bk. 2, p. 73.

77. The Underground Man is not a believer: this is the root of his dilemma, in Dostoevsky's view. He spins helplessly in a fate-bound world of his own making, lost in the "logical tangle" of his rationalistic consciousness. His lack of religious faith and his thirst for something in which he can believe is touched upon obliquely in chapter 10, the one that the censor mauled. The chapter opens with the line "You believe in the crystal palace." The Underground Man argues that he cannot believe in such an ideal. He wonders at the end of the chapter whether he is not so constituted as to be obliged to give up his desires for an ideal that he could respect. "Is it possible that the whole goal is in this?" "I don't believe so," he replies. The words *ne verju* may also mean "I do not believe," "I have no faith." Taken in this meaning, the phrase underlines the vicious circle in which he finds himself: he believes that his desires

for something to respect, to believe in, are valid, but he does not believe—he lacks the very ingredient that would not merely validate his desires but realize them. This play on the words *ne verju* may be all that is left of more direct indications in the uncensored chapter of the root cause of the Underground Man's tragedy.

78. The "ridiculousness" of Dostoevsky's Ridiculous Man is a kind of caprice, a kind of 2 + 2 = 5. After his dream in which he discovers his ideal, however, his so-called ridiculous behavior—preaching the ideal in the knowledge that the idea is impossible—takes on a creative character. He passes from an immobilizing nihilism to a new realistic idealism. See my discussion of "The Dream of a Ridiculous Man" in *Art of Dostoevsky*, pp. 276–87 (pp. 286–87 in particular).

79. Bakhtin, *Poetics*, p. 11.   80. Ibid., pp. 3, 4.
81. Ibid., p. xxvi.

Chapter 16

1. Leonid K. Dolgopolov, *Na rubezhe vekov* (Leningrad, 1977), p. 28. See also Emma Polotskaya, who writes of Chekhov as a writer who adhered to the "principle of equilibrium of contradictory forces." The "Chekhovian variant of human breadth in comparison with the Dostoevsky variant might be more precisely defined this way: his hero is neither an angel, nor a villain (instead of 'and' / 'and' we have 'neither / neither')"; Polotskaja, "Chelovek v khudozhestvennom mire Dostoevskogo i Chekhova," in *Dostoevskij i russkie pisateli* (Moscow, 1971), pp. 209, 211.

2. Dostoevsky, *PSS*, vol. 24, p. 49. The word *bezdokazatel'no*, here translated as "without proof," may also be translated as "unsubstantiated."

3. Somewhat analagous examples may be found in the notebooks to *The Brothers Karamazov*. Under the heading "Confession of the Elder," we read: "If you are an atheist and if you are in doubt, then love with an active love, you will return to God and you will see him." Or again: "Be *an atheist*, but through works of charity you will come to a knowledge of God" (*PSS*, vol. 15, pp. 243, 244).

4. Ibid., vol. 24, p. 50.   5. Ibid., pp. 49–50.
6. Ibid., vol. 21, pp. 38, 37.   7. Ibid., p. 10.
8. "Zu Rapps Kritik der 'Resignation,'" *Schillers Werke: Nationalausgabe*, ed. Julius Petersen and Hermann Schneider (Weimar, 1958), vol. 22, p. 178.

9. Dostoevsky, *PSS*, vol. 28, bk. 1, p. 176.

10. It is true that Dostoevsky seems to anticipate "proof" or "substantiation" that love for humanity is impossible without concurrent faith in the immortality of the human soul: "For the time being," he emphasizes, his assertion is "without proof" or substantiation. The suggestion here is not that immortality can be *rationally* substantiated. Dostoevsky's parenthetical remark sug-

gests, rather, the millenarian or apocalyptic mood that manifests itself in certain parts of his *Diary of a Writer*. One may surmise, perhaps, that the disaster that Dostoevsky sees befalling European civilization (socialism, materialism, the Tower of Babel) will itself constitute *evidence* that love for humanity cannot exist without concomitant faith in immortality, that virtue cannot survive in a world where men have lost their faith in God and immortality.

11. Dostoevsky, *PSS*, vol. 29, bk. 2, pp. 101, 102. Dostoevsky cites from Tyutchev's poem "Silentium."

Index

Library of Congress Cataloguing-in-Publication Data

Jackson, Robert Louis.
    Dialogues with Dostoevsky: the overwhelming questions / Robert Louis
Jackson.
        p.   cm.
Includes bibliographical references and index.
ISBN 0-8047-2120-3 (cl.) : ISBN 0-8047-2803-8 (pbk.)
    1. Dostoevsky, Fyodor, 1821–1881—Criticism and interpretation.
2. Dostoevsky, Fyodor, 1821–1881—Influence.   3. Russian literature—
History and criticism.   4. European literature—History and
criticism.   I. Title.
PG3328.z6J33   1993
891.73'3—dc20
92-38404   CIP

∞ This book is printed on acid-free paper.
It has been typeset in Adobe Caslon by
G&S Typesetters.

Designed by Eva Gavrielov